Palgrave Studies in Life Writing

Series Editors
Clare Brant
Department of English
King's College London
London, UK

Max Saunders
Department of English
King's College London
London, UK

This series features books that address key concepts and subjects, with an emphasis on new and emergent approaches. It offers specialist but accessible studies of contemporary and historical topics, with a focus on connecting life writing to themes with cross-disciplinary appeal. The series aims to be the place to go to for current and fresh research for scholars and students looking for clear and original discussion of specific subjects and forms; it is also a home for experimental approaches that take creative risks with potent materials.

The term 'Life Writing' is taken broadly so as to reflect the academic, public and global reach of life writing, and to continue its democratic tradition. The series seeks contributions that address contexts beyond traditional territories – for instance, in the Middle East, Africa and Asia. It also aims to publish volumes addressing topics of general interest (such as food, drink, sport, gardening) with which life writing scholarship can engage in lively and original ways, as well as to further the political engagement of life writing especially in relation to human rights, migration, trauma and repression, sadly also persistently topical themes. The series looks for work that challenges and extends how life writing is understood and practised, especially in a world of rapidly changing digital media; that deepens and diversifies knowledge and perspectives on the subject, and which contributes to the intellectual excitement and the world relevance of life writing.

More information about this series at
http://www.palgrave.com/gp/series/15200

Valérie Baisnée-Keay • Corinne Bigot
Nicoleta Alexoae-Zagni • Claire Bazin
Editors

Women's Life Writing and the Practice of Reading

She Reads to Write Herself

palgrave
macmillan

Editors
Valérie Baisnée-Keay
University of Paris-Sud
Orsay, France

Nicoleta Alexoae-Zagni
University of Paris 8
Vincennes-Saint-Denis
Paris, France

Corinne Bigot
University of Toulouse II Jean Jaurès
Toulouse, France

Claire Bazin
Department of English
Université Paris Nanterre
Nanterre, France

Palgrave Studies in Life Writing
ISBN 978-3-319-75246-4   ISBN 978-3-319-75247-1   (eBook)
https://doi.org/10.1007/978-3-319-75247-1

Library of Congress Control Number: 2018936514

This Palgrave Macmillan imprint is published by the registered company Springer International Publishing AG part of Springer Nature.
The registered company address is: Gewerbestrasse 11, 6330 Cham, Switzerland

ACKNOWLEDGEMENTS

The editors would like to thank our colleagues who have taken part in the meetings and conferences of the University of Paris Nanterre's Research group on Anglophone women writers (Faaam), whose discussions over the years have fed our thoughts and research. Faaam has been crucial to our research for many years. Most particularly, we would like to thank the participants to Faaam's conferences on women's life writing held at Paris Nanterre University in 2015 and 2016.

We also wish to thank Paris Nanterre's research group CREA, and more particularly Cornelius Crowley and Caroline Diamond, for their constant support for our projects.

Finally, we also wish to express our grateful thanks to Nigel Keay for his support and help.

Contents

Notes on Contributors

Nicoleta Alexoae-Zagni is Senior Lecturer at Paris 8 University. Her areas of research include Asian American, Ethnic and Postcolonial Studies. After a doctoral thesis on self-writing in the works of Maxine Hong Kingston and Shirley Geok-lin Lim, she is currently engaged in an exploration of non-Anglophone textual productions belonging to American literature (Yan Geling) as well as of contemporary Japanese-American fictional and self-referential representations (Ruth Ozeki). She has been involved in academic events, published articles and presented papers on subjects relative to her areas of scientific investigation and was also co-editor of *On the Legacy of Maxine Hong Kingston: The Mulhouse Book* (2014).

Valérie Baisnée-Keay is a Senior Lecturer in English at the University of Paris Sud. She holds a PhD in English from the University of Auckland, New Zealand. She has contributed to several published books and journals on twentieth- and twenty-first-century women's life writings. Her publications also include two books: *Gendered Resistance: The Autobiographies of Simone de Beauvoir, Maya Angelou, Janet Frame and Marguerite Duras* (1997) and *Through the Long Corridor of Distance: Space and Self in Contemporary New Zealand Women's Autobiographies* (2014). She is a member of the University of Paris Nanterre's research group on women writers (Faaam).

Claire Bazin is Professor of Nineteenth Century English Literature and Commonwealth Literature at Paris Nanterre University, France. She is the author of several books on Charlotte and Emily Brontë: *La*

Vision du mal chez les sœurs Brontë (1995); *Jane Eyre, le pèlerin moderne* (2005), *Jane Eyre: L'itinéraire d'une femme* (with Dominique Sipière). She co-authored *Janet Fame, Naissance d'une œuvre: The Lagoon* in collaboration with Alice Braun (2010) and is the author of *Janet Frame* in Writers and Their Work (2011). She has been head of the University of Nanterre's research group on Anglo-Saxon women writers (Faaam) for many years.

Corinne Bigot is a Senior Lecturer in English and Commonwealth Literature at the University of Toulouse Jean Jaurès, France. She holds a PhD in Canadian Literature from the University of Paris Nanterre and has published essays on Canadian women writers. Her publications also include books on Alice Munro's works: *Alice Munro, les silences de la nouvelle* (2014) and *Sunlight and Shadows: Alice Munro's* Dance of the Happy Shades, co-authored with Catherine Lanone (2014). She has been a member of the University of Paris Nanterre's research group, Faaam, for many years.

Nicolas Pierre Boileau is Senior Lecturer in English Studies at the University of Aix-Marseille, France. His PhD thesis was entitled *Experiencing the Impossible: Autobiographical Writing in Virginia Woolf's Moments of Being, Sylvia Plath's The Bell Jar and Janet Frame's An Autobiography* (2008). He has published papers on autobiography and psychoanalysis, and modernism, including an article on autobiography and gender criticism, and one on Janet Frame in *a/b: Auto/Biographical Studies*. He is a member of the British Association of Modernist Studies and of the French Virginia Woolf Society, and has recently worked on the translation and publication of *Mrs Dalloway* into French.

Elisabeth Bouzonviller is Professor of American Literature at Jean Monnet University in St Etienne, France. She is the author of *Francis Scott Fitzgerald ou la plénitude du silence* (2000), *Francis Scott Fitzgerald, écrivain du déséquilibre* (2000) and *Louise Erdrich. Métissage et écriture, histoires d'Amérique* (2014). She is a member of the F. Scott Fitzgerald Society and has contributed not only to its Review and Newsletter, but also to *A Distant Drummer: Foreign Perspectives on F. Scott Fitzgerald* (2007) and to *Fitzgerald in Context* (2013).

Joan Chiung-huei Chang is Professor of Comparative Literature at National Taiwan Normal University in Taipei, Taiwan. She is the author of *Transforming Chinese American Literature* (2000). She has edited special issues on Asian American Literature for *Chung-Wai Literary Monthly* 29.11 (2001) and *Concentric: Literary and Cultural Studies* 39(2) (2013). She is also the editor of *The Globalization of Comparative Literature: Asian Initiatives* (2004). She has published essays on the Asian American writers Maxine Hong Kingston, Henry David Hwang, Amy Tan, Shirley Lim, Milton Murayama, Chang-rae Lee and Ha Jin.

Stephanie Genty is a Senior Lecturer in English at the University of Evry, France. She holds a PhD in American Literature from the University of Bordeaux. Her dissertation focused on the representation and analysis of feminine "malaise" in the work of Marilyn French. She wrote the Afterword for French's 2006 novel, *In the Name of Friendship* and is currently preparing a literary biography of the author. She has studied the work of Nadine Gordimer, Margaret Atwood and, more recently, Patti Smith and plans to one day write a monograph on Patti Smith's poetry.

Ann Jefferson is Professor Emeritus at New College, Oxford, and former Professor of French Literature. She has published extensively on French literature, and, more recently, on French writers' biographies. Her recent publications include *Le Défi biographique* (2012), a translation of her *Biography and the Question of Literature in France* (2007). Her most recent book is *Genius in France: An Idea and its Uses* (2015) and she is currently working on a biography of Nathalie Sarraute.

Delphine Louis-Dimitrov is a senior lecturer at the Catholic University of Paris, France. She studied at the Ecole Normale Supérieure in Paris and holds a doctorate from the Sorbonne Nouvelle (Paris III). She has published extensively on Mark Twain's work. Her research more broadly deals with the connection between nineteenth- and early-twentieth-century American literature and history.

Anne-Claire Marpeau is a doctoral student preparing her PhD in comparative literature at ENS Lyon France and the University of British Columbia, Canada. Her research areas include the representations of the practice of reading (in novels and writers' autobiographies), and gender studies. An essay on Flaubert's Emma Bovary is forthcoming (to be published in *Revue Flaubert*), and she is currently working on representations and perceptions of sexual and sexist violence in literature as part of a research project headed by the French sociologist Christine Detrez.

Ludmila Martanovschi is Associate Professor at Ovidius University, Constanta, Romania, teaching Twentieth Century American Literature and Ethnic Studies. She is the author of *Decolonizing the Self: Memory, Language and Cultural Experience in Contemporary American Indian Poetry* (2009) and *Family Ties: An Introduction to Postwar American Drama* (2012).

Laure de Nervaux-Gavoty is Senior Lecturer in English at Paris-Est Créteil University. She has written articles on women's poetry as well as on the relationship between literature and the visual arts. Her recent work bears on the representation of illness and the body in American autobiography (Alice James, Lucy Grealy, Nancy Mairs). She has co-edited a collection of articles on experience in literature and the arts in the twentieth and the twenty-first centuries (*L'Expérience II*, 2013) and is currently completing another collection on inter- and transdisciplinarity. She is a member of *Quaderna*'s (an interdisciplinary and multilingual online journal) editorial board.

Anne-Florence Quaireau holds a PhD in Anglophone literature (2013) from the University of Paris Sorbonne, where she now teaches. Her PhD dissertation on Anna Jameson's *Winter Studies and Summer Rambles in Canada* received the 2014 SELVA (the French Society for Travel Writing) doctoral award. Her research focuses on travel literature, and she has published essays on Anna Jameson's travel narratives.

Virginia Allen-Terry Sherman is currently is a doctoral student at the University of Grenoble, France. Her PhD project is entitled "Diaspora and displacement: The evocation of traditions, origins and identity in culinary memoirs, an emerging literary genre." She has published several essays on culinary memoirs and is one of the co-editors of a collection of essays entitled *(Re)writing and Remembering. Memory as Artefact and Artifice* (2016).

Sidonie Smith is Mary Fair Croushore Professor of the Humanities and Director of the Institute for the Humanities at the University of Michigan. She is author of *Where I'm Bound: Patterns of Slavery and Freedom in Black American Autobiography* (1974); *A Poetics of Women's Autobiography* (1987); *Subjectivity, Identity, and the Body* (1993); *Moving Lives: Women's Twentieth Century Travel Narratives* (2001); and, with Kay Schaffer, *Human Rights and Narrated Lives* (2004). With Julia Watson, she has co-authored *Reading Autobiography: A Guide for Interpreting Life*

Narratives (2001; expanded edition, 2010) and co-edited five collections: *De/Colonizing the Subject: The Politics of Gender in Women's Autobiography*; *Getting a Life: Everyday Uses of Autobiography*; *Women, Autobiography, Theory*; *Interfaces: Women, Autobiography, Image, Performance*; *Before They Could Vote: American Women's Autobiographical Writing, 1819–1919*. Julia Watson and Sidonie Smith's most recent book, *Life Writing in the Long Run* (2017), gathers together 21 essays by Smith and Watson. Julia Smith is a former president of the Modern Language Association of America (2010).

Josette Spartacus holds a PhD in American literature from the University of Montpellier, France (2015). Her research focuses on the writings of Afro-American and Caribbean-American writers such as Toni Morrison, Edwige Danticat and Jamaica Kincaid.

Julia Watson is Professor Emerita of Comparative Studies and former associate dean of Arts and Sciences at The Ohio State University. With Sidonie Smith, she has co-authored *Reading Autobiography: A Guide for Interpreting Life Narratives* (2001; expanded edition, 2010) and co-edited five collections: *De/Colonizing the Subject: The Politics of Gender in Women's Autobiography*; *Getting a Life: Everyday Uses of Autobiography*; *Women, Autobiography, Theory*; *Interfaces: Women, Autobiography, Image, Performance*; *Before They Could Vote: American Women's Autobiographical Writing, 1819–1919*. Professor Watson's recent essays are on graphic memoir, post-humanism, voice, and, with Smith, online life narrative. Julia Watson and Sidonie Smith's most recent book, *Life Writing in the Long Run*, was published in 2017, and gathers together 21 essays by Smith and Watson.

LIST OF FIGURES

CHAPTER 1

Introduction

Valérie Baisnée-Keay

> *As a child, I found my home in books. I dreamed of writing one. But until I began to work on this memoir, I thought of writing as a solitary enterprise. To my surprise, I discovered it to be an intensely communal adventure, bringing me into ever-deepening contact with an ever-widening circle of people. Through the act of writing, I found my home in the world.*
> *Joyce Zonana,* Dream Homes *(2008)*

If moving from a home in books to a home in the world may be one of the metaphors for the process of life writing, the route that leads to writing is made of twists and turns. Joyce Zonana's journey well illustrates the dialectics of reading and writing, from a refuge of the self to a way for the self to connect to the world. As such, reading as a figurative activity and a process is central to women's life writing and the self/selves that emerge out of it. Thus, while reading and writing now have a distinct history, they are often reunited in life writing.

Life writing has often been thought as a transgressive genre, in the etymological sense of the term, that is a genre that crosses boundaries, such

V. Baisnée-Keay (✉)
University of Paris-Sud, Orsay, France

© The Author(s) 2018
V. Baisnée-Keay et al. (eds.), *Women's Life Writing and the Practice of Reading*, Palgrave Studies in Life Writing, https://doi.org/10.1007/978-3-319-75247-1_1

as fact and fiction, past and present, and also crucially between reading and writing. As a highly reflexive text/act, autobiography often illuminates that link between reception and production. As the author woos other readers to read her life, she also reads to write herself. This process entangles the self into other narratives. In exploring the reading/writing dialectics in self-writing, the theme of the conference from which this collection grew wished to acknowledge the fact the self is made up of stories told as well as read all through life.

In recent years, not only has there been a boom in autobiographical writing, but the field of autobiography has also become increasingly diverse in form, so that the term autobiography no longer covers all its subgenres. In the 1980s and 1990s, Donald Winslow and Marlene Kadar argued in favour of using the term "life writing" to accommodate a broader scope of texts, especially, as pointed out by Kadar, women's texts such as journals, diaries, oral narratives, anthropological life histories, and "blended genres" (Kadar 1993). In the preface to their seminal guide to life writing, *Reading Autobiography* (2010), Sidonie Smith and Julia Watson claim that the field of life writing has become "intergalactic," and the emergence of new forms and new media is profoundly changing the genre. The Latin origins of the words autobiography and biography, with their scholarly implications tend to screen so called non-literary forms of writing one's life. The term *autobiography* refers back to a certain Western literary tradition which started during the Enlightenment era and became represented by a few canonical works. As the genre increased in prestige, it also started to constitute around a canon which is now being contested, as new autobiographical texts continue to appear, and not only in the Western world. Although writers and critics alike tend to refer to the term *autobiography* rather than *life writing*, the latter was already in use in the eighteenth century as Donald Winslow (1980, xi) notes, while *autobiography* was introduced later. In her introduction to *Essays on Life Writing*, Kadar argues that "life writing" could be seen as a category to classify autobiographical works by marginalized social groups defined by race or gender (1992, 7). Hence her argument that the genre is related to gender (29). Finally, in their introduction to *Life Writing in The Long Run* (2017), Sidonie Smith and Julia Watson point out that even the terms "life narrative" and "life writing" cannot account for the ever-increasing modes available to present a "life."

Nonetheless, the broader phrase "life writing" encompasses forms of writing that are not purely literary while taking into account the diversity of autobiographical forms (written and visual). Crucially, the phrase also stresses that practice and process are just as significant as the finished product. The texts analysed in this collection reflect this variety: diaries, slave narratives, culinary memoirs, poetic memoirs, travel narratives, family memoirs, autobiographical essays, drawn memoirs and writers' autobiographies, including recent trends such as autoethnography. The corpus of nineteenth- to twenty-first-century writers is also diverse, ranging from the mainstream literary culture to the most marginal women: the former slaves. Geographical areas (America, Canada, Britain, New Zealand, France, China), social and ethnic backgrounds are also represented. Thus, the collection stresses the wide appeal, flexibility and creativity of the genre.

A BOOK OF ONE'S OWN: GENDERED PRACTICES OF READING

By choosing to focus on women's life writing practice, the collection acknowledges that there is a specificity to gendered practices and modes of reading in life writing. The book is premised on the idea that gender is a major factor affecting the way the reading experience is reconstructed or entangled in narratives of the self. Gender overdetermines and inflects the activity of reading, which is primarily a social activity, even in its most private forms. However, reading is not only affected by gender. Racial and class relations are also major factors as slaves' narratives so poignantly demonstrate.

In the richest countries, where the circulation of writing is the highest, today gender literacy discrepancy has almost disappeared. Yet, globally, illiteracy is still currently higher among adult women in the world; United Nations Education, Scientific and Cultural Organization (UNESCO) data reveal that the male adult literacy rate is 88% while the female literacy rate stands at 79%.[1] Demographically, a correlation has been established between literacy and reproduction: illiterate women tend to have more children. Women reading is not taken for granted in some regions of the world, as they do not enjoy the same access to books and education everywhere. The history of reading also reveals gender discrepancy.

Historians of reading[2] have identified two main trends in the gendered practice of reading since the eighteenth century: women have tended to read in private places, and have been more attracted to escapist books. However, historians have stumbled against the lack of evidence and treated women as homogeneous groups. The fact that women were not encouraged to write about their reading may account for this scarcity of evidence. Kathryn Lenore Steele, who has studied female reading in the eighteenth century, shows that for higher-class women reading had "its appropriate outlet not in writing, but in conversation" (Steele 2008, 51). Moreover, until the end of the eighteenth century women were taught to read, especially by the Church, but not to write, as it would have given them too much independence (Lyons 2001, 396). The history of reading, which has become disconnected from the history of writing, is even more so for women. Steele claims that the lack of evidence of women reading poses epistemological and methodological problems. First, this creates an over-reliance on individual accounts. Second, the scarcity of traces influences the way we may interpret women's silence, highlighting what Steele calls "oppositional reading," that is reading against authority, which is the type of reading historians tend to have traces of, while obscuring ordinary, submissive reading.

In the nineteenth century, a period when female readership increased significantly in the Western world, there was a certain anxiety about women's new passion for reading, and its consequence on traditional gender roles. As women turned massively to secular reading, any reading that was not religious or domestic was frowned upon, as it was regarded as a distraction from women's presumed primary role: motherhood. Reading and motherhood were perceived for a long time as mutually exclusive, and writing even more. For Kate Flint, who has examined the intense discussions surrounding "the woman reader" between the accession of Queen Victoria and the First World War, this "emphasis on presumed maternal functions is the one, ultimately, which has the most bearing on the question of women and reading" (Flint 1993, 69).[3] As reading was often viewed as a suspicious activity, women tended to hide in order to read, as numerous life writing accounts attest. "Reading novels for the first time during childhood or adolescence, often secretly, is one of the topoi of women's autobiographies," Christine Planté points out, looking at the fate of nineteenth-century French female authors (1989, 76; my translation). Faced with constraining roles and the pressure to conform, women found in reading, especially the reading of novels, a unique form of individual experience, and sometimes the only one possible (Planté 1989, 76). Reading novels and literature gave women the illusion of becoming subjects on their own, and encouraged them to become more critical of their lives. The diary of Alice James, analysed by Laure de Nervaux-Gavoty in this book, well illustrates this trend.

Intense scrutiny, restrictions, banning, on the one hand, prescriptions on what to read on the other put reading at the core of a nexus of power/knowledge relations for women. If we follow Foucault's definition of power, this can lead to two contradictory effects. On the one hand, reading is a source of empowerment: it gives access to knowledge and enlightens the reader. As such, it may become a potentially dangerous activity that can subvert the established social order. Hence the absolute ban on reading for slaves; they had to be kept in a state of ignorance. As a matter of fact, Muslim fundamentalist groups still ban reading for women. But while reading can be a form of individuation and even liberation, it may also be seen as a form of social control. Writers do not communicate directly to readers. Unless they are clandestine, texts reach readers through institutions that exercise different forms of control on discourses. In his lecture at the Collège de France in 1970, published as *The Order of Discourse*, Michel Foucault stressed that "in every society the production of discourse is at once controlled, selected, organised and redistributed by a certain number of procedures whose role is to ward off its powers and dangers, to gain mastery over its chance events, to evade its ponderous, formidable materiality" (Foucault 1971, 52). Similarly, conventions governing literary texts produce "structures of authority" to which the author-function and the whole institution of literature belong. The attribution of authorship to a text also lends it certain social characteristics that an anonymous text does not possess, among which that of tying an author to the legal and institutional systems that control the circulation of texts. Therefore, within the institution of literature, the reader only has an illusion of being a free agent, whereas writing seems to be a more independent act. Moreover, as children, subjects are socialized into discourses that tell them what is acceptable or not: many narratives of development recount such encounters with ideological discourses, and, in particular, children's literature is often used to mark gender roles. Books are thus also instruments to discipline the subject. In Althusserian terms, we could also say that the subject is interpellated by the text. Sentimental novels, for example, can be viewed as a way to remind women of their destiny: marriage and motherhood. So reading may act paradoxically: it gives the subject a sense of individuality, but also subjects it to authorized texts. When ethnic relations are involved, the power/knowledge regime can become overwhelming. 'Indian' schools were a case in point: they both empowered indigenous children by providing them with a formal education and a literary canon, and dispossessed them of their traditional cultures and knowledges. The collection *Here First: Autobiographical Essays by Native American Writers* (2000), discussed by Ludmila Martanovschi in this book, shows that maintaining traditional culture and claiming the literary canon as their own became a critical act for these writers.

Yet, as Foucault reminds us, power, in its very restrictions, also produces knowledge. Simply opposing subversive reading to ideological reading is not sufficient, and risks creating two categories of women, the rebels and the submissive. Furthermore, looking for the exceptional women contesting ideologies of gender may hide the mass of obedient female readers that accept guidance. Feminist critics have emphasized reading as a site of conflict, subversion, or empowerment, and women's life writing definitely contains a lot of examples of those conflicts. But exceptional lives are not representative. According to Steele, in the eighteenth century, most readers wanted to be guided in their reading. She points out that the individual reader who resists authority has been given more visibility, because we tend to apply our own modern conceptions about the "autonomous reader" to the past.

The concept of resistant reading, albeit crucial for the examination of women's reading practices, should thus be applied with caution to life writing, so as not to create a transhistorical and essentialized category of "resisting female reader." In her seminal text, Judith Fetterley (1978) defined resisting reading as "reading against the grain," a necessary act for women in the face of the domination of male writing. Women are confronted with an androcentric world of books, which render them powerless in several ways:

> To be excluded from a literature that claims to define one's identity is to experience a peculiar form of powerlessness—not simply the powerlessness which derives from not seeing one's experience articulated, clarified, and legitimized in art, but more significantly the powerlessness which results from the endless division of self against self, the consequence of the invocation to identity as male while being reminded that to be male—to be universal, to be American—is to be not female. (Fetterley 1978, xiii)

Reading as resistance may take on different forms: resisting the text and its stereotypes, resisting the social order through/with the text, reading multiple meanings in a text. In life writing, another dialectics of reading and writing emerges, as misreading can be another way to find a form of truth. For Harold Bloom, who has theorized misreading in relation to poetic influence, the "strong" reading act, as a later poet performs on an earlier one, is always an act of misreading (1975, 3). A case in point is Nicolas Pierre Boileau's examination of the links between Virginia Woolf's reading and writing practices in this collection: Virginia Woolf had to misread others to read herself, as she constantly oscillates between the act of reading and the act of writing. Life writing can shed light on the context that shapes women's reading as well as reveal how closely integrated to reading writing is.

Hence, in looking at reading practices in women's life writings, one must consider not only what is read, but also how women read: is reading obedient or resisting? Is obedient reading always a form of submission? And what is the purpose of reading? For Patrocinio Schweickart (1995), any feminist perspective on reading should link the questions of what and how women read, and that an inquiry into gendered practices of reading should be premised on the fact that the literary canon is androcentric. For feminists, the politics and poetics of reading are intimately related; thus, theories of reading that are only textual, and not contextual might not be sufficient to account for reading in life writing.

The Poetics of Women's Reading in Life Writing

On the poetic level, inasmuch as this can be separated from the cultural one, however reading is defined, it always implies using a code to construct meaning. There is a consensus among linguists and literary theorists today in considering reading as an active process, which therefore can be creative. Reading is not a passive act, a simple absorption of written information. As Charles Michel has demonstrated, a text acts on the reader and in turn the reading act transforms the text (1977, 86). Thus, current definitions of reading as a cognitive activity fall into two categories: one set of definitions emphasizes reading as a decoding process (a more linguistic one); the other one, reading as a meaning-making process.[4] Finally, whatever the category, it is assumed that reading implies a form of communication between a reader and an author, so that there is also a rhetoric of reading.

Since the 1970s, reader-response theory has developed around the assumption that readers participate in the reading process, and demonstrated how understanding the relationships between readers and texts affect perspectives on texts, producing new categories for literary analysis. For example, Umberto Eco in *Lector in Fabula* (1979) made a distinction between "open texts," which require an active participation from the reader, and "closed texts," where the reader's response is already predetermined and oriented, such as the detective novel. Wolfgang Iser (1972) has focused on the blanks or gaps in the texts that the reader has to fill in order to interpret a text. Going beyond the individual use of texts to take history into account, Hans Robert Jauss (1967) has advanced a hermeneutics of reception to focus on the public reception of works with his concept of a shared "horizon of expectations": "The new text evokes for the reader (listener) the horizon of expectations and rules familiar from earlier texts, which are then varied, corrected, altered, or even just reproduced" (12). The aesthetic value of a text is then determined by the distance between a work and its horizon of expectation, which the critic needs to establish for a given historical period.

These theories aimed at counterbalancing author-centred criticism which has dominated literary studies: they questioned the assumption that the author was the source of meaning to put forward the text instead. Reader-response theorists denounced the "intentional fallacy," which consists in finding the interpretation of a work from what the author had in mind at the time of writing. Rather, they looked for the effects of texts on readers, rather than focus on deciphering meaning from a disguised author's point of view. They tried to ascertain how the text predicts the reader. As such, the reader response theory is both an aesthetics and a hermeneutics.

There are some limits, however, to the reader-response theory, which have often been pointed out by various strands of criticism. The implied reader is always presented as an agent of unlimited creative and interpretive capabilities. This assumption puts a huge responsibility on the reader. As meaning-making rests further and further on the reader, reading becomes, in Ricœur's words, a picnic where the author brings words and the reader interpretation (1985, 308). In terms of a poetics of women's reading, the main limit is that these theories think about the reader as a role, sometimes a function of the text, and the reader is represented as a genderless, isolated literary figure. It is a theoretical reader who fills the gaps or predicts what comes next, and these processes have automatically been included in the text. Reader-response theory implies the presence of a universal reader, not marked by genre, class or race.

In his chapter "Reading as poaching" in *The Practice of Everyday Life*, Michel de Certeau defines reading both as a social and poetic activity. De Certeau suggests readers are nomads, poaching in fields they have not written. Reading involves tactics of wandering and improvisation: it is an "ephemeral dance" across textual space. Readers can be compared to travellers who pick and choose and resist authorized meanings. Although the reader is subjected to social hierarchy that imposes its information, she may invent meanings in the text. De Certeau concludes: "Reading is thus situated at the point where social stratification (class relationships) and poetic operations (the practitioner's constructions of a text) intersect" (1988, 172).

Life writings let us better understand the relationship between the theoretical reader and the actual reader through representations of acts of reading as a socio-cultural activity and a meaning-making process. However, like other experiences recounted in autobiography, the reading experience is never immediate (a given), but, as Smith and Watson remind us in *Reading Autobiography*, is mediated by language and memory. We have an interpretation of our past rather than an experience of it. Consequently, experience is always filtered through prevailing discourses. As Rita Felski points out, it is naïve to believe that any "text can transmit an unmediated representation of the real" (1989, 79), but that does not diminish the "strategic importance of feminist writing as a medium of self-exploration and social criticism" (79). While experience, a key term in second-wave feminism, has now fallen into disrepute, life narratives often document the materiality of reading and represent the reading act in its political, social and cultural context. Moreover, through individual histories of reading, some stereotypes about women and reading can be debunked, such as the idea that women read novels for romantic reasons, or that women's empathic qualities help them identify more easily with protagonists of novels. A phenomenology of reading becomes possible. However, one should be wary of extending the reading practices of exceptional women to all female readers.

At the juncture of textual/contextual practices, the material and physiological dimensions of reading are often mentioned in life writing, but ignored in theories of reading which insist on meaning-making. For Karen Littau (2006), reading cannot be reduced to a silent, intellectual activity, as it also involves the body, through posture and the various emotions that may affect the reader. Littau claims that literary studies have become overly cerebral; this contrasts with another tradition dating back from Antiquity that was concerned with literature not only as "sense making" but also "sensation." When the French writer Nathalie Sarraute describes herself as "*plongée dans un livre*" (immersed in a book), she shows how intense an experience reading is. When she is immersed in a book, she simply lives it. For her part, the Canadian writer Janice Kulyk Keefer, whose memoir Corinne Bigot analyses in this collection, explains that she "loses herself" in books, and often uses the word "haunting" to refer to her reading experiences.

Reading is not only about interpreting, but also experiencing through the body. The relationship of a reader to a book is also a relationship to another body, and while today reading is mostly a silent activity, it has not always been the case; in the past, reading aloud was even considered as physical exercise (Littau 2006, 2). Writers such as Nancy Huston and Jeanette Winterson recall the intense experience of listening to their family reading aloud, from stories to the Bible. From tears to laughter, the emotional, physiological reaction to reading has a rich changing history, well-illustrated and documented, which cultural theories of reading have overlooked, mostly because pathos has been thought incompatible with political activism. The bodily dimension of reading is particularly significant for women as it is in line with the feminist reintroduction of the body in theory, although we should be careful of any problematic identification of women with the body. In this perspective, the culinary memoirs analysed by Virginia Sherman in this collection offer another form of sensory experience, which underlines the bond between food, reading and memory as recipes are interwoven with autobiographical fragments. Thus, remembering can be both an intellectual feat and a feast for the senses. Culinary memoirs signal reading as both a form of consumption and a sensuous experience, even though some writers are careful not to be seen as reinforcing traditional female roles through this form of life writing.

Consequently, a poetics/rhetoric/politics of women's reading in life writing may include an examination of the following aspects: modes of reading (public/private, hidden), the materiality of reading, the staging of reading in an autobiography, and the various political or aesthetic responses to reading. The mode of narration should be taken into account: resistance reading implies distanciation while identification suggests closeness. Examining the way the memory of books affects the representation of the past is also crucial as well as whether life writings include *mise en abyme*, whereby the fictions women read act as mirrors to their lives. In this collection, two main aspects have emerged: the question of intertextuality, as in women's interaction with the code (language and/or the literary canon) and reading as a form of ontology or quest for identity.

READING AND INTERTEXTUALITY

As the sheer number of references to books and other authors attest, the practice of intertextuality is one of the key aspects of reading in life writing. Originally understood to refer to the relations between two or more texts, the term "intertextuality," which became popular in the late 1960s, was first designed as a structural approach to studying literary texts as opposed to historical or author-oriented approaches. As its most extreme structural level, intertextuality assumes "the dependence of every text on other texts," whether the reference to other texts is intentional or not. In its (ut)most structural definition, there is no more agency in the process. However, American theories, in particular, have reintroduced the notion of person and influence in their discussion on how texts are affected by other texts, and questioned the division between sources and influences on the one hand and intertextuality on the other. Jay Clayton and Eric Rothstein argue that "the discourse of intertextuality was already implicit in the study of literary influences as a methodology" (1991, 155). They point out that while Kristeva coined the term "intertextuality," she was herself indebted to Bakhtin as a source.

As in other genres of literature, there is an interweaving of other texts, as well as metatextual comments in life writing. The psychological and emotional responses to books is often noted, as well as the way books may have a real impact on women's lives: for example, Joyce Zonana's reading of de Beauvoir's *Memoirs of a Dutiful Daughter* determines her attitude to her own mother. Through intertextuality, the dialectical and dialogic process of reading is emphasized. Examining *The Bondwoman's Narrative* by Hannah Crafts in this book, Josette Spartacus suggests the slave enters into a dialogue with the text of *Jane Eyre* and *Bleak House*, and that the juxtaposition of texts is transformative. When Hannah Crafts immerses herself in Brontë's and Dickens's novels (some might say pilfering from them or plagiarizing them), she becomes Jane and Esther. She sees them not merely as characters but as the narrators of novelized autobiographies and she considers herself as the author of a narrative that is as powerful as the ones Brontë's and Dickens's narrators produced.

The specificity of intertextuality in life writing not only lies in the presence of intertexts, which is common to all literature, but also in determining the "culture of reading" and the socialization of women as authors. "One of the most important aspects of women's biographical and autobiographical productions is what they reveal of women's relationships to the sphere of the literary and to literary culture," Laura Marcus writes (1994, 268). Memoirs offer an insight into the way women are socialized into literature. By discussing sources and other authors, writers take positions in the literary field. In Anna Jameson's case, which Anne-Florence Quaireau analyses in this collection, travel writing is also travel reading, as the traveller travels through books and land. The travelogue is turned into a space where the traveller strikes up a discussion with her famous predecessors. In some instances, autobiographical writing becomes a metaphor for reading.

The confrontation with the canon is essential, for women often realize that the canon has excluded them or misrepresented them. Through reading, women writers learn the implicit or explicit hierarchy of genre and gender. They also use autobiographies to project an image of themselves as writers, or, in Marcus's words, "define, negotiate or contest their 'professional' identities as authors" (268–9). Anna Jameson quoted and paid tribute to Alexander Henry, the famous author of travel narratives, in order to present herself as both Henry's inheritor and the author of a new kind of travel narrative, one that would fill in the blanks in male travelogues. In her autobiography, New Zealand writer Janet Frame addressed her public image as a "mad" writer, and tried to reclaim control of her identity by writing in the first person.

READING AS SELF-TRANSFORMATION: AN ONTOLOGY OR SOCIAL TECHNOLOGIES OF THE SELF?

When personal histories of reading are integrated into autobiographical narratives, reading becomes intimately linked to the definition and representation of the self, a central concern in women's life writing. As numerous life stories testify, reading takes part in the construction of an identity, or the discovery of one's true identity, and the process of individuation. Reading may become a vicarious mode of living as it extends one's horizon. It is also a ubiquitous experience since memorialists find a world of its own in reading. One autobiographical model for writing's one life, the woman's story of development from childhood to adulthood (*Bildungsroman*) is particularly likely to interweave reading with self-development. Thus, Anne-Claire Marpeau in this collection establishes that Nancy Huston's *Bad Girl* concludes with the account of two births, the birth of the little girl and that of the writer.

Reading and identity are strongly interrelated in contemporary autobiographies, because of what is known as the "modern identity crisis": modern identities are no longer bestowed by social backgrounds (religion, class, ethnic background), but it is now up to the individuals to find their own path to individuation and identity, as several social theorists have demonstrated (Erhenberg 1998; Kauffman 2004). In their chapter on "postethnicity narratives" Julia Watson and Sidonie Smith point out that "new kinds of narratives have emerged that explore a postethnic identity that challenges earlier versions of ethnic identity as fixed in place, history and culture" (Smith and Watson 2010, 157).

In this respect, women's identity formation is more difficult to negotiate than men's, as traditional gender roles still confer identities on women creating diverse dilemmas and double-binds in their identity-making. The constraints of social structures and gender stereotypes are still heavier for women. Consequently, reading may help invent possible selves, protect women against constraining roles, but also be an impediment to identity formation. Psychoanalytical concepts of identification, transference and narcissism may be useful to analyse some of the most extreme phenomena of reader identification to a character, while constructivist theories of the self as a reflexive model present modern identity as plural and polyphonic. Many contemporary life writings stress the transformative power of reading in their life. Growing up, the narrator of *Dream Homes* refuses to learn cooking skills from her mother; instead, she turns to books as a way to escape from traditional gendered roles. In an illuminating scene, the narrator swaps the recipe books for the Thesaurus: "I evaluated synonyms in my bedroom, rifling through an old thesaurus, sampling the sounds: "*'Hunger,' I said to myself, 'appetite, craving, greed.'* 'Identity,' I pondered, 'agreement, likeness, self'" (Zonana 2008, 30). The words she samples and tastes are not only a metaphor for the writing experience, but also a gateway to her ultimate desires and a sense of identity. The relationship between identity, reading and writing united by food and language is striking here. With life writing, we may wonder whether identity is formed before reading, therefore already fixed, or shaped in the process of reading, thus in performance. In any case, reading works against essentialist assumptions about writing as an expression of the self.

For writers such as Louise Erdrich and the 15 indigenous women whose autobiographical essays were collected in *Here First* (2000), the relationship between reading, writing and the expression of the self remains complex. When discussing their art, indigenous women writers often reflect on the confluence between the oral and written strands in their work. Their identity as writers is informed by these two modes. They both write about the influence of the books they read and of the vital role of storytelling, paying tribute to their mothers and grandmothers as storytellers. As Elisabeth Bouzonviller argues in this collection, Erdrich's quest about the meaning of literature in *Books and Islands in Ojibwe Country* is closely linked to a quest for origins, which can only be found in her maternal ancestor's Ojibwe country. Louise Erdrich gives equal importance to the Ojibwe petroglyphs and other tribal signifiers she finds there, and reads, and to the books she surrounds herself with. In doing so, she explores her rhizomatic identity. All in all, reading is involved in the origin and process of writing a life; sometimes it becomes the ultimate goal of autobiography when, as Proust hoped in finishing *La Recherche*, the book furnishes readers with "the means of reading what lay inside themselves" (1927/1983, 3.1089).

The essays are organized around five parts that explore diverse aspects of the reading experience in female life writing. Thus, the collection begins with the recent and popular form of the graphic memoir that visually portrays women as readers in order to tell personal stories of artistic vocation, and presents reading as a means of "breaking the frames through which women have been read," as Sidonie Smith and Julia Watson demonstrate. Part I, "Reading, Writing & Othering/Authoring Themselves," considers how the graphic artists Alison Bechdel and Ellen Forney, the nineteenth-century English travel writer Anna Jameson, the American song writer Patti Smith and the English writer Jeanette Winterson have questioned representations of women and used literary foremothers and forefathers to create intersexual personae that enabled them to become writers. Part II, "Reading and Misreading the Canon," addresses the question of whether the woman writer should not misread rather than read the canon to write herself. The chapters focus on Virginia Woolf's autobiographical essays and on autobiographical works by Nathalie Sarraute, Monique Wittig, Hélène Cixous and Nancy Huston. They explore the female writer's relationship to the canon, including the canonic forms of autobiography, which these writers play with. Part III, "Reading as Resistance and Emancipation," a core section in the collection, considers how for women such as diarist Alice James, former slaves Harriet Jacobs and Hannah Crafts, and New Zealand writer Janet Frame, reading canonical works was a life-saving practice, enabling them to escape from physical and mental prisons and to find their voices. Part IV, "Reading to Write herself in the World," analyses a postethnic family memoir by the Canadian writer Janice Kulyk Keefer, a hybrid work by Ruth Ozeki, a half-Japanese half-Caucasian American writer who lives in Canada, and a poetic memoir by the Asian American writer Maxine Hong Kingston, in order to show that these writers read and write their lives with the lives of others, building bridges across countries and centuries, as they meditate on time or inscribe their personal history into History. Finally, Part V, "Reading Herself through Oral and Written Traditions," examines two culinary memoirs, autobiographical essays by Native American women writers, and two works by the American writer Louise Erdrich, showing that in these works, the woman writer's quest for identity rests on a tension between different cultural traditions that may be resolved or unresolved. "Books, Why?," the question Louise Erdrich asks in *Books and Islands in Ojibwe Country*, resonates throughout the life narratives and the essays that analyse them, providing an apt conclusion to the collection in the form of an open-ended question that will continue to be addressed by female readers.

NOTES

1. United Nations Education, Scientific and Cultural Organization [UNESCO] Institute of Statistics, September 2010.
2. Cavallo Gugliemo, Roger Chartier, *Histoire de la lecture dans le monde occidental*, 2ème ed. (Paris: Seuil, 2001); Manguel, Alberto, *A History of Reading* (New York: Viking/Penguin, 1996).
3. Female reading in the Victorian Age has been the object of a number of studies as the period not only witnessed an increase of female readership, but also a surge of discourses and images about women's reading. See also *Women's Reading in Britain, 1750–1835: A Dangerous Recreation*, by Jacqueline Pearson (Cambridge: Cambridge University Press, 1999), and *Images of the Woman Reader in Victorian British and American Fiction*, by Catherine Golden (Tallahassee: University Press of Florida, 2003).
4. Donna E. Alvermann, Norman Unrau, and Robert B. Ruddell, eds, *Theoretical Models and Processes of Reading* (Newark, DE: International Reading Association, 2013), 701.

REFERENCES

Alvermann, Donna E., Norman Unrau, and Robert B. Ruddell, eds. 2013. *Theoretical Models and Processes of Reading*. Newark: International Reading Association.

Bloom, Harold. 1975. *A Map of Misreading*. Oxford: Oxford University Press.

Cavallo, Gugliemo, and Roger Chartier. 2001. *Histoire de la lecture dans le monde occidental*. 2ème ed. Paris: Éditions du Seuil.

Charles, Michel. 1977. *Rhétorique de la lecture*. Paris: Éditions du Seuil.

de Certeau, Michel. 1988/1984. Reading as Poaching. In *The Practice of Everyday Life*, 165–176. Trans. S. Rendall. Los Angeles/London: University of California Press.

Eco, Umberto. 1979. *Lector in Fabula*. Milan: Bompiani.

Ehrenberg, Alain. 1998. *La fatigue d'être soi. Dépression et société*. Paris: Odile Jacob.

Felski, Rita. 1989. *Beyond Feminist Aesthetics: Feminist Literature and Social Change*. Cambridge, MA: Harvard University Press.

Fetterley, Judith. 1978. *The Resisting Reader: A Feminist Approach to American Fiction*. Bloomington: Indiana University Press.

Flint, Kate. 1993. *The Woman Reader, 1837–1914*. Oxford: Clarendon Press.

Foucault, Michel. 1981/1971. The Order of Discourse. In *Untying the Text: A Post-structuralist Reader*, ed. Robert Young, 51–76. Trans. Ian McLeod. Boston: Routledge and Kegan Paul.

Iser, Wolfgang. 1972. The Reading Process: A Phenomenological Approach. *New Literary History* 3 (2): 279–299.

Jauss, Hans Robert. 1967. Literary History as a Challenge to Literary Theory. Trans. Elizabeth Benzinger. *New Literary History* 2 (1): 7–37. Autumn 1970.

Jay, Clayton, and Eric Rothstein, eds. 1991. *Influence and Intertextuality in Literary History*. Madison: University of Wisconsin Press.

Kadar, Marlene. 1992. Coming to Terms: Life Writing—From Genre to Critical Practice. In *Essays on Life Writing: From Genre to Critical Practice*. Toronto: University of Toronto Press.

———. 1993. *Reading Life Writing, an Anthology*. Toronto: University of Toronto Press.

Kaufmann, Jean-Claude. 2004. *L'invention de soi: une théorie de l'identité*. Paris: Armand Colin.

Littau, Karin. 2006. *Theories of Reading: Books, Bodies and Bibliomania*. Cambridge: Polity Press.

Lyons, Martyn. 2001. Les nouveaux lecteurs au XIXème siècle: Femmes, enfants, ouvriers. In *Histoire de la lecture dans le monde occidental*, ed. Gugliemo Cavallo and Roger Chartier, 365–400. Paris: Éditions du Seuil.

Mangel, Alberto. 1996. *A History of Reading*. New York: Viking/Penguin.

Marcus, Laura. 1994. *Auto/Biographical Discourses: Theory, Criticism, Practice*. Manchester: Manchester University Press.

Planté, Christine. 1989. *La petite sœur de Balzac*. Paris: Éditions du Seuil.

Proust, Marcel. 1983/1927. *Remembrance of Things Past*. 3 vols. Trans. C. K. Scott Moncrieff and Terence Kilmartin. Harmondsworth: Penguin.

Ricœur, Paul. 1985. *Temps et Récit* 3. Paris: Éditions du Seuil.

Schweickart, Patrocinio P. 1995. Reading Ourselves: Toward a Feminist Theory of Reading. In *Readers and Reading*, ed. Andrew Bennett, 66–93. London: Longman.

Smith, Sidonie, and Julia Watson. 2010. *Reading Autobiography. A Guide for Interpreting Life Narratives*. Minneapolis: University of Minnesota Press.

———. 2017. *Life Writing in the Long Run: A Smith & Watson Autobiography Studies Reader*. [E-reader version].

Steele, Kathryn Lenore. 2008. *Navigating Interpretive Authorities: Women Readers and Reading Models in the Eighteenth Century*. PhD diss., Rutgers University, New Brunswick.

Winslow, Donald J. 1980. *Life-Writing: A Glossary of Terms in Biography, Autobiography, and Related Forms*. 2nd ed. Honolulu: University of Hawai'i Press.

Zonana, Joyce. 2008. *Dream Homes*. New York: The Feminist Press.

PART I

Reading, Writing & Othering/ Authoring Themselves

Contrapuntal Reading in Women's Comics: Alison Bechdel's *Fun Home* and Ellen Forney's *Marbles*

Sidonie Smith and Julia Watson

INTRODUCTION

In the 1960s and '70s, activists engaged in the project of feminist "consciousness-raising" sought to define a new praxis of self-reading as both an intensive scrutiny of experiential history and an analysis joining that personal story to the political history of women's oppression under capitalist patriarchy. In the 1980s and '90s American and British feminists argued that, for women readers, be they artists, writers, or activists, the project of claiming agency entailed a process of reading against the history of woman's status as an object to be read, and postulating a subject who acts. Similarly for French feminists of the 1980s and '90s, a

S. Smith (✉)
University of Michigan, Ann Arbor, MI, USA

J. Watson
The Ohio State University, Columbus, OH, USA

© The Author(s) 2018
V. Baisnée-Keay et al. (eds.), *Women's Life Writing and the Practice of Reading*, Palgrave Studies in Life Writing,
https://doi.org/10.1007/978-3-319-75247-1_2

preoccupation with language and linguistic processes was linked to "the temporal rhythms of the body ... closer to the sense[s] of touch and taste than sight" (Martin Jay in McBean 2015, 141 n. 70).[1] Such theorizing emphasized palpable embodiment and reclaimed women's bodies from the abject otherness projected on them by much psychoanalytic theory. Now, in the early twenty-first century, shifts in theoretical discourse to conceptual vocabularies focused on visuality, embodiment, spectatorship, agency, precarity, and affect, as well as the influence of interdisciplinary lenses drawn from queer theory and disability studies, suggest new strategies for reading contemporary genres of life narrative focused on documenting, representing, and bearing witness to women's experiential histories.

One robust site of feminist theorizing is the popular form of graphic memoir, which explores and exploits the potential of drawn lines in comics to tell personal stories of becoming and being an artist. Cartoonists as diverse as Marjane Satrapi, Phoebe Gloeckner, Lynda Barry, and Julie Doucet have produced graphic memoirs in the flourishing field of women's comics. Many of these graphic memoirs play with and ply the conjunctions of visuality and textuality to represent women as readers and women's reading as a transformative means of breaking the frames through which women have been read. Two such graphic memoirs that have increasingly become the focus of critical studies on autographics in courses at American colleges and universities are *Fun Home: A Family Tragicomic* (2006) by Alison Bechdel and *Marbles: Mania, Depression, Michelangelo, and Me* (2012) by Ellen Forney.

As an acclaimed graphic memoir, *Fun Home* has energized academic work at the intersection of sexuality studies and comics studies; as an award-winning play on Broadway it has also reached a diverse audience outside the academy and now circulates internationally.[2] While *Marbles* has traveled less widely, its exploration of an historical link between artistic genius and mental illness makes it potentially a key text at the nexus of feminist and queer disability studies and in debates about the medicalization of neuro-diversity as mental illness.

Our analysis of acts of reading in *Fun Home* and *Marbles* depends on four larger propositions about how reading is imbricated in practices of life narrative.

Proposition 1: Every autobiographical narrator is composed of at least two entities: the narrating "I", who tells her own experiential history; and an earlier version of herself, referred to as the narrated "I."[3]

Proposition 2: Most narrating I's configure their engagement with others either as *mentors* who read them helpfully or as *misreaders* who misunderstand them and must be addressed and potentially redressed.

Proposition 3: Within this interplay of self-reading, some narrating "I"'s emphasize explicit acts of reading and visualize or cite specific texts related to several processes: their shaping as subjects; their understanding of the salient subject positions they claim, inhabit, or resist; and their meta-commentary on the challenges and complexities of autobiographical remembering itself.

Proposition 4: The form of the graphic memoir heightens and thematizes readerly engagement in ways that are illuminating for the autobiographer as a reader of her own and others' life narratives. In drawing acts of reading, women graphic artists construct specific kinds of readers and reading occasions that engage us as their public in acts of looking, as well as acts of verbally engaging personal storytelling.

The above propositions underlie our focus on how contemporary autographic memoirs present the figure of the feminist reader at the intersection of drawn and textual media, and how the act of drawing affects the presentation and the reception of that reader. Both *Fun Home* and *Marbles* depict reading as a process in which the narrating "I" shows her younger narrated "I" engaging with writers and visual artists at the same time as that earlier self was encountering influential others who read her. These others include parents, family, and lovers in *Fun Home*, and a mother, friends, and a therapist in *Marbles*. Further, both comics spur readers to interrogate the frames of their comics against both the written text on the page and their own inherited belief systems, which include assumptions about contemporary issues that have generated anxiety-provoking crises for them: for Bechdel, the genealogical and psychical legacy of sexuality; and, for Forney, the psychodynamics of mental health.

Both of these comics require us to discern three figures of the reader: (1) the drawn figure of the narrated "I" as an earlier version of the graphic artist who enacts desperate misreadings; (2) the drawn figure of the narrated "I" as an earlier narrating "I" engaged in conversation or personal reflections about her struggles with sexuality and creativity; and (3) the drawn figure of the narrating "I" as an older artist rereading and reflecting on her past.

These multiple drawn figures of the artist-reader in the comics of Bechdel and Forney also invite readers to perform three kinds of reading of their graphic memoirs: (1) in *the visual mode*, involving how we "read" the comics' images and marks; (2) in *the textual mode*, involving how we read the assemblage compiled of numerous archival and written texts; and (3) in *the memorial mode*, involving how we read the narrating I's process of remembering and its effects. Taken together, these entwined acts of reading the complex narrative positions of autographics and engaging in their reading practices comprise a new mode of reading that is layered and continuously self-reflexive. We call this process a contrapuntal hermeneutic of reading, that is, reading attentive to the situated play of visual and verbal counter-narratives throughout the comics. As Hillary L. Chute asserts, "comics texts give shape to lost histories and bodies," thereby offering "a new seeing" (Chute 2016, 38). Thinking of the process of reading in graphic memoirs as a new kind of seeing that retrieves and represents what has been lost or suppressed argues for the importance of resituating reading not only as a mode of reception but a mode of active agency in the project of self-making.

ALISON BECHDEL'S *FUN HOME: A FAMILY TRAGICOMIC*

On its surface, Alison Bechdel's *Fun Home: A Family Tragicomic* is a hybrid graphic memoir about growing up in rural Pennsylvania in a family that runs a funeral ["fun"] home and is comprised of an artistic and autistic group of individuals who inhabit their home as if it is an "artists' colony" (134). Part of *Fun Home*'s story is daughter Alison's discovery of her identity as a graphic artist and a lesbian. She must also confront the death of her father at age 44 when she was 17, likely by suicide, and the suppressed history of his homosexuality that links his desire to her own. Beautifully drawn and wittily narrated, *Fun Home* is several things: a family memoir, a biographical portrait of a father, a coming-of-age narrative by a graphic artist, and a queer coming-out story.

And it is more. As Hillary L. Chute has observed, "Bechdel's drawing and, in some cases, redrawing of archival materials [is] an embodied repetition" (Chute 2010, 183). Nearly every page of the comic relates reading texts from a variety of literary and personal archives to reading oneself.

Fig. 2.1 Bechdel, 76. (From *Fun Home: A Family Tragicomic* by Alison Bechdel. Copyright © 2006, by Alison Bechdel. Reprinted by permission of Houghton Mifflin Harcourt Publishing Company. All rights reserved.)

References to the Modernist master narratives of Proust, James Joyce, F. Scott Fitzgerald, and others locate self-discovery within a family context that links artistic productivity to sexual repression in the twentieth century. Against these texts Bechdel juxtaposes a narrative of sexual diversity, drawn from feminist and queer counter-canons that emerged in the retrieval of works by Colette, Oscar Wilde, Radclyffe Hall, and others, and the publication of 1970s "coming-out" anthologies such as *Word Is Out* (Fig. 2.1). The assemblage of these narratives serves as a body of literary evidence that enables Alison to recognize her own and her father's sexuality as something other than "deviant" or perverted. Assembling a Modernist canon and a gay-and-lesbian counter-canon also challenges readers to extend their prowess in reading between words and images, as several critics of *Fun Home* have noted. Robin Lydenberg observes that "Bechdel arrives ultimately at her own understanding of reading as an ongoing struggle ... [and] teaches her readers to be attentive ... to the ... materiality of reading" (133). Robyn Warhol asserts that "a third layer, the division of the verbal between voiceover narration and dialogue ... breaks the dual structure of 'story' and 'discourse' by using 'the space between' words and pictures to extend possibilities for the representation of consciousness" (1). Julia Watson observes how readers engage reading as a material and embodied practice in *Fun Home*'s "interplay between the erotic and the necrotic [that] generates meanings as incarnate—in bodies ... connected to our own as we touch and turn the pages" (35).

If young Alison was a reader, she was also subjected to being read. In her narrative her father was her first reader, but one who misread her by trying to make her "feminine." The narrating "I" must work through the labyrinth of her father's misreadings to resolve how, despite them, his example of gay desire supported her. The Modernist narratives that he revered, as a high school English teacher, become her literary and bio-graphical model of the Proustian "network of transversals" by which the innate homosexual desire that linked them genealogically can be acknowl-edged as a core erotic truth (Bechdel 102). Three examples of kinds of reading in *Fun Home*—as intertextual, archival, and self-reflexive—suggest the multiple acts of reading in which the graphic memoir invites readers to participate.[4]

Reading Intertextually

The frames and gutters of the opening page of *Fun Home* visualize reading as intertextual in graphic terms. The bottom right frame depicts the child Alison "flying" on her father's feet, with Tolstoy's novel *Anna Karenina* lying on the oriental rug next to them. Its opening page famously begins: "Happy families are all alike; every unhappy family is unhappy in its own way" (3). Although the sentence is not cited, readers readily recall Tolstoy's beginning. And it offers a literary intertext to contextualize the introspec-tive and literary family in *Fun Home*. In the way the drawing places the daughter over her father's hands and feet, it enlists the reader to observe the three-dimensional quality of this apparently flat comic page (Bechdel 3) (Fig. 2.2). Visually, learning to "fly," a metaphor for growing up, is depicted as a complicated process, in which the figure of the child, of ambiguous gender when seen from behind, is not yet either male or female. The frame's dialogue boxes, one within and one outside it, signal how the narrative is set up: its narrating I will comment at both the discur-sive and the meta-discursive levels.

In these first pages the comic boxes that precede and follow the frame add further glosses about reading by making a lexical reference to the cir-cus acrobatics of "Icarian games" as a metaphor for the father–daughter relationship. The frame also implies the metanarrative of the Icarus–Daedalus story about both the benefits and the potential dangers of pater-nal mentoring in nurturing creativity through "flying." The Icarus myth, which is thematized and inverted throughout *Fun Home*, also links the father–daughter relationship to the spirals of mentoring in James Joyce's *A Portrait of the Artist as a Young Man* and *Ulysses*, an allusiveness that

Fig. 2.2 Bechdel, 3. (From *Fun Home: A Family Tragicomic* by Alison Bechdel. Copyright © 2006, by Alison Bechdel. Reprinted by permission of Houghton Mifflin Harcourt Publishing Company. All rights reserved.)

structures *Fun Home*. Bechdel incorporates these multiple layers of reading—drawn, cited, and formally enacted—into a personal story of origin staging young Alison's desire to achieve perfect balance in the father–child relationship and the inevitability of failing and falling.

Finally, these three initial comic frames situate the reader at three different angles of viewing. The first is a fourth-wall proscenium view, how an observer might regard the scene; the second is a worm's-eye view that suggests the child's subjective angle of vision; and the third is a bird's-eye view from the adult perspective of the narrating "I." Moreover, on turning the page, readers encounter a fourth frame with a rotated view: the child crashing to the floor as her father stops supporting her body. The sequence of these four frames introduces Bechdel's metacritical aesthetic of reading. The chronological sequence of moments, however, will be counter-balanced by a narrating "I" who reads her past contrapuntally, and invites the reader to continually juxtapose the linear time of narrative to the recursive and associative time of memory in her drawn frames.

Our close reading of *Fun Home*'s first four frames is emblematic of the multilayered intertextuality of Bechdel's graphic memoir as it "translates" Proust's literary structure of "transversals" across gendered difference into other styles of verbal and visual depiction. *Fun Home*'s intrinsically literary character, with citations from Modernist novels that serve as chapter titles, consistently filters and contextualizes the personal experience narrated in each. As several critics have observed, *Fun Home* is profoundly citational throughout. For example, Bechdel shapes a detailed sequence of exchanges between Alison and her father shortly before his death as a parallel to the structure of "the Ithaca moment" in Joyce's *Ulysses*. Characters also consciously model themselves on literary exemplars: Bruce, Alison's father, styles himself as Jay Gatsby in *The Great Gatsby*, and frequently cites from it. Helen, her mother, is an amateur actress who recites lines from Oscar Wilde's play, *The Importance of Being Earnest*, and "Sunday Morning" by Wallace Stevens, her favorite poet, to gloss familial life.

But teenaged Alison also draws on a different domain of literary references that illuminate the child's life, ranging from the domestic (Dr. Benjamin Spock's *Baby and Child Care*) to lesbian and gay counterculture. For example, Bechdel draws teenaged Alison riotously reading passages from a children's book, Roald Dahl's *James and the Giant Peach*, as she and her girlfriend engage in oral sex. Another frame depicts Alison's pleasure in reading Colette while she masturbates, and the narrator metatextually complicates this scene with a reference to how Joyce incorporates the Nausicaa episode of Homer's *Odyssey* in *Ulysses* (Bechdel, 10) (Fig. 2.3). For readers conversant with multiple literary contexts *Fun Home* glosses moments of the pleasures of reading as alternately comic and tragic, as its subtitle, *A Family Tragicomic*, suggests.

Reading Archivally

Another layer of texts to be read in *Fun Home* are the documents from several visual and verbal archives that it meticulously redraws throughout the comic; photographs are never used. The replications of documents are, as Chute suggests, part of the "'labyrinthine' structure" of the narrative in its recursive "returns again and again to picture and repicture central, traumatic events" (Chute 2010, 183). *Fun Home*'s redrawn documents include: several letters that were exchanged between Bechdel's mother and father during their courtship; the adolescent diaries of Alison, the budding artist; maps of the family's home town, Beech Creek,

Fig. 2.3   Bechdel, 10 (detail). (From *Fun Home: A Family Tragicomic* by Alison Bechdel. Copyright © 2006, by Alison Bechdel. Reprinted by permission of Houghton Mifflin Harcourt Publishing Company. All rights reserved.)

Pennsylvania, and reproductions of the house's décor and wallpaper; and pages citing passages not only from Modernist novels, but also dictionaries, catalogs, newspapers, and a police report. The replication of these numerous archives attests to the material quality of *Fun Home*'s textuality in Bechdel's concern to not just document but embody Alison's history.

The pages redrawn from Bechdel's adolescent diaries in the later chapters of *Fun Home*, for example, develop an extended narrative thread about adolescent Alison's foray into writing autobiographically. When, as a corrective to Alison's obsessive-compulsive disorder, her father gives her a funeral home calendar and tells her to "just write down what's happening," she responds by beginning a diary (140). Its daily chronicles, reproduced in the younger narrated "I"'s drawn child-scrawl, fill many pages with names and dates. But soon young Alison's emerging self-consciousness compels her to write "I think" after each sentence, and later to compress this marking of her perceptions into a drawn circumflex, making the entries all but unreadable (Bechdel 148) (Fig. 2.4). The diary's inauthenticity increases when Alison, because of her poor penmanship, is required to dictate "official" episodes of her daily life to her mother.

Young Alison's internal life as an adolescent beginning to explore her sexuality is illegible in another sense. For example, the narrated "I"'s diary has an entry on swimming, but none on getting her first menstrual period;

Fig. 2.4   Bechdel, 148 (detail). (From *Fun Home: A Family Tragicomic* by Alison Bechdel. Copyright © 2006, by Alison Bechdel. Reprinted by permission of Houghton Mifflin Harcourt Publishing Company. All rights reserved.)

such personal stories are censored in her formal family. As readers we move contrapuntally between reading the narrated "I"'s diary in the comic boxes and the older narrating "I"'s meta-commentary in the boxes above them on its inadequacies and omissions. That is, Bechdel reads into the silences of her younger self, interpreting scrawls and gaps as more revealing than her childhood comments.

Finally, when teenaged Alison abandons keeping a diary, Bechdel sums up this process as "the implicit lie of the blank page" (186). That blankness is the culmination of the narrating "I"'s substitution for the diary's reconstruction of her official history. And it bespeaks the experiential past of her unacknowledged sense of homosexual desire that she and her father share, which is formative for her sexuality. Ironically, then, Alison's failure in the conventional autobiographical form of the diary becomes the starting point for an innovative autographic self-presentation told contrapuntally in the tensions between comics images and the family story. As readers learn to read *Fun Home* intertextually, archivally, recursively, and metacritically, its depiction of reading and drawing instructs us in how to read differently, and read for difference, her construction of a multitextual and intermedial self.

Reading Photographs Self-Reflexively

Bechdel uses a redrawn photograph from the family album to open each chapter and redraws photographs at several other points. While these "photographs" cannot speak, the questions posed about them by the narrating "I" reference both the family's and the American nation's histories. Some photos allude to the secret past of her father's homosexual desire that she cannot directly access because he never "came out" while alive, despite his "dandy" qualities, but that she speculates about as his genetic legacy. A few of the photographs make visual, sexually explicit allusions to her father's secret past, which Bechdel underscores by marking the act of reading—hers of her past and the viewer's of *Fun Home*—with a drawn hand, life-sized or larger, that holds the drawn photograph and touches its subject.

For example, Alison's thumb and forefinger are drawn holding an old photograph of her father as a college student wearing a woman's bathing suit (Bechdel, 120) (Fig. 2.5). The narrating "I" within the frame muses, "[The] pose he strikes is not mincing or silly at all. He's lissome, elegant" (120).

Fig. 2.5 Bechdel, 120 (detail). (From *Fun Home: A Family Tragicomic* by Alison Bechdel. Copyright © 2006, by Alison Bechdel. Reprinted by permission of Houghton Mifflin Harcourt Publishing Company. All rights reserved.)

And the metatextual comment above the frame observes, "What's lost in translation is the complexity of loss itself" (120). Taken together, these musings both reflect on cross-dressing as a "translation" of sexual identity and probe the "loss" of knowledge of not just her father's hidden sexuality, but also the complex interchange of their "reading" of each other due to his suppressed homosexual legacy. As the narrating "I" reads this photo, the reader reads along with her even while "reading" her. Such acts of reading are, however, simultaneously prompts to the reader's curiosity about "dirty pictures" that invite voyeurism and thereby make readers conscious of their own suppressed desires. Thus, *Fun Home* both summons readers to intimate engagement and counteracts that impulse as it reflects on the act of looking at and reading others' confessional disclosures through the documents and images it redraws.

In sum, *Fun Home* prompts readers to read on multiple levels across the wide and diverse network of literary texts and archival documents that it assembles in tantalizing visual fragments. This process provokes cultural speculations about gender fluidity, filiality, embodied identification, and the historically conditioned processes of sexual identification. The few examples of intertextual layering from frame to frame that we have described in *Fun Home* suggest how its recursive structure of self-reflection implicates many domains of visual and verbal reading. This layering of drawn reading in a wide range of documents and texts requires readers to acquire a contrapuntal method of reading *Fun Home*'s disjunctions and the seeming incoherence it sets up between words and images across different contexts and temporalities. As readers traverse its spatial and historical gutters and gaps, they discover how the text constructs its narrative itineraries, and how literary metaphor may both veil and disclose erotic truth. *Fun Home* is, then, an autographic model for reading stories linked through at times ambiguous references and transverse logics that refuse the simple coherence of linear narrative for a different kind of reading, one that is multilayered, recursive, and ethically attuned.

Ellen Forney's *Marbles: Mania, Depression, Michelangelo, and Me*

In 1998, queer comicbook artist Ellen Forney was diagnosed with bipolar disorder. She spent nearly a decade in treatment and on various medications, eventually achieving relative stability. Published in 2012, *Marbles: Mania, Depression, Michelangelo, and Me* is an autographic that chronicles her journey from diagnosis to management achieved through a "trial-and-error" process of medication and therapeutic regimes. Intriguingly, Forney's graphic memoir went public as a story of "coming-out," not in the usual sense of a narrative of sexuality but as a coming-out narrative of being bipolar. *Marbles* is also a visual and textual meditation on the relationship of "madness" and artistic creativity. More specifically than Bechdel's, Forney's graphic memoir engages with the meaning of creativity as both an artistic process and a mental-health issue.

Structurally, the arc of Forney's quest story shifts between visual registers and personal readings of the effects and felt affects of the psychic states of mania and depression experienced by her younger narrated "I". Its chapters alternate between two kinds of stories: dyadically-oriented scenes of therapeutic encounters between her as patient and her analyst, the joined yet distinct readers of Ellen's symptoms through applications of the *Diagnostic and Statistical Manual of Mental Disorders IV* (henceforth referred to as *DSM*[5]); and Ellen's acts of self-reading and readings of visual and verbal texts by and about a roster of artists and writers that gradually become a compendium on the possible relationship of artistic creativity and mental illness. By rendering her acts and practices of reading, the narrating/drawing "I" tracks the narrated "I"'s search for evidence in several sources: the *DSM*, genealogy, the lives of artists and writers, and her own interpretive capacities. Her quest for a diagnostic identity is also a search for a deeper understanding of the vexed relationship between creativity and what she freely calls "craziness." Three kinds of reading thus engage the protagonist of *Marbles* and the readers she solicits: self-reading as a method of visualizing psychic states, reading as a diagnostic and therapeutic enterprise, and reading as a process of researching textual archives—scientific and artistic—in both visual and verbal modes.

Reading Psychic States Visually

Forney opens her graphic memoir *in medias res* on a manic high, with the drawing hand of her narrating "I" remembering and visualizing the effects of the frenetic, erotic energy of her exuberant younger artist-self. The younger Ellen is in the midst of a "transformation," feeling the pain and physical rush of the needles of a tattoo artist who is refashioning her "least favorite body part" with an elaborate tattoo inscribed across her back. The narrating "I" then takes the reader back a year by drawing an Ellen who composes the design and fitfully articulates the significance of the tattoo that is later inscribed across her back (Forney 6–7) (Fig. 2.6). Forney uses

Fig. 2.6 Forney, 6. (From *Marbles: Mania, Depression, Michelangelo, and Me*, by Ellen Forney. Copyright © 2012, by Ellen Forney. Reprinted by permission of Penguin Random House and Little, Brown Book Group. All rights reserved.)

this lavish two-page spread to project the affect of manic highs and the felt euphoria of creation itself. That is, in contrast to Bechdel, who in *Fun Home* often contains her story within the formal design of boxes and gutters characteristic of comics-page layout, Forney uses an early two-page spread to capture the disjunctive frenzy of manic thinking and its insight. The letters of "KRAK!!" express a synesthesia blaring out the electric charge of a sudden vision erupting in the mind. The pictures of lightning charges and ping-pong balls hopping from one word cloud to another, as well as the arrows drawn directionally but somewhat incoherently from one popcorn kernel of words to another, contribute to visualizing the way Ellen imagined her tattoo design as symbolic of her artistic uniqueness. In this messy two-page spread, Forney draws her avatar as a simplified face of eyes and mouth popped wide open. The narrated "I" is configured as a center of imagination, emitting insight and creativity. In projecting the instantaneity of Ellen's inspirations and ideas, the two pages both set a linear reading in motion and arrest our interpretation of it. As the narrating "I" remembers how she imagined which tattoo design would adequately represent her fantasy of transformation, her story of having the tattoo inscribed on her back stalls—its narration cannot be completed. With this disruption, Forney compels readers to vicariously inhabit the intensity of manic artistic creativity that the younger Ellen sought to enact as an artist driven by intense felt experience.

Visually and verbally, these two pages and succeeding ones of the narrated "I"'s remembered highs in the first three chapters have distinctive aesthetic features. In the drawings there is little white space, and drawn lines, sometimes straight, but often curvilinear, sprawl on the page. Word-thoughts unfold through the disorganized chains of a fractured logic. The sprawling lines and disorganized boxes of Forney's pages create visual and lexical axes that do not seem to align; rather, initially, they work as a manic succession that at times prods, at other times disrupts, readers' expectations of narrative. Lines radiate out from human figures and drawn objects. Images and words expand beyond the edges of frames and seem to pop off the pages. Even when episodes of manic highs are somewhat contained in regularized boxes, as in the series of pages (31–38) that show Ellen organizing and participating in a photographic shoot on lesbian sexuality (to document a project on pornographic comics), the boxes are irregularly placed on the page, overlapping at skewed angles. These lines and words explode off the pages to produce a portrait of the artist as an "in-your-face" personality, a presence who is exhausting, even alienating, to her friends represented inside the comic and to her readers outside it.

In Chap. 5 Forney turns to the felt experience of depression that inevitably followed these psychic highs. To reproduce these effects, she imports facsimiles of the sketchbook pages she made during these periods. The visual features of the imported sketchbook pages are as arresting as those on the felt experience of her highs: but here, the lines are thin, fragile, sometimes wispy to the point of disappearance (Forney 103) (Fig. 2.7).

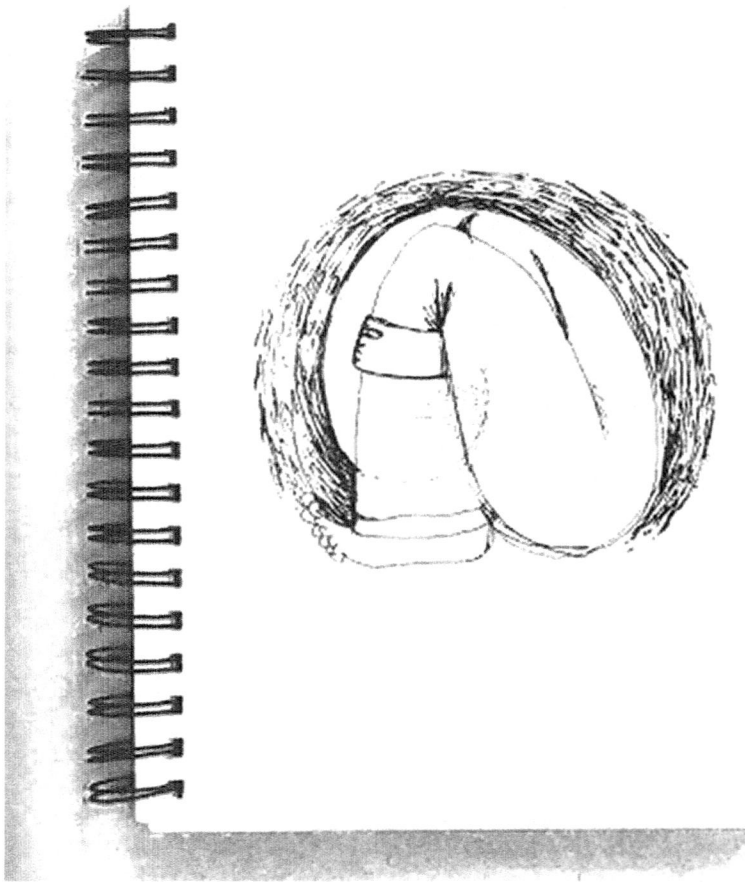

Fig. 2.7   Forney, 103. (From *Marbles: Mania, Depression, Michelangelo, and Me*, by Ellen Forney. Copyright © 2012, by Ellen Forney. Reprinted by permission of Penguin Random House and Little, Brown Book Group. All rights reserved.)

The figures are sedentary, drawn bodies without motion. Patches of solid black mark zones of bleak disappearance or inescapable constraint, a deadness at the figure's core.

In sum, then, Forney represents the visual corollary of the manic state as an explosive, hypersexualized woman who is out of control in her excesses. Similarly, she depicts bouts of depression as a woman abandoned to bloblike withdrawal into self-loathing and self-erasure. Throughout the first four chapters of *Marbles*, these visual representations of swings of the psyche in its felt experiences pose the conundrum of Forney as an artist in therapy tasked with inquiring about her own symptoms of dysfunction: How does the mind, when inside either a manic creative state or the inertia of a depressive state, analyse itself? In such states, the self-reading narrated "I" becomes a misreader, an artist misinterpreting her out-of-control mania and depression. One main way that she does this is by importing an imaginary of the mythologized figure of the tortured, crazy artist, to which we later turn.

Reading as Therapeutic Exchange

Chapter 3 introduces an alternative mode of reading and uses therapeutic scenes of dialogue to organize the unfolding of subsequent chapters. The therapist to whom Ellen turns as her life reels out of control becomes a companion reader of her experiential history. The opening page of this chapter depicts Ellen the patient and her therapist Karen, presented as a calmly neutral observer, in their first foray into the *DSM IV*. The next pages juxtapose two modes of visualization (Forney 16–18) (Fig. 2.8): on the left side of the page we see stacked, tidy boxes, bordered in simple drawn lines; these are boxes of calm and orderliness, in which the therapist's drawn finger is moving through the *DSM*'s catalog of symptoms of bipolar disorder. By contrast, on the right side of the page, the drawn boxes of chaotic content produce disorderly borders that stretch and overflow beyond the straight lines of the cartoon box; this disorder manifests the contents of the narrated "I"'s recollections of her experiences. The visual syncopation of these pages projects a sharp contrast between the calm orderliness of the therapist's intervention as a reader of both the *DSM* and her patient and Ellen's out-of-the-box frantic movements of self-projection as a creative artist.

Throughout *Marbles*, Forney depicts the therapist and patient engaged in acts of what we call symptomatic reading. Early on in representing the therapeutic process, this reading practice unfolds as the narrated "I" reads her life

Fig. 2.8   Forney, 17 (detail). (From *Marbles: Mania, Depression, Michelangelo, and Me*, by Ellen Forney. Copyright © 2012, by Ellen Forney. Reprinted by permission of Penguin Random House and Little, Brown Book Group. All rights reserved.)

in terms of the *DSM*'s set of diagnostic features constituting the identity of the person who has bipolar disorder. In this phase an identity is conferred on Ellen that she then retrospectively projects upon her past experience.

Symptomatic reading continues as the narrating "I" chronicles the treatment phase of Ellen's struggle. Ellen and her therapist read her bodily symptoms as a way to gauge the patient's response to medications for treating the disorder. In this phase Ellen comes to recognize that there is no easy "cure" through medication. Rather, there is the difficult work of taking agency in self-reading, or "managing," her behavior with the help of a usable drug cocktail (only achieved after four years of experimentation). That is, Forney presents self-reading as a multi-stage process in which Ellen initially adopts a set of tropes to shape her understanding of symptom, etiology, and psychopharmacology. Eventually she collaboratively develops a more malleable set of practices for making her bipolarity manageable.

In other words, the chronicle of *Marbles* initially moves toward Ellen's internalizing of the therapist's role to become a better self-analyst. But, as Elizabeth Tacke observes, Ellen is also on a quest to read beyond this medical model of interpretation. Forney chronicles this quest by depicting scene after scene in which Ellen engages with the works of other artists and writers. Forney as narrating "I" animates this quest by posing an artistic aesthetic that reframes the diagnostic terminology of the therapist through representing disjunction and incoherence. Tacke argues that eruptions of incoherence "demonstrate Forney's choice to represent her bipolarity and the results of that bipolarity in a nonlinear, poetic, and artistic style that resists a singular reading" (12) of the kind scripted by the *DSM*.

In the final chapter of *Marbles*, Forney absents the therapist from the boxes of dialogic therapy to present Ellen as both therapist and patient (Forney 235) (Fig. 2.9). Two Ellens are drawn together in orderly boxes of encounter. Forney, the narrating "I" who has achieved workable stability as "a high-functioning bipolar," gently assures Ellen, her younger narrated "I" of 1998 who was diagnosed as bipolar, that she will come through the struggle to achieve some kind of manageable balance and remain the creative artist she desires to be. In other words, the narrating "I" is presented as a woman who has successfully found a method of self-monitoring and mindful self-observation, a key aspect of cognitive behaviour therapy, yet does not slavishly adopt the tropes and definitions of the *DSM*.

Fig. 2.9 Forney, 235 (detail). (From *Marbles: Mania, Depression, Michelangelo, and Me*, by Ellen Forney. Copyright © 2012, by Ellen Forney. Reprinted by permission of Penguin Random House and Little, Brown Book Group. All rights reserved.)

Reading as Research

Marbles is not only a teleological narrative tracking Forney's journey from diagnosis in 1998 to self-monitoring balance a half-decade later; it is simultaneously a retrospective narrative of the artist moving from the position of an initially naïve misreader to that of a more enlightened reader of the lives of other artists and the nature of creativity. Throughout *Marbles*, Forney depicts Ellen reading the autobiographical narratives of writers and artists, from Leonardo to Virginia Woolf, and viewing the visual work of painters, especially their self-portraits, as well as rereading her own diaries and artist's journal. In incorporating her own autobiographical material, Forney performs acts of reading "sideways" or relationally, from her own life as an artist to biographical and autobiographical life writing about and by other artists.

Initially, her act of reading what she understands as her creative self through the *DSM*'s diagnostic category of bipolar disorder, which seems to closely describe her symptoms, troubles her. The narrated "I" observes: "My own brilliant, unique personality was neatly outlined right there, in that inanimate stack of paper" (19). Ellen's first response to this diagnosis is to embrace the identity of "crazy artist" that entwines her two identities as bipolar subject and artist. She is, as she quips, a member of "Club Van Gogh" with a membership card that reads, "The true artist is the crazy artist" (22). Chronicling this earlier moment, Forney, the narrating "I", presents Ellen as mythologizing the relationship of madness and creativity.

Her reading project thus begins as an effect of "CRA-DAR," her term for a kind of "radar" attuned to identifying "crazy" artists as role models of exceptional creativity. Similar to the symptomatic reading project of therapy discussed above, CRA-DAR is a mode of reading artists' works symptomatically for signs of their lived mental instability. For instance, early in her struggle the narrated "I" reads Van Gogh's and Edvard Munch's psychic states through viewing their paintings as expressive of a craziness legible in line and colour, as well as the aesthetic of their work (117–23). In chronicling the stages of her therapeutic journey, however, Forney draws Ellen becoming a different, less prescriptive kind of reader of artists' lives and work. For example, engaging with the poetry and fiction of Sylvia Plath, Ellen finds phrases and drawings that better describe the neurological aspects of her manic phase. Consequently, she comes to regard Plath's suicide at age 30 as a cautionary tale rather than a romantic

tale of the fate of a great genius (169–71). When Ellen views Georgia O'Keeffe's paintings she discovers there are no "signs of a mental disorder" in the work itself (142). In other words, the "craziness" in artists with unstable or volatile mental lives doesn't necessarily translate to their work; nor does work expressing disorder require an artist to be "crazy." Her supplementary reading on scientific theories of creativity in Chap. 9 enables her to assess in a more nuanced way how manic and depressive states can either enable or disable creative energy and productivity. When Ellen asks, "If I take meds to prevent my mood swings, am I choosing to be less creative?" (213), she begins to recognize and redress her fear that any achievement of balance will come at the expense of diminished creativity (Forney 201) (Fig. 2.10). By the end (of her journey and her graphic memoir) Forney comes to rest in inconclusive ambiguity about the "evidence" of the relationship between mental instability and creativity.

Forney offers this narrative of her life as exemplary, a reader's companion for other artists who seek "company" in their pain and their quest. *Marbles* can thus be read as a complex self-help narrative and an educational guide for readers seeking to survive their own disabling mental conditions, such as bipolarity. Forney's drawings and story capture for readers the exhilarating highs and enervating lows of bipolar disorder. They project a "you-are-there" intensity that draws the reader into the felt experience of mania and depression. As Teresa González-Gil observes of the effect on students of reading *Marbles*: "Helped by the text and images you can feel grandiose, you can become unusual *[sic]* talkative, you can increase goal directed activity, you can become a little bit agitated or, by contrary, you can feel immersed in a deep dark sadness with no exit" (2016, 1003). Further, images and story bring readers into the struggle to both find a diagnostic identity and qualify it in order to achieve a kind of balance. The reader is ultimately situated in the position of the younger Ellen in the final chapter, who is concerned about losing a sense of herself to the effects of medication. And, just as Ellen tries on the biographies of different artists and writers to assess whose stories match her own as models of what Kay Redfield Jamison termed the "unquiet mind" and William Styron called "darkness visible," Forney offers her own narrative as a model to help readers manage cycles of mania and depression or other mental instability (Forney 90). On the graphic memoir's final page, a simply composed figure of the artist, looking into the bathroom mirror as she brushes her teeth, addresses both herself and her reader by announcing "I'm okay!"

Conclusion: Reading Contrapuntally in Women's Comics

We have explored three aspects of drawn reading and the drawn reader in *Fun Home* and *Marbles*: the representation (textual and visual) of their narrating and narrated "I"s as queer artists and embodied feminist readers; the narrativization and visualization of different kinds of reading, including the authors' readings of their earlier autobiographical writing; and the narrating "I"'s addresses to their imagined readers as a means of soliciting an ethical reading.

The practices of these two graphic memoirs converge at several points. For both Bechdel and Forney, acts of reading become a way of constituting epistemological agency. And the act of representing reading drives the story of an emerging queer artistic identity. Both Bechdel and Forney arrive at parallel recognitions through re-reading their earlier experiments in life writing, such as diaries and journals, and forging new intermedial forms of self-representation. As avid readers of a range of high- and popular-culture texts, both read their own lives through others' texts, as well as the personal evidence produced by their research into family, public, and scholarly archives. Both Bechdel and Forney also construct an intimate relationship to their readers, using several kinds of visual address to invite their participation in collaboratively rethinking the place and status of women as cultural actors and agents.

The ways that both artists conceptualize and pursue the efficacy of reading for the queer comics artist are also congruent in several ways. While the figure of the reader often serves as a signpost enabling readers to identify with the narrating "I" and vicariously seek some form of repair, *Fun Home* is not concerned with psychic recovery *per se*, although Bechdel acknowledges the obsessive-compulsive disorder that led her to keep diaries and that distinguishes the exquisite care in her replications of photos and documents. Rather, her graphic memoir seeks to redress official histories about both Bechdel's family and the legacy of Modernism by recovering a suppressed subtext of gay and lesbian archives that can generate alternative stories about the relation of artistry and sexuality. Bechdel thus guides her reader toward a hermeneutic of contrapuntal reading that emphasizes how the form of comics enables reading to become an interrogative act of moving through her "circling, 'labyrinthine' structure," rather than a linear progression (Chute 2010, 183). *Marbles*, at one level, appears to be a quest for self-management through achieving a productive level of psychic stability, and thus a modicum of "recovery" from the devastations of alternating currents of mania and depression. But recovery is a problematic goal for this feminist artist whose self-concept is grounded in exuberant non-heteronormativity and violation of conventions of all kinds. Ellen moves from being an artist who mythologizes excess and craziness as a member of Club Van Gogh to an informed, empathetic reader by learning to read and visualize differently and to accept the ambiguities of living with bipolar disorder. Along the way she enlists helpful artistic interlocutors and co-readers of her symptoms, both through her therapist and the paradigm of diagnosis and self-management offered by cognitive behavior therapy. As a connoisseur of bipolar artists' lives and work, she offers herself as a model to readers seeking a different understanding of the relationship of creativity and mania-depression. Her tracking of Ellen's transformation from an initially unstable and often self-destructive artist to a relatively balanced composer of graphic memoirs invites the text's readers not only to legitimate her achievement but to imagine their own possible paths to recovery. For Forney, then, mental "disability" is presented alternatively, as a source of creativity, not a deviation from able-bodied normativity. Her project thus queers the concept of disability to an extent. To become "abled" is redefined as finding relief from the swings of bipolarity that threaten to diminish her eroticized creative powers by coming to a balance that acknowledges the condition of bipolarity.

The dynamics of reading in both Bechdel's and Forney's autographics provoke readers to perform and to think about the hermeneutics of reading. And their examples suggest that we ask more generally, What do scenes of reading in graphic memoir accomplish? We have observed that they suggest the contours and densities of the subjectivity of narrated and narrating "I"s in intermedial ways. Scenes of reading also arrest narrative's forward teleological drive by exposing traces of affective attachment, how it feels as a comics artist to be searching for identity, self-knowledge, and a way to retrieve and commemorate memory. Furthermore, scenes of reading position the narrating "I" in a genealogy by establishing literary and visual networks of citations that reach beyond the specific text to a transnational, transtemporal collective of artists and writers. Scenes of reading also become repositories to document lived histories in the memoirs' archives and displays by replicating heterogeneous materials, including books, photographs, letters, diaries, paintings, newspapers, and the like. The primacy of scenes of reading in Bechdel's and Forney's comics emphasizes the artists' relationship to readers, both imagined and real, as they model how to read the graphic memoirs of artists engaged in drawing their embodied selves and the embodied histories of others. In them the narrating "I" in the text and the reader of the text come to reside in analogous positions.

Hillary L. Chute argues that "Comics, both in its autographic aspect and in its constant juxtaposition of word and image, reveals a form that takes up the problem of reference as central" (2016, 19). In Chute's terms, comics work in two ways: as documentary, "a set of practices that is about and instantiates the presentation of evidence" in a temporally-driven form (18) that "materialize[s] history" (26); and as witnessing, "the attestation of truth, even if that truth … is elusive or 'unclaimed'" (29). That is, comics register both "documentary innovation" and "the complexity of witnessing" (35). In *Fun Home*, this dynamic generates a reading of how erotic truth is produced at the convergence of family genealogy, history, and artistic relationships; in *Marbles*, it generates a reading of psychic truth as interrogating the relationship of erotic energy and creativity to psychic restlessness and enervation.

In their projects, acts simultaneously of documenting and witnessing, both Bechdel and Forney remake common genres of life writing. Scenes of the narrated "I" reading in *Fun Home* and *Marbles* are often an interplay of evasions and illuminations. The story of *coming-out*—in Bechdel, sexual coming out, in Forney, coming out with a mental illness—becomes a collective pastiche incorporating others' works visually and citationally. Others' texts instruct them, as a transformation of the Bildungsroman's mentors into books. And, as an instantiation of the Künstlerroman, the memoirs incorporate the artist's own earlier drawn and written diaries. The convergence of these reworked genres gives these comics a metacritical dimension that reflects on the relationship of sexuality and creativity for queer women artists working at this time.

We must, however, acknowledge the ethical challenge presented by these drawn representations of reading extreme states. The use by both Bechdel and Forney of extensive personal and public archives linked to their urgent personal crises challenges readers to resist becoming voyeuristic spectators and to engage as witnesses to the artists' efforts to make a new kind of sense of the evidence assembled by their narrating "I"'s. Thus, the process of confronting extreme states becomes an entangled and interrogatory act of reading: in *Fun Home* about what the mid-twentieth century considered homosexual "perversion"; in *Marbles* about the relationship of bipolarity, in its combination of aggressive mania and enervated depression, to creativity. As readers encounter edgy, uncomfortable issues they must decide whether and where to trust these narrating "I"'s. As we learn to read the tactics and temporal shifts of *Fun Home* and *Marbles*, their narrators emerge as queer feminist artists engaged in acts of witness to their own psychic states and histories. Through drawing archives and making comics that foreground the figure of the reader and instruct audiences in how to read, Bechdel and Forney mobilize feminist intervention to devise new reading practices for the twenty-first century.

NOTES

1. The most influential French feminist theorists were Luce Irigaray, Julia Kristeva, and Hélène Cixous.
2. *Fun Home* was serialized in *Libération*, selected for the Angoulême International Comics Festival, and has been the subject of an academic conference in France. See Juliette Cherbuliez, "There's No Place like (Fun) Home." (Note—original sources no longer available.)
3. See our discussion of four kinds of autobiographical "I"s in "Acts and Practices of Life Writing" (Smith and Watson 2010, Chap. 3).
4. Although Robin Lydenberg's essay was published after this paper was first given in 2015, Julia Watson read an earlier version of it and greatly benefitted greatly from its perceptive observations. The Modern Language Association will publish *Approaches to Teaching* Fun Home, ed. Judith Kegan Gardiner, in 2018, which will contain more essays on the topic.
5. The *DSM* has been the official handbook of the American Psychiatric Association since 1952. It gives standard criteria for diagnosing and treating mental disorders that are used by mental health workers, and is revised periodically. Forney refers to the fourth edition, but the fifth has since been released.

REFERENCES

American Psychiatric Association. 2000. *Diagnostic and Statistical Manual.* Fourth Edition, Text Revision. Washington, DC: American Psychiatric Association.

Bechdel, Alison. 2006. *Fun Home: A Family Tragicomic.* Boston/New York: Houghton Mifflin Co.

Chute, Hillary L. 2010. *Graphic Women: Life Narrative and Contemporary Comics.* New York: Columbia University Press.

———. 2016. *Disaster Drawn: Visual Witness, Comics, and Documentary Form.* Cambridge, MA/London: Belknap Press of Harvard University Press.

Forney, Ellen. 2012. *Marbles: Mania, Depression, Michelangelo, and Me.* New York: Gotham Books (Penguin).

González-Gil, Teresa. 2016. Teaching and Learning by Comics: 'Marbles: Mania, Depression, Michelangelo, and Me' (By Ellen Forney). SCIMED Central. *JSM Schizophrenia* November 26. Online open access. https://www.jscimedcentral. com/Schizophrenia/schizophrenia-1-1003.pdf. Accessed 4 July 2017.

Jamison, Kay Redfield. 1995. *An Unquiet Mind: A Memoir of Moods and Madness.* New York: Random House.

Lydenberg, Robin. 2017. Reading Lessons in Alison Bechdel's *Fun Home: A Family Tragicomic. College Literature* 44 (2) (Spring 2017): 133–165.

McBean, Sam. 2015. *Feminism's Queer Temporalities.* London/New York: Routledge.

Smith, Sidonie, and Julia Watson. 2010. *Reading Autobiography: A Guide for Interpreting Life Narratives.* Minneapolis: University of Minnesota Press, Second, expanded edition.

Styron, William. 1990. *Darkness Visible: A Memoir of Madness.* New York: Random House.

Tacke, Elizabeth. 2016. Deconstructing the Diagnostic Urge: Counter-Diagnosis and the Quest in *Marbles.* Seminar Paper (course), University of Michigan.

Tolstoy, Leo. 1963. *Anna Karenina.* Trans. Constance Garnett. New York: Random House.

Warhol, Robyn. 2011. The Space Between: A Narrative Approach to Alison Bechdel's *Fun Home. College Literature* 38 (3) (Summer): 1–20.

Watson, Julia. 2008. Autographic Disclosures and Genealogies of Desire in Alison Bechdel's *Fun Home. Biography* 31 (1 Winter): 27–56.

———. 2012. The Pleasures of Reading in Alison Bechdel's *Fun Home. Life Writing* 9 (3) (September 2012): 1–11.

CHAPTER 3

Rimbaud's Daughter or Ginsberg's Son? Patti Smith's Literary Fathers and Mothers in *Just Kids* (2010)

Stephanie Genty

INTRODUCTION

Just Kids is a promise fulfilled. A promise made to an expiring "twin" to one day tell *their* story to the world, the tale of two youths in New York between 1967 and 1979, mutually supportive and dedicated to their respective artistic development.[1] Part biography of photographer Robert Mapplethorpe, who died of AIDS in 1989, part autobiography of Patti Smith, *Just Kids* fuses the two forms of life writing as it zeros in on the period of their lives that was shared. At first separate and alternating, the tales of each protagonist's childhood and adolescence soon merge into a common coming-of-age narrative, only to separate once again as the two became established artists in their own right. *Just Kids* "kicks in the wall" separating biography from autobiography and takes the relational narrative a step further.[2] The biography of Smith's significant other is not simply "embedded" in her own life story; it is its *raison d'être*, its beginning and

S. Genty (✉)
Université d'Évry, Évry, France

© The Author(s) 2018

V. Baisnée-Keay et al. (eds.), *Women's Life Writing and the Practice of Reading*, Palgrave Studies in Life Writing, https://doi.org/10.1007/978-3-319-75247-1_3

its end, an integral part of a shared auto/biography. However, although we might refer to *Just Kids* as an "autobiographical biography," this label would eclipse the presence of other modes of life writing in this relational and intertextual textual hybrid.

It is the death of Mapplethorpe that sets the narrative into motion and with which it closes, "bookends" that "frame the memoir as an act of saying 'goodbye'" (Watson 2015, xii). As Julia Watson puts it, *Just Kids* is a memorial that "morphed" into something else, something more (Watson 2015, 136). Initially a grief memoir (autothanatography), it is equal parts celebrity and cultural memoir (autoethnography), each genre reinvented by the mother of punk in her story of a tandem artistic becoming. Indeed, *Just Kids* is above all a *künstlerroman*, albeit a non-fictional one, in its focus on two young artists' quest for selfhood.[3] Historically, this descendant of the *Bildungsroman* was Romantic and masculine; the feminine version had to wrestle with the tradition of the passive female muse, with the lack of appropriate mythological metaphors, and with the tenacious romance plot in order to grant its heroines sufficient latitude to create.[4] Only in the feminist novels of the 1960s and 1970s do we see female protagonists coming of age as artists, although such emancipation is generally associated with the sacrifice of their "womanhood." The narrator of *Just Kids* is no exception to the rule, having resolved this dilemma by identifying herself as androgynous, by fashioning herself after male artists, and by remaining "just a kid," as we shall see.

This auto/biographical *künstlerroman* is characterized by its unique fusion of relationality and intertextuality. Indeed, *Just Kids* brings into play "different kinds of textual others—historical, contingent, or significant—through which an 'I' narrates the formation or modification of self-consciousness" (Smith and Watson 2010 [2001], 86). Although the late Robert Mapplethorpe occupies a special place in this narrative, our focus on relationality will involve other textually-significant significant others, i.e., the "mothers" and "fathers" that nourished the formation of Smith's poet persona. In this tale of artistic becoming, the narrator returns to her childhood to identify the sources of her love of words and of her desire to write, both of which are associated with maternal and female literary figures. Paul John Eakin's concept of narrative identity, which sees the self as fashioned through "signifying practices," most notably "narrative constructions or stories" (Eakin 1999, 21) is particularly useful here.[5] It is a concept that reaches back to Saussurian linguistics and incorporates recent work in neurology and developmental and narrative psychology. The narrator of *Just*

Kids singles out her parents and especially her siblings as essential to her acquisition of "narrative competence" (Eakin 1999, 67). This autobiographical *künstlerroman* illustrates well "the child's awakening to the call of stories as they are performed within the family circle and the larger community" (Eakin 1999, 118). The importance of books in the Smith family is portrayed as prefiguring her own relationship to them.[6] According to *Just Kids*, books and reading were vital to the couple Smith formed with Robert Mapplethorpe and to their development as artists. It is worth noting that the multitude of literary references woven into the narrative fabric and which also participate in the construction of her poetic persona were mostly penned by men. Two of them, Arthur Rimbaud and Allen Ginsberg, will be the focus of this study, primarily devoted to *Just Kids* but taking into consideration the poetry and songs of Patti Smith whenever useful. Our goal is to attempt to evaluate to what degree the androgynous author may incarnate the "daughter of Rimbaud," as Etienne Ethaire (2010) would have it, or the son of Ginsberg.

FROM MOTHER'S DAUGHTER TO ALCOTT'S ANDROGYNE: THE BIRTH OF A YEARNING

One of the first images recorded in Patti Smith's memoir is that of a child's walk along a river with her mother. A fantastic winged creature takes to the skies, whiter than the snow blowing on the day of the child's birth in Chicago, 1946: a swan, *cygne* in French, homophone for Ferdinand de Saussure's sign (*signe*), whose signifier is judged far too inadequate to communicate the experience of the bird's whiteness and its slow ascension into the clouds. This vision, presented as the narrator's recollection of an awakening to both the importance and the impotence of language, gives birth to a desire to one day find a way to express such moments of epiphany in words. Smith writes,

> *Swan* ... The word alone hardly attested to its magnificence nor conveyed the emotion it produced. The sight of it generated an urge I had no words for, a desire to speak of the swan, to say something of its whiteness, the explosive nature of its movement, and the slow beating of its wings. ... I struggled to find words to describe my own sense of it. *Swan*, I repeated, not entirely satisfied, and I felt a twinge, a curious yearning, imperceptible to passersby, my mother, the trees, or the clouds. (Smith 2010, 3)

In *Just Kids*, it is the mother who gives the daughter the word to name this marvellous sight, a waterbird whose sinuous silhouette evokes the letter "S"—as in Smith—and whose feathers evoke the leaves of a blank page. Its translation (*cygne/signe*) conjures up the linguistics of Saussure and the novels of Marcel Proust, whose *Amour de Swan* recounts that author's recovered past. The lines we draw from Patti Smith's swan to the French *cygne/signe* connect with her often-expressed love for France and French poets, beginning with Arthur Rimbaud and his *Illuminations*, stolen from a bookstall in Philadelphia at age 16 and with which she took off, symbolically and literally, when she packed up and left for New York a few years later. From the Big Apple she flew first to Paris and then to Charleville-Mézières, where her romanticized hero had begun his youthful ascension as a poet, daydreaming on the banks of the river Meuse.[7]

The narrator of *Just Kids* also associates her mother with the first form of poetry she would encounter, that of prayer: "Now I lay me down to sleep, I pray the Lord my soul to keep. If I should die before I wake, I pray the Lord my soul to take" (4–5). According to Smith, the recitation of these words each evening, under the watchful eyes of her mother, constituted a magical door onto the divine and creativity. What was the soul, the narrator recalls asking, and could she not invent her *own* prayer to express the secrets of her heart? (5). "Freed" from the evening ritual by her mother, young Patti began to explore the meanders of her imagination in bed at night and during periods of childhood illness. Books soon replaced prayers, and this evolution was also attended by the mother: "My love of prayer was gradually rivaled by my love for the book. I would sit at my mother's feet watching her drink coffee and smoke cigarettes with a book on her lap" (6). Smith, who could not yet read, describes being fascinated by books and especially by her mother's fascination with them. When the latter learns her daughter has hidden her copy of *Foxe's Book of Martyrs* under her pillow in order to somehow absorb its meaning, she teaches her daughter to read (6). Books inspire new desires, and among them the longing to tell her own stories:

> Oddly enough, it was Louisa May Alcott who provided me with a positive view of my female destiny. Jo, the tomboy of the four March sisters in *Little Women*, writes to help support her family, struggling to make ends meet during the Civil War. … She gave me the courage of a new goal, and soon I was crafting little stories and spinning long yarns for my brother and sister. From that time on, I cherished the idea that one day I would write a book. (10–11)[8]

It is significant that Smith, looking back at her girlhood, should connect the question of gender with the desire to write, and specifically attach herself to the "boyish" model of Jo, seen as a viable female role model. This identification foreshadows her adoption of an increasingly androgynous writer persona. Smith relates the pleasure associated with the invention of stories and adventures for her siblings (11), and we can imagine how these contributed to the development of her narrative competence. She tells of reading to them (Robert Louis Stevenson's *A Child's Garden of Verses*) and of discovering comics (*Superman, Little Lulu, Classic Comics, House of Mystery*) (7). Besides *Mother Goose* and *The Red Shoes*, Smith mentions reading *The Diary of Anne Frank, Alice in Wonderland, Peter Pan* and *Snow White and the Seven Dwarfs*. Among these, the story of Peter Pan will take on particular significance for her, as evident in the recurrent references to the character in *Just Kids*: "I was of the clan of Peter Pan and we did not grow up" (10). The narrator's identification with the eternal boy child points once more to her rejection of traditional femininity and of bourgeois values and lifestyle, as well as of responsible adulthood. Her father apparently introduced her to science fiction (Arthur C. Clarke) and to combing the skies for UFOs (112). The narrator tells of sharing these familial recollections with Mapplethorpe when they first met, drawing for him the contours of her emerging identity, a "tomboy" immersed in reading and storytelling (16–17).

From Reader to Writer: Feeding on the Words of Others

Before writing, Smith would read, and widely, storing up the words that would later serve her craft. The many literary references, over 180 in all, are so many stepping-stones placed in the river of her narrative, forming a bridge between the two banks of her life story, before and after Robert Mapplethorpe. In *Just Kids*, Smith refers to a variety of genres, beginning with art books. In the first pages of her text, the evocation of her former partner's passing involves a reference to a book of paintings by Odilon Redon. *The Fabulous Life of Diego Rivera* was a gift for her 16th birthday following a visit to the art museum in Philadelphia (12). She cites books on Modigliani, Dubuffet, Picasso, Fra Angelico, Albert Ryder, Jackson Pollack, De Kooning, and especially William Blake. Smith mentions reading the poetry of Arthur Rimbaud, Charles Baudelaire, Paul Verlaine,

Stéphane Mallarmé, and Blaise Cendrars, Walt Whitman, Vachel Lindsay, Art Carney, Dylan Thomas, Frank O'Hara, Sylvia Plath, Allen Ginsberg, Gregory Corso, Gerard Malanga, Mayakovsky, Robert Creeley, and Ted Berrigan. The biographies she lists include the memoir on Jackson Pollack by Ruth Kligman and Enid Starkie's biography of Rimbaud. *Crazy Horse: The Strange Man of the Oglalas* by Mari Sandoz is important, but Smith also mentions *Zelda Fitzgerald* by Nancy Milford. Novels by Jean Genet are recurrent in the memoir, as are books linked to France, such as *Love on the Left Bank* or Anaïs Nin's *Collages*, and books by André Gide, Gertrude Stein, André Breton, and Djuna Barnes.[9] We must also mention British and American authors Oscar Wilde, Henry James, Eugene O'Neill, Tennessee Williams, William Faulkner, Terry Southern, Thomas Wolfe, Jack Kerouac and Tony Ingrassia, and, above all, her admired friend William Burroughs.[10] A final, smaller category of books concerns religion, philosophy and esoteric science, with *Psychedelic Prayers* by Timothy Leary, *The Bible*, Plato and *The Golden Bough*. Paradoxically for an artist who is primarily known as a singer, only two books on music are cited: *The Anthology of American Folk Music* by Harry Smith, whom she befriended at the Chelsea Hotel; and *The Age of Rock II*, edited by Jonathan Eisen with an entry by Lenny Kaye, future guitarist of the Patti Smith Group.

Books are presented as accompanying and comforting her, as informing and inspiring her, and, above all, as nourishing her developing artistic identity. They also represented a source of income, thus figuratively and literally sustaining Smith and Mapplethorpe. According to *Just Kids*, between her arrival in New York in 1967 and 1972, Patti Smith was employed at Brentano's, Scribner's and the Strand bookstore. An informed reader, Smith was expected to read *The New York Review of Books* weekly in order to better serve the customers of the bookstores she worked in. She describes buying and reselling rare and special editions in order to make some extra money, exchanging books as gifts and reading passages aloud to lovers and friends, "like Wendy entertaining the lost children of Neverland" (57–58). Smith thus fed Mapplethorpe's creative pursuits: "I came home and there were cutouts of statues, the torsos and buttocks of Greeks, the *Slaves* of Michelangelo, images of sailors, tattoos, and stars. To keep up with him, I read Robert passages from *Miracle of the Rose*, but he was always a step ahead. While I was reading Genet, it was as if he was becoming Genet" (70).

Although the mother is credited with connecting her to language, verse, and books, and Louisa May Alcott with the initial idea to write, the daughter writes of turning to male models in order to hone her craft, breaking with female and familial filiation in her quest for artistic selfhood. Patti Smith does not write "as a woman" in the tradition of American feminist writers of the Second Wave, filtering her life experience through the prism of gender. Nevertheless, her relationship to her sex and assigned gender is presented as just as "troubled" as that of many women writers. As a girl-child she played barechested in the mannish manner of Peter Pan (10). As a young woman, when compared to folksinger Joan Baez, she responded by defiantly cutting her hair like Keith Richards, simultaneously distancing herself from folk music and the more feminine Baez. It was this haircut that apparently first earned her the label "androgyne" and landed her a role as a young man in an experimental play.[11] In *Just Kids*, Smith admits to modelling her physical appearance after male artists as when she evokes Jean Genet in her description of the men's dress shirts she purchased for the famously androgynous cover of *Horses* (1975): "the one I really liked … reminded me of a Brassaï shot of Jean Genet wearing a white monogrammed shirt with rolled-up sleeves" (249). Recalling her unexpected pregnancy at age 19, the narrator notes that she, "who [had] never wanted to be a girl nor grow up, would be faced with this trial … was humbled by nature" (17). This unwelcome reminder of her capacity to reproduce only reinforced her resolve to become a gender-less artist (18). Writing about women later forced her to connect with her female self, which Smith seems to situate at her core, invisible and inaccessible, as exemplified by her piece on Edie Sedgwick's death: "In writing an elegy to a girl like Edie, I had to access something of the girl in myself. Obliged to consider what it meant to be female, I entered the core of my being, led by the girl poised before a white horse" (176–7). Like many a male poet, Patti Smith observed women at a distance, as muses: "The girls interested me: Marianne Faithfull, Anita Pallenberg, Amelia Earhart, Mary Magdalene. I would go to parties with Robert just to check out the dames. They were good material … Some of them found their way into my work" (199). In a humoristic and telling passage of *Just Kids*, Smith recounts how Allen Ginsberg mistook her for an attractive young man when they first met, and bought her a sandwich before realizing his mistake (123). And while Mapplethorpe was becoming Genet, Smith was reading Rimbaud. The biography and work of the French poet were to provide her with the nutrients necessary for her artistic development.

RIMBAUD'S DAUGHTER

References to Arthur Rimbaud and his *Illuminations* abound in *Just Kids*, indicating the extent of the narrator's identification with the poet and of his influence on her poetry. Here is the central passage devoted to the French poet in Smith's memoir:

> I found solace in Arthur Rimbaud, whom I had come upon in a bookstall across from the bus depot in Philadelphia when I was sixteen. His haughty gaze reached mine from the cover of *Illuminations*. He possessed an irreverent intelligence that ignited me, and I embraced him as compatriot, kin, and even secret love. Not having the ninety-nine cents to buy the book, I pocketed it.
>
> Rimbaud held the keys to a mystical language that I devoured even as I could not fully decipher it. My unrequited love for him was as real as anything I had experienced. ... It was for him that I wrote and dreamed. He became my archangel, delivering me from the mundane horrors of factory life. His hands had chiseled a manual of heaven and I held them fast. ... I tossed my copy of *Illuminations* in a plaid suitcase. We would escape together. (23)

This passage illustrates well the subversive and sustaining power of *Illuminations*, which the narrator credits with literally liberating her from a dead-end life. Smith recalls reading and quoting Rimbaud, imagining writing a play in which she rivals Paul Verlaine for his heart and attempting to finance a trip to Ethiopia to recover a lost chest of manuscripts (216–17). At that time (1973), her project was to write a book on Rimbaud, hence her trip to Paris where she slept in "his" hotel-room bed, her visits to his museum[12] and grave in Charleville, seeking inspiration (225–32). Suggesting that she lived in the shadow of the French poet, Smith even equates her decision to give up her career and move to Michigan in order to have children and work on her poetry as a parallel to Rimbaud's move to Ethiopia. Smith is quoted as saying, "Rimbaud taught me a lot. I couldn't understand how he could leave Paris for Ethiopia. Now, I know. In my own way, I have made a similar voyage. I left New York to come here near Detroit. Michigan is my Ethiopia and this garden is my own coffee plantation" (*Les Inrocks* 1996, our translation).

She read Enid Starkie's biography of the French poet, and Starkie's analysis of Rimbaud's life and art can be felt in Patti Smith's. Her mentor had a very spiritual understanding of his prodigious talent and role as a poet, elements one finds in Smith's vision of the artist. In an interview with Tavis Smiley in December 2010, after *Just Kids* won the National Book Award, Smith is quoted as saying, "I do believe that being a true poet or being an artist, a true artist, is a special, God-given thing." Referring specifically to her capacity to improvise, she told Smiley, "I do have the ability to riff for quite some time and to go out there and hopefully speak to God a little and then come back and give it to the people" (Smiley 2010). These words indicate that Smith sees herself as a Rimbaldian figure, a divine intermediary, or oracle, as Starkie described Rimbaud in her biography of the French poet.

More than any other singer-poet of the 1960s and 70s, such as Bob Dylan, Lou Reed or Jim Morrison, Smith perpetuates the myth of Rimbaud that Etienne Etiemble analysed in 1954. The myth of the *poète maudit* that developed around Rimbaud, even before his death, made of him an archetypal antihero and an anti-establishment artist. Smith drew upon this in the construction of her poetic and performance persona, as Carrie Jaurès Noland (1995) and Daniel Kane (2012) have aptly noted. This persona, which she forged as she forged her art, was a hybrid identity, a fusion of poet and rock rebel. Indeed, in 1972 Patti Smith did a series of readings entitled "Rock and Rimbaud" with Lenny Kaye accompanying her on the guitar, noting in *Just Kids* the novelty of their project: "As Rimbaud said, 'New scenery, new noise'" (196).[13]

The French *poète maudit* had split from the poetic conventions of his time—the meters, rhymes, and stanzas—and enlarged the rift opened by Charles Baudelaire, one which paved the way for the textual "disorder" of contemporary poets and the treatment of taboo subject matter (Guyaux 1985, 10). In *Just Kids*, Smith notes that her second volume of poems, *Witt* (1973) pays tribute to the French Symbolists: "*Witt* was very different from *Seventh Heaven*. Where the poems in *Seventh Heaven* were lighter, rhythmic, and oral, *Witt* made use of the prose poem, reflecting the influence of French Symbolists" (225). Smith's poems support the idea of a textual filiation. They contain many explicit references to Verlaine, Nerval, Baudelaire and Rimbaud (Noland 1995, 587) and Smith's anthology *Early Work, 1970–1979* (1994) includes such titles as "Dream of Rimbaud" and "Rimbaud Dead." Her second album, *Radio Ethiopia* (1976), whose title is an explicit reference to Rimbaud, is appropriately dedicated to the French poet, and in commentary printed on the inner sleeve of the album *Easter* (1978), Smith links their respective rebellious destinies when she refers to Arthur as a "smith".[14] Carrie Jaurès Noland notes the parallels between the poetry of Smith and that of Rimbaud, among which the move from sin (Cain) to redemption (Christ),[15] and young Arthur's symbolic revolt against the church and capitalist repression of workers. Noland develops the notion of *babble*,[16] which she links to Rimbaud's *musique sourde* in "Being Beauteous" and to the pagan language in "Mauvais sang" (Noland 1995, 595). Noland points out the figure of the *nègre* in Smith's "Rock n Roll Nigger," and notes that the initial title of *Une Saison en enfer* was *Livre nègre*.[17] For her, both "Rock n Roll Nigger" and "Being Beauteous" contain calls for a redefinition of art (598–9). The way in which Smith alters the spelling of certain words— "rhythm" which becomes "rythumn," a hybrid mix of *rythme*, "hum" and "hymn"—is coherent with these poets' recurrent break with traditional codes, as is her experimentation with punctuation. Another parallel is Smith's use of the Rimbaldian thesis and anti-thesis (Noguez in Rimbaud 1991, 12; 14). The presence of these elements in the poetry of Smith reinforces the notion that the artist has succeeded in her quest to become Rimbaud's daughter. The autobiographical elements of *Just Kids* trace the evolution of the author's relationship to this very significant textual other—from lover to model to mentor—and demonstrate the constancy of her daughterly devotion.

GINSBERG'S SON

However, no androgyne can be reduced to "the daughter of," and in *Just Kids*, Smith claims Beat affiliation too. Although Allen Ginsberg is not always singled out as the principal Beat influence on her poetry or performance, he was a friend whose creative and supportive presence permeated her life as an artist. Their lifelong friendship took root in Smith's gender ambiguity and in Ginsberg's role as instructor. The poet who bought the hungry young "man" a sandwich would nourish her artistic self-realization in more ways than one: "he once asked how I would describe how we met. "I would say you fed me when I was hungry," I told him. And he did" (123).

Allen Ginsberg and Gregory Corso are mentioned as two of her "teachers": "Gregory made lists of books for me to read, told me the best dictionary to own, encouraged and challenged me. Gregory Corso, Allen Ginsberg, and William Burroughs were all my teachers, each one passing through the lobby of the Chelsea Hotel, my new university" (138). After William Carlos Williams,[18] Jack Kerouac and Allen Ginsberg had developed a style of writing close to the bebop of Charlie Parker, the objective being to distance themselves from the formal constraints of traditional poetry in English and to imitate the complex rhythms, rapid tempos and improvisation of jazzmen like Parker, Dizzy Gillespie, Thelonious Monk, and Charlie Christian.[19] In *Just Kids*, Smith foregrounds the influence of the Beat poets when she recalls that in the weeks preceding her first public reading accompanied by Kaye on electric guitar, she immersed herself in their poetry, in jazz and in rock, seeking inspiration:

> I was in a Beat humor. The Bibles were piled in small stacks. The Holy Barbarians. The Angry Young Men. Rummaging around, I found some poems by Ray Bremser. He really got me going. Ray had that human saxophone thing. You could feel his improvisational ease the way language spilled out like linear notes. Inspired, I put on some Coltrane but nothing good happened. I was just jacking off. Truman Capote once accused Kerouac of typing, not writing. But Kerouac infused his being onto rolls of Teletype paper, banging on his machine. Me, I was typing. I leapt up frustrated.
>
> I picked up the Beat anthology and found "The Beckoning Sea" by George Mandel. I read him softly, and then at the top of my voice, to get the sea he embedded in the words and the accelerating rhythm of the waves. I kept going, spitting out Corso and Mayakovsky and back to the sea, to be pushed off the edge by George. (177)

In this passage, the narrator reveals not only the aesthetic influence of these poets on her poetry, with the reference to the "human saxophone thing" and the "improvisational" flow of language, but also and especially the way books literally fed her development as a performer. Smith describes how she read, and how the reading aloud allowed her to access the power "embedded" in the words, which become waves "pushing" her "off the edge," and toward the stage.

Smith emphasizes the importance of rhythm in an oral performance, of improvisation too, and the reference to the sea's repetitive swelling may be linked to Allen Ginsberg's Buddhist chanting, whose goal was to bring on a higher state of consciousness and which resulted in a divorce between signifier and signified. In recitation, sound presides over meaning, a fracture Smith had experienced that day beside the river with her mother and when mouthing her nightly prayer to the divine.[20] As a performer, Patti Smith developed a shamanic chant, as John Rockwell first mentioned in his 1976 *Rolling Stone* review of *Horses*.[21] Twenty years later, in an album released the year of Allen Ginsberg's passing (*Peace and Noise* 1997), Patti

Smith recited his "Footnote to Howl," which she also performed with Philip Glass in an homage to their mutual friend. In it, Smith intones the holiness of all things, a legacy of both Buddhist Ginsberg and "grandfather" Blake whose *Auguries of Innocence* inspired the punk poet's volume of the same name.[22]

For her first rock poetry reading, on February 10, 1971, Patti Smith chose a venue where Allen Ginsberg had read, as she explains in *Just Kids* (180), with the Poetry Project at St. Mark's Church, where she performed under the protective eye of Rimbaud and the Beats: "My goal was not simply to do well, or hold my own. It was to make a mark at St. Mark's. I did it for Poetry. I did it for Rimbaud, and I did it for Gregory. I wanted to infuse the written word with the immediacy and frontal attack of rock and roll" (180). Commenting on this first public reading in the 2010 interview with Smiley, Smith explains, "What I wanted to do was merge poetry with rock and roll in the way that Jimi Hendrix or Jim Morrison or Bob Dylan had. I wanted to continue that tradition" (Smiley 2010). Rock and roll was the "jazz" of her generation, and in her fusion of poetry and rock she was merely applying the Beat poetry template to her own time. In this, the boyish girl Ginsberg first met in a downtown cafeteria may be considered his progeny. As *Just Kids* shows, the Beats' influence allowed our androgynous author to find her own "rythumn," and to take the stage, propelled by the swell of her literary forefathers.

CONCLUSION

In order to fulfil her promise to her lost twin and share their coming-of-age story with the world, Patti Smith had to create a hybrid memoir from different genres of life writing, the *künstlerroman* in particular. In our discussion of Smith's description of her artistic development, we have isolated some autobiographical elements of this composite narrative, specifically those related to significant others, whether familial or literary. We have tried to reveal the role given to certain women and men, family members and writers, and to certain books in the narrator's portrayal of her evolving sense of self. We have attempted to demonstrate that, for Smith, the development of her artistic identity is enmeshed in her relationships and her readings, and specifically in her relationship to reading.

Smith's narrative stance in *Just Kids* is that of a young girl at a loss for words to describe her experience and of a young woman who finds them in books. Reading equips her with the tools for self-expression and self-construction, and the auto/biographical *künstlerroman* provides her with an opportunity to pay tribute to those who gave her the tools to become the artist she is today. Above all, Smith associates her mother with her first awareness of the power of words to name reality and of their simultaneous powerlessness to do so. She credits her mother with introducing her to prayer and to poetry, to recitation and to reading, and with introducing her to the books that would inspire her to want to tell stories, notably the one of her artistic becoming. Smith's mother is thus portrayed as initiating the daughter into "a lifelong practice of self-narration" (Eakin 1999, 67). In *Just Kids*, Smith writes of her youthful identification with Peter Pan and with Jo of *Little Women*, characters that combine storytelling adventures with rebellion against societal and gender norms. This rebellion reappears in Smith's identification with Rimbaud, the *poète maudit* who is presented as a primary influence in her life, poetry, and persona. Smith describes herself as reading, writing, and finally "becoming" Rimbaud as she developed as an artist. Her development would only be complete when, under the influence of the Beat poets, she would fuse poetry and rock 'n' roll into a new form of self-expression with the invention of punk rock. Patti Smith, the androgynous *autodidacte,* is undoubtedly both the daughter of Arthur Rimbaud and the son of Allen Ginsberg, a punk Peter Pan who succeeded in remaining "just a kid."

NOTES

1. "Before Robert died, I promised him that I would one day write our story" (Smith 2010, Acknowledgements). Recurrent in the text is the idea that the two youths, both born on a Monday in 1946, were somehow twins and the only ones to truly understand the other. Patti Smith arrived in New York on July 3, 1967 and left for Detroit, Michigan with Fred Sonic Smith in the spring of 1979. See Thompson 2011, 27; 263.

2. The expression is borrowed from Julia Watson 2015, 131–51. In *Reading Autobiography: A Guide for Interpreting Life Narratives*, Sidonie Smith and Julia Watson defined the relational life narrative as one "bound up with that of another": "Relational narratives incorporate extensive stories of related others that are embedded within the context of an autobiographical narrative" (Smith and Watson 2010, 86). Susan Stanford Friedman (1985) is credited with coining the term to characterize the model of selfhood in women's autobiographical writing, against the autonomous individual posited by Georges Gusdorf. See Smith and Watson 2010, 278–9 and especially Chapters 3 and 8. Paul John Eakin has posited that all life writing is necessarily relational since all lives and all selves are relational.

3. *Künstlerromane* usually depict the hero as in conflict with society, his/her personal creative impulses pushing the protagonist into some form of exile, like that of Smith and Mapplethorpe in New York. See Beebe 1964, vi; 6.

4. Traditionally, the principal themes have been the divided self and the ideal of detachment. See Beebe 1964, vi. Among the first examples of the feminine *Bildungsromane* are Germaine de Staël's *Corinne ou l'Italie* (1807) and George Sand's *Consuelo* (1842). Masculine myths of creativity include Faust, Icarus, and Prometheus.

5. See Eakin 1999, 21. He is referring to Kerby 1991, 1. For Kerby and other "narrative psychologists," "self-narration is the defining act of the human subject, an act which is not only "descriptive of the self" but "fundamental to the emergence and reality of that subject."

6. In an interview, Smith once said, "Books were very important. My father read everything from Bertrand Russell to the Holy Bible. My mother read Mandingo. They were always reading, and I followed in kind. I had a very good education through books" (Talbott 2011, 9).

7. Patti Smith's first visit to France was in the summer of 1969. In October 1973, she returned to the French capital and took a train to Charleville-Mézières in order to see the Rimbaud museum and grave site (Smith 2010, 226–30). Enid Starkie writes that it was beside the Meuse that "Rimbaud, whenever he could escape his mother's vigilance, lay and dreamed, filling his mind with the images that were to become the substance of his later poems" (Starkie 1938, 23).

8. In an interview with Jeffrey Brown on PBS (2010), Smith elaborates on the importance of books during her childhood and how reading inspired her to want to become a writer.

9. In an interview given in 1996 to a journalist of the French rock magazine, *Les Inrocks*, Smith credits Albert Camus for giving her the idea for the infamous incipit to "Gloria," "Jesus died for somebody's sins but not mine," a call to arms for artists. See "Patti Smith—étoile filante," *Les Inrocks*, 5 June 1996.

10. Smith's admiration for the lives and works of many artists and writers is evident in her photography. Images of the beds, masks and tombs of the deceased, their slippers and belongings have been exhibited and published as catalogues. "I have photographed the bed of Keats, the life mask of Blake, the utensils of Rimbaud, the bandana of William Burroughs. I suppose it's my way of taking their portraits" (Talbott 2011, 10).

11. Her haircut brings the following reaction: "Someone at Max's asked me if I was androgynous. I asked what that meant. 'You know, like Mick Jagger.' I figured that must be cool. I thought the word meant both beautiful and ugly at the same time. Whatever it meant, with just a haircut, I miraculously turned androgynous overnight" (Smith 2010, 140). As for the play in which she had a role as a young man, it was *Femme Fatale* by Jackie Curtis, at La MaMa, New York (Smith 2010, 140–141).

12. See the 1996 interview for *Les Inrocks*. We should note that at the time of writing, Smith had just purchased the Rimbaud house/museum in Charleville-Mézières.

13. For Carrie Jaurès Noland, "In her work of the mid-seventies, Patti Smith was establishing a hybrid genre she dubbed "rock poetry," which implicitly aligned the techniques of poetry with a socially deviant lifestyle involving drugs and the performance of gender ambiguity" (Noland 1995, 587).

14. Text by Patti Smith, *Easter*, Arista Records, 1978.

15. Like Rimbaud in "Mauvais sang" and "Adieu" (Noland 1995, 594–595).

16. Smith published a book of poems entitled *Babel* (New York: G. P. Putnams Sons, 1974).

17. Dominique Noguez notes in his presentation of *Saison en enfer* that the title of the book, begun some five months earlier, was "Livre païen ou Livre nègre," "texte de crise et de cris" ["Pagan book or 'nigger' book," "a text of turmoil and of screams"] (Rimbaud 1991, 8). My translation.

18. Williams was apparently the first to incorporate the rhythms of jazz in his poetry, those of white jazzman Mezz Mezzrow (Darras 2002, 30).

19. In an essay on the genesis of "Howl," Allen Ginsberg describes his stream-of-consciousness-like technique, quick and without revision, with "long saxophone-like chorus lines" (Parkinson 1961, 28). The repetition of "who" at the beginning of each line forms a rhythmic foundation which the poet leaves and then returns to repeatedly. The aspirated "who" is literally the breath of the poet, the length of each line corresponding to his lung capacity.

20. In "Reflections on the Mantra" (1966), Ginsberg writes that a poetics of mantra speech presupposes a trust in words that extends beyond their referential function; mantra recitation produces a relationship between speech and action in which "the original thin-conscious association with meaning disappears and the words become pure physical sounds uttered in a frankly physical universe" (Triglio 2007, 88). Dominique Noguez makes a similar remark about Rimbaud's *Saison en enfer*, which he characterizes as a "performative" text, "simultaneously action and text" (Noguez in Rimbaud 1991, 12; 14).

21. "Patti Smith is a rock & roll shaman and she needs music as shamans have always needed the cadence of their chanting" (Rockwell 1976). Her third album, *Easter* (1978), contains a good example. In "Ghost Dance/We Shall Live Again," Smith combines "the sounds and rythumns" (*sic*) of indigenous tribal dances with an incanted refrain, the goal being to create a greater tribal community. See liner notes for Smith's commentary on the song.

22. "Underlying the wide compassion of the 'Auguries of Innocence' is Blake's reiterated doctrine that "Everything that lives is Holy"—all Forms of Being one and identical in the Divine Humanity" (Sampson, in preface to Blake 1921, xviii). It is possible to trace a lineage from Smith back to Blake through Ginsberg.

References

Beebe, Maurice. 1964. *Ivory Towers and Sacred Founts: The Artist as Hero in Fiction from Goethe to Joyce*. New York: New York University Press.

Blake, William. 1921. In *The Poems of William Blake*, ed. John Sampson. London: Chatto and Windus.

Brown, Jeffrey. 2010. Patti Smith Reflects on Power of Words, *Rock 'N' Roll*. PBS News Hour, 29 December. http://www.pbs.org/newshour/bb/entertainment/july-dec10/pattismith_12-29.html. Accessed 15 Apr 2012.

Darras, Jacques. 2002. *Allen Ginsberg. La voix, le souffle*. Paris: Jean-Michel Place.

Eakin, Paul. 1999. *How Our Lives Become Stories. Making Selves*. Ithaca: Cornell University Press.

Ethaire, Etienne. 2010. *Patti Smith Fille de Rimbaud*. Camion Blanc: Rosières en Haye.

Etiemble, Etienne. 1954. *Le mythe de Rimbaud: Genèse du mythe, 1869–1949*. Paris: Éditions Gallimard.

Guyaux, André. 1985. *Poétique du fragment: Essai sur "Les Illuminations" de Rimbaud*. Neuchâtel: Éditions de la Baconnière.

Kane, Daniel. 2012. 'Nor Did I Socialise with Their People': Patti Smith, Rock Heroics and the Poetics of Sociability. *Popular Music* 31 (1) (January): 105–123.

Kerby, Anthony Paul. 1991. *Narrative and the Self*. Bloomington: Indiana University Press.

Noland, Carrie Jaurès. 1995. Rimbaud and Patti Smith: Style as Social Deviance. *Critical Inquiry* 21 (3) (Spring): 581–610.

Parkinson, Thomas. 1961. *A Casebook on the Beat*. New York: Thomas Y. Cromwell.

Rimbaud, Arthur. 1991. *Une Saison en enfer suivi de Illuminations*, ed. Dominique Noguez. Collection Orphée. Paris: Éditions La Différence.

Rockwell, John. 1976. Patti Smith: Shaman in the Land of a Thousand Dances. *Rolling Stone*. February 12. http://www.oceanstar.com/patti/crit/760212rs.htm. Accessed 9 Aug 2015.

Smiley, Tavis. 2010. Interview with Patti Smith. December 21. http://www.pbs.org/wnet/tavissmiley/interviews/singer-songwriter-patti-smith/. Accessed 15 Apr 2012.

Smith, Patti. 1972. *Seventh Heaven*. Philadelphia: Telegraph Books.

———. 1973. *Witt*. New York: Gothic Book Mart.

———. 1974. *Babel*. New York: G. P. Putnams Sons.

———. 1975. Horses. Arista Records.

———. 1976. Radio Ethiopia. Arista Records.

———. 1978. Easter. Arista Records.

———. 1994. *Early Work: 1970–1979*. New York/London: W. W. Norton and Company.

————. 1996. Patti Smith – étoile filante. Interview. *Les Inrocks*, June 5. http://www.lesinrocks.com/1996/06/05/musique/patti-smith-etoile-filante-11233578/. Accessed 24 Sept 2016.

————. 1997. *Peace and Noise*. Arista Records.

————. 2008 [2005]. *Auguries of Innocence*. New York: HarperCollins.

————. 2010. *Just Kids*. London: Bloomsbury.

Smith, Sidonie, and Julia Watson. 2010 [2001]. *Reading Autobiography. A Guide for Interpreting Life Narratives*. Minneapolis: University of Minnesota Press.

Starkie, Enid. 1947 [1938]. *Arthur Rimbaud*. London: Hamish Hamilton.

Talbott, Susan Lubowsky. 2011. *Patti Smith. Camera Solo*. Hartford, Connecticut: Wadsworth Atheneum Museum of Art and New Haven and London, Yale University Press.

Thompson, Dave. 2011. *Dancing Barefoot. The Patti Smith Story*. Chicago: Chicago Review Press.

Triglio, Tony. 2007. *Allen Ginsberg's Buddhist Poetics*. Carbondale: Southern Illinois University Press.

Watson, Julia. 2015. Patti Smith Kicks In the Walls of Memoir: Relational Lives and 'the Right Voice' in *Just Kids*. *a/b Auto/Biography Studies*. 30 (1): 131–151.

CHAPTER 4

Reading and Rewriting Herself: Anna Jameson's Literary Exploration of Canada

Anne-Florence Quaireau

INTRODUCTION

Irish-born authoress Anna Jameson (1794–1860) was already a seasoned traveller when she sailed to Canada in October 1836, complying with her husband's request[1] and regretfully leaving Europe just as her literary career was taking off—she had penned six books which revealed her interest in life writing, hers or others'. Her first work, *The Diary of an Ennuyée* (1826), first published anonymously under the title "A Lady's Diary," was based on her Grand Tour, performed when she was working as a governess for a wealthy English family; it drew immensely from her experience as a reader, more particularly from Madame de Staël's *Corinne; ou l'Italie* and Lord Byron's *Childe Harold* (Fowler 1982, 145). The supposedly heartbroken heroine was also inspired from her own experience.[2] An avid reader, Anna Jameson was very interested in the depiction of women in literature and saw this as a point of entry into a reflection on the female character, as shown by her popular work *Characteristics of Women, Moral, Poetical and Historical* (1832). Jameson's interest in life writing had

A.-F. Quaireau (✉)
Sorbonne Université, Paris, France

© The Author(s) 2018
V. Baisnée-Keay et al. (eds.), *Women's Life Writing and the Practice of Reading*, Palgrave Studies in Life Writing,
https://doi.org/10.1007/978-3-319-75247-1_4

produced several similar female biographies: *Memoirs of the Loves of the Poets* (1829), *Memoirs of Celebrated Female Sovereigns* (1831), and *Memoirs of the Beauties of the Court of Charles II* (1831). Through literature and a study of *characters*, Jameson discussed female *characteristics*, in other words female identity.

In this study of the role reading plays in women's life writing, travel writing provides a compelling case to analyse. Travel writing is a genre that challenges boundaries. According to Charles Batten, "[t]he travel book's autobiographically determined narrative ... suggests that it is merely a specialized form of biography describing the events in an author's life during a trip" (Batten 1978, 31–32). As a form of life writing dealing with a specific context in the life of the person, the travel narrative revolves around the traveller, who is both narrator and character. The travel narrative "I" is even more complex since "the voice narrating the journey may appear quite distinct from the 'real' author, for example when the narrator is posing or controlling him or herself in accordance with certain aims or social expectations" (Korte 2000, 12). Travel writing is also close to the genre of the *Bildungsroman* (Viviès 1999, 164), whose plot follows the evolution of a character through time, often narrated in retrospect by a character looking back and taking stock of his or her transformation. Even though the relation between truth and fiction in travel writing is a complicated one, at the beginning of the nineteenth century, veracity was still a criterion in the assessment of travel narratives, and it was even more the case for women whose writing "was more prone to accusations of lying" (Mills 1991, 116). Very much concerned with questions of authority, the genre enables unlikely people to become *authors*, through the pretext of their travelling, of their being first-hand witnesses, but the question is also that of being an *authority* on a topic, and to bring back from a trip something more than memorabilia—a certain position. Travel writing could as well be called *travel reading*. The traveller travels through books as well as through a physical land, either before or along their trip. Intertextual *par excellence*, the genre opens a space for travellers to strike up a discussion with their predecessors, as illustrated by the practice of footnotes for instance. Thus, travel writing appears as a literary space suited to reinventing oneself, all the more so as the geographical itinerancy may come to parallel the evolution of the individual, through both travelling and writing.

With a study of Anna Jameson's Canadian travel narrative, *Winter Studies and Summer Rambles in Canada* (1838), I would like to explore her life writing when that life is her own, and analyse the articulation between studying and reading on the one hand and acting and writing on the other, explicitly stated in the binary structure of the narrative. Even if Jameson did not bring the books she had been reading in Toronto along on her rambles, she regularly referenced and incorporated them into her own narrative, rewriting male versions of first encounters, and authoring herself and promoting women's rights in Britain in the process. I will therefore suggest that she uses her reading to rewrite herself as the heroine of her own life, creating an androgynous intertextual persona for herself, neither completely male, nor female, but always going from one to the other.

READING AND WRITING TO COMBAT ENTRAPMENT

Winter Studies and Summer Rambles in Canada provides a striking example of the blending of three forms of life writing: journal, letters and travel writing. As the narrative of Jameson's time in Canada from December 1836 to August 1837, it is usually considered a travel narrative. And yet, its author introduces it as "'fragments' of a journal addressed to a friend" (Jameson 2008, 1). This led Helen Buss to call it an "epistolary dijournal":

> This formal blend allows for multiple subject positions to be presented as coexisting rather than 'competing' and therefore eliminates the need for resolution into unitary selfhood that the term 'competing' implies. The term 'epistolary dijournal' is meant to imply the values of correspondence and alterity that the epistolary form suggests, as well as those values of intimate self-disclosure and self-construction suggested by our contemporary concept of 'diary', along with the facticity and externalisation present in the travel 'journal'. (1992, 44)

The original addressee of the epistolary part can be identified as Ottilie von Goethe, although all specific mentions have been omitted. It would partly explain all the references to German literature and culture present in this book about Canada. This "epistolary dijournal" entails that Jameson is reading and writing for a female friend as well as for herself; therefore, "the letter can be seen to recreate, in *mise-en-abyme* fashion, a paradigmatic Jamesonian narrative pattern, a feminocentric discursive universe in which narrator, narratee and narrated are all significantly female and woman-oriented" (Friedwald 1986, 62).

In the first part of Jameson's journey in Canada, and in the first part of her narrative, entitled "Winter Studies," reading is dramatized as a way to escape Toronto's winter and her solitude, just like German literature is presented as a way to bridge the physical gap between Ottilie von Goethe and herself. She refers to her reading *Corregio* by Danish playwright Adam Oehlenschläger, *Die Schuld* by German playwright Adolf Müllner, comments on German actresses Sophie Müller, Anna Krüger, and Antoinette Adamberger, and more often than not paraphrases Eckermann's *Gesprache mit Goethe*. Reading is presented as the activity enabling her to survive Canada and her solitude. The divide between the two parts of the book is built on a series of binary divisions: winter/summer, indoors/outdoors, solitude/companionship, intellectual/physical activity, stasis/movement, entrapment/freedom, and death/rebirth. In January 1837, as the cold permeates everything, her thoughts become frozen too, as the simile with the ink suggests: "I lose all heart to write home, or to register a reflection or a feeling;—thought stagnates in my head as the ink in my pen—and this will never do! I must rouse myself to occupation; and if I cannot find it without, I must create it from within" (Jameson 2008, 23). This simile can also be read as a metonymy, suggesting that the pen stands for the activity of writing that is threatened too. The threat of entrapment is physical as well as intellectual and resistance will come from her reading and translating. When she quotes Mademoiselle de l'Espinasse (1732–1776), who was a French salon holder and letter writer, the activity that enables the writer's survival and even escape, reading, is emphasized by the *mise en abyme* of reading:

> Ce qui est *moins* que moi, m'éteint et m'assomme: ce qui est *à côté* de moi m'ennuie et me fatigue: il n'y a que ce qui est *au-dessus* de moi qui me soutienne et m'arrache à moi-même". This is true—*how* true, I *feel*, and far more prettily said than I could say it; and thus it is that during these few days of illness and solitary confinement, I took refuge in another and a higher world, and bring you my ideas thereupon.
>
> I have been reading over again the Iphigenia, the Tasso and the Egmont of Goëthe. (74)

While Jameson mentions the activity of reading, by quoting de l'Espinasse in French, she shows herself into the action of reading. The foreignness of the French in the English text draws the reader's attention to the fact that she seems to be reading and quoting from it directly. Reading is also construed as a means of resisting her husband's power, since he took her away from Europe and her budding literary career. Anna Jameson keeps reading Goethe as if it brought her closer to Ottilie von Goethe, but also other books, which she introduces as "a remedy" (103).

Jameson repeatedly stages herself reading, using direct speech to convey her reaction and stage direction-like phrases to dramatize her reactions. She tends to analyse what she reads in relation to life and society, pointing out the connection she makes between literature and life, between fiction and real life: "The heroine, Galathée, dies quietly of a broken heart. 'The more fool she!' I thought, as I closed the book, 'to die for the sake of a man who was not worth living for!' but ''tis a way we have'" (197). Although at first reading and acting seem to be opposed in the binary structure of *Winter Studies and Summer Rambles,* the two activities prove more similar, and are even superimposed as Jameson sets the scene of her reading in the Canadian wilderness: "Imagine me alone in the very centre of *this vast wild country,* a storm raging *without,* as if heaven and earth had come in collision—lodged and cared for, *reclining on a neat comfortable bed,* and *reading* by the light of one tallow candle" (267, my emphasis). Although the opposition of the indoors and the outdoors is carefully constructed, the two spaces are here, in this wild Canada, similar to a blank page waiting to be written on, brought together. After reading before travelling, Jameson now reads while travelling.

Jameson spent the whole winter isolated in Toronto, whiling away the time reading and trying to translate Eckermann's *Gesprache mit Goethe* into English. As she supported her parents and her sisters financially, she was always already thinking of the next book, which she saw as a means to earn a living, and had planned on making a book out of her Canadian experience from the beginning of her stay there. Although she never completed this editorial project, her reading, about both Europe and Canada, features prominently in her travel narrative. Come spring, she took to the road and travelled into the Canadian wilderness in order to meet Anishinaabe people (also called Ojibwe in English), and in particular women, as she explains to Ottilie von Goethe in a letter in June 1837: "But when I go up the wild country I must leave my books behind me. I am anxious to see with my own eyes the conditions of women in savage life, and that is the principal reason of my venturing so far" (Needler 1939, 93). This process was in fact part of Jameson's writing method: to read beforehand, then to experience and take notes, and to rework notes (Thomas 1967, 137). This practical reference to her travelling conditions and the necessity to travel light may also be read as a metaphorical hint that, after thinking and living by proxy, she was now about to have experiences and become an active heroine.

AUTHORITY THROUGH INTERTEXTUALITY

Jameson's exploration of Canada is both literary and physical. After the literary exploration of Europe from Toronto, the geographical, literal exploration of Canada is doubled with a literary exploration of companion texts on Canada. Although in 1837 Upper Canada was no longer *terra incognita*, Anna Jameson claimed to be the first European *gentlewoman* to have *written* about what she experienced there, in particular her meeting of Anishinaabe people: "While in Canada, I was thrown into scenes and regions hitherto *undescribed* by any traveller, (for the northern shores of Lake Huron are almost new ground,) and into relations with the Indian tribes, such as few European women of refined and civilised habits have ever risked, and none have *recorded*" (Jameson 2008, 1, my emphasis). The account of her peregrinations thus presents itself as a *literary* exploration. With her liminal remark, Jameson draws attention to her sex ("few European women") and consequently to so far unnamed male companion texts. Her statement that she was one of the first European women to have had relations "with the Indian tribes" and to have recorded these suggests that male counterparts mainly had paved the way, and a few women too. Captain Frederick Marryat and Harriet Martineau had both preceded Jameson in Sault Ste Marie, while undertaking their American tour. And indeed, in her narrative, Jameson acknowledged one of her predecessors in particular. She makes numerous references to Alexander Henry's *Travels and Adventures in the Years 1760–1776* (1809) and emphasizes that it "struck [her] so much as to have had some influence in directing the course of [her] present tour" (394). Alexander Henry (1739–1824), a famous explorer and fur trader, told in *Travels and Adventures in Canada and the Indian Territories Between the years 1760 and 1776* (1809) of his time among the Anishinaabe, the attack on the fort Mackinac and how he was rescued from death by an Anishinaabe, Wenniway, who adopted him as a brother.

The significance of intertextuality in travel writing needs no longer to be proven. Referring to other texts on a similar subject in order to legitimize one's discourse is common practice (Said 1979, 20, 23; Mills 1991, 73–4). Jameson's reliance on previous texts—written by male authors—assumes further import. Her numerous references to Henry establish him as a role model and a mentor and thus she gains in authority through *his* authority. After introducing him to her reader/friend, she adds: "Mr. Henry is to be my travelling companion, or rather *our* travelling companion, for I always fancy *you* of the party. I do not know how he might have figured as a squire of dames when living, but I assure you that being dead he makes a very respectable hero of epic or romance" (395). Jameson humorously calls attention to her position as a woman travelling alone and to her need to assert her femininity and ensure her respectability. The reference to and inclusion of an addressee partake of this strategy. Through her reading of his narrative, Alexander Henry, although dead, is going to vicariously take part in the travel. It is a commonplace, which Jameson builds on, to say that, when reading a travel book, the reader travels along with the author, but Jameson rewrites the cliché. Reversing situations and roles, she turns Henry, the male author *she* read, into a "travelling companion," a guardian of her femininity, while she, the woman, leads the way. In this sentence, she obliterates his role as a predecessor and a mentor, which she acknowledged a few lines earlier. What is more, "he makes a very respectable hero of epic or romance" tends to suggest that her narrative is an epic or a romance and that she is also likely to be a heroine of these genres.

A similar reversal takes place with Jameson's quoting from Henry's *Travels*. She frequently resorts to quoting to legitimate her assessments, thereby showing that an authority on the matter concurs with her. But what is particularly striking is that she creates the impression that she is the one who confirms Henry's assertion and transfers her authority onto him, thus becoming the authority in the first place: "Henry declares that the flavour of the white-fish is 'beyond any comparison whatever', and I add my testimony thereto—*probatum est*!" (486). While quoting is the most obvious mark of intertextuality, it is also, according to Antoine Compagnon, "the primitive interdiscursive relation" (Compagnon 1979, 54, my translation). Compagnon analyses the *process* of quoting and emphasizes its significance, relegating the quote itself to a secondary role: "it no longer is possible to speak of the quote for itself, but only of its work, of quoting" (36).[3]

In Sault Ste Marie, Jameson addresses the subject of fisheries, after expressing her will to write "a chapter of geography, and topography, natural philosophy, and such wise-like things" (Jameson 2008, 482). Her decision to come to grips with this subject is built around an opposition between two attitudes: one characterized by "solemn reveries on starlit lakes" with "too much—of self and self-communings" (482) and the other characterized by natural sciences, enumerated above. It is tempting to read these attitudes according to nineteenth-century gender roles. Jameson seems to be implying that she is now adopting a more serious, scientific approach to her subject and leaving egotism on one side. Thus, she decides to devote a section to the white fish found in the region and how tasty they are, highlighting her authority on the matter through her first-hand experience (486), and then Henry's concurring. Jameson also gains in authority through inheritance: she presents herself as following in Henry's steps, both geographically and literarily. On reaching the Missasagua river (nowadays Spanish river), while voyaging down Lake Huron, she intimates that she meets the same Indians as Henry, fore-grounding the continuity between them: "This is the river called by Henry the *Missasaki*, where he found a horde of Indians who had never seen a white man before ... There is a remnant of these Indians here still" (530). Focusing on the "remnant of these Indians," she contends that she is Henry's successor, thus acquiring legitimacy and authority.

DEPARTING FROM THE (LITERARY) BEATEN PATH

Having acquired authority through the lineage she creates between Henry and herself, Jameson also needs to single herself out. If, as she writes, "Henry is the Ulysses of these parts" (395), what does that make her? Is she his spiritual son, a Telemachus figure, or Penelope? Jameson creates an androgynous intertextual persona for herself, neither completely male, nor female, but always going from one to the other. Karen Lawrence's study of women's travel writing inquires into the figure of Penelope, "the weaver and teller of the story of male absence," when she is both traveller and narrator and studies "how femininity [is] constructed when its relation to the domestic is radically altered" (Lawrence 1994, x). She shows the tension between inscribing oneself into a tradition and breaking away from it: "[w]omen writers mapped these voyages in narratives that appropriated literary traditions developed by male writers to trace the itineraries of men. ... 'Questions of travel,' to use Elizabeth Bishop's phrase, are also questions of travel writing, of departing literarily as well as literally from the beaten path" (Lawrence 1994, x). By constantly recalling that she is a woman, partly in a traditional strategy of disclaimer, Jameson subversively claims to offer a *new* point of view. She repeatedly proclaims the specificity of her feminine point of view, "femininely speaking" (Jameson 2008, 496), or when she writes: "Let but my woman's wit bestead me here as much as my womanhood, and I will, as the Indians say, 'tell you a piece of my mind,' and place the matter before you in another point of view" (556). This is made possible and supported by the authority acquired through the literary means I have just highlighted. The lands she travels may no longer be completely unfamiliar, yet she explores them all the same, bringing to the fore other elements, *renewing* the experience through her feminine viewpoint and expression.

This endeavour culminates in her narrative of encounters, all the more invaluable since she completes Henry's unfinished work. A lyrical passage where she compares him to Ulysses and his journey to Ulysses' Odyssey ends on the remark that his narrative does not include encounters with Native women (395). The superimposition of the *Odyssey* and Henry's *Travels and Adventures* serves to point out a lack in Henry's work, which Jameson wants to fill in by taking his place. As Henry's substitute, she too becomes an impersonation of Ulysses, the archetype of the (male) traveller, and the very antipode to Penelope, whom as a woman Jameson also symbolizes. Jameson thereby seems to refuse to assume the part of Penelope, or of Calypsos for that matter, donning the costume of the male traveller, becoming the hero while insisting on her femininity. Jameson in turn takes on a male or female persona, never settling on one or the other. While Marian Fowler has evidenced Jameson's donning of a Byronic persona (Fowler 1982, 145), others have analysed her cautious preservation of femininity, for instance through her emphasis on using objects seen as feminine (parasol, gloves, etc.) (Johnston 1997, 113–114; Roy 2005, 24).[4]

FILLING IN THE BLANKS

Jameson rewrites Henry's narrative by filling in the blanks and writing about her encounters with Anishinaabe *women* who are made prominent in her narrative. This is particularly manifest in her rendition of the Johnston sisters: Jane Johnston Schoolcraft and Charlotte MacMurray, daughters of a famous fur trader and "a woman of pure Indian blood, of a race celebrated in these regions as warriors and chiefs from generation to generation, who had never resided within the pale of what we call civilised life" (Jameson 2008, 490). Just as Jameson was leaving Toronto, she was introduced to Mr. MacMurray, a missionary from Sault Ste Marie, and his wife, Charlotte MacMurray. This chance encounter (as it is constructed in the narrative) proved very beneficial to Jameson as it facilitated her meeting of Anishinaabe in Sault Ste Marie. Her interaction with these women also provides an illustration of Sara Mills's point that women's travel narratives "differ from the writings of male travel writers in the stress they lay on personal involvement and relationships with people of the other culture and in the less authoritarian stance they take *vis-à-vis* narrative voice" (Mills 1991, 21). Jameson remarks that "Mrs. Schoolcraft's features are more decidedly Indian than those of her sister Mrs. MacMurray" (Jameson 2008, 405). Describing Mrs. MacMurray's "refined" features, the "fawn-like softness" of her eyes, she concludes on her voice, accent and intonation which resemble "the voice and accent of some of [her] German friends" (205). The evocation of her German friends brings to mind Ottilie von Goethe and draws attention to the triangle drawn between Anishinaabe women and European women through Jameson. Moreover, she finds Mrs. MacMurray "unlike the specimens of Indian squaws and half-cast women [she] had met with" (205) but we may wonder who they are, since no mention is made of them in her letters or in the narrative, apart from the previous description of a group of Indians in Erindale, and it could be argued that she did not really meet them but simply observed them from a distance.

Considering Jameson's repeatedly expressed desire to meet Native *women*, it could be contended that if she had indeed met "squaws," she would have dedicated an important part of her narrative to the relation of these encounters. My contention is that these "Indian squaws" with whom she contrasts Mrs. MacMurray could be *literary* encounters. Several times in her narrative, Jameson evokes her literarily acquired knowledge about Anishinaabe:

> I am not going to tell you here of well-known Indian customs, and repeat anecdotes to be found in all the popular books of travel. With the general characteristics of Indian life and manners you are already familiar, from reading the works of Cooper, Washington Irving, Charles Hoffman, and others. I can add nothing to these sources of information; only bear testimony to the vigour, and liveliness, and truth of these pictures they have drawn. I am amused at every moment between what I see and what I have read... (433)

Strikingly, Jameson cites famous authors of fiction, most obviously referencing *The Last of the Mohicans* and possibly thinking of Washington Irving's travel narrative *A Tour on the Prairies* (1835). Her experience with Anishinaabe was indeed very much influenced by her readings, as exemplified by her conclusion after her first meeting with three Anishinaabe in her home in Toronto. Commenting on their "swarthy countenances, their squalid, dingy habiliments, and their forlorn story" which "filled [her] with pity" and disappointment, she adds "my previous impressions of the independent children of the forest are for the present disturbed" (21). She is aware that her encounters are both informed by her readings and that this literary-acquired knowledge is inadequate:

> Notwithstanding all I have heard and read, I have yet but a vague idea of the Indian character; and the very different aspect under which it has been represented by various travellers, as well as writers of fiction, adds to the difficulty of forming a correct estimate of the people, and more particularly of the true position of their women. (21)

On several occasions, Jameson admits to being greatly influenced by her readings. She was not immune to preconceptions, despite this cautionary remark: "In former times, when people travelled into strange countries, they travelled *de bonne foi*, really to see and learn what was new to them. Now, when a traveller goes to a foreign country, it is always with a set of preconceived notions concerning it, to which he fits all he sees, and refers all he hears" (162). Jameson does it as well and the comment about Cooper's and Irving's Indians in fact comes up towards the end of her narrative, showing that she never completely breaks free from these literary-constructed images.

In fact, Jameson rewrites in a feminine version the "transracial love stories that proliferated in late eighteenth-century narratives [which] were shaped in many ways by antecedents in classical expansionist literature, notably the *Odyssey* and the *Aeneid*" (Pratt 1992, 96). Mary-Louise Pratt further points out that "the colonized heroes and heroines of European sentimental literature are rarely 'pure' non-whites or 'real' slaves. [T]hey are typically mulattoes or mestizos who already have European affiliations" (100). Mrs. MacMurray and her sister, Mrs. Schoolcraft, were the daughters of a fur trader and an Anishinaabe woman, and were both married to white men. They might not be representative of Anishinaabe women, yet Jameson sets them up as paragons of their people, underlying their Native origins to impart more authenticity and value to her experience and narrative, while underlining their elegance and sophistication. The traditional transracial love story is turned into a story of friendship and even of sisterhood. The special relationship that is presented as taking place between Jameson and Mrs. MacMurray is forecast by her precise description, in particular of her face. Indeed, "[t]he conventional facial sketch of the non-European love object distinguishes her or him from the stereotypic portraits of slaves and savages" (Pratt 1992, 100). Jameson's special relationship with and attitude to the sisters is related to the fact that they are women: "there are a thousand quiet ways in which woman may be kind and useful to her sister woman. Then [Mrs. Schoolcraft] has two sweet children about eight or nine years old—no fear, you see, that we shall soon be the best friends in the world!" (Jameson 2008, 405–6). The striking phrase "her sister woman" prefigures the Anishinaabe adoption Jameson stages for herself, which turned Mrs. Schoolcraft and Mrs. Johnston into her sisters. She thus protracts and literalizes the metaphor of sisterhood between the sisters and herself.

Authoring Herself

One of the most famous passages from *Winter Studies and Summer Rambles* is Jameson's Indian baptism, symbolized by her shooting down the rapids at Sault Ste Marie and her subsequent renaming and adoption by Mrs. Johnston. This passage climaxes the narrative of Jameson's relationship with "[her] Indians" (499). She stresses the dangers involved in her canoeing "those glancing, dancing rapids" (498) and turns it into an initiatory rite: "I was declared duly initiated, and adopted into the family by the name of Wah,sàh,ge,wah,no,quà … and by this name I am henceforth to be known among the Chippewas" (499). However, two narratives contradict Jameson's version of events. Captain Frederick Marryat's description of the rapids differs substantially: "The rapids from which the village takes its name are just above it; they are not strong or dangerous, and the canoes descend them twenty times a-day" (Marryat 1839, 54). Mrs. Schoolcraft's summary of events to her husband also presents a contrastive account: "While here, George came down the rapids with her in fine style and spirits. She insisted on being baptized and named in Indian, after her sail down the falls" (Schoolcraft 1851, 563). Both sources point out the absence of danger, and Mrs. Schoolcraft's account reveals Jameson's intervention and stage directions. In her narrative, Jameson rewrote the reality so as to author herself.

Strikingly, Jameson's narration of her adoption once again revives literary recollections. Victoria Brehm identifies in this scene a "refiguration of the traditional Indian captivity narrative": "Jameson parodied the central scene of captivity, where the captive is baptized and renamed, but unlike true captives (or dissatisfied wives), she used it to celebrate her power and freedom" (Brehm 1999, 82). Jameson pretends to comply with the *scène-à-faire*, inscribing her narrative within a tradition, but recasts it in a positive light. She counters the vision traditionally spread by the captivity narrative of the Indian as barbarous and evil and subverts the traditional norm. Moreover, her orchestration of her rebirth recalls another specific narrative, that of Alexander Henry. Earlier, she mentions Henry had escaped Michilimackinac during the attack of the fort "through the friendship of an Indian (Wa'wa'tam) who ... had adopted him as his brother" (Jameson 2008, 417). Jameson thus appropriates Henry's story, reliving it but altering it, turning it into a feminine version. What is striking is that through this (literary) act, not only does she assert again her authority, claiming to be a worthy successor to Henry—even his equal—; she also inscribes herself within a literary lineage. What is more, she also inscribes herself within the Anishinaabe lineage, purporting to become *other* (Wah,sàh,ge,wah,no,quà) in order to become *herself*. The change of name, apart from the Indian colour it gives to the narrative, is highly symbolical for this woman in an unhappy marriage, who thus symbolically sheds her husband's name and her ties to him.

CONCLUSION

Winter Studies and Summer Rambles chronicles the evolution of Jameson in Canada from reader to writer, from spectator to actress of her own life. In fact, the text does more than record this evolution, as a *Bildungsroman* would; it *performs* it. Through intertextuality with Henry's text, Jameson created an intertextual persona for herself and gained in *authority* and *authorship*. Thus sanctioned, she was at liberty to stage her rebirth as a free and powerful woman. This literary enactment foretokened Jameson's separation from her husband. Jameson's work as a whole was both descriptive and prescriptive: "To supplement, indeed profoundly to revise Western biographical history by representing the attainments and attributes of women, and to provide role models to an audience of her peers, was a mission for Jameson" (Booth 1999, 259). Jameson's reinvention of herself thus has implications for her female readers as well. Although quite forgotten today, this close friend of Lady Byron and Ottilie von Goethe was at the time the "idol of thousands of young ladies" (Strachey 1978, 89). Mirroring Jameson's process, these readers could emulate her and become the heroines of their own lives.

NOTES

1. Her husband, Robert Jameson, the attorney general of Upper Canada, had requested her presence by his side, probably to facilitate his promotion. Following his various appointments abroad, the couple had been living separately for seven years. After a year and a half on the North American continent, Jameson obtained a separation agreement from her husband and a small allowance.

2. The editor's preface purports the book to be the true diary of a heartbroken lady: "The following Diary is published exactly as it was found after the death of the Author; varied only by the omission of certain names" (Jameson 1826, np). Jameson's first work already blurred the line between fact and fiction, between creating a fictitious character and writing about herself. She undertook the Tour right after her (first) engagement with Robert Jameson had been broken. *The Diary of an Ennuyée* interwove the notes she had taken during her Tour and literary archetypes gleaned from her reading.

3. The original French reads, *la relation interdiscursive primitive; il n'est plus possible de parler de la citation pour elle-même, mais seulement de son travail, du travail de la citation* (my translation).

4. For other examples, see "the driver, who had been selected from among the most respectable settlers in the neighbourhood as a fit guide and protector for a lone woman" (Jameson 2008, 307); "We breakfasted on an island almost covered with flowers, some gorgeous, some strange, and unknown, and others sweet and familiar; plenty of the wild-pea, for instance, and wild-roses, of which I had many offerings. I made my toilette in a recess among some rocks" (576).

REFERENCES

Batten, Charles. 1978. *Pleasurable Instruction: Form and Convention in Eighteenth-Century Travel Literature*. Berkeley-Los Angeles: University of California Press.

Booth, Alison. 1999. The Lessons of the Medusa: Anna Jameson and Collective Biographies of Women. *Victorian Studies* 42 (2): 257–288.

Brehm, Victoria. 1999. Inventing Iconography on the Accessible Frontier: Harriet Martineau, Anna Jameson, and Margaret Fuller on the Great Lake. *Prospects* 24: 67–98.

Buss, Helen. 1992. Anna Jameson's *Winter Studies and Summer Rambles in Canada* as Epistolary Dijournal. In *Essays on Life Writing: From Genre to Critical Practice*, ed. Marlene Kadar, 42–60. Toronto: University of Toronto Press.

Compagnon, Antoine. 1979. *La Seconde main ou le travail de la citation*. Paris: Éditions du Seuil.

Fowler, Marian. 1982. *The Embroidered Tent: Five Gentlewomen in Early Canada: Elizabeth Simcoe, Catharine Parr Traill, Susanna Moodie, Anna Jameson, Lady Dufferin*. Toronto: Anansi.

Friedwald, Bina. 1986. 'Femininely Speaking': Anna Jameson's *Winter Studies and Summer Rambles in Canada*. In *A Mazing Space: Writing Canadian Women Writing*, ed. Shirley Neuman and Smaro Kamboureli, 62–73. Edmonton: Longspoon.

Jameson, Anna. 1826. *The Diary of an Ennuyée*. London: Henry Colburn.

———. 2008. *Winter Studies and Summer Rambles in Canada (1838)*. Toronto: McClelland & Stewart, The New Canadian Library.

Johnston, Judith. 1997. *Anna Jameson: Victorian, Feminist, Woman of Letters*. Aldershot: Scolar Press.

Korte, Barbara. 2000. *English Travel Writing: From Pilgrimages to Postcolonial Explorations*. New York: St Martin's Press/Palgrave.

Lawrence, Karen. 1994. *Penelope Voyages: Women and Travel in the British Literary Tradition*. Ithaca: Cornell University Press.

Marryat, Frederick. 1839. *Diary in America, with Remarks on Its Institutions*. New York: Wm. H. Colyer.

Mills, Sara. 1991. *Discourses of Difference:An Analysis of Women's Travel Writing and Colonialism*. New York: Routledge.

Needler, George Henry, ed. 1939. *Letters of Anna Jameson to Ottilie von Goethe*. London: Oxford University Press.

Pratt, Mary Louise. 1992. *Imperial Eyes: Travel Writing and Transculturation*. London: Routledge.

Roy, Wendy. 2005. *Maps of Difference: Canada, Women, and Travel*. Montreal: McGill-Queen's University Press.

Said, Edward. 1979. *Orientalism*. New York: Vintage.

Schoolcraft, Henry Rowe. 1851. *Personal Memoirs of a Residence of Thirty Years with the Indian Tribes on the American Frontiers: With Brief Notices of Passing Events, Facts, and Opinions, A.D. 1812 to A.D. 1842*. Philadelphia: Lippincott, Grambo and Co., Successors to Grigg, Elliot and co.

Strachey, Ray. 1978. *The Cause: A Short History of the Women's Movement in Great Britain (1928)*. London: Virago.

Thomas, Clara. 1967. *Love and Work Enough: The Life of Anna Jameson*. Toronto: University of Toronto Press.

Viviès, Jean. 1999. *Le Récit de voyage en Angleterre au XVIIIe siècle. De l'inventaire à l'invention*. Toulouse: Presses Universitaires du Mirail.

CHAPTER 5

"The Trouble with a Book…": Reading, Writing and Transgression in Jeanette Winterson's *Why Be Happy When You Can Be Normal?*

Valérie Baisnée-Keay

INTRODUCTION

Despite the growing popularity of memoirs among contemporary writers, British novelist Jeanette Winterson has never wholeheartedly embraced the genre. Her best-known novel, *Oranges Are Not The Only Fruit*, published in 1985 and adapted for television can be read both like the semi-autobiographical story of her upbringing as an adopted child among Pentecostal evangelist parents in the north of England and as a postmodern story interweaving fantasy and realist tales. With *Why Be Happy When You Can Be Normal?*, published in 2011, Winterson returned to the story of her beginnings to commit herself to a more factual account of her life and unravel the story of her adoption.[1] But she opts for a non-linear

V. Baisnée-Keay (✉)
University of Paris-Sud, Orsay, France

© The Author(s) 2018
V. Baisnée-Keay et al. (eds.), *Women's Life Writing and the Practice of Reading*, Palgrave Studies in Life Writing,
https://doi.org/10.1007/978-3-319-75247-1_5

account, omits events, and does not seal any pact of truth, even teasing the reader at times: "I have a memory—true or not true," she asks (11).

The story of Jeanette Winterson's development evinces multiple departures from the typical artist's autobiography. As many writers before her, Winterson emphasizes the key role books played in her life, from Bible reading in her childhood, the discovery of English literature at the public library in her teenage years to her reading of contemporary feminist works at Oxford University. Her reading experience, although as illuminating and life changing as other writers have recorded, is marked through and through by transgression, of which this chapter will decline the various forms.

Transgression is usually defined as "that which exceeds boundaries or exceeds limits," and is thought to be a characteristic of human experience.[2] Through its Latin origins, the word *transgressere* implies the crossing of boundaries and displacement, which is recorded in Winterson's memoir in the form of class and gender identity crossing. Furthermore, displacement also characterizes Winterson's postmodern aesthetics as noted in her criticism (Pykett 1998). In the traditional moral sense, transgression means breaking rules imposed from the outside, by religion especially, which, in the memoir, is staged as a major mother/daughter conflict. But limits can come from the inside as well. Winterson, whose whole existence may be a transgression since she was adopted, therefore displaced, constantly needs to push limits to find her own self as well as her art.

RECLAIMING A WORKING-CLASS IDENTITY THROUGH STORYTELLING: A CULTURAL TRANSGRESSION

By reclaiming her working-class cultural background and breaking the literary codes of bourgeois culture, Winterson performs political acts of transgression. Born in 1959 in Manchester, Jeanette Winterson grew up in the 1960s and 70s, a period of mill and pit closures during which the Lancashire region underwent major social change and worsening living conditions. The Winterson household smacked of poverty, lack of comfort and sometimes food. In this context, religion was a form of relief. In the city of Accrington (Lancashire), the narrator's early life revolved around the Pentecostal community with its preaching, Bible reading and summer camps. In both *Oranges* and *Why Be Happy*, a similar representation of Jeanette Winterson's childhood and adolescence emerges, featuring ingredients of Victorian literature: an adopted child, depicted as isolated, lonely and marginalized at school, an evil and crazy adoptive mother, and poverty.

Reviewing working-class autobiographies in *Landscape for a Good Woman*, historian and author Carolyn Steedman, a working-class daughter herself, found that tales of hardships are typical of the genre (1986, 9). In *Why Be Happy*, however, the humour and irony of the distanced narrator as well as of resistance of the character do not convey the victimization and passivity that Steedman sees as common to those tales.

Although she did not grow up surrounded by books like other writers, the narrator stresses that the Northern working-class nonetheless had a rich and unique oral culture based on storytelling: "For the people I knew, books were few and stories were everywhere, and how you tell 'em was everything" (Winterson 2011, 30). Spinning a tale was everyone's ability; stories could be heard everywhere, even in conversations on the bus. The pervasiveness of stories and imagination is thus not reserved to the upper class. It is that heritage that Winterson wants to reclaim as she establishes the significance of storytelling in her writing, which has become the cornerstone of her fiction. For Peter Childs (2005, 265), the recurring phrase of her novel *The Passion*—"Trust me, I'm telling you stories"—could be applied to Winterson's fiction as a whole. In an essay published in 1936, *The Storyteller,* Walter Benjamin claims that the traditional practice of storytelling has been marginalized by the advance of print culture, and that the once-powerful voice of the storyteller has been silenced.[3] Unlike Benjamin, however, Winterson does not lament the loss of an archaic voice to print culture, the domination of information and silent reading. Her fiction is an effort to make that voice heard again.

Among the oral culture she draws on, fairy tales hold a special place. They provide Winterson with a moral explanation for her characters as well as with the fantasy necessary to her art. In this respect, Winterson is close to Benjamin's view that "the first true storyteller is, and will continue to be, the teller of fairy tales" (Benjamin 2000, 89). Thus, to explain her mother, a woman who was "too big for her world" (35), the narrator refers back to her novel *Sexing the Cherry* (1989), whose main character is a giantess called The DogWoman who lives on the River Thames (Winterson 2011, 36). For Benjamin, the educational role of fairy tales is to imprint a spirit of resistance in children: "The wisest thing—so the fairy tale taught mankind in olden times, and teaches children to this day— is to meet the forces of the mythical world with cunning and high spirits" (89). Accordingly, Winterson's young self identifies with the small and smart fairy tale characters, such as Tom Thumb and Jack in the story *Jack and the Beanstalk*, in which the boy resists giants and ogres (34–35).

Being steeped in oral culture gives the narrator a sense of the materiality of reading. Reading is not only an intellectual process but also a sensual and emotional experience. In this oral culture, powerful language stands out, hence the importance of poetry: "a tough life needs a tough language" (40) says the narrator. Poetry can trigger a strong emotional response: Jeanette is moved to tears by T.S. Eliot's poetry. The power of texts, especially the Bible, also comes from a working-class tradition of reading aloud. At home, Mrs. Winterson read the Bible to her husband and daughter, and according to the narrator, she read well: "She read the Bible as though it had just been written," says the narrator (27). This way, language is both absorbed and embodied.

This working-class culture, represented as spontaneously creative, contrasts with the bourgeois culture the narrator encounters later in her life, where aesthetic experience is clouded by class, gender and racial prejudice. Working at the Accrington library as a teenager, she discovers that the library classification system, however scientific it may sound, is already a form of literary judgement. The narrator discovers Gertrude Stein in the humour section, because one librarian deemed she "was too modern a modernist for English literature A-Z" (128). Literature A-Z is presented as the ultimate canon of great works, which contains a handful of women and excludes marginal writers. Later, the narrator realizes that the elite literary culture is imbued in prejudice and social hierarchy, which makes working-class culture sound even more genuine. At Oxford University, she discovers she is "the working-class experiment" while another woman in her group represents "the black experiment" (142). Their tutor is "malevolently gay" and ignores them. She learns that the best way is to subvert the system by making her own way through literature, as well as trusting the texts before everything else. At the University of Oxford she sets up a parallel reading group, and establishes her own canon of contemporary female writers: "Suddenly I was reading Doris Lessing and Toni Morrison, Kate Millett and Adrienne Rich. They were like a new Bible" (142). Winterson condemns the elitism of upper class culture which wants to claim knowledge, therefore power for itself: "The more I read the more I fought against the assumption that literature is for the minority—of a particular education or class. Books were my birthright too" (143).

Similarly, Winterson finds it difficult to insert her working-class self into the bourgeois discourse of traditional autobiography, a linear "womb to tomb" (154) story about a great person. When she wrote *Oranges* in 1985, "it wasn't the day of the memoir" as she notes in *Why Be Happy*

(Winterson 2011, 3). Not only did the memoir appeal less than fiction, but it was also considered as a minor genre. Moreover, like a majority of women writers, Winterson felt autobiography contributed to the devaluing of women's writing. She "was trying to get away from the received idea that women always write about 'experience'" (Winterson 2011, 3). Yet there is no denying that *Oranges* is based on her own life. So she took an ambivalent, 'sitting on the fence' stance towards its status, feeling the need to write about her own experience, and rejecting autobiography for political and aesthetic reasons: "Is *Oranges* an autobiographical novel?," she asks in the preface, only to reply "No not at all and yes of course" (Winterson 1991, xvi). By 2011, Winterson had somewhat revised her position towards autobiography. The memoir had become commonplace and recognised as a literary genre in itself, while the diversity of autobiographical styles had opened doors to new creative ways of writing the self. Although she still finds it impossible to write a linear "womb to tomb" (Winterson 2011, 154) story and commit to a pact of truth, the reflexive autobiographical *I* remains the best way to recount the traumas of her childhood.

STORIES: FROM NETS TO MAPS

Despite working-class storytelling, the domestic scene is also marked by violence and conflict in the powerful struggle that opposes mother and daughter. The mother/daughter relationship is one of the leitmotivs of the memoir. Reading and writing in Winterson's narrative also take the familiar shape of a narrative of transgression and prohibition within the religious family background.

In the Winterson household, Mrs. Winterson is the dominant figure, the one who controls language, which allows her to dominate daughter and husband: "My mother was in charge of language. My father had never really learned to read—he could manage slowly, with his finger on the line, but he had left school at twelve and gone to work at the Liverpool docks. Before he was twelve, no one had bothered to read to him" (27). The Bible is the only book allowed in the household, although Mrs. Winterson also reads detective novels borrowed from the library. Life in the Winterson household is ruled by the Bible's prescriptions, quotes and prohibitions, told ironically or dramatically according to the distance chosen by the narrator. Thus, she remembers her mother sending her to school with the following quote embroidered on her gym bag:

"THE SUMMER IS ENDED AND WE ARE NOT YET SAVED" (7). A certain version of the Bible, the dark, gloomy one (Life as a Vale of Tears) is upheld by the mother who aggrandizes and dramatizes it like a prophet: "God is forgiveness—or so that particular story goes, but in our house God was Old Testament and there was no forgiveness without a great deal of sacrifice" (9). The narrator's adopted mother becomes the central figure in the memoir, a complex and ambivalent figure. She is portrayed not only as a religious fanatic, but also as an eccentric woman who "hated being a nobody" (1). She is even dubbed a "monster," a word that applies to her in the literal sense. A monster is a being that cannot live in the normal order of things as it exceeds its borders.[4] This is the case of Mrs. Winterson, who was "too big for her world" (35). Mrs. Winterson's conduct is also transgressive, as her actions also exceed boundaries and limits, but the mother's transgression cannot find a proper outlet outside herself, whereas the daughter finds creative energy in pushing limits.

There is a mythical subtext to the story: in order to read and write, the daughter has to reclaim language from her mother and transgress religious prohibitions on reading and storytelling. The conflict can also be read in terms of a master–slave dialectic: both mother and daughter demand recognition from the other. Ultimately, they struggle for the control of the other's story: "I can't remember a time when I wasn't setting my story against hers" (5), the narrator writes. Mrs. Winterson draws her power from the literal use of the biblical discourse, which gives a definitive version to life. She particularly revels in the Apocalypse, which appeals to her sense of drama and suits her dark moods. While the Bible tells life in a complete predictable theological manner from the origins to the end—Mrs. Winterson didn't believe in resurrection—English Literature often takes readers to unusual places. By possessing/embodying the Bible Mrs. Winterson, explains both the origin and the end of the narrator, an adopted child, a net that the daughter must disentangle herself from: "It took me a long time to realise that there are two kinds of writing: the one you write and the one that writes you. The one that writes you is dangerous" (54).

Unsurprisingly, the mother/daughter competition reaches its climax in a battle of books, leading to the narrator's departure from the family home: "In many ways it was time for me to go. The books had got the better of me, and my mother had got the better of the books" (41). The mother's prohibitions on reading open a space for the narrator to contravene them, according to Georges Bataille's rule that prohibitions prompt a desire to transgress.[5] Prohibitions confer a sacred aura on literature, and increase the daughter's desire to discover it. But when Mrs. Winterson finds out that Jeanette has hidden books under her mattress, she burns them in the garden (42). Once again, the episode is told like a fairy tale story: Jeanette starts accumulating books under her bed so that the bed rises like the Princess and the Pea (40). It also ends with a moral: on that day Jeanette realizes she will become a writer so that stories will never be taken away from her. This writing epiphany, common in autobiographies, is born out of destruction, which is turned into a positive event.

The symbolic confrontation between secular and religious texts is also displayed in the order of discourse. In the memoir, the chapter "English Literature A–Z" follows directly "The Apocalypse" in which the narrator recounts her coming out, and her mother turning her out of the house after a failed attempt from the Pentecostal community to "exorcise" her. The order of events (reality) is manipulated to fit in with the order of the narrative (ideological): in fact, Jeanette had started working in the library before she was expelled from the house. Thus, literature seals her departure from her mother's rigid religious world, as the daughter enters a new symbolic one, English literature with its own codes and rules, but potentially life-changing. Although the Bible left a profound influence on Jeanette Winterson, as the first book she had access to, it had been appropriated by the mother to submit the daughter. The chapter "The Apocalypse" ends with Jeanette justifying herself by saying she's happy, and her mother replying "'Why be happy when you could be normal?'" (114). This is actually a rhetorical question as Mrs. Winterson stresses the importance of conforming to normative heterosexuality at the expense of well-being. Mrs. Winterson herself had got married for the sake of conformity even though she refused to sleep in the same bed as her husband.

Crucially, therefore, transgression also represents an access to self: symbolic actions against the mother are highlighted and presented as landmarks that help form the narrator's new identity. For Winterson, individuality comes with the pushing of limits. In the preface to *Oranges*, she writes: "Everyone, at some time in their life, must choose whether to stay with a ready-made world that may be safe but which is also limiting, or to push forward, often past the frontiers of commonsense, into a personal place, unknown and untried. This quest can be of sexuality as well as individuality" (Winterson 1991, xiv).

Finally, prohibitions on reading are linked to sexuality, although sexuality is the greater transgression in a religious sense: "I was sixteen and my mother was about to throw me out of the house forever, for breaking a very big rule—even bigger than the forbidden books. The rule was not just No Sex, but definitely No Sex With Your Own Sex" (Winterson 2011, 38). Anthropologists have argued that the biggest taboos are linked to the body. Transgressing the boundaries of gender identity is a major breach of social roles. That is why queer feminist critics have located the origins of Winterson's transgression in her gender identity. In *Transgressing Boundaries in Jeanette Winterson's Fiction*, Sonia Front (2009) argues that "Jeanette Winterson's characters live in the patriarchal culture in which gender entails the attribution of social roles, appearance and sexual orientation. As they do not identify themselves with these significations inscribed on their bodies, gender becomes a burden for them. They decline to be bestowed identity on the basis of gender, and therefore they seek to reformulate their selves" (19).

Ironically, the first book that Mrs. Winterson discovers under Jeanette's mattress is D. H. Lawrence's *Women in Love*, whose title in this context echoes the narrator's sexual life, even though the novel is a heterosexual love story. While this love story is embedded in the narrative as a mirror image of the narrator's sexual identification, it is also displaced: the book is used to mean something else, a homosexual instead of her heterosexual story, which is another form of transgression, and a characteristic of postmodern literature.

Ultimately, transgression leads to a discovery of the true self, as the narrator experiences a double epiphany: I can write my own books and I can assume my own identity. She comes out as a lesbian at 15 in a "moment of recognition and desire" (78) just as the destruction by fire of her books leads to the realization that she would be writer. Winterson's transgressive acts are fundamentally reflexive, as they do not lead to destruction or subversion: her aim is not to reverse the order of things (she chooses to leave the family home) but to find herself by crossing some limits. Religious exorcism is replaced by an exorcism though literature: she expulses herself from her dysfunctional home to find a new self in the library. Exorcising the self given by others to become someone else is also reflected in the act of writing an autobiography as an exorcism from an authoritarian past. Consequently, the experience of limitlessness allowed by transgression has become Winterson's motto in her art and life alike.

But finding the self also means finding what she calls the "doubleness at the heart of things" (168) created by the trauma of her adoption, a much harder limit to transgress.

Breaking Away from the Stigma of Adoption

Jeanette Winterson was adopted at a time when adoption was still surrounded by secrecy and taboo. In Britain, the 1926 act made adoption a closed system, based on the complete severance of ties with the birth family. The birth parents were supposed to be forgotten about, and adopted children assumed the name of the adoptive family. As the narrator writes, until the 1976 Adoption Act, "mothers and children alike were assured of lifetime anonymity" (182). For Kerry O'Halloran (2015), the adoption process in Britain was "wrapped in a distinct aura of taboo" (74). The first step in breaching the secrecy of the adoption process was to give the right to an adopted person to obtain a copy of their original birth certificate (O'Halloran 2015, 20). Thanks to this new legal development Jeanette Winterson found out the name of her birth parents.

Adoption made Winterson's very existence a transgression. She is fundamentally a displaced person. She had to face the stigma and taboos of adoption as a child, as recounted in both *Oranges* and *Why Be Happy*. Jeanette grew up with the belief that either her biological parents were morally deficient creatures or there was something wrong with her for having been given up. "All adopted children blame themselves" (2011, 39), the older narrator notes, a statement that is confirmed by social workers. This was reinforced by her mother, Mrs. Winterson, who often used adoption as a disciplining tool against her daughter: when Jeanette was misbehaving, her mother told her she was "the wrong crib" (1). Jeanette was also violently beaten up for asking if her birth mother had come for a visit.[6] In order to cope with this, she had to shut out the whole story of her adoption, and live as if she had never been adopted: when she finds her adoption papers as a little girl, as related in *Why Be Happy*, she is not curious to find out who her birth parents were. Clinicians and psychologists have shown that this shutting out of the past is a common coping strategy among adoptees and what they are expected to do. But this strategy leaves marks on the psyche, as Jeanette will realize later.

To break the taboo surrounding her adoption, Winterson turns it into a chance, fuelled by her reading and writing. The narrator of *Why Be Happy* explains that "the missing past can be an opening, not a void" (5).

Adoption gives Jeanette the possibility to recreate herself, turning necessity into opportunity: "Adopted children are self-invented because we
have to be; there is an absence, a void, a question mark at the very beginning of our lives" (5). Adoption gives the illusion of an identity tabula rasa
which coincides with new cultural formulations of identity. Winterson is
also writing her memoir at a time when historically identities are no longer
given as an essence and have become a question of self-invention and
choice. Adoption as self-invention becomes both a means to make sense of
the past and a narrative principle: *Oranges* is a hybrid of fantasy and reality.
The main plot—a girl's development among Pentecostal parents and a
religious community—is interspaced with fairy tales and Holy Grail stories
as metaphoric renderings of her adoption. Sir Perceval and Winnet Stonejar
are her alter egos: the name Winnet Stonejar itself contains that of Jeanette
Winterson. For that reason, the novel was hailed as postmodern, not only
for mixing genres of discourse, but for projecting a postmodern sense of
subjectivity which says that there is no single identity but rather a series of
shifting selves. For Paulina Palmer (1993), the novel is truly postmodern
since it rejects "a unitary model of subjectivity in favour of a delineation of
fantasy identities and multiple selves" (30). These fluid selves are constructed in the act of storytelling. Furthermore, the postmodern stance is
more than just an aesthetic choice for Winterson: fantasizing is also an
activity that adopted children have in common (Groza & Rosenberg
2001, 44). What matters for Winterson is the ability to transform oneself
into someone else in the story.

Self-invention, on the other hand, implies shutting out the past and
denying the psychological effects of adoption. Part of her identity is built
on denial and on the negation of her real self, which makes it difficult to
reach out to the others and acquire a social identity. The adopted subject
cannot develop feelings of belonging: self-invention goes hand in hand
with social isolation: "I was a loner. I was self-invented. I didn't believe in
biology or biography" (Winterson 2011, 155), Winterson writes in *Why
Be Happy*.

Dealing with the trauma of adoption becomes necessary later in her life.
In the second part of the memoir, the narrator tells about the midlife
depression she went through, which led her to enquire about her birth
mother. Finding out about her origins became a question of survival, for
she was contemplating suicide. Like a lot of adoptees, Winterson had the
impression of living among ghosts: the ghost of her birth mother and the
ghost of the child she might have been had she stayed with her birth
mother. Her identity had become a haunted house.

Looking back at her origins forces Jeanette Winterson to experience her identity as split into two, which is common to adopted people. Betty Jean Lifton, an American psychotherapist who has written extensively about adoption, tells about the experience of doubleness in *Lost and Found: The Adoption Experience* (1979): "The Adoptee ... forced by circumstances to lead a double life, is haunted by a series of doubles" (34). Winterson explains this doubleness by her origins: "I had been twice born already, hadn't I—my lost mother and my new mother, Mrs. Winterson—that double identity, itself a kind of schizophrenia—my sense of myself as being a girl who's a boy who's a boy who's a girl. A doubleness at the heart of things" (Winterson 2011, 168). This fundamental split at the core of her identity is further reinforced by her homosexuality, which sets her apart socially but also confuses her gendered identity. Coincidently, Lifton's memoir is entitled *Twice Born: Memoirs of an Adopted Daughter* (1975).

As a result, *Why Be Happy* is a broken narrative as the story of adopted children often is. Narrative strategy mirrors a psychic strategy: to separate one part of the self from the rest of the self after a trauma is known as dissociation, numbing, or splitting. Thus, *Why Be Happy* is divided into two parts which are not connected. The first part completes and corrects the narrative of *Oranges*; the second part opens after a gap of 25 years with the story of her quest for her biological mother, whom she meets at the end of the narrative. Autobiographers usually want to make sense of life across time. Winterson cannot reconcile her two births, and is forced to play what Lifton (1979) calls the Adoption Game:

> The Adoption Game—as I call it—requires Adoptees to lead a split existence. Cut off as they are from knowledge of their origins, they go underground emotionally. While seeming to live entirely in the "real" world with their adoptive parents and friends, they are inhabiting a subterranean world of fantasies and fears governed by demons, which they can share with no one. (8)

Winterson's identity quest demonstrates the limits of a constructivist approach to identity in the face of trauma. However "self-invented" the narrator insists she is, this does not suffice to sustain a coherent sense of self. She had lost ontological security as a child in the trauma of adoption. Knowing where you belong is also important as no one is born out of nowhere. Origins cannot be bypassed or forgotten about. Erikson has defined "a sense of identity" as "a sense of personal sameness and historical continuity" (1968, 17).[7] While *Oranges* insisted on self-invention and turned identities into the creation of oneself, the memoir also acknowledges the importance of sameness and the way identities are also inscribed in the body and produced by society. As a result, transgressing the boundaries of fact and fiction becomes the ultimate transgression, as a way of integrating the reality of her life into a fiction of herself.

READING MYSELF AS A FICTION

A final form of transgression for Winterson consists in crossing the boundaries between fact and fiction in the recounting of her past. In both *Oranges* and *Why Be Happy*, a pact of truth with the reader is unachievable because of the narrator's doubleness and absence of origins. Jeanette Winterson's identity as an adoptee makes it impossible for her to write a linear account of her life, as in a traditional autobiography, while she can make sense of herself through fiction, and thus transgress the limits of facts—the inescapable reality of her adoption and abandonment—for the limitlessness of imagination: "The womb to tomb of an interesting life—but I can't write my own; never could. Not Oranges. Not now. I would rather go on reading myself as a fiction than as a fact" (Winterson 2011, 154). Winterson's self is absent, and its presence can only be felt in reading and writing. While autobiographers often want readers to believe in the truth of their life story, Winterson cannot make such a claim. In the introduction to her novel *Weight* (2005), she writes that what matters is authenticity:

> *Weight* has a personal story in the First Person, indeed almost all of my work is in the First Person, and this leads to questions of autobiography. Autobiography is not important. Authenticity is important. The writer must fire herself through the text, be the molten stuff that melds together disparate elements. I believe there is always exposure, vulnerability, in the writing process, which is not to say it is either confessional or memoir; simply, it is real. (2005, xviii–xix)

The opposition fact/fiction, however, is far from being as clear-cut as Winterson would like it to be, for fact and fiction are always mixed in the act of narrating as a number of autobiographical critics have stressed.[8] In *Fictions in Autobiography: Studies in the Art of Self-Invention* (1985), Paul J. Eakin in particular claims that "autobiographical truth is not a fixed but an evolving content in an intricate process of self-discovery and self-creation," and adds that "the self that is the center of all autobiographical narrative is necessarily a fictive structure" (3). From a psychoanalytic point of view, the fictional elements in autobiographies come from the impossibility for a subject to tell his/her own origins. Following Lacan, Judith Butler (1990) argues that "the constitutive identifications of an autobiographical narrative are always partially fabricated in the telling" (85). Similarly, fiction is never pure invention; facts are mixed in it as well. The terms fact and fiction are therefore not antithetical in an autobiography. So what does the opposition between fact and fiction really mean for Winterson?

To make sense of her own self, Winterson needs to be able to read herself in stories, that is to connect stories to the understanding of her identity. In this sense, reflexive identity is more unifying than aesthetic postmodern identity. Reflexivity must be dialectical. First, the very act of narrating allows speakers/writers to disassociate the speaking/writing self from the act of speaking, to take a reflective position towards the self as character. Second, reading stories let her enter into an exchange with others that in return helps to define who she is. Thus, Winterson can keep the story of Jeanette going. This is what British sociologist Antony Giddens argues in his book *Modernity and Self-identity:*

> A person's identity is not to be found in behaviour, nor—important though this is—in the reactions of others, but in the capacity to keep a particular narrative going. The individual's biography, if she is to maintain regular interaction with others in the day-to-day world, cannot be wholly fictive. It must continually integrate events which occur in the external world, and sort them into the ongoing 'story' about the self. (1991, 54)

Antony Giddens makes a crucial distinction between identity and self-identity. Identity is what results from a biographical trajectory while self-identity is "the self as reflexively understood by the person in terms of her or his biography" (53). Self-identity implies reflexivity and a narrative, whether explicit or not. Accordingly, autobiography is "at the core of self-identity in modern social life" (Giddens, 76).

The postmodern fragmentation of identities cannot produce a self-identity. For Giddens, "a self-identity has to be created and more or less continually reordered against the backdrop of shifting experiences of day-to-day life and the fragmenting tendencies of modern institutions" (186).

Thus, Jeanette's autobiography, in Giddens's sense, is a reordering of a battered, double identity through literature. Doubly marginalized and stigmatized as an adoptee and a lesbian, she uses literature to find a definition of herself outside prescribed identities, to reach out to the world and find a form of agency, rather than shut herself from it: "Literature isn't a hiding place. It's a finding place," says the narrator (Winterson 2011, 40). After the "Apocalypse" of her coming out, which marks the end of her old world, the narrator describes her entrance into a new world order. At the local library, she systematically explores English literature, reading it alphabetically. Literature becomes her new home in many ways, from the library to the room offered by her English teacher at school at her place. "Books, for me, are a home" (61), Winterson says.

Two books especially, Virginia Woolf's *Orlando* (1928) and Gertrude Stein's *The Autobiography of Alice B. Toklas* (1933), introduce Winterson to the instability and playfulness of identity in the text, as well as different modes of transgressing the border between fact and fiction. In *The Autobiography of Alice B. Toklas*, she finds a narrator, Stein, telling her story through her lover, Toklas, thus blurring the boundaries between narrating self and narrated self. The author appears as a fiction of her own self. In *Orlando*, subtitled "a biography" and dedicated to Woolf's lover Vita Sackville-West, Woolf plays with the serious factual genre of biography. Born in the Elizabethan Age, Orlando is a young nobleman at the beginning of the story, and a modern woman three centuries later. In this text, the limits of time, space and sexual identity are blown over. The change of sex is not problematic for Orlando, as Woolf stresses his/her androgynous nature. This use of fantasy in portraying characters is crucial for Winterson. Woolf, like Winterson, didn't believe that a person couldn't be grasped through biography. Both books became a model for Winterson's understanding of the self as fiction: "For me, fascinated with identity, and how you define yourself, those books were crucial" (Winterson 2011, 119). In a collection of essays, *Art Objects*, Winterson wrote extensively on Woolf and Stein, pondering on the link between fact and fiction, transfigured in the act of storytelling: "Are real people fictions? We mostly understand ourselves through an endless series of stories told to ourselves by ourselves and others. The so-called facts of our individual worlds are highly coloured and arbitrary, facts that fit whatever fiction we have chosen to believe in" (Winterson 1995, 59). In this comment, fact is not opposed to fiction. Rather, the two are mixed in autobiography, which nonetheless tends towards fiction.

Literature opens to a lot of possible identity scripts, and gives one the illusion of escaping from prescribed roles. Both books especially prove that identity is not fixed. Through Stein and Woolf, Winterson learned one can fictionalize oneself with biographical material, as well as with the effects of narrative discourse. This way she can transgress the borders of fact and fiction.

With reading and writing Winterson believes that she can force destiny: "Reading yourself as a fiction as well as a fact is the only way to keep the narrative open—the only way to stop the story running away under its own momentum, often towards an ending no one wants" (2011, 119). Death is the only limit that cannot be transgressed, and it is also the reason for all transgressions, as Bataille has demonstrated. Yet, if storytelling is a powerful source of agency, it cannot make you an author in the sense defined by Hannah Arendt in *The Human Condition* (1958/1998): "Although everybody started his life by inserting himself in the human world through action and speech, nobody is the author or producer of his own life story because every story must have an ending and no agent can both act his and tell it at the same time" (184).

A storyteller cannot be an author. Life has no beginning, no end and no author.

CONCLUSION

As a writer, Winterson believes in the power of stories and books to create identities, and to go beyond the restrictions imposed by others and by institutions. But identity is something one can only invent from what is already there, so she cannot erase the story of her adoption. Telling stories about herself and others is a way to keep her identity in movement against the fixity of other people's images of herself and to reduce her sense of a discontinuity in the temporal experience of being "twice born." Reading and writing, therefore, must always be transgressive. Hence travelling may be the overarching trope in *Why Be Happy*, but not in the traditional linear sense. Winterson borrows its meaning from Gertrude Stein: life is a road to find yourself as much as to get lost.

NOTES

1. The following editions of Winterson's works are used in this article: *Oranges Are Not the Only Fruit* (London: Vintage, 1991); *Why Be Happy When You Can Be Normal?* (New York: Grove Press, 2011).
2. Chris Jenks. *Transgression.* (London: Routledge, 2003), 7.
3. The full title of Benjamin's essay is "The Storyteller: Observations on the Works of Nikolai Leskov" (1936).
4. The Oxford English Dictionary defines "monster" as: "Originally: a mythical creature which is part animal and part human, or combines elements of

two or more animal forms, and is frequently of great size and ferocious appearance. Later, more generally: any imaginary creature that is large, ugly, and frightening" (OED, 2nd ed., Oxford: Clarendon Press; New York: Oxford University Press, 1989).

5. "The taboo is there in order to be violated" (Georges Bataille 1986, 68).

6. This episode is referred to as the "Awful Occasion" in *Oranges*, 128–129 and in *Why Be Happy*, 11–12.

7. "...which ... is based on two simultaneous observations: the perception of the fact that selfsameness and continuity of one's existence in time and space and the perception of the fact that others recognize one's sameness and continuity" (Winterson 1968, 50).

8. The inevitably fictive nature of the autobiographical text has been stressed in the criticism of the genre. On this topic, see also Paul De Man, "Autobiography as De-facement," in *The Rhetoric of Romanticism* (New York: Columbia University Press, 1984).

REFERENCES

Arendt, Hannah. 1998. [1958] *The Human Condition*. 2nd ed. Chicago: University of Chicago Press.

Bataille, Georges. 1986. *Erotism: Death and Sensuality*. First published 1957. Trans. Mary Dalwood. San Francisco: City Lights Books.

Benjamin, Walter. 2000. The Storyteller. In *Theory of the Novel: A Historical Approach*, ed. Michael McKeon, 77–93. Baltimore/London: The John Hopkins University Press.

Butler, Judith. 1990. *Gender Trouble: Feminism and the Subversion of Identity*. London: Routledge.

Childs, Peter. 2005. Jeanette Winterson: Boundaries and Desire. In *Contemporary Novelists: British Fiction Since 1970*, 255–273. New York: Palgrave Macmillan.

Eakin, Paul J. 1985. *Fictions in Autobiography: Studies in the Art of Self-Invention*. Princeton: Princeton University Press.

Erikson, Erik H. 1968. *Identity, Youth and Crisis*. New York: W. W. Norton.

Front, Sonia. 2009. *Transgressing Boundaries in Jeanette Winterson's Fiction*. Frankfurt: Peter Lang.

Giddens, Anthony. 1991. *Modernity and Self-identity: Self and Society in the Late Modern Age*. Stanford: Stanford University Press.

Groza, Victor, and Karen F. Rosenberg, eds. 2001. *Clinical and Practice Issues in Adoption: Bridging The Gap Between Adoptees*. Westport: Bergin & Garvey.

Jenks, Chris. 2003. *Transgression*. London: Routledge.

Lifton, Betty Jean. 1979. *Lost & Found: The Adoption Experience*. 3rd ed. First published 1979. Ann Arbor: The University of Michigan Press.

O'Halloran, Kerry. 2015. *The Politics of Adoption: International Perspectives on Law, Policy and Practice.* 3rd ed. Dordrecht: Springer.

Palmer, Paulina. 1993. *Contemporary Lesbian Writing: Dreams, Desire, Difference.* Buckingham: Open University Press.

Pykett, Lyn. 1998. A New Way With Words? Jeanette Winterson's Post-Modernism. In *'I'm Telling You Stories': Jeanette Winterson and the Politics of Reading,* ed. Helena Grice and Tim Woods, 53–60. Amsterdam: Rodopi.

Steedman, Carolyn. 1986. *Landscape for a Good Woman: A Story of Two Lives.* London: Virago Press.

Winterson, Jeanette. 1991. *Oranges Are Not the Only Fruit.* London: Vintage.

———. 1995. *Art Objects: Essays on Art and Effrontery.* London: Jonathan Cape.

———. 2005. *Weight.* Edinburgh: Canongate Books.

———. 2011. *Why Be Happy When You Can Be Normal?* New York: Grove Press.

PART II

Reading and Misreading the Canon

CHAPTER 6

The Art of Mis-Reading: Life's Writing in Virginia Woolf's Essays

Nicolas Pierre Boileau

INTRODUCTION

As she wonders how she should raise the question of "Women and Fiction," Virginia Woolf asserts: "One must strain off what was personal and accidental in all these impressions and so reach the pure fluid, the essential oil of truth" (*A Room of One's Own*, 20).[1] This statement suggests an opposition between the personal and truth that could set us on the wrong track regarding the function of life writing in Woolf's work. Woolf's modernist style is, on the contrary, widely regarded as foregrounding the personal experience, and she seems to sponsor a vision of truth that is highly subjective and contingent. In her monograph on Woolf's aesthetics of the essay, Elena Gualtieri precisely emphasizes the role played by the personal:

N. P. Boileau (✉)
Aix-Marseille Univ, LERMA, Aix en Provence, France
e-mail: nicolas.boileau@univ-amu.fr

© The Author(s) 2018
V. Baisnée-Keay et al. (eds.), *Women's Life Writing and the Practice of Reading*, Palgrave Studies in Life Writing,
https://doi.org/10.1007/978-3-319-75247-1_6

> [Woolf's] approach to the history and to the nature of the genre was always marked by an attempt to identify within what she saw as a male tradition an alternative line of descent to which she could affiliate herself. This she outlined by stressing the connection between the essay and autobiography, but a type of autobiography which she insisted was essentially non-narrative and presented the self as a conglomeration of moments of perception and reflection. (Gualtieri 2000, 49)

This description perfectly applies to *A Room of One's Own*, because the essay also combines personal affects ("moments of perception") with a coherent demonstration ("reflection"), playfully working its way through the *terra incognita* of women's relation to fiction by offering a discourse that presents itself as an alternative to the patriarchal one. Woolf's assertion, quoted at the beginning of this chapter, may indeed come as a surprise to those who readily associate Woolf with feminism, for it seems to oppose women, the object of the essay, and the personal, when it has become customary to consider that it was from their position or situation, through the personal, that the category "woman" could be addressed (Smith and Watson 1998, 4–21). This is why Woolf's short writings were reappraised favourably only recently, and stopped being discarded for their autobiographical nature (Reynier 2009; Amselle 2008; Adorno 1984). Critics' slow recognition of the value of these texts were also caused by Woolf's opinion about life writing at large, which seems ambivalent: exhorting historians to take a look at women's "infinitely obscure lives" that remain "to be recorded" (*AROO*, 77), she still criticizes women for resorting to autobiography, which she seemingly regards as an uncreative form: "She may be beginning to use writing as an art, not as a method of self-expression" (*AROO*, 68).

It is this complex negotiation between essay and life writing that I wish to analyse in this chapter, through the question of reading, which Woolf uses to define her art. Stripping the text of its personal dimension does not amount to a rejection of the autobiographical: in order to highlight this, I want to look at Woolf's "critical essays" as pertaining to the same continuum as her autobiographical ones, insofar as they also serve to construct her image, her story and to reflect the process by which the incidental becomes the essential. Woolf's interest in the telling of lives (her own or that of others) lies in each individual's singular trajectory towards truth.

So as to explore this aspect, it is necessary to try and delve into Woolf's proposal concerning the choices of reading. In the beginning of *A Room of One's Own*, Woolf invites us to "follow" her as she tries to answer the question of women and fiction. Her essay therefore starts like an autobiographical account by situating the writing subject in the anecdotal through the description of her surroundings, and her menial activities (*AROO*, 20). Despite the change of name (and the multiplication of what could be called "aliases" is an indication of its fictional nature), *A Room of One's Own* does not follow "Mary Beton, Mary Seton, Mary Carmichael" (*AROO*, 2), but another Virgin, Virgin-ia. We are asked to "follow" "I" (before Twitter—and it is a pleasant idea to think that Woolf is prefiguring the Twitter accounts of today, that is the promotion of personal opinions that must be followed, and derives from the current collapse of any guarantee of truth), an "I" that paradoxically offers herself to view in confessing her lack of knowledge. The "I" of the essayist inescapably stages her reflection in a way that undermines the traditional answers given to the question she asks, providing a very personal answer to a general question: "Every page in my notebook was scribbled over with notes. To show the state of mind I was in, I will read you a few of them, explaining that the page was headed quite simply, WOMEN AND POVERTY, in block letters" (*AROO*, 23). The materiality of the text that is underlined here evokes the act of portraying that will continue throughout the essay to offer not "the truth," but "a truth" derived from the articulation of thought that the essay proffers, and the subject that writes it. In this chapter, I intend to follow Woolf in her autobiographical acts of (mis)reading the other in order to read herself. The word itself "mis-reading" comes from Woolf's essays, and casts a shadow of doubt on the possibility of any reliable knowledge that could be attained without the misleading track of fiction. I will argue that her celebration of acts of mis-reading corresponds to the delineation of an *Ars Poetica* of life writing that in turn enables Woolf to create breakthroughs in auto/biographical writings.

ON MIS-READING OTHERS

Woolf starts *A Room of One's Own* with a personal anecdote. Lunching in Oxbridge has fostered many questions that, as suggested before, strike the reader as an attempt at finding universal laws rather than emphasizing subjective experience: "Why did men drink wine and women water? Why was one sex so prosperous and the other so poor? What effect has poverty on fiction?" (*AROO*, 20). In order to answer these questions, Woolf wants to enter the Oxbridge library, and other places of knowledge like the British Museum, in order to pursue an investigation that is doomed to fail:

when it comes to the History of Women, there is no fact to be found, but only layers of fiction—an opposition between facts and fiction that does not run counter to establishing some form of truth. The official reason for this absence has a cultural explanation: Oxbridge and the British Museum were patriarchal institutions designed by men for men's benefit, and the deployment of a masculine rationality that has since been debunked in its self-representation as the norm. Perhaps the reason why there is only fiction to be told can also be related to the type of question the essayist is raising: as her study is meant to observe *all* women, she necessarily embarks upon a reflection that will situate her on the side of the phallocratic, universal truth. However, the pleasure of her text derives, not only from the sarcasm of the educated lady confronting the domineering male "professor" of Oxbridge, who would then have been the educator of the British Museum curator (and probably still is), but from the fact that these grand questions are taken down to the level of the subject(ive), the personal, contrary to what she affirms. When Woolf asks why men drink wine and women water, what she really does is to show how she, a subject, responds to that truth that can only be fiction (men drink wine and women do not), and why it is that she should be struck by that truth. In other words, Woolf develops the various answers she can find to the questions, and in so doing distracts our attention from the fact that it is the truth of the question itself that should be challenged. For it is that aspect which is revealing of herself.

Her interpretation of facts can be likened to the way she reads. Woolf, like Clarissa Dalloway, reads obsessively: "Like most uneducated Englishwomen, I like reading—I like reading books in the bulk" (*AROO*, 94). What she mostly reads is lives (Snaith 2000, 96–104; Raitt 2000, 29–49); but it is also what she mostly writes (about). The number of books she read and commented on throughout her life is impressive. Her multivolume diary and autobiographical fragments reveal an interest in the reading of books—fiction and non-fiction—and her obsession with finding the right way of telling other people's lives: she is the renowned author of biographies *Roger Fry, Flush*—Barrett Browning's dog—or *Orlando*—a thinly veiled portrait of her lover, Vita Sackville-West. These (auto)biographical acts were prolonged into a larger spectrum that could be called "autobiographical space," following in the footsteps of Philippe Lejeune and my own reading of it (Lejeune, 1975; Boileau 2007, 217–229). Woolf writes about reading as much as she reads about writing, because it is in reading that she finds the truth that goes missing in the very places where she expects it to

belong, and this is how she constructs her own experimental stance in relation to, or against, other writers she has criticized: on starting her work on
"women and fiction," she immediately turns to books (to find that there are
none). As a result, *A Room of One's Own* as a whole can be said to be a conversation in reading (despite the absence of any reliable books). Reading
exposes Woolf to the complexity of her being, as reader, and the constraints
of her art, but also to the kind of writer she is and the more complex question of her womanhood—a question that always surfaces in her reviews.
The link between Woolf's writing and her reading has been stressed by
many (genetic) critics, who looked at the importance of intertextual references in her work (Davison 2014). However, what remains to be seen is
whether the act of reading opens up a critical space for the author to half-say
her truth and suggest other ways of reading her self.

In an article on "Two Women," Alice Wood comments on an essay,
largely forgotten even in Woolfian circles (Wood 2011, 51–62). Woolf's
essay, "The Wrong Way of Reading" (May 1920), is the review of a biography of Mary Russell Mitford, who was a country novelist in the beginning of the nineteenth century. "The Wrong Way of Reading" is crucial
because it interweaves the questions of reading and of life writing regarding the essay as such, but it also gives insights into Woolf's own conception of her art. Besides, Alice Wood argues that this short text was the
origin of *A Room of One's Own*. Woolf's essay advocates that a reader can
be licensed to forge her own opinion of the subject she reads about, and is
therefore allowed to wander off the trodden paths offered by the author
(Wood 2011, 52). It is paradoxically in mis-reading that truth can be
found. In other words, Wood claims that Woolf finds in reading a way of
escaping the "obstinate arbitrariness of 'what happened'" (Furbank,
quoted by Wood 2011, 53) that enslaves the author, especially the author
of life writings. This is Wood's conclusion, but I would like to take the
problem the other way around, and start with the idea that reading is a
way to escape the obstinate arbitrariness of "what is written." For it seems
that Woolf's essays on the books that she has read would be likely to fail
the Oxbridge tests that academics promote. The possibility for Woolf to
mis-read (or "half-read" to parody Lacan's "*mi-dire*") is of paramount
importance, and the effects of this are multifarious in her appraisal of texts
and genres. Woolf's unreliable ways of reading will not be a great surprise
to those familiar with "On Not Knowing Greek," which explores the
effect of a language she could not read, speak or understand: for all the
phonological, and cultural reasons that are named, what interests Woolf in

Greek—as a language and the culture it is the vehicle of—is how she interprets it without being able to understand it: "There is a cruelty in Greek
tragedy which is quite unlike our English brutality" (Woolf 1984, 25).[2]
Woolf chooses to 'not read' Greek from the perspective of the English's
sense of propriety, which means that what she is reading is a negative portrait of herself as English (in terms of rank, class, religion, education, etc.)
and no analysis of the language *per se*. This is an observation that can be
made about many essays: this does not suggest that she could not read the
books she commented upon, but her opinion of them was very much personal, if not biased, and based on an appreciation of the reflexive act of
self-portraits they inspire. She thus claims that life writings are the only
reliable texts: "other people may evade us, but our own features are almost
too familiar" (*CR*, 58). This statement appears in an article on "Montaigne,"
which is of paramount importance for the argument developed here, as it
is an essay on the genre of the essay as well as an essay in reading another
essayist who will then become the figurehead of Woolf's own style.

Woolf's essays often raise the question of the representation of life and
the definition of generic patterns: the essay on Montaigne continues with
an argument in favour of "laying down rules" (*CR*, 59) in order to undermine the absence of correspondence between language and life, the former stable and the latter changing. And yet, elsewhere, she worries about
the expansion of biographical writings because this genre threatens the
interest in the written text itself, and may endanger forms of writings that
are deemed more complex to understand: "How far we are going to read
a poet when we can read about a poet is a problem to lay before biogra-
phers" (Woolf 1986, 202).[3] Likewise, in an essay on "Lewis Carroll,"
Woolf comments on 'our' failure to grasp Carroll: "The complete works
of Lewis Carroll have been issued … in a stout volume of 1293 pages. So
there is no excuse—Lewis Carroll ought once and for all to be complete.
We ought to be able to grasp him whole and entire. But we fail—once
more we fail. … In order to cement it, we turn to the Life" (Woolf 1948,
81). The "Life" seems to be the easy response to avoid the more difficult
task of analysing the work of fiction. Yet these passing remarks are largely
overbalanced by the amount of essays focusing on autobiographical writings, and, if not, being twisted in a way that sees every fiction as an autobiographical act in disguise.

Woolf develops an *Ars Poetica* through the mis-reading of all these
texts: staging herself as reader, Woolf is first and foremost a critic of literature whose review is marked by the impossible-to-escape figure of the

critic that is usually sought to be erased out. Theodor Adorno, for example, endorses the commonly-held criticism that essays are often reproached for leaving out the person's point of view (Adorno 1984, 23). Interestingly, Woolf's essays are the opposite, promoting her vision in the way she selects the works she writes about; she seldom writes about one particular text, and the titles of her essays often correspond to the name of the author rather than the title of the texts she comments on, as if works and author were one and the same. For example, "Defoe," which takes a broad view at the whole *oeuvre* of the English writer, reads as follows:

> The interpretation that we put on his characters might therefore well have puzzled him. We find for ourselves meanings which he was careful to disguise even from his own eye. ...
>
>   The advocates of women's rights would hardly care, perhaps, to claim Moll Flanders and Roxana among their patron saints; and yet it is clear that Defoe not only intended them to speak some very modern doctrines upon the subject, but placed them in circumstances where their peculiar hardships are displayed in such a way as to elicit our sympathy. (*CR*, 92)

The primary objective of this is to reveal that reading is unstable, not fixed, and that a text escapes the scope that was initially intended by its author: it is a justification of mis-reading others. This seems to confide the readers in the construction of the text's meaning, as shown in the quasi-absence of quotes in Woolf's essays. Her texts unfold as if they were mere ramblings detached from the text(s) that triggered off her reflexion. According to Elena Gualtieri, in Woolf's introduction to the first collection of her essays, "[she] stressed both the humble character and the mediating nature of her ideal reader, whom she envisaged as a sort of third term, escaping the two extremes of either inaccessible scholarship or mindless consumption" (Gualtieri 58–59).

Reading was certainly one of Woolf's major concerns. Numerous essays focus on the act of reading, such as "Reading," "On Re-Reading Books," "Reviewing,"[4] or "How Should One Read a Book?", not to forget the titles of two of her published collections of essays in book form. Reading is often placed in relation to the taxonomical aspect of generic boundaries (*CR II*, 259), and Woolf both strengthens the function of genre distinctions while promoting the liberty of readers to freely accept the category the writer has chosen for his/her texts. This often creates a reader figure that is akin to that of reviewer or critic, an expert in reading whose subjective response predominates. Her criticism of her own texts, which is on a par with the criticism she offers of other texts, creates, as I have suggested elsewhere, the figure of an expert writer that knows better (Boileau 2011):

> The only advice, indeed, that one person can give another about reading is to take no advice, to follow your own instincts, to use your own reason, to come to your own conclusions. If this is agreed between us, then I feel at liberty to put forward a few ideas and suggestions because you will not allow them to fetter that independence which is the most important quality that a reader can possess. ("How Should One Read a Book?", *CR II*, 258)

The liberty of the author/reader as defined here is such that it amounts to an affirmation of power, as if indeed Woolf's opinion derived from the reading of other texts had contributed to improving her capacity to form notions and objects. Therefore, one may not be surprised that after asking for her readers' consent that they will not begrudge her for taking liberties with the texts she reads, she warns them elsewhere against certain ways of reading that would be fatal: "But let us, as we approach the danger-zone of Hardy's philosophy, be on our guard. Nothing is more necessary, in reading an imaginative writer, than to keep at the right distance above his page. Nothing is easier, especially with a writer of marked idiosyncrasy, than to fasten on opinions, convict him of a creed, tether him to a consistent point of view" (*CR II*, 254). It seems that her vision of the reader's liberty dovetails with the ideal of a reader who is in the know, a reader that is less common than she claims hers to be. In other words, there is an art of mis-reading and this art pertains to a delicate combination between the text and its author, the impression(s) and the fact(s), the style and the woman. Throughout her essays, Woolf seeks to track down the personality of the author. Christine Reynier helps us understand this aspect in her illuminating study of "Personalities":

> Woolf's universality does not presuppose a unified subject; for her, a universal art form cannot be ascribed to a single voice but to a double one, both male and female, and even to a pluralist voice. In other words, instead of being emptied out and disappearing as in Eliot's case, the authorial voice becomes an anonymous and universal or collective voice, "the common voice singing out of doors", the voice of a multiple self and multiple selves, a polyphonic voice, what Gillian Beer calls "the nameless multiple author" in reference to Woolf's "Anon" that she compares with Walter Benjamin's "storyteller". (Reynier 2009, 24)

This plurality of the author's voices and selves do not jeopardize the auto-biographical project. It only means that this project finds many voices through an incessant, repetitive practice that only fails to complete the story.

ON MIS-WRITING AUTO/BIOGRAPHY

Amongst the various examples that could be taken to explore this aspect, I would like to take her essay "William Hazlitt" because it starts with a celebration of the presence of this overwhelming voice that unifies all his texts: "[Hazlitt's] essays are emphatically himself. He has no reticence and he has no shame. He tells us exactly what he thinks, and he tells us—the confidence is less seductive—exactly what he feels" (*CR*, 173). After this remark, Woolf launches in a biographical account based on her impressions of reading his essays. Woolf here interestingly directs her criticism at another essayist and points out the subjective experience that his essays are, when they would have certainly been appreciated for the objective, rational writing of a man of letters, at the time when the essays were published and when Woolf reviewed them. The liberty of reading Woolf advocates is linked to the importance for her to break free from the constraints of literary genres, and especially from the genres linked to the representation of lives, despite the strength she gives them in "How One Should Read a Book": "It is simple enough to say that since books have classes—fiction, biography, poetry—we should separate them and take from each what is it right that each should give us" (*CR II*, 259). *A Room of One's Own* offers itself as scholarly lectures on the question of women. Instead of abiding by the traditional rules of objectivity, Woolf prefers to launch into the personal account of her encounter with the absence of women in fiction, both as characters and writers. This is the result of the very path she found in reading De Quincey's autobiography.

As Catherine Lanone argues, "Woolf is fascinated by De Quincey's subversive displacement of autobiography, his refusal to make it fit the ethical constraints of the day, to shape his tale into a normative narrative" (Lanone 2011, 40). Yet, when she writes about De Quincey, Woolf at first seems to find more to criticize than to praise: "Together with his fatal verbosity and weakness of architectural power, De Quincey suffered too as an autobiographer from a tendency to meditative abstraction" (*CR II*, 137). This sounds anything but praise and shows that Woolf, despite her failing to have written any substantial work of autobiography in 1932 when the essay first came out, once again stresses her capacity to identify failings in the works of others. However, what she finds worthy in De Quincey is his attention to dreams and vision that supplant facts in his recounting of his life. She thus lays the emphasis on his use of prose to record visions that cannot be reduced to observable facts and therefore show his personality. In so doing, he can be likened to what she finds interesting in Hardy's "moments of vision," an expression she uses from one of his poems and collection of poems. This cannot but echo the "moments of being" which she uses as a theory at the heart of her own autobiography, which she writes in "between the acts," as it were, of her novel and in between the bombings that were going to precipitate her death.[5] De Quincey, like Hardy (and Shakespeare, Coleridge and Keats if we are to trust *A Room of One's Own*), is a poet of prose, which both writers use to an end that Woolf agrees with: she writes that he "treats prose as a humble beast of burden, … as an impure substance in which dust and twigs and flies find lodgement" (*CR II*, 132). The personification of prose or fiction is a recurring motif of Woolf's essay that we find again in "The Art of Fiction," her response to Forster's *Aspects of the Novel*. What matters here is to see how reading still means reviewing and forming a criticism that sounds like a programme for herself rather than a stock of the current situation: "To tell the whole story of life the autobiographer must devise some means by which the two levels of existence can be recorded—the rapid passage of events and actions; the low opening up of single and solemn moments of concentrated emotion" (*CR II*, 139). The use of the modal verb "must" is an injunction that can be read as self-directed and that will then be used in the texts she was writing at the same time (*c*.1929): "Fiction here is likely to contain more truth than fact. Therefore I propose, making use of all the liberties and licenses of a novelist, to tell you the story of the two days that preceded my coming here—how, bowed down by the weight of the subject which you have laid upon my shoulders, I pondered it, and made it work in and out of my daily life" (*AROO*, 2). This quote points to the absence of a clear-cut opposition between fact and imagination, as truth can lodge itself in either. And this is something she found in her reading great male authors: "Lamb, Browne, Thackeray, Newman, Sterne, Dickens, De Quincey—whoever it may be—never helped a woman yet, though she may have learnt a few tricks of them and adapted them to her use" (*AROO*, 65). The word "adapt" is another trace of that operation by which a reader appropriates his or her own version of that story s/he is told. Moreover, the essay is presented as the work of a novelist—and at that time Woolf had been the successful writer of *Mrs. Dalloway, To the Lighthouse* and the lighter in tone, but rather successful *Orlando*. This can be read as an attempt to do what she suggests De Quincey should have done, or did at times; Woolf combines facts with the power of prose writing, in order to account for the personal emotions created the reality that she writes about. *A Room of One's Own* can thus be seen as the end of the journey Woolf embarked upon as reader and finished as writer, conscious as she had become that truth lies in the things that are half-said in the same way that books are mis-read: "Truth is only to be had by laying together many varieties of error" (*AROO*, 91). It is not so much that texts are not read as they should be, but that reading is a form of interpretation by which things understood supplement the things that were actually written, prompting the writer to work on the ways in which her text will be in turn mis-read.

Jean Starobinski defines life writing as impure, in the sense that it is always contaminated by other forms, other concerns, an impurity that Woolf was fascinated by, as shown by Catherine Bernard and Christine Reynier's collection of essays (2002):

> The Autobiographer is free to "contaminate" the story of his/her life by the narrative of events s/he was the distant witness of: the autobiographer will then become a chronicler … s/he is free to precisely date the different times of his/her writing and to comment on the time when s/he wrote: the diary then comes to contaminate the autobiographical work and at times the autobiographer becomes a diarist. As can be seen, the conditions of autobiography are only a large framework for a great variety of specific styles to manifest themselves. It is therefore essential to avoid speaking of a style or a form linked to autobiography, for there is no expected style or form in this case. Here more than in any other genre, the style will depend on the subject. (Starobinski 1970, 110, my translation)[6]

The "subject" here is pleasantly equivocal, meaning both the object of study and the subject of writing that is changed by the mission. The absence of stability, and even the objective impurity of the genre, cannot but have appealed to Woolf, especially as she was progressing in her novelistic experimentations whose story reflect her changing attitudes towards fixed forms and definitions. She was comforted by the reading of others as an exercise in her own creative powers, derived from the observation of their failings and successes, as if she could place herself in the cracks and nooks of their shortcomings in order to establish herself as a writer: "How far is it safe to let the man interpret the writer?... /But also we can read such books [lives and letters] with another aim, not to throw light on literature, not to become familiar with famous people, but to refresh and exercise our own creative powers" ("How should one...", *CR II*, 263). That complex balance between autobiography and essays, between the serious tone of the researcher and the lighter tone of the novelist, was achieved through a prolonged work on the image of the *flâneuse* and the form of the essay which enabled her to escape from dominant discourses and wander freely between texts, references and the point of view she's arguing (Lanone 2011, 49; Bowlby 2011, 19–38). Woolf's essays, derived as they are from the works of others, are the expression of her own tentative approach to art, which is the best self-portrait she could draw and which corresponds to Adorno's viewpoint:

> The relevance of the essay is that of anachronism. The hour is more unfavourable to it than ever. It is being crushed between an organized science, on one side, in which everyone presumes to control everyone and everything else, and which excludes, with the sanctimonious praise of 'intuitive' or 'stimulating,' anything that does not conform to the status quo; and, on the other side, by a philosophy that makes do with the empty and abstract residues left aside by the scientific apparatus, residues which then become, for philosophy, the objects of second-degree operations. The essay, however, has to do with that which is blind in its objects. (Adorno 2000, 170)

Conclusion

I think reading Woolf's development as reader, which remains inseparable from her activity as writer, enables us to move away from a strict understanding of how form and genres played a role in her art. Woolf's invitation to mis-read, or read as one pleases, is another example of her *flâneuse* attitude and reveals more about her than any confession she could have made to a priest or a psychoanalyst (*AROO*, 26). For it is in her artistic stumbles and ambiguities that her figure comes to life behind the well-written prose of her essays. Notwithstanding her self-confessed refusal of autobiography, she resorts to "I", an "I" that at the very beginning of *A Room of One's Own* she defines as "only a convenient term for somebody who has no real being" (*AROO*, 2). What this suggests in the economy of *A Room of One's Own* is that, as woman indeed, Woolf and others had no real being. But it could be argued that the writing of the essay, which exposed the absence of her being, was a way to fill in the absence with fiction "desiring to remain veiled" (*AROO*, 42). Woolf's respect of form is a way for her to suggest we mis-read her and look for her truth, always relative and subjective: what she seems to praise at first, the mechanics of the Oxbridge student, capable of "[extracting] pure nuggets of the essential ore every ten minutes or so" (*AROO*, 22), is only another criticism in disguise, because this student is also the one that remained blind to the absence of women in fiction, despite his well-crafted technique of text analysis. In *A Room of One's Own*, she was witness to a world that was changing with incredible and probably unprecedented pace, in the aftermath of a Suffrage movement that didn't go without its drawbacks (*AROO*, 85). This is how she may have fostered the idea that far from being narcissistic, autobiography was another form of writing to survive:

> They have been great egotists. That too was forced upon them by their circumstances. When everything is rocking round one, the only person who remains comparatively stable is oneself. When all faces are changing and obscured, the only face one sees clearly is one's own. So they wrote about themselves—in their plays, in their poems, in their towers. No other ten years can have produced so much autobiography as the ten years between 1930 and 1940. No one, whatever his class or his obscurity, seems to have reached the age of thirty without writing his autobiography. But the leaning-tower writers wrote about themselves honestly, therefore creatively. (Woolf 1948, 148)

Woolf's judgement here is unambiguously positive (*c.*1940) and towards the end of her career she may have managed to find a (temporary?) answer to the long-running question of the validity of life writing in relation to art. She also points to current research in the fluid nature of the genre that is often expressed in the spelling of auto/biography—or its more encompassing version found in the use of the term "life writing."

NOTES

1. Virginia Woolf, *A Room of One's Own*, with an introduction by Hermione Lee (London: Vintage Classics, 2001 [1929]). All references to this edition in between brackets, *AROO*.
2. "On Not Knowing Greek," in Virginia Woolf, *The Common Reader*, introduction by Andrew McNeillie (New York: Harcourt Inc., 1984 [1925]). All subsequent references to this text between brackets, *CR*.
3. Virginia Woolf, *The Second Common Reader* (New York: Harcourt Inc., 1986 [1932]). All references to this text noted *CR II* in brackets.

4. "The ambivalence towards the commodification of literature and literary journalism that is evident in 'Reviewing' sits uneasily with the celebration of women's access to the profession of literature for which Woolf is best known." (Gualtieri 2000, 69).

5. Virginia Woolf, "Sketch of the Past," in Jeanne Schulkind ed., *Virginia Woolf's Moments of Being* (London: Pimlico Edition, 2002).

6. My translation of the following French text: *L'autobiographe est libre de "contaminer" le récit de sa vie par celui d'événements dont il a été le témoin distant: l'autobiographe se doublera alors d'un mémorialiste ...: il est libre aussi de dater avec précision les divers moments de sa rédaction, et de faire retour sur lui-même à l'heure où il écrit: le journal intime vient alors contaminer l'autobiographie, et l'autobiographe deviendra par instants un « diariste ». On le voit, les conditions de l'autobiographie ne fournissent qu'un cadre assez large, à l'intérieur duquel pourront s'exercer et se manifester une grande variété de styles particuliers. Il faut donc éviter de parler d'un style ou même d'une forme liés à l'autobiographie, car il n'y a pas, en ce cas, de style ou de forme obligés. Ici, plus que partout ailleurs, le style sera le fait de l'individu.*

References

Adorno, Theodor. 1984. L'Essai comme forme. In *Notes sur la Littérature*. Paris: Flammarion.

———. 2000. *The Adorno Reader*. Trans. Bob Hullot-Kentor and Frederic Will. Oxford: Blackwell.

Amselle, Frédérique. 2008. *Virginia Woolf et les écritures du moi: le journal et l'autobiographie*. Montpellier: Presses Universitaires de Montpellier.

Bernard, Catherine. 2002. In *Le Pur et l'impur*, ed. Christine Reynier. Rennes: Presses Universitaires de Rennes.

Boileau, Nicolas Pierre. 2007. Places of Being: Janet Frame's Autobiographical Space. *a/b: Auto/biography Studies* 22 (2): 217–229.

———. 2011. Virginia Woolf's AutoReading in *Moments of Being*. In *Woolf as Reader/Woolf as Critic, or the Art of Reading in the Present*, 127–138. Montpellier: Presses Universitaires de Montpellier.

Bowlby, Rachel. 2011. Real Life and Its Readers in *Mrs Dalloway*. In *Woolf as Reader/Woolf as Critic, or the Art of Reading in the Present*, 19–38. Montpellier: Presses Universitaires de Montpellier.

Davison, Claire. 2014. *Translation as Collaboration*. Edinburgh: Edinburgh University Press.

Gualtieri, Elena. 2000. *Virginia Woolf's Essays: Sketching the Past*. London: Macmillan.

Lanone, Catherine. 2011. Stereoscopic Displacement in Virginia Woolf's 'Street Haunting'. In *Woolf as Reader/Woolf as Critic, or the Art of Reading in the Present*, 39–50. Montpellier: Presses Universitaires de Montpellier.

Lejeune, Philippe. 1975. *Le Pacte autobiographique*. Paris: Éditions du Seuil.

Raitt, Susan. 2000. Finding a Voice. In *The Cambridge Companion to Virginia Woolf*, ed. Sue Roe and Susan Sellers, 29–49. Cambridge: Cambridge University Press.

Reynier, Christine. 2009. *Virginia Woolf's Ethics of the Short Story*. New York: Palgrave Macmillan.

Smith, Sidonie, and Julia Watson, eds. 1998. *Women, Autobiography, Theory: A Reader. Madison, Wisconsin*. Madison: The University of Wisconsin Press.

Snaith, Anna. 2000. My Poor Private Voice': Virginia Woolf and Auto/biography. In *Representing Lives: Women and Auto/Biography*, ed. A. Donnell and P. Polkey, 96–104. London: Macmillan.

Wood, Alice. 2011. "Virginia Woolf's 'Two Women'; or 'The Wrong Way of Reading'," in Bernard, Catherine. ed. 2011. *Woolf as Reader/Woolf as Critic, or the Art of Reading in the Present*, 51–62. Montpellier: Presses Universitaires de Montpellier.

Woolf, Virginia. 1948. *The Moment and Other Essays*. London: Harvest Book.

———. 1984. On Not Knowing Greek. In *The Common Reader, First Series*, ed. Andrew McNeillie. New York: Harcourt Inc. (The Hogarth Press, 1925).

———. 1986. In *The Second Common Reader*, ed. Andrew McNeillie. New York: Harcourt Inc. (The Hogarth Press, 1932).

———. 2001. In *A Room of One's Own*, ed. Hermione Lee. London: Vintage Classics (The Hogarth Press, 1929).

CHAPTER 7

Plunged in a Book: Nathalie Sarraute, Monique Wittig, Hélène Cixous and the Literature of Experience

Ann Jefferson

> *… It is rather when*
> *We gloriously forget ourselves, and plunge*
> *Soul-forward, headlong, into a book's profound,*
> *Impassioned for its beauty and salt of truth—*
> *Tis then we get the right good from a book.*
> *Elizabeth Barrett Browning,* Aurora Leigh *(1857)*

INTRODUCTION

By way of introduction to my three women readers, I shall make a brief excursus via four male writers, André Gide, Maurice Blanchot, Jean-Paul Sartre, and Michel Leiris because it is from them that I take the notion of a "literature of experience." Blanchot coins the expression in the title of an essay written in 1947, "Gide and the Literature of Experience," where he

A. Jefferson (✉)
New College, Oxford, UK
e-mail: ann.jefferson@new.ox.ac.uk

© The Author(s) 2018
V. Baisnée-Keay et al. (eds.), *Women's Life Writing
and the Practice of Reading*, Palgrave Studies in Life Writing,
https://doi.org/10.1007/978-3-319-75247-1_7

presents Gide as strung out between two alternative conceptions of literature, "that of traditional art which places the good fortune of producing masterpieces above everything, and literature as experience which cares nothing for works and is ready to ruin itself to attain the inaccessible" (Blanchot 1995, 224–225).[1] This tension between the work of literature and literary experience is most fully exemplified in the life writing which became one of the most salient features of the French literary landscape in the second half of the twentieth century, and to which women writers—including the three under discussion in this chapter—have made important contributions. It is largely by means of autobiography that writers (of both sexes) have been able to explore and establish the phenomenon of a literature of experience.[2]

Early autobiographical examples of the phenomenon of literature as experience are *Manhood* (1939) and *The Rules of the Game* (1948 ff.) by Michel Leiris, and Sartre's *The Words* (1964). As Leiris says in his preface to *Manhood*, his aim is to "write a book that is an act." Instead of the formal elegance of what he calls "the vain grace of a ballerina," he envisages a practice of writing that would be the equivalent of a bullfight where artistic skill becomes a matter of life and death for its author (Leiris 1968, 14). For Leiris, autobiography is the genre that provides the greatest chance of incorporating this potentially fatal "horn of the bull" into writing, or, in other words, of ensuring the element of risk which for him is the guarantee of literature as experience. The same issues are at stake in Sartre's *The Words*, except that here the values are reversed. This is because literature in Sartre's eyes is inherently and inescapably inauthentic, and the risk that it poses to both author and reader is that it seeks to pass itself off as having a reality that it does not in fact possess. Sartre turns his back on literature because of his realization that it implies an equivalence of text and experience that can only falsify the lived experience of those who allow themselves to be taken in by this imposture.

These, then, are the issues out of which the twentieth-century autobiographical tradition in France emerged, defining literature in experiential terms, and doing so primarily by means of a narrative of the author's own path to writing. Beginning with Gide's *If it die...* (1926), and confirmed by the examples of Leiris and Sartre, the emphasis is very firmly on the autobiographer as writer. The critic Gérard Genette famously summed up the narrative of Proust's *In Search of Lost Time* with a four-word formula, "Marcel becomes a writer" (Genette 1983, 30). And the same formula could be applied to the autobiographies of Gide, Leiris, and Sartre, each of which can be summarized as "André/Michel/Jean-Paul becomes a writer." There is nothing intrinsically gendered about this narrative, but the terms in which each of Leiris and Sartre adhere to literature as experience nevertheless carry distinctly male overtones. Leiris establishes his literary value system by opposing the art of a very macho torero to "the vain graces of a ballerina." And when Sartre denounces his misplaced faith in literature, he does so in the same masculinist terms by maintaining that "For a long time, I took my pen for a sword" (Sartre 1964, 253). The writer Leiris that aspires to become is a torero, and the one that Sartre had mistakenly believed himself to be was a knight.

However, not all autobiographies gender the writer in such extreme terms, nor do they necessarily tell the story of how their author "became a writer." In the examples I have chosen to discuss here—Nathalie Sarraute's *Childhood*, Monique Wittig's *The Opoponax*, and Hélène Cixous's *Manhattan*—it is by means of a focus on *reading* rather than on writing that literature is presented as experience. This is in no way to suggest that women read and men write: the three women in question are most certainly writers, and, equally, the autobiographies of Gide, Leiris, and Sartre all contain important scenes of reading. Indeed, the first half of Sartre's *The Words* is entitled "Reading." But the three autobiographical texts by Sarraute, Wittig, and Cixous make no reference to their authors' future literary career, and their conception of literature as experience emerges from their exploration of reading rather than that of writing.

While very different from each other on several counts, and separated by intervals of almost two decades, their books collectively form a kind of metanarrative that goes from *childhood* with Sarraute's book of the same name (published in 1983) towards the end of her career), to *adolescence* in Wittig's *The Opoponax* (the autobiographical novel with which she began her career in 1964), and, finally, to *youth* with Cixous's mid-career, generically indeterminate *Manhattan*, subtitled *Letters from Prehistory* (2002). None of the texts proclaims itself explicitly to be autobiography: Sarraute's *Childhood* bears no rubric, although the paratext of the *folio* paperback edition, which includes a recognizable photograph of Sarraute as a child, certainly encourages assumptions about its status as autobiography. Wittig's *The Opoponax* defines itself as a novel, but any biographical knowledge of its author will retrospectively inflect a reading with an autobiographical slant. And while Cixous's *Manhattan* gives no indication as to its generic status, the narrative content, its first-person mode, and familiarity with Cixous's other work where boundaries between fiction and autobiography are frequently blurred, all invite an autobiographical reading, however problematized. In their different ways, all three texts lend strong support to Paul de Man's claim that "Autobiography... is not a genre or a mode, but a figure of reading or of understanding that occurs, to some degree, in all texts" (De Man 1984, 70).

In addition to the developmental metanarrative through which I am linking them, the three texts also chart the evolution of a relation to literature, which starts in Sarraute with a combination of total immersion and profound suspicion, continues in Wittig with a highly personal appropriation, and concludes hyperbolically in the work of Cixous with an unshakeable passion. This narrative is of my own devising, but the three writers knew and read each others' work, and so it would not be entirely fanciful to see a sequence of evolving variations on a single theme in the autobiographical texts under consideration here. At each stage, the experiential sequence progresses though an engagement with reading, where the three authors repeatedly portray themselves as plunged in a book—"soul-forward," as Elizabeth Barrett-Browning has it in the above quotation from *Aurora Leigh*—with no reference to their future as writers. Nathalie Sarraute insists that "The idea of becoming a writer never occurs to me" (Sarraute 2013, 191). The possibility is so far removed from *The Opoponax* that the question does not even arise, especially in the case of a child who has such difficulty mastering basic penmanship at school, where the nib of her pen is always snagged with paper fibres, her fingers covered in ink, and her exercise book spoiled by splotches. Hélène Cixous's narrator states quite categorically (and without punctuation) that at the time portrayed in *Manhattan*, "I had absolutely no desire to write I was a passionate reader the books I would have needed to write already having been written I had only to read them like nobody else" (Cixous 2002, 87, my translation).[3] These, then, are readers who have no ambition to write, but who, as Cixous puts it, "read like nobody else."

CHILDHOOD

To begin with Nathalie Sarraute's *Childhood*, where the young Natacha reads voraciously. She says of herself that she had read a great deal for her age, and the book is scattered with memories of reading, whether sitting in the Luxembourg Gardens as her writer-mother tells her stories from her own books, or as she is warned that she will ruin her eyesight if she continues to read the books in the popular children's series, the "Bibliothèque

Rose," to which she is devoted. The list of titles read by Natacha includes *Uncle Tom's Cabin* (whose pages bore the marks of the tears it had inspired), *Struwwelpeter* (whose great tall tailor terrified her), *Max and Moritz*, the tales of Hans Christian Andersen, Mark Twain's *The Prince and the Pauper*, *David Copperfield*, Hector Malot's *No Relations*, Lazhechnikov's *House of Ice*, various westerns by Mayne Reid, along with novels by popular but now mostly forgotten writers of the day, such as René Boylesve, Andre Theuriet, or Pierre Loti. She is so unable to tear herself away from Ponson du Terrail's adventure series, *Rocambole*, that her father feels obliged to apologize to a visitor for her antisocial behaviour by explaining that she was "immersed [*plongée*] in Rocambole" (Sarraute 2013, 237). But though the friend claims to sympathize, Natacha is convinced that no other person could possibly understand the hold that the book has over her. No reading experience could be as all-encompassing as hers.

For the child, reading is a total experience. Natacha not only reads but also *re*reads many of these books. The lives of David Copperfield and Rémi in *No Relations* become her own, but even they do not have quite the same power over her as *The Prince and the Pauper*, about which she writes, "I don't think there was any other book that I lived in as I lived in that one" (67–68). Reading for Sarraute's Natacha is a form of wholesale plunging, and to be plunged in a book is to quite simply to live it. The books survive in her adult memory thanks to images that have remained intact and are just as intense as they were in childhood, when she *re*lives them, unchanged, nearly eighty years later. (Sarraute was 83 when *Enfance* came out.)

Nevertheless, this reading is given no status as a form of a literary apprenticeship. The books Sarraute recalls in *Childhood* are not among those she cites in her critical essays or in interviews as having contributed to her development as a writer. On the contrary, however absorbing the books of her childhood may have been and may still be, they pose a serious threat to the very writing in which they are recalled. Throughout *Childhood*, the narrator and the alter ego with whom she conducts a running self-commentary worry that the autobiographical narrative is being inappropriately modelled on the kind of literature she read as a child. These worries start on the first page of *Childhood* where the alter ego suggests that the very intention "to evoke childhood memories" introduces the risk of cliché to a writing whose stated aim is precisely to avoid the ready-made and to ensure that its subject matter remains "still faintly quivering," untouched by any "written word, [or] word of any sort" (3).

The alter ego constantly intervenes in the narrative with warnings about the danger of literary cliché, as happens in the episode where Natacha sits with her mother in the Luxembourg Gardens. The narrator's description of the scene is cut short as the alter ago interrupts to ask: "don't you think that ... with that cooing, that chirruping you haven't been able to resist introducing something a little bit prefabricated?" (12). The narrator herself wonders at one point whether her portrait of Vera, Natacha's stepmother, hasn't turned her into the wicked stepmother of fairy tales, and that her narrative has "[lost] touch with reality [and] tak[en] off into fiction ..." (115). In another episode, where a maid comments, "What a tragedy, though, to have no mother" (105), Natacha's immediate impulse is to try and extricate herself from association with the heroes of Dickens and Hector Malot in whose own "tragic" lives she had been so thoroughly immersed. The literary overtones of the tragedy suggested by the well-meaning maid are felt by the child to obliterate her own experience, however distressing it may at times have been. She feels trapped by a misfortune whose origins are literary: "the tragedy that strikes children in books, in *No Relations*, in *David Copperfield* ... has pounced on me, it grips me, it has me in its claws" (106). Natacha may have lived the lives of these children as she read the books that tell their unhappy stories, but her unhappiness is not theirs.

Sarraute curtails any potential for reading *Childhood* as the narrative of a literary apprenticeship by portraying Natacha's youthful attempts at writing as failures. This is because they draw on her reading, rather than on her own experience. Her school composition on the subject of "My first sorrow" is written with words she has borrowed from schoolbook anthologies, classroom dictations, and the work of René Boylesve, André Theuriet, and Pierre Loti. Neither the puppy that dies under the wheels of a train, nor the words that narrate the event were ever hers. Equally, the more ambitious "novel" that she writes at her mother's instigation is written with words she has sought "far away from home." This unfamiliar language leads her into equally unfamiliar territory, and she ends up losing her way "in places where [she] has never lived" (75–76). Even her young hero is a stranger to her, and she has never met the "pale young man with the blond curls, lying down beside a window through which he can see the mountains of the Caucasus," coughing blood and doomed to die in the following spring (75–76). When a writer friend of her mother's criticizes Natacha's novel for its poor spelling, this puts a merciful end to her modest literary ambitions.

Although reading is the source of an experience that has genuine literary value, the books that are the source of that experience cannot be imported into the books the adult novelist will subsequently write. Whether for the Caucasian tale written by the young Natacha or for the autobiography written by the eighty-year-old Nathalie Sarraute, the books which were lived with such intensity by the reader constitute a permanent danger for the writer. Reading does not automatically open the way to writing, and most certainly not to a writing of the self.

ADOLESCENCE

Monique Wittig's *The Opoponax* is also a story of reading as it recounts the emotional and literary apprenticeship of its reader-protagonist, Catherine Legrand. Although not ostensibly an autobiography, Wittig's first novel lends itself peculiarly well to being read as such. By implicitly presenting her narrative as fiction, and by ascribing the events to a third-person Catherine Legrand rather than to a first-person Monique Wittig, Wittig short-circuits any direct causal link between Catherine Legrand's apprenticeship in reading and the novelist's subsequent writing. Reading is the focus of the narrative, and much of it takes place in the Catholic girls' school which Catherine Legrand attends and where most of the teachers are nuns. What the girl learns from her reading is not always what the nuns and the curriculum have intended.

Her skills as a reader are laboriously acquired as she learns the rudiments by deciphering sentences such as "The miller's wife mills the maize. The miller leads [*mène*] the sheep [*moutons*]" (Wittig 1966, 11). The pedagogical purpose of these sentences has nothing to do with the miller's wife, the maize she mills, or the sheep her husband removes, but is designed to develop recognition of the letter "m." For the teachers, reading is merely a pretext for acquiring a rule, whether the letters of the alphabet or, in due course, the use of the reflexive in Latin. The same goes for moral precept, as is implied by the "the story of a holy little boy who was stoned to death when he tried to take the host of Our Lord to a sick person," which is used to illustrate the Christian duty which the girls are encouraged by the nuns to emulate (28). But by presenting these examples through the child's eyes, Wittig shifts her own reader's attention onto the narrative content of the tale which is made all the more vivid in this case through the omission of the boy's saint's name (Tarcisius, for the adults who already know their

Lives of the Saints), so that what remains in the memory are details, such as the discovery of the host concealed on the boy's body between his skin and his clothes.

As the girls' reading becomes more extensive, they appropriate it for ends that are very different from those that their teachers seek to inculcate. In the section where the class slowly ploughs through *Aliscans,* a twelfth-century *chanson de geste* about the Albigensian crusade, the teacher (who goes by the name Mother of the Infant Jesus) insists on its patriotic lesson, according to which "there has never been a civilization that can compare with that of this land" (103). But outside the classroom, the text is put to quite other uses as it provides a verbal accompaniment to a fierce game of volleyball in the school yard: "Nicole Marre runs off to get the ball … passes Laurence Bouniol yelling, *rois Desramés a sa barbe jurée,* and Laurence Bouniol replies as she goes by, *ke Guibors ert à cevaux trainée*" (104). (The published English translation makes visual and linguistic distinctions between text and quotation that are not present in Wittig's original French.)

This divergence between pedagogical purpose and the young readers' own interest increases as the novel progresses, and it becomes the principle of Catherine Legrand's response to everything she reads. However uninspiring the ten-line literary extracts the girls are given to study and analyse, Catherine makes a point of selecting one in order to make it her own by repeating it over and over. Frustrated by having no access to the complete texts by Chrétien de Troyes, Marie de France, or Charles of Orleans from which the extracts are taken, she copies two lines from Charles of Orleans— *tout a part moy en mon penser m'enclos et fait chasteaulz en Espaigne* (everything within me enclosed me in my mind and created castles in Spain)—into her exercise book so that she can refer to them whenever she wants, "and even say them aloud when she is alone" (117). The lines become a kind of motto for Catherine Legrand, and the private use to which they are then put is very far removed from the introduction to Old French or to medieval literature envisaged by the teachers or the authors of the school textbooks.

Despite the inauspicious beginnings with the miller's wife, Catherine Legrand becomes an avid reader, and she discovers that the most interesting girls—the ones she is drawn to as friends—are also the most assiduous, and the most independent readers. She comes across Valérie Borge plunged in a book that she doesn't know (and which is therefore not one that figures on the syllabus), while the mysterious Dominique Vurse retreats to the school dormitory to smoke *gauloises* and read Rousseau's *La Nouvelle Héloïse* in secret.

Literature—both licit and illicit—provides the girls with a language that allows them to communicate with each other. Most importantly, however, it gives Catherine Legrand the words with which to speak her love for— and also to—Valérie Borge. She copies a line from Leopardi into the album she is compiling for the girl, and when Valérie Borge drops her handkerchief, a line from *Délie* by the sixteenth-century French poet, Maurice Scève, immediately comes to mind—*Suave odeur mais le goût trop amer* (A sweet smell, but the taste too bitter, 160). As with the lines from Charles of Orleans, neither author nor title is named in the text, as if to suggest that the significance of the quotations has nothing to do with the sort of knowledge that is dispensed in the classroom and tested in exams.

In fact, none of the numerous extracts in *The Opoponax* is signalled as such, as there are no inverted commas, no capital letters, and in the original French, no italics, to mark the distinction between the poetry of the quotations and the prose of Wittig's text. At times, the quotations are slightly modified to make them more meaningful for the speaker, as happens with the line from Tibullus's *Elegies*, "quam lento Marathus me torquet amore," which is given much more urgently as "lento me torquet amore" (145). The final chapter of Wittig's text is woven through with repeated quotations from Baudelaire's "L'invitation au voyage," and the book concludes with six continuous lines from the poem, end-stopped by a further line from Scève's *Délie* in modernized spelling, "*tant je l'aimais qu'en elle encore je vis*" (so much did I love her that in her I still live, 189). Where Flaubert, for example, makes reading the source of Emma Bovary's unrealistic fantasies about love, for Wittig's heroine, books become the sole means whereby she can live and speak her love for Valérie Borge. But what is equally clear from Catherine Legrand's reading and the uses she makes of it is that love for Valérie is indistinguishable from a love of literature. To speak of one is necessarily to speak of the other.

YOUTH

This overlay of human and literary love objects also lies at the heart of Hélène Cixous's *Manhattan*, which recounts the effects of reading and an unconditional love of literature that the narrator shared with her boyfriend of the time. Narrator and author are ambiguously related in a narrative that can plausibly purport to be the "prehistory"—but not the history—of Cixous's emergence as a writer. The context for the narrative is the year the narrator-protagonist spends in the US on a Fulbright Scholarship when, as Cixous herself had done, she visits a number of major research libraries for a thesis on Montaigne and a project devoted to the theme of banishment. Reading in this text is pursued in these prestigious libraries by a narrator who repeatedly states—and always in italics—"*I loved literature above all else*" (Cixous 2002, 77). And she continues: "life is this I thought … I open a book, there is light, language immediately begins its tale, I constantly remake myself with these molecules of literature." (77) For her, real life is books. And it is in a library—the Beinecke Library in Yale—that she falls for another great lover of literature, Gregor. A shared love of literature triggers a grand passion between the two of them in a clear case of "contagion by literature" (38).

On the narrator's part it is the story of love for a person who is constructed entirely of literary references and allusions. Gregor gives himself out to be the new great American novelist, and if his name is Gregor—like the character in Kafka's *Metamorphosis*—there is nothing to confirm that it has any legitimacy. His talk is laced with literary quotations, but since, at the time, she had read neither Kafka's *Letters to Milena* nor Mandelstam's poetry, Cixous's narrator fails to recognize the literary origins of the things her lover says and writes to her, and she allows herself to fall under their literary spell. She also allows herself to be taken in by the image presented by Gregor who, like the hero of Natacha's Caucasian tale, coughs blood, will (allegedly) die in the spring, and who for the time being also lies gazing out of a window. The only literary element that he lacks are the blond locks of Natacha's young prince.

As the narrator says, "[her] imagination was moved by the abnormally literary character of the person playing the part of the dying man." But she later discovers that "the dying Gregor was just a temporary and cobbled-together figure, a fabulous montage-assemblage of references borrowed from world classical and extremely modern literature" (85). By the end of the book she has finally realized that she "had only ever loved the shadow of a book clothed in the body of a young man" (223), whose death she had feared as "the death of Literature" itself (231).

To love Gregor was, through him, to love Literature, most often with a capital L. It was also an extravagant way of living literature, living it as experience. But loving Literature in this mode also led to being taken in by an impostor and mythomaniac, and several episodes in the book reveal the extent to which Cixous's narrator is complicit with the mystifications of her lover and what she calls her own "self-enchantment" (108). However, unlike Sartre, or even Nathalie Sarraute, Cixous makes a virtue of the deceptions exercised by literature and she refuses either to condemn literature for its inauthenticity or—as the narrator's mother regularly does—to blame her own naivety. The passionate reader who loves literature "*above all else*" wants nothing more than to fall under its spell.

In retrospect, her regret is not that she was taken in by Gregor's counterfeit genius, but that she failed to appreciate that his true genius was for counterfeiting as such. And, in Cixous's estimation, this counterfeiting is the very genius of the literature that she loves above all else. "You can't read without believing," she writes. "When you read, you believe" (20). And of course this applies with equal force to her own text which, despite the deceptions perpetrated by Gregor, the narrator's mythomaniac lover, invites its own reader's belief that what it narrates is true, that the events actually happened in the real life of its author. The "omnipotence" with which Cixous credits literature operates precisely through its ability to "spread its illusioning powers over the world." Because, quite simply, thanks to the reader's willing complicity, "What is written, is" (Preface).

Conclusion

What emerges from each of these three narratives is a picture of reading as a certain experience of literature which transcends the individual and fairly eclectic texts that are the pretext for the experience. None of the three authors suggests that any of the books they read in their childhood, adolescence, or youth served as a model or an apprenticeship for the literary works they would subsequently write. Indeed, for Sarraute they serve mostly as entirely negative examples whose potential influence has constantly to be averted. In any case, none of the three writers presents herself explicitly in these books *as* a writer, and their status as such has to be inferred from the empirical fact of their authorship. Sarraute and Cixous were already established as writers when *Childhood* and *Manhattan* appeared, but for Wittig, *The Opoponax*, being her first book, defined her as a writer only through her signature on the cover. Any connection between the experiences of reading that the books describe and the writing that describes them has to be made by their own readers in the present. And even then, these narratives are not so much covert accounts of a path to authorship, as they are an appeal for their readers to share a certain kind of literary experience, and to plunge in their turn, "soul-forward" and "headlong" (to hark back to Elizabeth Barrett Browning) into a book whose "salt of truth" lies more in the quality of the experience of reading than in its narrated content. Or to put it in the terms suggested by Blanchot in his discussion of Gide, the success of these books as *works* of literature is implied by their respective authors to derive from an *experience* of literature which each of them discovered in the practice of reading.

Notes

1. Translation slightly modified by me. The essay was first published in the journal *L'Arche*.
2. I have discussed these issues more extensively in Jefferson (2007).
3. All further quotations from the text are my translation. Pages references are to the 2002 French edition.

References

Blanchot, Maurice. 1995. *The Work of Fire* (1949). Trans. Charlotte Mandell. Stanford: Stanford University Press.

Cixous, Hélène. 2002. *Manhattan: Lettres de la Préhistoire*. Paris: Galilée.

De Man, Paul. 1984. *The Rhetoric of Romanticism*. New York: Columbia University Press.

Genette, Gerard 1983. *Narrative Discourse. An Essay in Method* (1972). Trans. Jane E. Lewin. Ithaca: Cornell University Press.

Jefferson, Ann. 2007. *Biography and the Question of Literature in France*. Oxford: Oxford University Press.

Leiris, Michel. 1968. *Manhood, Preceded by The Autobiographer as Torero (1946)*. London: Jonathan Cape.

Sarraute, Nathalie. 2013. *Childhood* (1983). Trans. Barbara Wright. Chicago: The University of Chicago Press.

Sartre, Jean-Paul. 1964. *The Words* (1964). Trans. Bernard Frechtman. New York: Braziller.

Wittig, Monique. 1966. *The Opoponax* (1964). Trans. Helen Weaver. London: Owen.

CHAPTER 8

Nancy Huston's *Bad Girl: Classes de littérature*: When the Autobiographer Plays Hooky

Anne-Claire Marpeau

INTRODUCTION

Truth? What truth? Truth might be that I don't exist. What exists, what might begin to exist one day, if I am very lucky, are my books, a few novels, an œuvre, if I dare to use that word. The rest is simply literature. (Romain Gary)[1]

Romain Gary's words, quoted by Nancy Huston as an epigraph of her account of the writer's life (Huston 1995, 10), could very well serve as an epigraph to *Bad Girl: Classes de littérature*, her latest attempt at self-writing. What kind of "truth" *does* the narrative tell about the writer-to-be? The book's subtitle and synopsis suggest a coming-of-age novel depicting the genesis of a literary calling, but *Bad Girl* will not match the reader's expectations. It does not depict a self-centred itinerary from class to class, from readings to literary encounters, until the birth of Nancy

---

A.-C. Marpeau (✉)
ENS Lyon, Lyon, France University of British Columbia, Vancouver, Canada

© The Author(s) 2018
V. Baisnée-Keay et al. (eds.), *Women's Life Writing and the Practice of Reading*, Palgrave Studies in Life Writing,
https://doi.org/10.1007/978-3-319-75247-1_8

Huston the writer. Rather, it is the story of the Canadian childhood and teenage years of a girl named Dorrit, the story of her ancestors, as well as a fictitious account of her life before birth, from the womb of her mother, until the day she was born. Short essays and explanations about some of Nancy Huston's writing themes occasionally interrupt the narrative.

This is not the first narrative in which Nancy Huston interlaces fiction and reality. As Adina Balint-Babos puts it, some of Nancy Huston's novels and essays belong to this generation of "heterogeneous" writing pertaining to the autobiographical tradition, but distancing themselves from it by building an "unsteady subject," a "discursive construction and escaping horizon, without solid features or metaphysical certainty"[2] (Balint-Babos 2012, 42). However, in *Bad Girl: Classes de littérature*, Nancy Huston seems to go further and deeper into the paradoxical exploration of the self and her search for the appropriate way to write it. While the work clearly contains autobiographical elements, the narrator/author constantly seems to deconstruct the conventions of autobiography by using narrative techniques that replace, or displace, the situation of enunciation and the horizon of expectations of canonical autobiographical works. As Philippe Lejeune puts it, the "autobiographical pact," which is a requirement of the autobiographical genre, requires "the affirmation in the text of [the] identity [of the name (author-narrator-protagonist)]" (Lejeune 1989, 14). Lejeune underlines the importance of the contract since it actually determines the attitude of the reader: if the identity is not stated positively, the reader will attempt to establish resemblances, in spite of the author; if it is positively stated (as in autobiography), the reader will want to look for differences (errors, deformations, etc.). Confronted with what looks like an autobiographical narrative, the reader tends to pretend to be a detective, that is, to look for breaches of the contract (whatever the contract) (Lejeune 1989, 14). In the case of *Bad Girl*, however, literary theory is contradicted by literary practice. Paradoxically, the narrative seems to adopt fictional traits in order to appear more faithful and truthful to Nancy Huston's life and her effort to tell it. The reader does not quite know which stand to take while reading what could be a novel or a life story. In a way, the writer plays hooky with the autobiographical literary tradition and offers her own version of what life writing is. She also skips literature classes to locate the literary experience off the beaten track, far away from schools and libraries, at the heart of her Canadian home and heritage.

My contention is that by refusing to construct a teleological account of a French-speaking writer's life—from the first glance at a book to the inevitable first word on a page—and by shifting attention from the "*classes de littérature*" to the genealogical account of her Canadian family, Nancy Huston wishes to keep part of the literary emotions and events which make her the writer she is to herself; it is as if describing and dissecting the effect of literature on her was more intimate than the story of her family traumas. At the same time, she offers the reader a new form of life writing, a *genre* that is less an autobiographical narrative than an autobiographical dialogue, less a predetermined construction than an exploration of the possibilities to speak truthfully about oneself. This original piece of life writing raises the following questions: "Whose education are we reading about? Is it the writer's or the reader's?"

A NAUGHTY WRITER: DECONSTRUCTING AUTOBIOGRAPHY

Why This Title?

The "space between" effect of Nancy Huston's writing, as Nicola Danby puts it (Danby 2004, 83), is identifiable from the moment one reads the title. *Bad Girl: Classes de littérature* creates several expectations, which don't seem to be fulfilled after the first reading. Nancy Huston is originally from Alberta, but she has been studying and living in Paris for more than forty years. She writes mostly in French. The bi-title (bilingual and in two parts) of her autobiographical text appears to play on the contrast between the English phrase "You bad girl!" and the quaint academic world conjured up by the French expression "classes de littérature" (although in France nowadays, we would rather say "*cours de littérature*" or else "*cours de lettres*"). "*Classes*" could also be an Anglicism, reminding the reader of the author's English-speaking childhood. We are then instantly confronted with the double geographical and metaphorical space in which the story takes place.

Even more troubling, "Bad girl" is in itself an ambiguous phrase, since it could refer to a child who has been mischievous as well as to a young woman who has committed a more transgressive act. Translating it in French would force one to choose between *mauvaise fille* and *méchante fille* and the first suggestion would be more appropriate to preserve the ambiguity of the message (the oscillation between "bad" and "naughty"). As for the second part of the title, it forces the reader to wonder about the location, the dates or else the language of these literature classes. According to the reading contract, these questions are supposed to be answered by the text. But the title plays with the reader's expectations: one may suppose that the book will portray a heroine who was a naughty girl in class, or else, that literature classes turned a good girl into a naughty girl, too well-educated by the book's lesson.

On the one hand, the title does stage the writer's life story, born and educated in an English-speaking environment until she became a French writer. On the other hand, it could be a literary game played by Nancy Huston, the ex-literature student, who plays with the conventions of the autobiographical genre (showing how well she learned her lesson), but also creates her own *genre*. Speaking of "literature classes" may be a pretext to dismiss the literature once learnt in the classroom.

A Library of Critics

The text seems to be addressing French critics who have shaped the expectations of academic readers and literature students when it comes to autobiography. The canonical autobiography was defined in France by Philippe Lejeune as a "retrospective prose narrative written by a real person concerning his or her own existence, when the focus is his or her individual life, in particular on the story of his or her personality" (Lejeune 1989, 4). This book was released in French in 1975, when Nancy Huston was living and studying in France, under the supervision of Roland Barthes. If we are to rely on Lejeune's definition, referring to *Bad Girl* as an autobiography is partly accurate. The work is a retrospective, mostly chronological narrative in prose that puts the emphasis on the individual existence of a feminine character who lived a life similar to Nancy Huston's, and deals with the specific theme of the birth of a writer's personality. But it is not that simple. *Bad Girl* only partly fits the definition. In *Bad Girl*, it seems that the outline of the canonical autobiography is still visible through the methodical deconstruction of its narrative features.

First of all, even though the members of the narrator's family bear the names of Nancy Huston's family, the narrator is not called Nancy Huston. The real person whose social and literary identity is supposed to be established through the use of a real name is given a name reminiscent of a famous character: Dorrit is probably borrowed from the eponymous novel by Charles Dickens, *Little Dorrit*—Dorrit is repeatedly called "little Dorrit" in *Bad Girl*. Dickens's Dorrit is one of those poor heroines who survives in the harshness of nineteenth-century London by demonstrating kindness and virtue. She is also a character who has no mother and no home, but only a prison she has to move out of. Why then choose this name for the main character of *Bad Girl*? Did the writer give this name to the little girl she was as an interpretation of her own life because she experienced no less than 18 moving-outs (Huston 2014, 160)?[2] Or was it the nickname her mother gave her after she left home, as suggested by what the narrator says about Alison's letters (254)?

For Philippe Lejeune, one cannot talk about "autobiography" when a writer does not use his or her biographical name since "in any case, there is no identity of author, narrator, and hero" (Lejeune 1989, 15). Fiction therefore enters the book from its very first page, as the very first words of the narrative underline the similarity between Dorrit and a fictitious protagonist: "You, it's you, Dorrit. She who writes. You at every age, and even before being old enough, before writing, before being a self. She who writes and therefore also, sometimes, one hopes, he/she who reads" (Huston 2014, 11, my translation).[3] Dorrit is both the writer and the reader. The only certainty about her identity is that she is a female when she writes, just like Nancy Huston, and both genders when she/he reads. But still, the hypothetical tone of the sentence and the absence of Nancy Huston's name allow Dorrit to be both a fictional and an autobiographical character.

Besides, the epigraph of the book likens the whole narrative to fiction. The quote, *"Tout ceci doit être considéré comme dit par un personnage de roman"* (259)—the usual translation of which is "All this must be considered as having been said by a fictional character"—is in fact an excerpt from Roland Barthes' autobiography, entitled *Roland Barthes by Roland Barthes*, which was also published in 1975 in French. Barthes challenges the man who, according to Lejeune, is the autobiographer *par excellence*, Jean-Jacques Rousseau, who wrote both *The Confessions* and *Dialogues: Rousseau, Judge of Jean-Jacques*. In his own autobiography, Roland Barthes mixes fiction and distance to ask the question of what a so-called real writing of the self would be. Even though the title seems to gather author, narrator and protagonist into the single identity of 'Roland Barthes,' the narrative as a whole plays with the possibility of reading autobiography as fiction. Barthes' book was followed in 1977 by Serge Doubrovsky's *Fils*, which the author defined as an "autofiction." "Autofiction" has several definitions but they all include what Laurent Jenny calls "a fictive misappropriation of autobiography":

[A]utofiction appears as a fictive misappropriation of autobiography. But according to a first type of stylistic definition, the metamorphosis of autobiography into autofiction lies in certain effects connected to the type of language being used. According to a second type or referential definition, autobiography turns into autofiction depending on its content and the relationship of this content to reality. (Jenny 2003, my translation)

Following the example set by her professor Roland Barthes, Nancy Huston blurs the borders of fiction and reality in her own autobiographical work as if, within the book, reading and writing, life and literature were one and the same. The writer seems to be aware of the fictional aspect inherent to autobiography when she calls Romain Gary's *Promise at Dawn*, "a very romanticised autobiography" (Huston 2014, 145). The literary critic in Nancy Huston notices that an autobiographer has to embellish and rewrite his or her own life.

Furthermore, in *Bad Girl*, the narrator uses the second person singular *tu* to speak to Dorrit. In France, people use *tu* when talking to family members, friends and people they consider close enough (in age, social hierarchy … etc.). The choice of the second person is a recurrent stylistic feature in Nancy Huston's work. For example, in 1995 she wrote *Tombeau de Romain Gary*, a biography in which she addresses Romain Gary while recounting his life. Ten years later, she picked up the pronoun she used in the biography for her autobiographical novel, as if speaking about oneself was, inevitably, to speak to and about another. According to the narrator, the multiplicity of the self is a central feature of Dorrit's personality: "*Little idiot* is the epithet you will hear the most. Coming from you. Or else, from one of your selves talking to another self. Because you have multiple selves. Avoiding finding themselves together at the same place and the same time is what they will invent as a survival strategy" (Huston 2014, 195).[4]

The distance allowed by this very specific situation of enunciation can be interpreted both as a criticism of the autobiographical genre as it underlines the illusion of pretending to be able to talk about one's own personality, and as a safeguard against the lies one might tell since this distance gives the narrator's voice a semblance of objectivity. The back cover of the French edition of *Bad Girl* signals that Nancy Huston is aware of the dangers and illusions of speaking about herself, noting that "you" is used throughout the book to speak to the foetus she once was. In *Bad Girl*, Nancy Huston herself traces this choice back to the recommendations made by her mother throughout their continuous correspondence:

Her letters will help you to stay alive, and when, later, you start to write books, the second person will always be the one you prefer, given the fact there is not enough room in this world for I, and that he or she would set too much distance between you and your favourite characters, you want to speak to them always, as if they were in the room with you, this is why, books after books, you will say *tu, tu, tu* and you, you, you, and so, Dorrit, you will do the same with this book, in which your life itself will be turned into letters, and you—will, won't—a funny courageous little chamois who has become an aging lady, into a *femme de lettres*. (254)[5]

In this passage, the similarities between Dorrit and Nancy Huston can't be questioned. The literary person "you" is explained by the author's life. An intimate trauma of abandonment is healed by epistolary practice, which is said to have been the origin of literary writing. The writer confides in the reader through comments on her own style and the impossibility to say I. She makes a show of sincerity by acknowledging the difficulty she experiences in speaking in the first person.

Another deviation from the autobiographical genre is to give an account of the lives of others. The narrative is not merely focused on the writer's life but also on that of her ancestors. The story is shaped like a linear family tree. Short chapters, rarely longer than one page, follow each other, containing miniature portraits of past generations, starting with her great grandparents. These miniature portraits are interwoven with the imagined account of Dorrit's life while in her mother's womb, and with the story of her future life analysed retrospectively. The text concludes with the account of a birth, both that of the little girl and that of the writer. This structure, which interlaces the life of a central self with the lives of others, creates an intersubjective and intergenerational (auto)biography, in which the I appears in others and other people appear in the I.

The traditional autobiographical form therefore undergoes some transformation since the story is told in the future tense, and in dialogue form, as if the narrator's voice was clairvoyant. The myth of a linear, spontaneous and unpremeditated confession is debunked. The future tense shows that the autobiographer's voice knows what will happen. Everything that is told was already written, because every narrative is essentially a retrospective construction. Thus, the illusion created by all chronological narratives is exposed.

Playing with the reader's expectations and the limits of autobiographical writing, *Bad Girl* is a narrative which, like *Roland Barthes by Roland Barthes*, is built on the close bond between stories and fiction: the narrative structure, which shapes all stories, whether they are life stories or fairy tales, is in itself a construction which introduces fiction in the written work. But *Bad Girl* does not only play with the limits of the genre of the autobiography. The writer offers the exploration of an itinerary, an intimate journey through literature which gives its full meaning to the expression "life writing." She just doesn't do it by the book.

When the Reader Plays Hooky: Skipping Literature Classes

Reading Before Class

Literature classes in *Bad Girl* don't look anything like what the title suggests. Although there are reading scenes in the book, these scenes never take place in class. They don't appear to be staged by the writer. This contrasts with Sartre's autobiography *Les Mots* where childhood reading is staged so as to show the birth of a writer through the young Sartre's choice of books.[5] In Huston's *Bad Girl*, reading scenes are evoked through allusions to texts and short scenes in the narrative, in what seems to be a random, non-chronological order. Despite the title, the first reading experiences are mentioned late in the book. Besides, neither the titles nor the literary reputation of the books recommended in class (the Classics) matter: Dorrit's reading is truly eclectic.

The first reading scenes take place in the family home. One story in particular, when told by the father, is unforgettable: it is the story of the "little blue engine," the moral of which had a "lasting impact" on the child (80). Here, Dorrit is not in class, her father is not reading, but he is telling the story, and she listens. At the origin of storytelling there is a voice, an oral reading, as most children hear stories at first. Moreover, the morality of the story is given, and not forced into the child's head, and therefore considered as more efficient than if learnt at school or at church (81). The mother's nursery rhymes and songs are also part of the child's education (180; 197). Childhood literary classes take place outside school, in the family home, and the textbook is replaced by texts that are told or sung: "you will experience literature as a music lover would. On the quicksand of your childhood, language and music will be the invisible, unmovable, weightless scaffolding that you can always grasp" (167).[6]

Learning to read silently has the effect of disturbing Dorrit's life. The writer describes the neurological process of silent reading that transforms written words into "sounds of silence." When she uses the word "save" to explain the effect of reading on her, this should be understood literally and figuratively:

> Learning how to read will save you. The flow of voices won't stop. Throughout your life, human voices will worm their way into your brain through your eyes to bloom into sounds of silence. You will read in the morning and at noon, in the evening and at night. You will read while walking, while eating and while going to the bathroom; you will read with a flashlight while hiding under your bed ... (163)[7]

From what will the child be saved? By taking a closer look at the vocabulary used in this extract, one realizes that reading amounts to hearing: "flow of voices," "human voices," "sounds of silence" resonate in the sentences. The text seems to be heard in silence. Silent reading is like internal music, both tune and dialogue with fictional characters. Another feature of reading is that it literally takes place everywhere, and informs every aspect of Dorrit's daily life, both temporal and spatial: this overwhelming presence consoles her from maternal abandonment, which the story will tell, by filling the void with sentences and stories as the narrator warns Dorrit that she will hear the voices of the books she reads, "[c]hanting, singing and quarrelling, making invisible vocal cords, safety cords vibrate ... all the human voices, including yours" (165).[8] Writing outside her mother tongue is interpreted by the narrator as a way for Dorrit to recreate the void left by the silenced maternal voice since "Ten thousand pages written in a foreign tongue won't cover the painful delight of hearing words-notes coming out of the ruby-red lips of Alison in a good mood" (155).[9]

Soon, Dorrit builds herself an intimate world of sounds-words: for years she has believed that "misled" is the past participle of a verb she imagines to be "misle" (163). Behind the humorous anecdote, which might remind the readers of their first (mis) steps, lies the very serious story of a fundamental change in Dorrit's life and personality. It will help her change the way she speaks. It also constitutes her first act of literary creativity, a play with words (see also Huston 2014, 247; 253). The use of the future tense lends this anecdote prophetic overtones, though this prophecy is a secular one, taking place away from church benches. Indeed, silent reading soon conflicts with the religious discourse that invades the child's universe: "The novel is movement, poles apart from the family prayer. It moves, and it moves you. In silence and in secret, thanks to reading, stories are woven in your head. You are alone and yet, in wonderful company. You read and read and read and read and read and read and read and read and read" (243).[10]

The character looks for alternative rituals to fight the religious influences of her childhood. Religious reading is later replaced by yoga (244). This practice brings together reading, Christianity and Hinduism into a same purpose—knowing how to create a sacred space (244).

The child's bookshelf, then, is non-elitist. Amongst her favourite books and the key titles of her literary education are all sorts of writings. Once again, autobiographical writing seems to mock the pretention of showing a writer's perfect itinerary, telling the story of a little genius who was inclined to read the classics from an early age. Here, the text displays no erudition, no literary showing off. Amongst the texts quoted by Nancy Huston is "a marvellous Golden Book," with a red cover, a maternal gift filled with fairy tales, short stories and poems (Huston 2014, 228). She also mentions *Hi and Lois, a comic strip* (238); *The High Chamber,* a journal (242; 243); the Bible her aunt reads; Hoffman's tales (249); the novel *Pierre, or The Ambiguities* by Melville (250); and even the lyrics of the song "Supercalifragilisticexpialidocious" from the movie *Mary Poppins* (249).

Literature Outside of Class

Quid then of the scholarly reading scenes? Of literature in class? In *Bad Girl*, what is called "literature classes" has very little to do with school. Dorrit does not learn how to read at school but at home, at four and a half, thanks to her brother. Interestingly enough, this precociousness is not acknowledged by the school system since she isn't allowed to enrol before the appointed age (163). The years of literature studies at Sarah Lawrence, "the excellent uni located in the North of New York," are barely mentioned (66). The same goes for the first years of what she calls "her French life," which Nancy Huston spent studying in Paris, and which she wrote about in other texts (29).

Several non-literary experiences are likened to "literature classes," in a narrative where life is the writer's first teacher. For example, Dorrit learns how to write when she is confronted by her family's religious austerity or by her father's "mental confusion" after a concussion (128). This confusion is said to provoke in Dorrit an obsession for organised and rational writing:

> What a literature class! Your desk will always be perfectly tidy. The tabletop will be bare when you are away. You will enjoy nothing as much as focusing on the same task, day after day. To see words follow each other, paragraphs line up, pages pile up. To keep going in a continuous and coherent fashion. To read, to rewrite, to correct, to improve. To trim. (129)[11]

The frantic pace of her family life is mentioned as yet another literature class. Dorrit learns to read in the chaos of moving out and moving in, a chaos she can flee by dreaming of another universe, and putting herself in other people's shoes (158). "Literature classes" for Dorrit take a different meaning here: they enable her to experience other environments, communities, and social *classes*.

Many experiences forge Dorrit's education as a writer. Playing the piano, for example, is another form of literature class, "maybe even the most important of all" (176), because she will learn how to "express [her] own emotions through other people's emotions" (176). Learning how to play an instrument teaches the writer how to work on her text, in a melodic way, with a Flaubertian obsession for precision, and the musical context of this teaching could remind the reader of the *gueuloir* used by the French writer. Classical tunes are used as mediums for interpretation and imagination, and not as unreachable models. Art is at the service of life and its lessons. The narrative tells as much about life as writing lessons. Nancy Huston retraces what made her: in Dorrit's life and in events around her, in her past, and in her experiences of the other. With this book, one learns to read life as a book, and to read literature outside books.

A Life Before Books: She Writes to Read Herself

At the heart of the writer's autobiography lies the question of the origins of literary creativity. It is a question that psychoanalysis, sociology and literature have tried to answer. As the narrative mixes psychology, genetics and education, Huston explores the relationship between life and what she calls "literature." Writing allows the writer to look into her past and see what made her so.

Psychology and Causality: Understanding the Writer's Past

The autobiographical enterprise starts with the premise that present life can be explained by the past. The relationship between the daughter Dorrit and the writer Nancy Huston is a relationship of causality. Writing is perceived as the consequence of Dorrit's past life, the life of her ancestors and her own childhood. One chapter recounts a sort of internal seism that happens when Dorrit is told by critics that one of her novels illustrates the principles of transgenerational psychology (150). The writer is surprised when she is confronted by reviews and perceptions of her novel. The expression of doubt might be a way to question intergenerational transmission, which will later be a leitmotiv in a narrative such as *Bad Girl*. A question is asked, that of the psychological and psychoanalytical causality at play in someone's life. Neither Dorrit nor Nancy Huston explicitly answer this question, but the shadows of the Freudian *id* and of the Lacanian *'dyad'* become apparent throughout the exploration of what might have shaped a being even before it became a being (49). What part does a mother play in her children's personality? Are our personalities shaped by our own "narratives" or the fruits of our mother's legacy (9)? What did the mother imprint on her children when they were "mingled in her body" (150–151). When Dorrit gets home, she learns that her partner, "the Painter," spent his day painting a series of aquarelles entitled *Foetuses as Storytellers* (150–151).

Knowing how much life before life shapes one's relationship to literature, to reading and writing, is a vital question in the literary field and in all fields. The anecdote of the painter's aquarelles is significant since it leaves the question of the randomness or necessity of creation unanswered in the text. Is it a coincidence or a necessity that Dorrit's day, the writer's, and her partner's day revolve around the same topic? Since no definite conclusion is given here, the interpretation is left to the reader. Indeed, the writer and her readers share the interpretive reading allowed by the retrospective point of view in an autobiographical narrative. As she is reading herself through the distance allowed by the dialogue between Dorrit and the narrator, Nancy Huston looks for the signs of an intra-uterine education, a desire, an innate taste for writing before words and books. Without ever hiding the part of fiction and storytelling which lies in all reading and all writing, she writes to read herself.

The causality which makes writing a consequence of her life is palpable in the affirmation that Dorrit's books reproduce her life, that her work is a metaphor for her life: "Decades later, people will ask you why you completely change the setting in each novel. The answer is simple: it is the pace you got used to as a child. Being wrenched away each year (sometimes more often) from what was familiar. Moving. Starting all over again. Somewhere else" (154).[12] This simple answer should call for cautious reading. Even if the autobiography suggests one interpretation for the life and creation of the writer, the reader can still doubt it. Indeed, while *Bad Girl* seems to be written against one myth, which Nancy Huston calls the Sartrian myth of self-generation, this might be to create another illusion.

Quotation, Summary and Illustration: Using the Words of Others

In an autobiographical essay entitled *Nord perdu* ("Lost North") first published in 1999, Nancy Huston criticises the Sartrian model of self-generation:

> For a long time now I have been working (and this includes writing, thinking, and speaking) against Sartre's model, against his belief in a self-engendered man, his belief that one's existence is entirely cultural, that one can say 'I choose myself, I, as an adult, rational, free and independent being'. ... And it's not just Sartre of course—Kundera, Beckett, Kafka, the whole antikitsh tribe: Down with mothers! Down with family love! (Huston 2004, 66)[13]

Further in the chapter, she reflects on the generation of French thinkers such as Sartre, Camus, Barthes, and Bataille who "dreamed of being the sons of their work" (68). Instead of representing herself as the offspring of her own work, in a world where literature precedes life and existence precedes essence, Nancy Huston conjures up another illusion: for the writer of *Bad Girl*, life precedes literature. A closer look at the way texts are quoted in the narrative reveals how books are used to illustrate life events: quoting and summarizing authors both help the writer illustrate and explain her own existence. The narrative construction conveys the feeling that books were written to validate life experiences through words and images.

For example, abortion is dealt with through Annie Ernaux's *L'Événement*, as if another writer's words better express a personal and intimate event (25). In another chapter, the father's "mental confusion" is portrayed and explained through a case study discussed by Antonio Damasio in *Descartes' Error* (119–122). These texts are chosen and quoted because they say something about Dorrit's life. But she also quotes other texts because they elucidate her writing practice. Another relationship between life and literature thus emerges, one based on a form of parallelism.

Instead of presenting herself as a reader, the autobiographer leads her reader through the books she wrote. She reads her own texts, which she interprets, analyses and compares to others. In Beckett she finds her "graphomany" (99), in Gary her "desperate empathy" (146), in Anaïs Nin, her overpoweringly seductive novel writing. The transformation of men into characters is said to empower both writers:

> You will put up with all kinds of men, including the worst … , you will put up with them because as you smile at them and nod your head, you take careful note of their behaviour, knowing you will get your revenge one day by turning them into characters. When you write, you will have the upper hand, you will handle them as if they were puppets. (207)[14]

The comparison with Anaïs Nin allows Nancy Huston to fantasize that her own writing is an inversion of power: life is changed by literature and women dominate men. From life to reading to writing, intertextuality in *Bad Girl* is a receptive and creative process which reverses relationships and covers the usual tracks. As a reflection of Nancy Huston and the heir of other writers, Dorrit therefore becomes a writer character.

The Family Novel: Rewriting the Writer's Past

In *Nord perdu* (*Lost North*), Nancy Huston was distancing herself from her favourite student books, such as Barthes' or Beckett's works, texts that she also mentions in *Bad Girl*. There, the writer pays a "bilingual tribute to Beckett" in a parodic essay where the narrator tells Dorrit that she will "mock him kindly as he pretends to remember his intra-uterine life" (140–141). But she also compares little Dorrit to the famous writer, as if one could accurately remember what happens in the mind of a five-year-old: "At the age of five, your mind will dive into Beckett-like spirals of logic" (165). The young reader has become a writer, and it's her turn to teach yet another literature class, one in which one learns to free oneself. Dorrit and Nancy Huston together pay their (dis)respect to models, by turning their ancestors' words and worlds into fiction: the "family novel" (232) becomes the novel *Bad Girl.*

The first writerly act of Dorrit, the little bookworm, the very foundation of her writing is not to stage herself as a model reader, but to create images for her texts, to invent them, to imagine fictive friends: her first characters, a group of friends called Trixi (238). She then starts to turn her world into fiction. Similarly, when she reads her mother's letters, Alison becomes her "favourite heroine in [her] favourite novel" (254). This childhood creative process is repeatedly interpreted as the first stone on which Dorrit will build her house as a novelist: "You will speak to yourself using the third person, turning each of your gestures into a scene, and your daily life into a novel" (165).

The autobiographical narrative offers several examples of transcribing and transforming Dorrit's ancestors' texts, as if writers' blood ran in the family. Some letters written by Dorrit's grandmother are copied out without a single comment on when and how Dorrit read them, as if they were just intended to be read in *Bad Girl* through the intermediary of Nancy Huston's work. These letters therefore become part of the narrative, the novel and the writer's work. In *Bad Girl*, they become literature. Another example of this 'novelistic' work is shown in the way the narrator analyses a letter from Dorrit's grandfather as if it were a novelist's text: "According to you, Dorrit, could a novelist have invented such a letter?" (75) The letter, describing a Reeves locomotive, is copied over four pages, in three fragments interrupted by the analytic work of the autobiographical voice, which becomes a literary critic, and turns the grandfather into another Proust whose *petite madeleine* is a Reeves locomotive (79). Thus, the writer's work, which has been shaped by life, is transformed by it in return. The letter becomes a novel, the daily writing a fictive work. By allowing us to read her grandfather's letter, Nancy Huston changes her (his)story into another story, a story in which her grandfather would have been a writer. Just like her "father's fiction" builds a world for his children where the poor have the same rights to culture as the rich (73), Nancy Huston's fiction turns Dorrit's life into a novel. The loop is closed, life leads to literature and literature leads to life, reading leads to writing and writing leads to reading.

Conclusion: "The Rest Is Simply Literature"

Bad Girl: Classes de littérature is a work in which the autobiographical pact and *genre* are deconstructed to be rebuilt. The refusal to give the protagonist the name "Nancy Huston" signals the advent of autofiction, together with stories about others' lives and the confusion between fiction and essay. One could argue that exploring how to write about oneself is another way to write truthfully about oneself, freeing the autobiographer from the conventions learnt in literature classes and giving the reader freedom of interpretation. One could then interpret the quote from Roland Barthes' autobiography—"All this must be considered as having been said by a fictional character"—as an invitation to read both autobiographies in parallel, and to deconstruct the idea of truth and fiction: should we really read the text given to us as told by a character in a novel? And does it prevent the text from being true?

On the one hand, the honesty and sincerity of the autobiographer may lie in the refusal to create for herself the mythical destiny of an intellectual *femme de lettres* bound to give her life to literature since first reading the classics in class. The narrative is the frank story of a little girl who becomes a French writer far away from the glory of the classics and academia, on the other side of the ocean, in a broken then rebuilt Canadian family which faces social tensions, abandonment, abortion, and extreme religious austerity. The text seems to argue that the need to write is not a gift, but is spawn from the events that took place in the family's past. Nancy Huston is not a self-generated writer. She does not choose her existence as a writer: she reads and writes because "she has it in her blood" (74), because she needs to, because literature is a land of exploration and comfort. Ironically, this story of an autodidact who learnt literature outside of school and became a writer despite the humiliation generated by her lack of money (73), cannot but remind the reader of another self-story, written by the father of French autobiography, Jean-Jacques Rousseau.

On the other hand, the absence of emphasis on literature classes and reading scenes is still to be questioned in regard to the title of the narrative. Books in *Bad Girl* are quoted alongside other life experiences to explain the birth of a writer; they are subjected to comments; they represent steps in the main character's life. But in comparison to other experiences in Dorrit's life, reading is rarely described emotionally; the writer herself seldom explores the intimacy of her feelings when she reads. The narrative becomes more pressing as if the writer could not take the time to describe the feelings reading awoke in her as she grew up. Perhaps speaking about such matters is already giving in, giving too much, saying more than when speaking of abortion, violence, sadness, and abandonment. The absence of the writer's self-representation as a student moved by the content and beauty of specific literary texts, as a learner subject to aesthetic pleasure and emotions, may be a way to construct the autodidact identity of Dorrit the character. But it is also a "survival strategy" and an opportunity to hide something about Nancy Huston's personality, to keep some matters of the heart secret. The first reading experiences are times of initiation, which, as all rituals, may be shared with the community, but, as all epiphanies, may remain individual and secret. The intimate reading scene shall not be made a public event, even in an autobiography. Nancy Huston foregrounds the obstacles a subject faces when she decides to analyse her own life, or else, when one becomes a life writer.

NOTES

1. The original reads as follows: *La vérité? Quelle vérité? La vérité est peut-être que je n'existe pas. Ce qui existe, ce qui commencera à exister peut-être un jour, si j'ai beaucoup de chance, ce sont mes livres, quelques romans, une œuvre, si j'ose employer ce mot. Tout le reste, c'est de la littérature* (my translation).
2. Page references are to the French edition.
3. The original reads as follows: *Toi, c'est toi, Dorrit. Celle qui écrit. Toi à tous les âges, et même avant d'avoir un âge, avant d'écrire, avant d'être un soi. Celle qui écrit et donc aussi, parfois, on espère, celui/celle qui lit.* The translations of all the excerpts from *Bad Girl* are mine.
4. *Petite idiote sera l'épithète que tu entendras le plus souvent. Venant de toi-même. Ou plutôt, d'un de tes soi s'adressant à un autre. Car tes soi sont multiples. Ne pas se trouver tous au même endroit, au même moment, c'est ce qu'ils sauront inventer de mieux comme stratégie de survie.*
5. *Ses lettres t'aideront à rester en vie, et quand, plus tard, tu te mettras à écrire des livres, la deuxième personne sera toujours celle que tu préfères, étant donné qu'il n'y a pas assez de place dans le monde pour je, et que il et elle mettraient trop de distance entre toi et tes personnages bien-aimés, tu veux leur parler tout ce temps, comme s'ils étaient dans la pièce avec toi, c'est pourquoi, livre après livre, tu diras* you, you, you *et tu, tu, tu, et il en ira de même, Dorrit, pour ce livre-ci, où ta vie elle-même sera transformée en lettres, et toi, veux, veux pas, drôle de petit chamois vaillant devenu dame vieillissante, en femme de lettres.*
6. *Tu vivras la littérature en mélomane. Sur les sables mouvants de ton enfance, langage et musique seront des échafaudages invisibles, amovibles, sans poids, auxquels tu pourras toujours te cramponner.*

7. *L'apprentissage de la lecture te sauvera. Le flot de voix ne s'interrompra plus. Ta vie durant, les voix humaines se glisseront par tes yeux jusque dans ton cerveau pour y éclore en sons de silence. Tu liras matin et midi, soir et nuit. Tu liras en marchant, en mangeant et en allant aux toilettes; tu liras avec une torche électrique en te cachant sous ton lit ...*

8. *Tu entendras les voix des livres que tu lis. Psalmodiant, chantant et se chamaillant, faisant vibrer d'invisibles cordes vocales, cordes de sécurité ... toutes les voix humaines, y compris la tienne.*

9. *Dix mille pages écrites dans une langue étrangère n'effaceront pas le douloureux délice d'entendre ses mots-notes sortir d'entre les lèvres rouge rubis d'une Alison de bonne humeur.*

10. *Aux antipodes de la prière familiale, le roman est mouvement. Il se meut, et il t'émeut. En silence et en secret, grâce à la lecture, des histoires se tissent dans ta tête. Tu es seule et pourtant en compagnie merveilleuse. Tu lis et lis et lis et lis et lis et lis et lis et lis et lis.*

11. *Sacrée classe de littérature. Ton bureau sera toujours parfaitement rangé. La surface de ta table de travail quand tu n'y es pas, sera nue. Tu n'aimeras rien tant que t'appliquer à la même tâche, jour après jour. Voir les mots se suivre, les paragraphes s'aligner, les pages s'empiler. Avancer de manière suivie et cohérente. Relire, retravailler, corriger, améliorer. Élaguer.*

12. *Des décennies plus tard, les gens te demanderont pourquoi tu changes complètement d'univers à chaque roman. La réponse est simple: c'est le rythme auquel on t'a habituée, petite. S'arracher tous les ans (voire plus souvent encore) à ce qui t'était familier. Déménager. Recommencer à zéro. Ailleurs.*

13. *Cela fait longtemps que je travaille (écris, réfléchis, parle) contre le modèle sartrien de l'auto-engendrement, du « tout culture », du je me choisis, moi, adulte, rationnel, souverain, entièrement libre et autonome. ... Il n'y a pas que Sartre bien-sûr; il y a Kundera, Beckett, Kafka, toute la smala antikitsh: à bas les mères! à bas l'amour familial ....*

14. *Tu supporteras les hommes de toutes sortes, y compris la pire ..., tu les supporteras parce que ... tu enregistres leur comportement, certaine de prendre un jour ta revanche en les transformant en personnages. Écrivant, c'est toi qui auras le dessus, toi qui les manipuleras comme des marionnettes....*

REFERENCES

Balint-Babos, Adina. 2012. Nancy Huston: penser l'identité multiple. *Cahiers Franco-Canadiens de l'Ouest* 24: 41–55.

Danby, Nicola. 2004. The Space Between: Self-Translator Nancy Huston's *Limbes/Limbo*. *La Linguistique* 40: 83–964.

Jenny, Laurent. 2003. L'autofiction, *Méthodes et problèmes*. Genève: Département de français moderne. http://www.unige.ch/lettres/framo/enseignements/methodes/autofiction/ last. Accessed 1 July 2017.

Huston, Nancy. 2014. *Bad Girl: Classes de Littérature*. Paris: Actes Sud.

———. 1995. *Tombeau de Romain Gary*. Paris: Actes Sud.

———. 2004. *Nord perdu*. Paris: Actes Sud.

Lejeune, Philippe. 1989. *On Autobiography*. Trans. Katherine Leary. Minneapolis: University of Minnesota Press.

PART III

Reading as Resistance and Emancipation

CHAPTER 9

The Diary of Alice James: A Portrait of the Artist as a Reader

Laure de Nervaux-Gavoty

Introduction

Sister to Henry, the novelist, and William, the psychologist and philosopher, Alice James (1848–1892) won fame posthumously thanks to her diary. She started it in 1889, at the age of 41, five years after she settled in England, to try to mitigate, she wrote, the "sense of loneliness and isolation" caused by her invalidity (A. James 1964, 25). Despite its crucial importance for the author, the existence of this diary remained a secret during her lifetime. Henry and William became apprised of it in 1894, two years after her death, when they both received one of the four copies privately published by Katherine Peabody Loring, Alice's closest friend. The diary was republished in a truncated form forty years later, by one of Alice James's nieces, with a long introduction devoted to Alice's lesser-known brothers, Robertson and Garth Wilkinson, under the title *Alice James, Her Brothers, Her Journal* (A. James, 1934). It was not until

L. de Nervaux-Gavoty (✉)
Université Paris-Est Créteil, Créteil, France

© The Author(s) 2018
V. Baisnée-Keay et al. (eds.), *Women's Life Writing
and the Practice of Reading*, Palgrave Studies in Life Writing,
https://doi.org/10.1007/978-3-319-75247-1_9

1964, however, that the original text was made available to the public, when Leon Edel published a new edition faithful to the original manuscript and to Katherine Peabody Loring's version.[1]

One of the striking features of this little-known text is the wealth of intertextual references it contains. Gifted with exceptional intellectual talents but confined to her room by illness, Alice James was an avid reader whose curiosity ranged across all genres, from fiction to drama through memoirs; she was familiar with English and European classics, but also with contemporary French literature and her brothers' works. Her interest was not limited to literature: well-versed in politics, she was also a keen reader of the press. Many diary entries are thus prompted by her reactions to books and articles she had read; some even include quotations of passages that captured her attention.

Alice James's attraction to books was not merely the expression of her intellectual appetite, however; there was actually much more at stake in it: "J. Lemaître says in a sentence of someone else what I blundered through a page in trying to say of him—'A book that gives me the impression of expressing my inner being and that makes me aware of myself as more intelligent than I believed myself to be'" (A. James 1964, 40, my translation).[2] Alice James was looking in books for no less than the revelation of an unclear identity, the passage suggests.

This need to make sense of herself was the result of two converging and closely linked factors: first of all, her position in the James family as the sister of two remarkable writers; and, secondly, her condition as an invalid suffering from what was then called hysteria. Reading, which found its accomplishment in the diary, allowed her to define her identity and to bring a self into being. The first section of this chapter will show that the diary can be analysed as an extension of the practice of reading—reading books but also reading the body. The second section will examine some major intertextual influences that enabled her to assert herself as an individual subject.

READING BOOKS, READING THE BODY, READING THE SELF

Creative Reading: From the Commonplace Book to the Diary

The specific meaning reading came to take for Alice James is first of all the result of complex family relationships. She was born in a literary family who set a crucial value on the life of the mind; but while the talents of her brothers Henry and William were valued and nurtured, Alice's own gifts were not taken seriously. Intellectual achievement was considered as a male prerogative in the James family: Jean Strouse, Alice James's biographer, notes that Henry James Sr "placed negative value on female intelligence" (Strouse 1980, 275) and that "to be a James and a girl ... was a contradiction in terms" (Strouse 1980, xiii).

The ban implicitly put on writing invested reading, the one legitimate intellectual activity available to her, with a crucial meaning. Alice James turned it into a form of personal expression by starting a commonplace book which she kept between 1886 and 1888 (Edel 1964b, 1–2). In it, she copied down quotations from authors as varied as Shakespeare, Edward Fitzgerald, George Eliot, Carlyle, Montaigne, George Sand, La Bruyère, Flaubert, Dumas fils, Anatole France or Tolstoy, to cite just a few names.[3] Reflecting Alice James's preoccupations, the quotations are striking for their consistency: Jean Strouse, who had access to the commonplace book, notes that they reveal "her absorption in the idea of triumph over worldly adversity, of private peace in the face of pain and death" (Strouse 1980, 268). Because of the process of selection, juxtaposition and appropriation it implies, her notebook can thus be read as an embryonic form of literary composition and as a personal narrative.

This text was clearly the cocoon out of which the diary emerged, when Alice James, tired of borrowing other people's voices, decided to speak for herself. While the commonplace book, which includes dates, foreshadows the diary, the latter bears signs of its origins as a collection of quotations: the dialogue with other texts is one of its crucial characteristics. Like the commonplace book, the diary remains a paradoxical form of expression, however; the choice of this minor genre can be read as a compromise between a desire for self-expression and a deep feeling of illegitimacy linked to her status as a woman. The unthreatening minor genre of the diary was the only form of literary expression which Alice, who was highly reluctant to compete with other writers in general and with her brothers in particular, allowed herself (Strouse 1980, 274–275). As if self-expression, even purely private, was already a form of trespassing, however, she kept its existence a secret, only betraying her suppressed literary ambitions in her occasional addresses to an imaginary audience, to a mysterious "dear Inconnu" (A. James 1964, 129) in particular, and in the wish she expressed at the end of her life that the diary be typewritten and published: "though she never said so, I understand that she would like to have it published," Katherine Peabody Loring wrote to explain why she decided to have four copies printed (Edel 1964a, v).

Coming to Terms with Bodily Dislocation

The meaning of reading, in Alice James's case, must also be examined in the light of her nervous disorders. As Jean-Marie Goulemot explains, "[o]ur body reads, but not just through our eyes and our mind, for our understanding of a book is deeply influenced by our consciousness of illness, health or death" (Goulemot 2003, 122, my translation). Alice James underwent several nervous breakdowns as an adolescent and was diagnosed in 1868 as suffering from hysteria (Strouse 1980, 123). Her condition deteriorated over the years and, by the time she started her diary, she was unable to leave her bed and had to be assisted by a nurse in her daily life.

Making the condition it refers to a specifically feminine disorder, the word "hysteria" functioned as a convenient term labelling an illness that eluded doctors and science in general. In hysteria, the body becomes an indecipherable text: symptoms abound, but cannot be assigned to a pathological cause, an organic disorder (Didi-Huberman 1982, 74). Weir Mitchell, the inventor of the rest cure, aptly called it "mysteria" (Showalter 1987, 130).

Alice James repeatedly rants in her diary about doctors' incapacity to treat her, lamenting, in a characteristic passage, "the ignorant asininity of the medical profession in its treatment of nervous disorders" (A. James 1964, 150). Drawing upon her brother William's analysis of hysteria in "The Hidden Self," she describes her condition as "a fight simply between [her] body and [her] will … in which the former was to be triumphant to the end" (A. James 1964, 149). In her diary, her body appears as the prey of centrifugal, dislocating movements, its organs always threatening to become autonomous. Her stomach and her heart are thus frequently personified and depicted as unruly creatures—a "dissipated organ" (129); a "jumping jack" (73)—which have to be disciplined, "towed … back into harbor" (74).

The very indecipherability of her body and the sense of opacity she experiences in connection with it underlie her experience of reading. The latter becomes a way of fighting off the threat of inner shapelessness: "books," she notes, "clarify the density and shape the formless mass within" (A. James 1964, 113). Literature, it seems, reintroduces what is missing between the subject and her body: language, as science's failure to name her disorder suggests. By giving a shape to "a formless mass," books also offer a reader deprived of status by illness, figures, forms of identity that can help her to define herself.

Reading as Individuation

Reading is in fact crucially related, in Alice James's case, to the delineation of an otherwise inchoate identity. Books work for her as mirrors reflecting back a fully formed self: "What one reads, or rather all that comes to us is surely only of interest and value in proportion as we find ourselves therein, form given to what was vague, what slumbered stirred to life" (A. James 1964, 27). As Marielle Macé, a French critic, explains, reading is by no means a purely aesthetic activity cut off from our daily life. It can actually inflect the direction of the latter by offering models of identity: "Books offer to our perception, our attention and our capacity for action unique configurations which include a wealth of potential 'paths' to follow. The patterns they enclose are not lifeless; they are not pictures placed before the eyes of the reader but *oriented* possibilities of existences" (Macé 2011, 14, my translation). Reading can therefore become part and parcel of a process of self-definition, or, as Macé puts it, of "individuation": "Reading can be regarded as a form of individuation ... Through books, we are constantly invited to recognize, 'refigure' ourselves, in other words to constitute ourselves as subjects and reclaim our perception of ourselves through a discussion with other forms" (18, my translation).

In the case of Alice James, the process of "refiguration" described by Macé finds its expression in the diary itself, in other words in the conversion of reading into writing. The two are closely interwoven in this text which offers itself as a constant dialogue with quoted authors or with less explicit but equally crucial influences, as well as with other literary genres and non-literary forms of textuality. Through this conjoined activity of reading and writing, Alice James claims legitimacy for herself as an invalid, in other words a sick body excluded from traditional roles, but also as a highly intelligent, independent-minded woman, and as a member of the James family gifted with literary talents. Deeply aware of the fragility of her body, she calls attention to the powers of her mind, borrowing from various authors and genres to turn herself into a highly perceptive consciousness endowed with acute discriminating powers.

DEFINING A SELF: VARIETIES OF READING

French Literature or the Life of the Mind

As an invalid, Alice James was faced with the difficulties of a life full of restrictions, but also open to suspicions of idleness. "America reproached the chance not taken," Jean Strouse explains (Strouse 1980, 233); the diary makes it clear that Alice James found her condition easier to bear in England.[4] Books, contemporary French literature in particular, also helped her to give meaning to a life confined to immobility.

References to late nineteenth-century French authors—often cited directly in French—abound in the commonplace book[5] and in the diary. Jules Lemaître's defence of a personal, impressionistic response to works of art, as well as Paul Bourget's, Anatole France's or Pierre Loti's departure from naturalism in favour of psychological novels probing the complexities of the human mind were then laying the foundations for a new form of literature in which mental rumination took precedence over action proper. This emphasis on the life of the mind, on interiority as opposed to action, or rather on the inner life *as* a form of action appealed to Alice James for it helped her claim value for her own experience.

Reacting energetically to a neighbour's incomprehension of her secluded life and her occupations—"She asked me with the greatest conviction if I didn't get 'awfully tired of reading!'" (A. James 1964, 35)—she retorts by quoting a passage from Anatole France's *Les Désirs de Jean Servien* (Paris: A. Lemerre 1882), praising the value of dreams, obscurity and resignation in one's lot.[6] Taking her cue from *Jean Servien*, as it were, Alice James keeps reasserting the value of immobility and of obscure lives like her own: "The paralytic on his couch can have if he wants them, wider experiences than Stanley slaughtering savages" (A. James 1964, 146).

Far from being a pleasant way to while away the time, reading becomes a way of living for Alice James, and the impressions it yields, an absolute form of experience. Her entranced responses to Jules Lemaître's work are particularly eloquent in that respect. Physical metaphors applied to mental operations enact a striking form of displacement, as if the brain had taken on the functions of the other organs; body and mind seem to merge, turning reading into an almost erotic experience:

I have now read three vol[ume]s of Jules Lemaître *Etudes et Portraits*. ... [H]ow grateful shall I ever be for the intensity of that first impression, two months ago, my whole being vivified with the sense of the *Intelligent* revealed! One's mind stretching to the limits of his, absorbing him with every sense, such a subtle flattery emanating from his perfection in 'putting it' as to make an absolutely ignorant creature like me vibrate, as with knowledge, in response to the truth of the myriad of his exquisitely subtle perceptions! Then his humour, his irony and his humanity! (30)

Alice James's responses to French authors thus emphasize the value and intensity of the inner life for sensitive minds. One last dimension of these works may explain their attraction. As a passage taken from Anatole France's *Vie littéraire* praising the value of pain suggests, the dialogue with this author and his contemporaries actually seemed to warrant the possible transformation, thanks to her diary, of the humble material of her life into a silent, inner work of art: "... the science of pain is the only science of life ... Under this inspiration the most humble existences can become works of art far superior to the most beautiful symphonies and the most beautiful poems. Are the works realized in oneself not the best? Those that are thrown out of oneself on canvas or paper are only images, shadows" (A. James 1964, 55, my translation).[7]

Becoming an Active Centre of Consciousness

The emphasis laid in the diary on the life of the mind and on the value of impressions owes a lot to French literature, but it must also be related to the influence of her brother Henry. In "The Art of Fiction," published in 1884, Henry James notes that novels are written from experience and that "experience consists of impressions" (H. James 1956, 13). Insisting on the importance of careful observation, he invites aspiring novelists to be "one of the people on whom nothing is lost!" (13) The pictorial metaphor runs throughout the essay, revealing James's interest in the deep connections between the sister arts and the high premium placed on visual perception in his work.

The primacy of perception and impressions culminates in a narrative technique centred on the question of point of view. Right from the beginning of his literary career, Henry James's prefaces clearly articulate his project to write novels reflecting the way reality is filtered through a sensitive mind; thus, commenting on *Roderick Hudson*, he notes, "The centre of interest throughout 'Roderick' is in Rowland Mallet's consciousness, and the drama is the very drama of that consciousness" (H. James 1934, 16).

Alice James was a great reader and admirer of her brother's work; it seems that his writings helped her convert a limitation imposed by her condition into a structuring figure of the diary: faced with a fragile, uncontrollable body which resists her, Alice James reasserts the power of her mind by turning herself into a perceiving I/eye, an active centre of consciousness. The value of impressions as the most intense form of experience appears clearly in the evocation of one of her rare outings. The "I" becomes a pure consciousness, an eye acutely receptive to the outside world:

> Yesterday I was lying in a meadow at Hawke's farm, absorbing like blotting paper hay-ricks, hedges and trees composing themselves into a multitude of pictures with that felicity alone known to this island, the foreground grey, with ghostly slants of sunshine, vanishing to reappear in the distance, so succulent, so smooth and so slow, so *from* all time and so for all time, when Somers came suddenly within view and there he was the peasant of these fields! (A. James 1964, 33–34)

With the image of the "blotting paper," Alice James positions herself not just as sensitive mind but as a writer. The description, which brings to mind the opening lines of *The Portrait of a Lady*,[8] is carefully composed, and the play of light reminiscent of an impressionist painting. The pictorial devices intensify the epiphanic dimension of the moment by removing it from the flow of time and turning it into a tableau. Distinctly belonging to Alice, however, is the comic note closing the passage: epiphany turns into comedy when the description of the idyllic pastoral scene is interrupted by the arrival of Somers's lumbering, clownish figure.

Priding herself on her powers of observations, Alice James clearly claims an identity as a James in her diary, as the following comment on the scene above suggests: "How grateful I am that I actually do see, to my own consciousness, the quarter of an inch that my eyes fall upon; truly the subject is all that counts!" (A. James 1964, 31).[9] The restriction of her field of vision makes her intensely aware of the subjective dimension of perception, which becomes much more important than the object described.

If Alice's debt to her brother is clear, she nonetheless turned their common interest in observation and the value of impressions into something distinctly personal by merging his influence with other intertextual reminiscences. As Brigitte Galtier points out, her confinement at home afforded her an unusual point of view on conditions sharply different from hers, allowing her to meet people with whom she would have had very few interactions, had she led a more traditional life (Galtier 1997, 80). One of the most striking characteristics of the diary lies, therefore, in its minute observation of the working class and in its focus on everyday life. Far from being trivial, the commonplace becomes fraught with meaning under Alice's pen: "It's amusing to see how, even on my microscopic field, minute events are perpetually taking place illustrative of the broadest facts of human nature" (A. James 1964, 48).

Many pages are thus dedicated to the Bachelers, a family she helped occasionally while living in Leamington, and whose life she followed through Nurse's regular reports. Anecdotes which would not have attracted anybody's attention are described with great precision and turned into comic scenes or embryonic narratives often reminiscent of Dickens's novels:

> Owing to an unprecedented condition of affluence, Mrs. Bacheler has joined the '*Bew*rial Soc[iety];'[10] hitherto only one could belong (two pence per week) and that one was naturally her lord and master. But she was not without her support for the dread moment, for she had an ancient night-gown of mine which she is cherishing for her shroud. It seems to be the climax of existence for 'em and one can't wonder for the thought of being buried higgledy-piggledy with odious creatures whom one has spent one's days in fighting with, must offend the aesthetic sense. This is another link with the great, it seems that the Prince has the same passion for deaths and burials as his mother. (49)

In a characteristic manner, Alice James deftly merges the morbid, the comic and the grotesque here. Vivid details abound, bringing the scene to life—from Mrs. Bacheler's mispronounced words to the carnivalesque night-gown turned into a shroud, or the surprisingly comic image of bodies piled up "higgledy-piggledy". Far from restricting her biting wit to the social ambitions of the poor, she also pokes fun at two royal figures' morbid interest in burials, thus hinting at the deep similarity of mankind across social classes.

These scenes build up a narrative taken up at unpredictable intervals in which Alice James anatomizes human nature, asserting herself as both a moralist and a comic writer making the best possible use of her restricted field of observation.

The Self as Spectator and Stage Director

The triumph of point of view, of the life of consciousness, as well as Alice James's comic genius also express themselves in her theatrical approach to life. The room where she is confined becomes a vantage point from which she observes and comments on the world. She takes up the position of both spectator and stage director, turning exclusion into a source of endless delight in the comedy of life: "to sit by and watch these absurdities is amusing in its way" (49). Although she mentions very few classical authors—apart from Shakespeare—there is every reason to believe that, as a highly cultivated woman, she had an excellent knowledge of the English canon. Her favour, however, seems to have gone to French nineteenth-century dramatists, such as Lemaître, Bourget, Daudet and Dumas fils. Her brother Henry's unfortunate venture into drama also looms large in the diary; several pages are devoted to the representations of *The American* and to the mixed reactions of the critics (161–163).

Asserting herself as a controlling mind, Alice James reorganizes the material she observes with categories borrowed from drama. Individual voices fascinate her and her diary shows an extreme attention to the materiality of living speech and to comic, individual distortions. Nurse, in particular, becomes a stage character in her own right, a comic figure whose naïve, unexpected remarks, idiosyncratic pronunciation ('ab-borrance', A. James 1964, 186), or way of dressing are carefully noted; her grotesque hat is thus turned into a regular stage accessory in one of the entries. Revealingly, the reader is never told her real name; she is always referred to through her function, "Nurse," thus making her transformation into a type, a stage character, complete.

Showing prevails over telling in the diary, which becomes an imaginary stage; Alice James loves to stage the anecdotes she has been told by Henry or Katherine Loring as they happened—or as she thinks they did—and to let the characters reveal their shortcomings through their attitudes and through dialogues. The many voices resounding in her diary stand in sharp contrast to her isolation, recreating the lively polyphony of an outside world from which she is cut off. Thus, in a miniature drama played out in one of the entries, Alice James gives full expression to her comic talent and her mastery of dramatic composition: human vanity and the absurdity of social codes are condensed in an absurd dialogue revolving around the appropriateness of wearing gloves at lunch (93).

Alice James's theatrical imagination had a lot to do not just with her invalidity, however, which forced her into the position of the spectator, but also with hysteria itself. The symptoms of hysteria, which masqueraded as those of other diseases but were divorced from real organic damage, had something theatrical, and hysterics were often accused of faking them. The theatrical potential of this disorder was fully exploited by Charcot, who made his patients "perform" spectacular crises for an audience (Showalter 1987, 148). Paradoxically, the latent theatricality of her condition becomes a way for Alice James to come to terms with her status as an invalid and define herself on her own terms. Echoing the prevalent negative view of invalids in self-ironic passages, she repeatedly presents herself as a grotesque figure, describing herself for instance as a freak, a "Barnum Monstrosity" (A. James 1964, 63). Her awareness of the constructed dimension of identity and of the fixity of the roles appears clearly in one of her self-deprecating remarks: "my glorious role is to stand as sick headache for mankind" (48). The language of drama thus becomes a way to deconstruct these fixed positions and claim an identity, as an entry occasioned by the rewriting of her will suggests. Describing a scene in which she should feature as a vulnerable, if not ridiculous figure, from an unexpected point of view, Alice James changes its meaning altogether. The theatricality and role playing involved in illness, which assigns fixed positions to everyone, are exposed:

> The arrival of this august personage the Consul naturally caused me to 'go off' and I had to be put to bed—when the most amusing scene followed. I lay in a semi-faint, draped in as many frills as could be found for the occasion, with Nurse at my head with the thickest layer of her anxious-devoted-nurse expression on, as K. told me after, when thro' a mist I vaguely saw five black figures file into my little bower, headed by the most extraordinary little man, all gesticulation and grimace, who planted himself at the foot of the bed and stroking my knees began a long harangue to the effect that he and his wife had both 'laid upon a bed of sickness' which seemed to constitute uncontrovertible reason for my immediate recovery. (89–90)

Most remarkable here is the implicit shift in the source of vision. From pitiful object of the gaze, trapped in the role of the meek, passive invalid, Alice James asserts herself gradually as the secret controlling source of vision. The consul, who embodies the authority of the state, is cast as the central comic character of the scene, a grotesque, fulsome puppet whose dislocated body performs a ridiculous pantomime in Alice's mental—and written—theatre.

In *The Given and the Chosen*, contemporary poet Ann Lauterbach writes that "certain givens, or inheritances, which cannot be factually altered, can be 'reconfigured' sometimes beyond all recognition. This reconfiguration does not abandon the initial, individuated reality but alters its internal shape, its syntax if you will, to allow new possibilities" (Lauterbach 2011, 16). One of the most striking features of the diary is no doubt its capacity to turn invalidism and isolation into a privileged position of observation of the human comedy, in other words, to transform an incapacitating condition into a literary gesture.

Redefining Private and Public Spaces

Alice James wrote her diary at a time when men's and women's activities took place in what has been called "separate spheres": the public arena of action was men's exclusive province while women were confined to the private space of the home.[11] The way Alice James was brought up perfectly reflects this constricting ideology which denied women any political status. Her diary, however, becomes a way to question this rigid partition and redefine male and female spaces. Highly concerned with political and social issues, Alice James spent a significant amount of time every day reading the press and many entries are prompted by her responses to articles from *The Atlantic Monthly*, *The Nation*, *The Pall Mall Gazette*, *The Speaker*, *The Standard*, *Truth* and other reviews.[12] She quotes them and comments on them acidly, giving free vent to her political opinions and to her satirical turn of mind.

Quite remarkably, the diary also contains pasted clippings which had particularly drawn her attention. These unusual collages bring into contact two completely different worlds: the private world of Alice's personal life and the public world of politics. They reflect her wish to be part of a debate from which her outsider position as a foreigner, a woman and an invalid excludes her. The inclusion of newspaper clippings can thus be read as a political gesture, a form of "subjectivation" to quote Jacques Rancière's words: "subjectivation creates a common ground ... by bringing together what was not common, by declaring as stakeholders of the common those who were only private persons, by identifying as relevant to public debate issues which used to belong to the domestic sphere" (Rancière 2009, 314, my translation). The juxtaposition of domestic anecdotes and political comments and the overlap between the private and the public world it produces question the ideology of the separate spheres. Cutting and pasting clippings become a way for the author to assert herself as a political subject and to redefine a space of her own, well beyond her room.

In her response to politics, Alice James takes issue with the brutal patriarchal ideology which expresses itself in Britain's aggressive imperialism abroad, in its dealing with the Irish claim for independence, or in the church's narrow-mindedness. Social issues such as poverty, the inequity of justice, or women's status as second-class citizens also loom large. In some entries, Alice James comments at great length on the passage cited or pasted. Such is the case in one of the entries where she pokes fun at both the church and the monarchy (A. James 1964, 124). Elsewhere, however, Alice James refrains from expressing any comment, making full use of the possibilities of juxtaposition offered by the cuttings to compose an ironic, contrasted picture of contemporary life. In one of the entries, for instance, she juxtaposes three clippings—two taken from *Truth* and one from the *Standard*—to illustrate the absurd way "justice is meted out A.D. 1890" (A. James 1964, 91), the different treatment one gets according to one's social position: while a swindler of noble descent accused of forgery gets off with a relatively light sentence, two poor men found guilty of minor offences are submitted to ruthless severity (91–92). Gender issues also figure prominently, exposing the double standard at work in British society, as suggested by an excerpt from *Truth* soberly introduced by the following sentence: "This is valuable as showing the relative value of women and herring" (118). In both cases, Alice James relies on the clipping's blunt presence and disruptive effect to give full resonance to revolting anecdotes; the events are left to speak for themselves and reveal their full absurdity and cruelty through the contrast built within the entry. Through these comments and these cuttings, Alice James claims for herself a distinctive voice which goes well beyond introspection: a voice which, although trapped in a sick body and within the confines of a room, is concerned with the outside world at large—the voice of a satirist and a moralist who asserts her right to a political opinion.

Conclusion: Reading, Individuation and Subjectivation

Reading, in the case of Alice James, cannot be envisioned simply from an aesthetic point of view, as an influence which helped her find her style; it is actually bound up with a quest for self and part of an "individuation" and "subjectivation" process, to quote Marielle Macé's and Jacques Rancière's words. Expanding on the definition offered by the first theorist, one could say that her sustained dialogue with contemporary French literature, with Henry James's and Charles Dickens's novels, as well as with the genre of drama enables her to give shape to an otherwise indecipherable and illegitimate self. Drawing upon this multiplicity of literary influences, she claims legitimacy for herself as a sick, but nonetheless intellectually active woman and as a genuine—although hidden—writer gifted with a keen sense of observation and a ruthless satirical mind. Refusing to submit to patriarchal dictates, she also asserts herself as an autonomous political subject, a "stakeholder of the common" as Rancière would say; in other words, as a lucid observer of political life who refuses to be confined to its margins.

Alice James's family background gives her quest for individuation special poignancy. Suffocating though her family was,[13] she couldn't free herself from it; as this chapter has tried to show, she had to define herself as a James and did it by turning herself into an active I/eye highly receptive to impressions, a triumphant centre of consciousness on which nothing was lost. The diary had a life of its own, however, and while her brothers' work influenced Alice James's perception of the outside world, she managed, through her dark humour, her attention to ordinary life, her satirical awareness of class matters and her interest in politics, to turn these Jamesian formulas into something intensely personal.

Notes

1. For more details about the history of the successive editions, see Edel's preface to his own edition (Edel 1964a, v–x) and the afterword of Jean Strouse's biography of Alice James (Strouse 1980, 319–326).
2. The original quote reads as follows: *un livre qui me donne cette impression qu'il m'exprime tout entier, et me révèle à moi-même plus intelligent que je ne pensais.* (Alice James 1964, 40).
3. For a list of the authors quoted in the commonplace book, see Leon Edel's 'Portrait of Alice James' (Edel 1964b, 2) and Jean Strouse's biography of Alice James (Strouse 1980, 268–9).

4. "It's rather strange that here, among this robust and sanguine people, I feel not the least shame or degradation at being ill, as I used at home among the anaemic and the fagged" (A. James 1964, 36).

5. Strouse notes that "[w]ell over half the entries were in French" in the commonplace book (Strouse 1980, 269).

6. "has she ever dreamed 'un songe merveilleusement délicat, comme la solitude et le malheur en forment seuls dans les âmes qu'elles arrachent aux rudesses de la vie commune; l'idée d'une belle vie pleine d'ombre, vouée tout entière sans salaire ni retour, à la bonté et à la résignation?'" (A. James 1964, 35, quotation in French). The passage in French could be translated as "a wonderfully delicate dream, as solitude and misfortune alone can form in the souls they rescue from the roughness of common life; the idea of a beautiful life full of shadow, devoted entirely, without salary or reward, to goodness and resignation?" (My translation).

7. The original quote reads: ... *la science de la douleur est l'unique science de la vie ... Sous cette inspiration les existences les plus humbles peuvent devenir des œuvres d'art bien supérieures aux plus belles symphonies et aux plus beaux poèmes. Est-ce que les œuvres qu'on réalise en soi-même ne sont pas les meilleures? Les autres qu'on jette en dehors de soi sur la toile ou le papier ne sont que des images, des ombres* (A. James 1964, 55).

8. "Real dusk would not arrive for many hours; but the flood of summer light had begun to ebb, the air had grown mellow, the shadows were long upon the smooth, dense turf. They lengthened slowly, however, and the scene expressed that sense of leisure still to come which is perhaps the chief source of one's enjoyment of such a scene at such an hour. From five o'clock to eight is on certain occasions a little eternity; but on such an occasion as this the interval could be only an eternity of pleasure" (H. James 1963, 59).

9. Her remark resonates with Henry James's above mentioned essay and preface, but also with a passage of the diary in which she praises her brother's power of vision: "He is just back from Paris, as amusing as ever about his experiences, seeing things that no one else does" (A. James 1964, 64).

10. The *Encyclopedia Britannica* defines burial societies as follows: "a form of friendly societies, existing mainly in England, and constituted for the purpose of providing by voluntary subscriptions, for insuring money to be paid on the death of a member, or for the funeral expenses of the husband, wife or child of a member, or of the widow of a deceased member."

11. "The ostensibly 'separate' arenas of men's and women's activities emerged as the ideological counterpart to the economic shift in the 1830s and 1840s, a shift predicated on commerce outside the home and the attendant rise of the middle class; hence the 'domestic' or bourgeois woman was invented" (Bauer and Gould 2006, 5).

12. Alice James mentions fourteen British and American periodicals and two French newspapers (*Le Figaro* and *Le Journal des débats*) over the course of the diary.
13. See Jean Strouse's already mentioned biography of Alice James.

REFERENCES

Bauer, Dale, and Philip Gould. 2006. Introduction to *The Cambridge Companion to Nineteenth Century American Women's Writing*, ed. Dale Bauer and Philip Gould, 1–16. Cambridge: Cambridge University Press.

Didi-Huberman, Georges. 1982. *Invention de l'Hystérie: Charcot et l'iconographie photographique de la Salpêtrière*. Paris: Macula.

Edel, Leon. 1964a. Preface to *The Diary of Alice James*, ed. Leon Edel, v–x. New York: Dodd, Mead & Company.

———. 1964b. Portrait of Alice James. In *The Diary of Alice James*, ed. Leon Edel, 1–31. New York: Dodd, Mead & Company.

France, Anatole. 1882. *Les Désirs de Jean Servien*. Paris: A. Lemerre.

Galtier, Brigitte. 1997. *L'Écrit des jours. Lire les journaux personnels*. Paris: Honoré Champion.

Goulemot, Jean Marie. 2003. De la lecture comme production de sens. In *Pratiques de la lecture*, ed. Roger Chartier, 119–131. Paris: Payot & Rivages.

James, Alice. 1934. *Alice James, Her Brothers, Her Journal*, ed. Anna Robeson Burr. New York: Dodd, Mead and Company.

———. 1964. *The Diary of Alice James*, ed. Leon Edel. New York: Dodd, Mead & Company.

James, Henry. 1934. In *The Art of the Novel. Critical Prefaces by Henry James*, ed. Richard P. Blackmur. New York/London: Charles Scribner's Sons.

———. 1956. The Art of Fiction (1884) *Longman's Magazine* 4. Reprinted in *The Future of the Novel*, ed. Leon Edel, 3–27. New York: Vintage.

———. 1963. *The Portrait of a Lady (1881)*. New York/London: Penguin.

Lauterbach, Ann. 2011. *The Given and the Chosen*. Richmond: Omnidawn Publishing.

Macé, Marielle. 2011. *Façons de lire, manières d'être*. Paris: Editions du Seuil.

Rancière, Jacques. 2009. La communauté comme dissentiment. In *Et tant pis pour les gens fatigués. Entretiens*, 313–324. Paris: Editions Amsterdam.

Showalter, Elaine. 1987. *The Female Malady: Women Madness and English Culture, 1830–1980*. London: Virago Press.

Strouse, Jean. 1980. *Alice James. A Biography*. Cambridge, MA: Harvard University Press.

CHAPTER 10

Reading as Emancipation in Harriet Ann Jacobs's *Incidents in the Life of a Slave Girl* (1861)

Delphine Louis-Dimitrov

INTRODUCTION

Literacy was a rare and dangerous privilege among slaves in antebellum America, even before slavery anti-literacy laws were passed following the publication of David Walker's abolitionist *Appeal to the Coloured Citizens of the World* in 1829 and Nat Turner's rebellion in 1831. For a slave, the ability to read and write meant intellectual freedom, if not the possibility to gain actual freedom through abolitionist connections. *Incidents in the Life of a Slave Girl* (1861), an autobiographical slave narrative written by Harriet Ann Jacobs (1813–97) under the pseudonym of Linda Brent, explores the redemptive power of reading in its articulation with emancipation. The text fuses different narrative and discursive modes, fictional and non-fictional, to present a life the threads of which are fully interwoven within the canvas of history, the life of a woman who uses her reading skills to fight for freedom and emancipation—from slavery, as well as from cultural and intellectual bondage. This chapter argues that reading turns

D. Louis-Dimitrov (✉)
Institut Catholique de Paris, Paris, France

© The Author(s) 2018
V. Baisnée-Keay et al. (eds.), *Women's Life Writing and the Practice of Reading*, Palgrave Studies in Life Writing,
https://doi.org/10.1007/978-3-319-75247-1_10

out to be the specific site through which the narrator progressively gains her emancipation, a site that materializes into concrete spaces marking the different stages of her fight for freedom. Thus, the forbidden activity of reading creates a secret, mental space of freedom that becomes actualized into the physical space of the small garret in which she remains hidden for nearly seven years, with hardly any other activities than reading and sewing; it further materializes into the free and open space of the North—the site of her enlightenment through reading, and *in fine* of her proper emancipation from slavery—where she finds a home, gets access to libraries and even runs, with her brother, an Anti-Slavery Reading Room. Far from having the contextual value of mere backdrops, such sites are literary spaces where reading progressively articulates with writing to eventually give form to the narrative itself, whereby her emancipation is fulfilled. They are narrative as well as political sites, "unhomely" as Homi Bhabha in "The World and the Home" (1992) writes of spaces that blur the borderline between literature and history, the private and the public, "the home and the world" (141, 148). Linda's progression through those metaphorical and actual spaces of emancipation brings patterns of hybridity, liminality and in-betweenness into play, showing how a marginal and interstitial perspective challenges discourses of racial and cultural domination. I will use Homi Bhabha's postcolonial reflection on processes of cultural hybridization from a minority's interstitial perspective in *The Location of Culture* (1994) to demonstrate that her position gives Jacobs the capacity to contest or interact with authoritative discourses while reinscribing the cultural and literary traditions of the dominant culture. I argue that in bondage first of all, Linda's ability to read turns her into a hybrid figure who reaches beyond her condition to challenge patterns of racial domination. In the intermediate stage of her emancipation, the garret in which she hides forms a liminal space dangerously posited on the borderline between freedom and imprisonment, home and the outside world, redemptive textuality and deadly aphasia. As a complex "in-between" space, the garret nonetheless becomes the breeding ground of a dialogical literary identity eventually fulfilled through authorship once in the North.

THE READING SLAVE: A HYBRID AND LIMINAL FIGURE

Literate slaves were few in antebellum America. The narrator of *Incidents in the Life of a Slave Girl* owes her ability to read—as well as sew—to the benevolent mistress who owned her in childhood between the ages of six and twelve: "While I was with her, she taught me to read and spell; and for this privilege, which so rarely falls to the lot of a slave, I bless her memory" (Jacobs 1987, 8). As often in slave narratives, the acquisition of literacy is a "marker of freedom" (Soto 2009, 34)—of intellectual independence to start with—which singles her out among the slaves; it makes her a prominent figure to whom others turn for instruction, and, as such, an agent of subversion liable to spread political, religious and moral awareness in the community. As Linda points out when an old black man entreats her to teach him how to read, the prohibition of instruction was then an instrument of racial oppression: "it was contrary to law; … slaves were whipped and imprisoned for teaching each other to read" (72). Texts such as newspapers, the Bible and letters play a central part in her own emancipation, giving her access to forbidden sources of meaning and anti-slavery connections.

The reading of newspapers endows Linda with a historical and political understanding which contrasts with the misconceptions of other slaves, who have but "confused notions" of their having allies in the "Free States" (44–5) or believe that the abolitionists have legally made them free already, but that their masters prevent the law from being enforced. Focusing on the example of a slave woman who entreats her to get a newspaper and read it over to her, she denounces the political and historical ignorance that stems from illiteracy:

> She said her husband told her that the black people had sent word to the queen of 'Merica that they were all slaves; that she didn't believe it, and went to Washington city to see the president about it. They quarrelled; she drew her sword upon him, and swore that he should help her to make them all free.

> That poor, ignorant woman thought that America was governed by a Queen, to whom the President was subordinate. I wish the President was subordinate to Queen Justice. (45)

Being a symptom of imposed ignorance, the woman's narrative functions as a tool in the narrator's abolitionist discourse. Taking up the erroneous notion of a Queen governing America, the latter weaves the anecdote into a political indictment of slavery pinpointing not just its lack of justice but also the denial of education. The narrator in that context occupies a dual position, being both the mouthpiece of "[her] sisters who are still in bondage" (29) and an emancipated figure who transcends her condition through her linguistic skills and political instruction. Her hybridity, in

Bhabha's sense, resides in her liminal position. Being both inside and out-side, placing herself both within the community of the slaves and beyond, she stands as a hybrid figure able to reach beyond her original condition and to challenge cultural and discursive boundaries. She contests political power and racial domination from the margin, through a discourse that here integrates the voice of the disempowered.

Just like the reading of newspapers, the slaves' access to the Bible undermines their masters' domination. Religious awareness is indeed an instrument of spiritual resistance liable to crystallize into actual rebellion. As stated in chapter XIII ("The Church and Slavery," 68), it was consid-ered as a threat to the institution of slavery until the Nat Turner insurrec-tion when some carefully framed religious instruction became tolerated for the sake of the masters' own safety. Yet for the old black man who entreats Linda to teach him his "A, B, C" (72), the reading of the Scriptures is first and foremost an instrument of spiritual salvation: "After spelling out a few words, he paused, and said, 'Honey, it 'pears when I can read dis good book I shall be nearer to God. White man is got all de sense. He can larn easy. It ain't easy for ole black man like me. I only wants to read dis book, dat I may know how to live; den I hab no fear 'bout dying'" (73). Beyond the undeniable proximity and complicity of the two slaves, the man's dialectal pronunciation contrasts with the narrator's own standard diction. Its transcription is essentially an instrument of characterization and effect which functions as a linguistic marker of her own education, placing her, for that matter, on an equal footing with white people rather than with other slaves. Linguistic disjunction materializes the distance between her and illiterate slaves, though the narrator of *Incidents* is not consistent in her use of this strategy (reported speech in the previous example was indeed transcribed in standard English, except for "America", reduced to "'Merica"). The rendering of African-American speech rests on several techniques that had by then become staples of Black American dialect writing, such as the use of apostrophe to indicate omission of a let-ter, changes in *th*, etc.[1] Such strategies were essentially to be found in the stereotypical representation of black characters in fiction by white writers, where they sometimes sounded like "phonological caricature" (Holton 1984, 63).[2] Through its contrast with the hegemonic language of the nar-rator and of white protagonists, "Black English" was then "contextualized as at best a source of humor, at worst of condescension or parody" (Simpson 1986, 16–17), as in Brackenridge's *Modern Chivalry* (1792–1815) and Poe's "The Gold-Bug" (1843), or was exploited for local color, as in Stowe's *Uncle Tom's Cabin* (1852). Shelley Fisher Fishkin observes that "an author's decision to have a black character speak in dialect often signalled the limits to the human qualities the novelist was willing to assign him" (Fishkin 1993, 95). African-American writers themselves did not make much use of dialect until Charles W. Chesnutt's stories in the 1880s and Paul Laurence Dunbar's poems in the 1890s (Fishkin 1993, 96). In that context, the transcription of dialect in *Incidents* again reinforces the narrator's "hybridity," creating what Bhabha calls a "difference 'within,' a subject that inhabits the rim of an 'in-between' reality" (Bhabha 1994, 19). As a spokeswoman with a distinct voice, the narrator linguistically sets herself out of the sphere of slaves while remaining essentially alien to the world of masters; she dwells in otherness.

If the Bible and newspapers are potentially subversive reading, the most threatening textual objects for the masters are letters, for they weave networks of human relationships that may lead to rebellion, escape and solidarity towards runaway slaves. Right after the outbreak of the Nat Turner insurrection, as a patrol of brutal "low whites" disrespectfully searches her grandmother's house for incriminating evidence, they come across a text that Linda received from a friend—a poem they mistake for a letter, in any case a sign of literacy and as such a hint at potential subversion. Enraged at her being able to read, and even more at her refusing to follow his orders and yield all her letters, the captain of the patrol loses his temper and inquires: "Who writes to you? half free niggers?", which triggers her biting reply, "O, no; most of my letters are from white people. Some request me to burn them after they are read, and some I destroy without reading" (65–6). The double irony of her retort is that it turns over the humiliating indictment of "half free niggers" into that of lecherous whites, while discrediting the slave-owning aristocratic white males in front of the "low whites" that Linda obviously also despises. Racist drives being here more powerful than social resentment, this only increases their anger so that the soldiers depart pronouncing "a malediction on the house" (66). The humiliation of the white soldiers enacted by Linda as a character is further emphasized by narrative style. As William L. Andrews remarks, it is here "southern whites, not slaves, [who] speak in a dialect removed from dignified English"; besides, the narrator "reconstructs the scene with a freedom approaching that of a caricaturist," transforming the "rampaging 'demons' into bumbling dimwits who are easily made the butts of ridicule" (Andrews 1986, 278–9). Literacy turns out to be the instrument whereby Linda, both as a character and as a narrator, overturns racial hierarchies.

But the slave's literacy is a double-edged tool that the master also makes use of to assert his own power. The end of the passage hints at the dissimulation and slyness of white men, and more precisely at her abusive master's attempted manipulation of her literacy—some of the unread letters being his. When he finds out that Linda can read, Dr. Flint indeed retains his anger and attempts to use her skill to his own purposes. Having failed to seduce Linda through verbal intimidation, he slips notes into her hand to the aim of winning her while circumventing the suspicion of his wife. Her refusal to read those letters is but one aspect of her victory, which resides even more in her ability to potentially weave sentimental relationships that he cannot control: "He knew that I could write, though he had failed to make me read his letters; and he was now troubled lest I should exchange letters with another man" (40). Her literacy for that matter clearly undermines his power. Letters indeed sustain the weaving of an underground network of emancipation, the scope of which is not just political but also sentimental. They create a sphere of privacy that the slave is otherwise denied and that undermines the master's power much more effectively than any other kind of text.

The Garret as Reading Space: Liminality and Emancipation

The activity of reading offers the slave a secret and tiny sphere of freedom and resistance that comes to be materialized by the liminal space of the garret in which she remains hidden for about seven years, as a means of escaping her master's harassment and blackmail before being able to reach the "Free States" of the North. Her "den"[3] is an oppressive place teeming with rats and mice, initially completely devoid of any light and air, so exiguous that she can only "sit or lie in a cramped position" (114). She calls it her "cell" (100, 123, 132, 133, 144, 145), a "prison" (121, 134) and a "dark hole" (131), considers herself, in gothic terms, "the poor captive in her dungeon" (133) and refers to this episode as one of "imprisonment" ("my body still suffers from the effects of that long imprisonment, to say nothing of my soul" [148]), yet she likes it better than slavery and perceives her confinement as a step towards freedom: "I tried to be thankful for my little cell, dismal as it was, and even to love it, as part of the price I had paid for the redemption of my children" (123).

It is a paradoxical place, both a prison and a matrix of freedom, the spot from which her actual escape is contrived. Significantly placed on the borderline of her grandmother's house, in a small shed added to the latter's house, the garret is literally and metaphorically a liminal space, "interstitial" (Green-Barteet 2013), in-between the spheres of slavery and freedom. It is an extraterritorial place neither fully at home nor elsewhere. Its ambivalence encapsulates the "unhomeliness" that Bhabha sees as "the condition of extra-territorial and cross-cultural initiations" (Bhabha 1994, 9). It is a bridge between the private space of home and the public sphere of freedom she perceives through the hole that she bored in the wall, using the gimlet that her uncle had left sticking when he made the trapdoor to her hiding place—a crucial hole only an inch square that allows her moments of "relief to the tedious monotony of [her] life": "My eyes had become accustomed to the dim light, and by holding my book or work in a certain position near the aperture I contrived to read and sew" (116). The hole in the wall is thus a site of enlightenment and redemptive intercourse, the point through which her den opens onto the outside world, visually and textually.

This is in fact the only reference to her reading in that place, but it is a powerful one. What she reads there is not stated in the text, which actually makes the activity of reading a relief in itself, an absolute the value of which does not depend on its object. Through this conciseness and simplicity, the image of the hidden slave reading in her tiny garret becomes an icon of mental emancipation. Unsurprisingly, knowing her thirst for spiritual support and her interest in political and social issues, her biography states that she was reading deeply from the well-worn Bible of her grandmother (who was free) and, when possible, from snippets of newspapers (Yellin 2004, 50). The interconnectedness of reading and sewing ("I contrived to read and sew" [116]) also reveals the connective function of textuality in the slave's life. Reading, like sewing, fastens and binds things together; it here creates the cohesive fabric of emancipation, weaving together the threads of religious and political discourses. Besides, if sewing—contrary to reading—is one of the regular activities of a slave woman, both activities entail a mental space of privacy that slavery cannot reduce—the space of consciousness. Repeatedly in the narrative, needlework proves propitious to reflection or introspection.

While Linda finds relief in such activities, sewing nevertheless cannot be here "a harmonious domestic image" as it usually is in Virginia Woolf's fiction for instance, nor can it link women "across boundaries of race and class" as is does for Mrs. Dalloway and Rezia (Cuddy-Keane 2003, 191). In the context of antebellum America, the figure of the slave woman reading and sewing in her cramped garret ironically evokes and thwarts the stereotypical image of domesticity, one of the four cardinal virtues of the "Cult of True Womanhood" that Barbara Welter identified as a central feature of the dominant patriarchal culture of the period 1820–60.[4] The ideology of domesticity defined the home as women's proper sphere; they were "to keep busy at morally uplifting tasks" and in particular "to master every variety of needlework" for their leisure moments (Welter 1966, 164–5). Sentimental fiction, popular magazines, textbooks and children's novels carefully framed the subject of sewing as "a hobby for females in respectable households" and "an attribute of gentility" (Perry 2006, 53), leaving aside other non-genteel forms of needlework. As for reading, the "Cult of True Womanhood" disapproved of novels, which might "ruin" girls, but permitted the reading of history, religious biography and women's magazines (Welter 1966, 165–6). It essentially encouraged women to read the Bible to their children—a key practice indeed in the Victorian culture of antebellum America, which promoted the association of domesticity and Christianity.[5] Lithographs accordingly pictured women at home peacefully reading the Bible to their children and husbands.[6] Linda likewise sews and reads the Bible, yet slavery makes it impossible for her to fit in the values of "True Womanhood" and separate sphere ideology. The slave woman indeed is denied access to domesticity, having a right neither to a house, nor to matrimonial choice, nor to the fruits of her labor, nor even to her own children; she is only an instrument in the domesticity of others. So, while the feeling of proximity that the narrator attempts to establish with her contemporary female readers may be sustained by her allusion to their common activities, the image of the slave reading and sewing in the garret is rich in critical potentialities. It comes into ironical contrast with the stereotypes of domesticity and challenges the "Cult of True Womanhood," proving it to be a cultural and ideological artifact in spite of its essentialist positioning.

The garret is not just an extraterritorial place located between the private and public realms and between freedom and imprisonment; it is also posited on the edge of life and death, threatening language itself as well as the viability of texts. The wretchedness of her life conditions in the small garret impedes Linda from carrying on her reading and sewing when winter comes, for the cold is such that she can only lie wrapped up in her blankets, freezing. No longer able to sit at her loophole to read and sew and to spy on people, she loses all agency and connection with the world and becomes engulfed in darkness. The second winter, the cold literally drives her to paralysis and aphasia: "My limbs were benumbed by inaction, and the cold filled them with cramp. I had a very painful sensation of coldness in my head; even my face and tongue stiffened, and I lost the power of speech" (122). The inability to speak is for sure a result of physical distress and of sensory deprivation; but it is also a symbol, a sign of the life-threatening failure of language in such conditions of physical and mental confinement. Deprived of any verbal or textual intercourse, she becomes fully engulfed in spiritual obscurity: "I was left with my own thoughts—starless as the midnight darkness around me" (127). Imprisonment within the cell of the self is a mental ordeal that significantly leads her to a state of delirium and to loss of consciousness, on the verge of death. She only manages to fight on for the sake of freedom, planning to take her children North (127).

As a mental prison, the garret stands in ironical contrast with the private space that Virginia Woolf calls for in *A Room of One's Own* as a requirement for a woman's literary creativity— a "silent, private" room with "a lock on the door" and enough money to support herself (Woolf 2015, 176, 79). Exposing the limits of this theory in a passage of *In Search of our Mothers' Gardens*, Alice Walker observes that it does not account for the creativity of slave women burdened with domestic chores, for whom literature was barely conceivable: "What then are we to make of Phillis Wheatley, a slave, who owned not even herself?", she asks (Walker 1983, 235). Taking up Virginia Woolf's notion of "contrary instincts" thwarting and hindering literary creativity—a euphemism for slaves afflicted with "chains, guns, the lash, the ownership of one's body by someone else, submission to an alien religion" (Walker 1983, 235)—Walker claims that the source of creativity for slave women who produced literature in spite of their oppressive life conditions is to be sought elsewhere.[7] As distant as it is from a writer's study or from other protective sites of artistic creation, Linda's garret is nonetheless a literary space in which reading articulates with writing, making her emancipation from slavery and patriarchy possible.

FROM READING TO WRITING: FORGING A DIALOGICAL LITERARY IDENTITY

As a complex in-between space, Linda's "loophole of retreat" (114) is the breeding ground of a dialogical literary identity in the sense that it is produced as a mode of fight and contestation and retains a hybrid quality. As Bhabha observes, "in-between" spaces, being sites of cultural difference, "provide the terrain for elaborating strategies of selfhood—singular or communal—that initiate new signs of identity". Subjects, like communities, are formed "in-between," where "the exchange of values [and] meanings ... may not always be collaborative and dialogical, but may be profoundly antagonistic [and] conflictual" (Bhabha 1994, 2). The garret as a liminal and interstitial space is indeed a site of exchange, redefinition and emancipation. Linda's dialogical and antagonistic relationship with the space of slavery beneath the garret takes the form of an epistolary war with her master whereby she makes a first step towards authorship. Seeing that after several years he still has not given her up and is laying traps for her to come back to her grandmother's home,[8] she resolves to "match [her] cunning against his cunning" (128) and writes him a letter dated from New York, using a newspaper "to ascertain the names of some of the streets" and resorting to her network of friends and relatives to have it "put in the post office there" (128). The device also includes a fake letter she writes to her grandmother asking her to send her children to her in the North, which she knows will first be read by Dr. Flint (128–9). The dialogical quality of her intercourse with the slaveholding world is materialized by the use—and instrumentalization—of a pro-slavery newspaper as a tool of emancipation: "I seated myself near the little aperture to examine the newspaper. It was a piece of the New York Herald; and, for once, the paper that systematically abuses the colored people, was made to render them a service" (128). The opening in the wall becomes a point of contact between the sphere of emancipation within the attic and the slaveholding world outside—the site through which the newspaper's values, meaning and identity circulate and become redefined.

Linda's ploy triggers an epistolary contest (a "competition in cunning" [128]) in which the slave girl keeps the upper hand, since she is never fooled by Dr. Flint's letters while he is fooled by hers. The garret becomes the war cell from which she manipulates him into believing that she has gone North. Setting her a trap in his turn, Dr. Flint reads a fake letter to her grandmother, saying that she desperately wants to come back home, in hope to have Linda's grandmother and uncle bring her back: "He broke the seal, and I heard him read it. The old villain! He had suppressed the letter I wrote to grandmother, and prepared a substitute of his own" (130). In this instance as well as later on in the North where the epistolary duel continues, she proves to be a skilful literary critic able to decipher her master's letters, to understand his hidden purposes and to unmask him through his writing style when he uses a persona like his daughter's name to fool her. In this literary fight—her first step towards literary authorship—Linda's critical reading skills become an instrument of survival.

The epistolary war she wages on her master from her garret bears a theatrical quality, as she comically leads him astray to different places in search for a slave girl hidden at home. Like a stage director, she stands off stage and, as Yellin puts it, directs the performance, manipulating Dr. Flint and watching him play the fool (Introduction to *Incidents*, xxviii). As with Cassy in the garret episode of *Uncle Tom's Cabin* (1852), the contest results in a "carnivalesque" power reversal in Bakhtinian terms (Bakhtin 1984) with the trickster-like slave girl controlling the master, overthrowing culturally constructed hierarchies of race and gender.[9] Linda's authorial power is a retort to her master's vain attempts at asserting his own power on her through letters and then other pieces of writing, the "wanted" posters in which he defines her through her literacy—"she can read and write" (97). The fight between master and slave is indeed a matter of reading and writing; it rests on the power of written language.

Like the well-known "madwoman in the attic" of Victorian literature, Linda—though far from mad—is a rebel who defies, threatens and humiliates white patriarchy. Quite significantly, one of the books that she reads once in the North is *Jane Eyre* (1847) (Yellin 2004, 145), in which Bertha Mason, locked up in the attic by her husband, was to become the archetype of the woman-in-the-attic pattern (Gilbert and Gubar 2000, xii). Though dramatization of captivity and escape in Linda's case goes well beyond the symbolic dimension the pattern entails for most nineteenth-century female protagonists, her emancipation is first enacted on a textual mode. Like Victorian women writers figuratively trapped in the fangs of patriarchal power, she fights back with literary weapons, primarily through the epistolary relationship in which she catches her master.

Her thinking of herself in gothic terms as "the poor captive in her dungeon" (133) is unsurprising considering the prominent role of intertextuality in her writing, a sign of the narrator's broad reading. The figure of the narrator as reader is implicitly present throughout the book, delineated through numerous allusions to other texts, whether literary, historical or religious. Leaving aside the iconic figure of the slave woman poring over the Bible in the garret, the image of the reader only becomes fully actualized in chapter XXXIII ("A Home Found"), lightly sketched through the allusion to the redemptive "enlighten[ment]"[10] the first Mrs. Bruce, for whom she works as a nurse, offers her in New York after her effective flight from slavery: "My narrow mind also began to expand under the influences of her intelligent conversation, and the opportunities for reading, which were gladly allowed me whenever I had leisure from my duties. I gradually became more energetic and more cheerful" (169). In contrast with the oppression of slavery and captivity in the garret, the enlightenment she finds in her new home allows her mind to widen out. As Bhabha writes of Henry James's heroine Isabel Archer in a fully different context, "the world" for Linda "first shrinks ... and then expands enormously" (Bhabha 1992, 141)—an expansion that largely results from her literary initiation. Foster notes that the Willis [Bruce] home was "a gathering place of the New York literati," as Nathaniel Willis was brother to the best-selling novelist Fanny Fern and a prominent editor and author in his own right. As a servant, Jacobs was consequently familiar with the white literary establishment and silently "absorb[ed] the critical questions and details of literary production" (Foster 1993, 101). Although what she reads during that period is not stated in the text, it comes out through the numerous intertextual allusions interspersed in the narrative and through the influences stamped on her style.

The literary identity that takes shape in the book is a hybrid one, dialogical in its incorporation of other texts and genres. The text's "hybridity" in Bhabha's sense depends on the "on-going negotiation" of cultural difference. "The 'right' to signify from the periphery of authorized power and privilege," Bhabha explains, "is resourced by the power of tradition to be reinscribed through the conditions of contingency and contradictoriness that attend upon the lives of those who 'are in the minority'" (Bhabha 1994, 3). In other words, Jacobs's ability to speak from the margin and come in dialogical contact with the dominant culture depends on the possibility for literary tradition to be reshaped through new contextualization. The narrator frequently reads her own experience through a literary prism, using literary references as paradigms for the events of her life. She, for instance, compares her joy to Robinson Crusoe's when she finds the gimlet that will allow her to dig a hole in the wall of her garret: "I was as rejoiced as Robinson Crusoe could have been at finding such a treasure" (115). Hinting at Bunyan's allegorical "City of Destruction," she calls New York the "City of Iniquity" (199) because it serves as a hub for the hunting of fugitive slaves, thus casting an allegorical dimension on a historical situation. Linda's "loophole of retreat," an emblem of her emancipation in the dialogical space of the garret, is itself a dialogical phrase testifying to the multilayered quality of her language. Initially borrowed from "The Task" (1785), a poem by William Cowper, an evangelist and preromantic writer who supported the abolitionist movement, the phrase was quoted in an African-American column of New York's *Freedom's Journal* in 1838.[11] Intertextuality also provides a figurative dimension to her own experience, as when she quotes Mary Howitt's fable-like lines from "the Spider and the Fly" to comment upon the letter slyly sent by Dr. Flint's daughter (187), using the image of the spider's web as a metaphor for her captivity: "'Come up into my parlor,' said the spider to the fly; / 'Tis the prettiest little parlor that ever you did spy'" (187). Conversely, the original images of the "City of Destruction," the "loophole of retreat" and the spider's web acquire an additional layer of meaning within the context of slavery. For Stover, the Bakhtinian concept of "heteroglossia" (Bakhtin 1981) aptly accounts for the intertextual quality of Jacobs's narrative, whereby the meaning of assimilated texts is altered by their integration within a new historical context (Stover 2003, 138–9).

Beyond its specific intertextual references, the narrative incorporates various literary traditions ranging from Puritan autobiography and jeremiad to sentimental fiction and the dime novels of the nineteenth-century. The use of novelistic conventions as an instrument of persuasion tends to blur generic boundaries, lending an appearance of fiction to a narrative which she otherwise claims to be a straightforward, autobiographical account of her life: "I have My dear friend—Striven faithfully to give a true and just account of my own life in Slavery" (letter to Amy Post, June 21, 1857, quoted by Yellin 2004, 135). Taking up the traditional, initially Puritan view of autobiography as a form of testimony, she attempts to include her readers in a community of experience so as to make them aware of the reality of slavery: "I want to add my testimony to that of abler pens to convince the people of the Free States what Slavery really is. Only by experience can any one realize how deep, and dark, and foul is that pit of abominations" (*Preface by the Author*, 1–2). Contrary to the other most prominent African-American female writers of the antebellum period (Jarena Lee, Zilpha Elaw, Nancy Prince, Harriet E. Wilson, Frances

E.W. Harper), she explicitly targets women, whom she desires "to arouse … to a realizing sense of the condition of two millions of women at the South, still in bondage" (1) (Foster 1993, 83). Blending the codes of Puritan narratives with the conventions of seduction novels and the melodramatic style of the dime novels that were then flooding the market,[12] she recurrently makes confessions, deplores her moral failings and presents herself to be judged by the reader, appealing for compassion and forgiveness:

> Pity me, and pardon me, O virtuous reader! You never knew what it is to be a slave; to be entirely unprotected by law or custom; to have the laws reduce you to the condition of a chattel, entirely subject to the will of another. … I know I did wrong. … The painful and humiliating memory will haunt me to my dying day. Still, in looking back, calmly, on the events of my life, I feel that the slave woman ought not to be judged by the same standard as others. (55–6)

While confessing to her moral failings, Jacobs eventually diverts the blame to place it on slavery. Novelistic conventions meanwhile participate in a narrative and rhetorical strategy of seduction, leading her white female readers to experience empathy and moral proximity with her in spite of her failings and of the irreducible difference in their life conditions, a purpose that has been repeatedly emphasized by critics: she thus "challenge[s] her audience's unwillingness to accept the authority of a slave speaker" (Gunning 1996, 133) and attempts to create a "bond of sisterhood" (Stover 2003, 134) between these white female readers and herself, to write "across the color line" as she "mediate[s] between the races" and asserts that they have "mutual concerns" (Foster 1993, 96). Here, as in many other instances, her melodramatic and confessional style intersects with the abolitionist discourse which is the proper purpose of her narrative.

Jacobs's struggle for emancipation once achieved in life goes on textually, for the sake of her "sisters" still "in bondage" (29). To this aim, *Incidents* is interspersed with long abolitionist developments—sometimes full-length chapters—instructing the Northern reader on slavery-related issues like religious practice (for instance, chapter XIII, "The Church and Slavery") or discussing such events as the Nat Turner insurrection (chapter XII, "Fear of Insurrection") and the 1850 Fugitive Slave Law (chapter XL). Reaching beyond the scope of literature, intertextuality here again plays a central part. Jacobs's abolitionist language was essentially shaped through her reading of the weekly anti-slavery press and of the political writings her brother John and his activist circle introduced her to in the North (Yellin 2004, 101, 145), especially in the Anti-Slavery Office and Reading Room she briefly ran with him in Rochester, a city which abolitionists endeavored to make a regional hub of the movement. Situated on the second floor of Frederick Douglass's office for *The North Star*, the place supplied free reading materials (books and pamphlets, works dealing essentially with slavery and other moral questions) to activists and reformers, who would meet there regularly to gain information in regard to the progress of their cause and discuss political and moral issues like slavery. Women more specifically would gather there on Thursdays "to sew, knit, read, and talk for the cause" (Yellin 2004, 102)—another revealing connection, here extradiegetic, between reading, sewing and weaving a network of emancipation.

Though *Incidents* but briefly alludes to this place—essentially to point out its failure (189)—Jacobs herself drew much profit from her reading and her political connections, which included such prominent abolitionists as Frederick Douglass and Amy and Isaac Post. In spite of its failure and of the 1850 Fugitive Slave Act, which makes the North (as she writes about Massachusetts more specifically) "a 'nigger hunter' for the [S]outh" (131), the Anti-Slavery Reading Room of Rochester is a figuration of a free reading space, the open and public counterpart to the confined hiding place of the garret where she read on her own. The letters that she then penned in secret develop into the open letters that she now publishes in *The New York Daily Tribune* as a prelude to her slave narrative—cautiously but eloquently signing herself "A Fugitive Slave" in the first letter (June 21, 1853) and "Fugitive" in the second one (July 25, 1853) (Yellin 2004, 122–3).

Literary authorship remained a challenge for Jacobs in her lifetime and beyond. Though the subtitle states that the book was "Written by Herself," the 1861 title page bears not her name but that of the editor, Lydia Maria Child, a white woman and prominent abolitionist writer who accepted to provide the preface that was required by publishers after Harriet Beecher Stowe had refused (Yellin 2004, 119–21). The black woman who struggled her way to freedom and authorship textually retreats behind the editorial presence of the white woman mentioned on the title page, while remaining hidden throughout the text behind the mask of her fictitious persona, Linda Brent. As a result, for most of the twentieth century the academic consensus was that the book had been written by Lydia Maria

Child; it was accordingly considered as biography, if not as fiction in the guise of autobiography—a feeling that was reinforced by the novelistic style of some passages. Jacobs's authorship, in fact, was not established until the 1980s, when her biographer, Jean Fagan Yellin, discovered an illuminating bunch of letters she had exchanged with Lydia Maria Child (Yellin 2004, xvi–xvii). The long-lasting denial of Jacobs's authorship among readers and critics ironically runs counter to the crucial process of emancipation that articulates reading with writing and only becomes fully accomplished with the publication of the book itself.

CONCLUSION

As a form of resistance, enlightenment and empowerment, reading is the slave's primary act of emancipation from slavery. Linda's capacity to break the chains of slavery comes to maturity in the literary space of written texts—books, letters and newspapers. Way beyond the topos of the slave's emancipating literacy, reading here materializes into literal and figurative spaces, from the liminal space of the garret, where readability is reduced to its last extremity, to the Anti-Slavery Reading Room and, more broadly, the whole space of (semi-)freedom in the North where books are bountiful and freely available. It is eventually with two last items of reading that Linda obtains freedom, the first one a newspaper saved from fire announcing the arrival of Dr. Flint's family in New York obviously to bring her back to slavery (196–7), the second one a brief letter from the new Mrs. Bruce which, as a consequence thereof, informs her of her newly paid-for freedom (199–200). The persona's emancipation from slavery in the last chapter of the text remains ambivalent, however, for Linda objects to her being *sold* into freedom—which, to her now enlightened mind, amounts to a perpetuation of the logic of slavery—before discarding this note of failure and frustration to eventually celebrate freedom, regardless of the way it was obtained and of its ironically stated restrictions: "Reader, my story ends with freedom; not in the usual way, with marriage. I and my children are now free! We are as free from the power of slaveholders as are the white people of the north; and though that, according to my ideas, is not saying a great deal, it is a vast improvement in *my* condition" (201). In contrast to the expectations of sentimental fiction, the narrative claims to find its accomplishment in the long-fought-for emancipation of the heroine and her children, thereby identifying itself first and foremost as a slave narrative—

but a female one, offering a model fully distinct in its stakes from the *Narrative of the Life of Frederick Douglass, an American Slave* (1845) and other male slave narratives. While humbly presenting itself through its title as a sequence of anecdotal, unimportant events—an obvious understatement considering the historical and political reach of the text—*Incidents* emphasizes the female identity of the slave, a mere "slave girl" who fights to become a free woman. For what is at stake in the book is the narrator's emancipation as a slave and as a woman, simultaneously and inextricably. Instead of the domestic fulfillment prescribed by the "Cult of True Womanhood" and even of the alternative ideal of "Real Womanhood,"[13] the ending proudly presents a woman's victory over slavery, which also entails a textual, generic act of emancipation from "usual" women literature. However, what the narrator presents as her emancipation from the ideology of domesticity adds yet another level of ambiguity to the ending of the text, for the persona's "dream of [her] life" remains a domestic one, as yet unfulfilled: "The dream of my life is not yet realized. I do not sit with my children in a home of my own. I still long for a hearthstone of my own, however humble. I wish it for my children's sake far more than for my own" (201). The persona/narrator thus fully frees herself neither from slavery nor from the ideology of domesticity. Emancipation nevertheless is fulfilled on a literary mode, through authorship. In fact, her real emancipation is not achieved until she writes her autobiography and converts herself from the object she was as a slave into author. Her actual emancipation is a literary one: the very writing of her autobiography is a "painful" (201) but empowering process whereby she writes herself into freedom, creating a dialogical literary identity which incorporates various genres and traditions. More meaningful yet than the title itself is therefore the subtitle "Written by Herself," a powerful expression of her literary emancipation.

NOTES

1. As Fishkin points out, McDowell credits Cooper with introducing techniques that would become staples of American dialect writing, such as "the apostrophe to indicate omission of a letter" (McDowell 1929, 294, quoted by Fishkin 1993, 94; 192).
2. Holton here refers to Brackenridge's representation of "Black English" in *Modern Chivalry.*
3. She repeatedly calls her hiding-place a "den" (114, 115, 116, 120, 122, 126, 140, 141, 148, 149, 150, 153, 165, 170).

4. The four tenets of "True Womanhood" are piety, purity, submissiveness and domesticity (Welter 1966, 152).

5. Colleen McDannell writes that "The Cult of True Womanhood promoted the association between domesticity and Christianity to the extent that mothers were considered to hold the key to the salvation of their children" ("Victorian Bibles," in Laderman and Léon 2003, 429). Mothers would gather their children and peacefully read the Bible to them, hence the importance of family Bibles in the Victorian home as a "critical element in domestic worship and maternal instruction" (430).

6. See, for instance, "Young woman reading the Bible". Lithograph, c. 1848 (Library of Congress). Reproduced in Laderman and Léon 2003, 430.

7. Her hypothesis is that the "creative spark" was handed down to them by their mothers and grandmothers (Walker 1983, 240).

8. "Every now and then he would say to my grandmother that I would yet come back, and voluntarily surrender myself; and that when I did, I could be purchased by my relatives, or any one who wished to buy me. I knew his cunning nature too well not to perceive that this was a trap laid for me" (128).

9. Benjamin writes that "From Joel Chandler Harris's Aunt Nancy to Harriet Jacobs's Linda Brent, the folkloric and symbolic emergence of the black female trickster points to an alternative trickster tradition where women complement the work of their male counterparts" (Benjamin 2009, 51).

10. "The more my mind had become enlightened, the more difficult it was for me to consider myself an article of property" (199).

11. William Cowper, "The Task", IV. 88–90: "'Tis pleasant, through the loopholes of retreat, / To peep at such a world, —to see the stir / Of the great Babel, and not feel the crowd". As Yellin points out, Jacobs was not the first African-American to borrow Cowper's phrase. It was used as an epigraph to "The Curtain," a column in *Freedom's Journal* (New York) in 1838. *Incidents*, note 1 to chapter XXI, 277.

12. The use of conventions of sentimental fiction in *Incidents* has been studied by many critics. See, for instance, Yellin (2004), Foster (1993), Patton (2000) and Stover (2003).

13. Cogan defines "Real Womanhood" as a competing ideal to "True Womanhood" among middle-class American women in the mid-nineteenth century. "Real womanhood" was "a survival ethics" promoting "intelligence, physical fitness and health, self-sufficiency, economic self-reliance, and careful marriage" (Cogan 1989, 4).

REFERENCES

Andrews, William L. 1986. *To Tell a Free Story: The First Century of Afro-American Autobiography, 1760–1865*. Urbana: University of Illinois Press.

Bakhtin, Mikhail. 1981. *The Dialogic Imagination: Four Essays*. Ed. Michael Holquist, trans. Caryl Emerson and Michael Holquist. Austin: University of Texas Press.

———. 1984. *Rabelais and His World*. Trans. Hélène Iswolsky. Bloomington: Indiana University Press.

Benjamin, Shanna Greene. 2009. A Trickster in Transition. In *Loopholes and Retreats: African American Writers and the Nineteenth Century*, ed. John Cullen Gruesser and Hanna Wallinger, 45–58. Münster: Lit Verlag.

Bhabha, Homi K. 1992. The World and the Home. *Social Text* 31/32: 141–153.

———. 1994. *The Location of Culture*. New York: Routledge.

Cogan, Frances. 1989. *All-American Girl: The Ideal of Real Womanhood in Mid-Nineteenth Century America*. Athens/London: The University of Georgia Press.

Cuddy-Keane, Melba. 2003. *Virginia Woolf, the Intellectual and the Public Sphere*. Cambridge (UK)/New York: Cambridge University Press.

Fishkin, Shelley Fisher. 1993. *Was Huck Black? Mark Twain and African American Voices*. New York/Oxford: Oxford University Press.

Foster, Frances Smith. 1993. *Written by Herself: Literary Production by African American Women, 1746–1892*. Bloomington/Indianapolis: Indiana University Press.

Gilbert, Sandra M., and Susan Gubar. 2000. *The Madwoman in the Attic: The Woman Writer and the Nineteenth-Century Literary Imagination*. 2nd ed. New Haven/ London: Yale University Press.

Green-Barteet, Miranda A. 2013. 'The Loophole of Retreat': Interstitial Spaces in Harriet Jacobs's *Incidents in the Life of a Slave Girl*. *South Central Review* 30 (2): 53–72.

Gunning, Sandra. 1996. Reading and Redemption in *Incidents in the Life of a Slave Girl*. In *Harriet Jacobs and Incidents in the Life of a Slave Girl: New Critical Essays*, ed. Deborah M. Garfield and Rafia Zafar, 131–155. Cambridge (UK)/New York: Cambridge University Press.

Holton, Sylvia Wallace. 1984. *Down Home and Uptown: The Representation of Black Speech in American Fiction*. Rutherford: Fairleigh Dickinson University Press.

Jacobs, Harriet Ann. 1987. *Incidents in the Life of a Slave Girl, Written by Herself* (1861). Ed. Jean Fagan Yellin. Cambridge, MA: Harvard University Press.

Laderman, Gary, and Luis Léon, eds. 2003. *Religion and American Cultures: An Encyclopedia of Traditions, Diversity and Popular Expressions*. Vol. 2. Santa Barbara: ABC-Clio.

McDowell, Tremaine. 1929. Notes on Negro Dialect in the American Novel to 1821. *American Speech* 5 (1): 291–296.

Patton, Venetria K. 2000. *Women in Chains: The Legacy of Slavery in Black Women's Fiction*. Albany: State University of New York.

Perry, Claire. 2006. *Young America: Childhood in 19th-Century Art and Culture*. New Haven/London: Yale University Press.

Simpson, David. 1986. *The Politics of American English, 1776–1850*. New York: Oxford University Press.

Soto, Isabel. 2009. 'The Spaces Left': Ambivalent Discourses in Harriet Jacobs and Frederick Douglass. In *Loopholes and Retreats: African American Writers and the Nineteenth Century*, ed. John Cullen Gruesser and Hanna Wallinger, 31–42. Münster: Lit Verlag.

Stover, Johnnie M. 2003. Nineteenth-Century African American Women's Autobiography as Social Discourse: The Example of Harriet Ann Jacobs. *College English* 66 (2): 133–154.

Walker, Alice. 1983. *In Search of Our Mothers' Gardens: Womanist Prose*. New York: Harcourt Brace Jovanovich.

Welter, Barbara. 1966. The Cult of True Womanhood: 1820–1860. *American Quarterly* 18 (2): 151–174.

Woolf, Virginia. 2015. *A Room of One's Own*. In *A Room of One's Own and Three Guineas (1929)*. Oxford: Oxford University Press.

Yellin, Jean Fagan. 2004. *Harriet Ann Jacobs: A Life*. New York: Basic Civitas Books.

CHAPTER 11

Hannah Crafts' Dialogizing Autobiography, *The Bondwoman's Narrative*

Josette Spartacus

INTRODUCTION

The Bondwoman's Narrative by Hannah Crafts is a crux in many ways. Henry Louis Gates Jr. bought the manuscript in 2001, published it in 2002, and dozens of scholars have tried to unravel the enigma which surrounds what might be termed the "proto-novel" of African-American writing since then. There is still a shroud of mystery around this narrative since to this day no one knows who "Hannah Crafts" (the name on the manuscript) was. A book of critical essays on the manuscript entitled *In Search of Hannah Crafts* (2004) proposes different and sometimes divergent analyses of this text, even if all assume that *The Bondwoman's Narrative* was written between 1856 and 1861 by a black female author.[1] Gates explains that the writer was afraid of being caught if identified, as evidenced by a reference to a character called Wheeler: "Hannah Crafts was living in the gravest danger of being discovered by Wheeler and returned to her enslavement under the Fugitive Slave Act" (Gates 2003, lxii; lxxiii).[2] Slavery was still thriving in the South and had not completely

J. Spartacus (✉)
Lycée Malherbe, Caen, France

© The Author(s) 2018
V. Baisnée-Keay et al. (eds.), *Women's Life Writing
and the Practice of Reading*, Palgrave Studies in Life Writing,
https://doi.org/10.1007/978-3-319-75247-1_11

disappeared in the North. Yet it seems that the desire to write was stronger than the danger, fear and anxiety of being discovered and sent back to slavery.

The full title of the manuscript reads as follows: *The Bondwoman's Narrative by Hannah Crafts, a Fugitive Slave Recently Escaped from North Carolina*. As such, it defines a horizon of expectation for the reader, which Philippe Lejeune calls an autobiographical pact between the author and the reader (Lejeune 1996, 26). The reader is told she is about to read a slave narrative, written by a former slave named Hannah Crafts. However, we are faced here with an *incognegro* writer, so to speak. Hannah Crafts' manuscript was not edited by any editor, it was not adapted to the usual slave narrative readership, and was not preceded by the kind of paratext slave narratives were usually fitted with.[3] It therefore did not contain any foreword by a famous editor or well-known person vouching for its authenticity, i.e., its autobiographical, rather than fictional, nature. Crafts was an interstitial author who eluded identification, and escaped the constraints of the mediation and authority of an amanuensis editor, as well as the constraints of the traditional slave narrative. In other words, her manuscript shows her to be free from any bonds. My contention is that Hannah Crafts' narrative illustrates the concept of "novelized black autobiographies," or "dialogizing autobiographies," William Andrews puts forward:

> … we must pay attention to the fact that novelized black autobiographies take an increasingly revisionist attitude toward authority of all kinds, moral, social, intellectual and aesthetic. Dialogizing autobiographies in novel ways may very well have arisen out of doubts about the capacity of the slave narrative in its traditional form to render certain aspects of reality in an authoritative way. (Andrews 1986, 276)

According to Andrews, by the mid-nineteenth century "self-expressiveness preside[d] over retrospective mimesis" in black autobiographies such as Douglass's and Jacobs', because of these writers' "commitment to the ideal of freedom" (280), which was "a characteristics of their style of writing" (280). My contention is that Hannah Crafts chose a specific form of life writing, a dialogizing autobiography relying on nineteenth-century writers, the Bible, and the romance and Gothic genres, in order to convey one message—namely that she "was not a slave," as she herself put it (Crafts 2003, 17), whoever she was. If we assume that Hannah Crafts was a Black woman and a former slave, we can assume that her choice of a dialogizing novelized autobiography to write her life enabled her to render certain aspects of reality in a novel, authoritative way, as Andrews puts it. If Hannah Crafts was a white woman's *nom de plume* (which no scientific evidence allows us to ascertain, even if the text contains clues that are not incompatible with this possibility), her aim could have been to author a text with a feminist message of freedom. The text and the scientific evidence we possess on Hannah Crafts having been a black woman are my starting points.

NINETEENTH CENTURY NOVELS AND THE "TALKING BOOK TROPE"

Hannah Crafts' life narrative illustrates the "talking book trope" Henry Gates identifies as crucial in Afro-American life writing (Gates 1988, 136–138). The genesis of the talking book trope dates back from the narrative of Ukawsaw Gronniosaw, first published in 1772, in which the slave's desire to hear a book speak to him the way a book seems to talk to his master, is crushed.[4] The narrative of the slave who understands that the book does not speak to him because he is black, also points to the absence of books that speak about him. So Gronniosaw writes a book that "speaks his face into existence among the authors and texts of the Western tradition" (Gates 1988, 137–138). Gates' argument is that Gronniosaw's desire to read and write is what triggered the autobiographical tradition in Afro-American writing.

Two rather obvious examples of intertextuality show that Hannah Crafts found her voice by borrowing from nineteenth-century writers and integrating their narrative voices into a dialogic novelized autobiography. Hannah Crafts, who, as her narrative shows, was well read, used the literary canon to which she had access[5] to write a book that would appeal to both black and white readers. A first crucial instance of Crafts' borrowing from the canon is to be found in the third chapter in which she appropriates a reading scene from Charlotte Brontë's *Jane Eyre*. Hannah (the protagonist) is hiding behind a window curtain, sitting on what may appear as a window-seat, and reading by stealth:

> My mistress was very kind, and unknown to my master she indulged me in reading whenever I desired. The next morning I descended to the parlor, and seated myself with a book behind the heavy damask curtains that shaded the window. In this situation I was entirely concealed. In a few moments the echo of a light footsteps [sic] was heard on the stair; then the door opened, and mistress entered. (Crafts 2003, 37)

There is no doubt that the reading scene was inspired from the scene in *Jane Eyre* in which Jane slips into the small breakfast room adjoining the drawing room, and mounts into the window-seat to read, hidden behind the curtain (Brontë 1996, 14).[6] When Jane overhears a conversation, she leaves her hiding place to speak for herself, shouting at the 14-year-old boy whom she has to call "Master Reed": "'Wicked and cruel boy!' I said. 'You are like a murderer—you are like a *slave-driver*—you are like the Roman emperors!'" (17, my italics). The word "slave-driver" suggests a similarity of predicament between Jane and Hannah: this is a particular instance of "heteroglossia" as Crafts appropriates the situation and diegesis of another writer to inflate it with her own intention (i.e., to write about slavery). However, Hannah Crafts makes Hannah stronger than Brontë's heroine: while Jane Eyre exposes herself and is sent away to Lowood after this, Hannah remains in her hiding place, which enables her to overhear a whole conversation. She acquires an "omniscient view" which provokes *her* decision to flee. Thus, and this is a recurring device,[7] Crafts turns Hannah into a "typical hero[ine] of romance," since Hannah is "superior in degree to other men [women] and to his [her]environment" (Frye 1973, 33).

Crafts' chapter thirteen starts with a description of Washington which borrows heavily from the incipit of Dickens's *Bleak House*,[8] from its structure to its rhythm:

> Washington, the Federal City. Christmas holidays recently over. The implacable winter weather. The great President of the great Republic looks perhaps from the windows of his drawing room, and wonders at the mud and slush precisely as an ordinary mortal would. … Gloom everywhere. Gloom up the Potomac; where it rolls among meadows no longer green, and by splendid country seats. Gloom down the Potomac where it washes the sides of huge warships. (Crafts 2003, 161–62)

Blurring geographical boundaries, Crafts turns the English capital into the American capital, the Lord Chancellor into the President, the English river into an American river, and fog into gloom, thus creating a narrative that speaks to her and about her. The similarities between the two "beginnings" (the incipit of *Bleak House* and Hannah's arrival in Washington at the beginning of chapter thirteen) not only signal re-appropriation of someone else's words (heteroglossia), but also suggest that Hannah Crafts sees herself as a critical eye/I, a critical observer of life and people. She sees herself on a par with Dickens's narrator. In both cases (Dickens and Brontë) Hannah Crafts is at the same time within the "talking book trope" as defined by Gates, and inside her own heteroglossia. The third phenomenon she adds is her femininity, black or white, since she could pass off as white.

THE BIBLE: A DIALOGIC EVIDENCE OF FREEDOM

Crafts also dialogizes her narrative through biblical allusions to the stories of David and Jacob, which enables her to offer her views on freedom and slavery. In her preface, the author reveals that her text is a "record of plain unvarnished facts," which further ascertains the autobiographical principle of the venture as announced by the full title, *The Bondwoman's Narrative by Hannah Crafts, a Fugitive Slave Recently Escaped from North Carolina*. However, the preface also claims that the narrative is a confrontation between the righteous and the wicked, and must be read by adopting a moral viewpoint: "Being the truth it makes no pretentions to romance, and relating events as they occurred it has no especial reference to a moral, but … [those] of pious and discerning minds can scarcely fail to recognize the hand of Providence in giving to the righteous the reward of their works, and to the wicked the fruit of their doings" (Crafts 2003, 4).

In other words, Crafts places her narrative at a crossroads between three kinds of narratives: a slave's narrative, a novel, and the genre of the romance in which retribution is granted. Hers is a story that is neither fancy nor reality, neither truth nor fiction but which is akin to belief, whether it be for the unbelievers or the believers. Hence the crucial role of her biblical allusions through which Hannah Crafts "dialogizes" her narrative in order to deliver her authorial message—that she is not a slave. Crafts' narrative comprises 21 chapters, with all but three of the chapters headed by a quotation from the Bible. Of these eighteen quotations,[9] two are from Psalms, three are from "Solomon" and six from David. As David was Solomon's father and the alleged author of the Psalms, 11 of the 18 quotations are centred on David, the shepherd who was chosen by God first to soothe King Saul's ailments with his songs and his harp, and who became King after Saul's death. He was a poet, a musician and a successful warrior who killed Goliath with a sling and a stone. David was also the founder of Israel through a covenant with God, as clearly stated in the Book of Samuel.[10]

Crafts uses David's story to point out that once a person is chosen by God, he or she is protected by Providence without his or her personal intervention, provided he or she can pray and believe. This enables Crafts to redefine slavery as lack of belief. In *The Bondwoman's Narrative* Hannah is literally chosen and repeatedly rewarded, which also signals the mode of romance. Thus, the child who desperately wants to be able to read is approached by a gentle old woman who teaches her how to read in the neat little cottage she shares with her beloved husband. This lasts for what appears to be a few years and the little girl believes that she has found a place forever: "How I wished to be with them all the time—how I entreated them to buy me, but in vain. They had not the means" (Crafts 2003, 10). At this stage, she does not wish for freedom but for another mistress, which will also happen several years later after the death of her mistress. A good many pages are devoted to the trials and tribulations of Hannah who, with her mistress, flee in order to escape from the clutches of a blackmailer called Mr. Trappe before they are caught and imprisoned, and there is no denying that the influence of the genre of romance is very strong in the episode. After her mistress's death, Hannah is sold to a Mr. Saddler, but an accident saves her and punishes the villain: the man's carriage is overturned and Saddler, quite fittingly, gets off his saddle as it were, and dies. Hannah is then taken care of by a gentle white lady. After her recovery Hannah asks Mrs. Henry to buy her: "I do not ask you to buy me and then set me free. ... Let me perform the menial service of your household—let me go to the fields and labor there— ... all I ask is to feel, and know of a certainty that I have a home, that someone cares for me" (Crafts 2003, 129–130). Many critics, including John Stauffer, argue that the author's attitude towards freedom and slavery is "ambivalent" in these two scenes: "[Crafts] articulates ambivalent and problematic attitudes toward freedom, which are part and parcel of her experimental style. At times, she resigns herself to slavery and even blurs the distinctions between freedom and bondage" (in Gates and Robbins 2004, 55).

However, my contention is that Crafts' biblical references enable her to depict herself as a "David" who is chosen and who is looking for that place promised by God through his covenant. The story of David sheds light on a passage in which Hannah is discovered to be able to play the harp when her mistress Mrs. Wheeler asks her if she is musical: "I had played a little on the harp, and so I told her. She bade me get it, and play softly, very softly on account of her nerves. ... My music, however did not suit her. It was sharp, or flat, or dull, or insipid anything but what she wished"

(Crafts 2003, 157). However surprising Hannah's musical talent is, it must be read in connection with David's story: at first his playing the harp soothes Saul (Samuel 16–17), but when Saul takes a dislike to David, the harp is so loathsome to him that he throws a javelin at David, which triggers David's flight (Samuel 19). The fact that Mrs. Wheeler is not charmed by Hannah's harp playing signals that Hannah's flight is imminent. However, the allusion to David indicates that Hannah will flee, not because she is a slave who needs to flee from her masters, but because she is the chosen one to whom God has already given a place to live in peace protected from all kinds of oppression. Several interpretations can be offered to explain Crafts' intertextual references to David's story, among which I offer two: as a black woman, Crafts would have been arguing that although not the son or the daughter of Esau, she could still have played a part to free the land from Goliath, while a white woman would have been arguing that a woman could have been a David, believing and arguing that gender was no obstruction.

The reference to David also suggests that she has a place where she will be able to unify the several kingdoms (white and black here) through a written covenant, her own narrative, which she addresses to both black and white readers. Thus, throughout her narrative Crafts repeatedly blurs the white/black divide. She suggests that white people such as Mrs. Wheeler, the white mistress to whom she is sold, or Mr. Trappe, the villain of the story, can be slaves. In the words of Mr. Trappe: "We are all *slaves* to something or somebody. A man perfectly free would be an anomaly and a free woman yet more so. Freedom and slavery are only names attached surreptitiously and often improperly to certain conditions" (Crafts 2003, 101). She also blackens Mrs. Wheeler in the comic episode of the beautifying facial powder that turns her mistress into a slave of her vanity. When in Washington, Hannah is asked to buy a beautifying facial powder for Mrs. Wheeler, who is going to request a post in her husband's stead. When Mrs. Wheeler comes back, her face is blackened (a side effect of the powder) and it emerges that her husband did not get the post since both he and she were believed to be "colored" (173). Hannah, who purchased the beautifying powder, is the only one in the know since she read an account in a newspaper which explained that it would suddenly "blacken the whitest skins" (172). Reading (even a newspaper) empowers the slave. As Ann Fabian puts it: "Hannah Crafts has the last word, exposing all and turning all she has learned into her novel" (in Gates and Robbins 2004, 51). She also uses all she has read. The dialectic here deals with "freedom *from* the self" and/or "freedom *for* the self" as developed by William L. Andrews (1986, 46). Crafts uses this comic episode to both turn Mrs. Wheeler into a slave, and so to "blacken" her, and show that Hannah is not a slave since she is the slave of no passion.

The passage is a turning point in the narrative. As Mrs. Wheeler is blackened in front of Hannah, she has no other alternative than to make her slave blacker than she appears to be (Hannah is almost white in complexion), by blaming her, and, eventually, by sending her off to the negro quarters. At this point Hannah Crafts changes her biblical intertext, switching from David to Jacob. This is shown when Hannah, who has taken the decision to flee, opens her Bible and opens it "as chance directed," at the place where Jacob fled from Esau: "to me it had a deep and peculiar meaning. 'Yes' I mentally exclaimed. 'Trusting in the God that guided and protected him I will abandon this house and the Mistress who would force me into a crime against nature'" (Crafts 2003, 213). For a black woman, the crime against nature was being raped at a very early age. Hannah Crafts, who is still a maiden at 18 or 20, although she is white in complexion and therefore the object of lust from white and black men, decides to flee on the day when she should become a field hand and be forced into sexual relationships.

The explicit reference to Jacob and its "peculiar" meaning is crucial since Jacob usurped his brother by being anointed by his blind father Isaac instead of his twin brother Esau. Apart from the idea of the foundation of a new order (Jacob eventually gives birth to 12 sons who are supposed to be the founders of the 12 tribes of Israel), what is fundamental is the existence of a twin brother to whom he is reunited later in life. As we shall see, many intertextual references point to Crafts' belief in the existence of her twin or twins, who could either be black or white. Crafts is telling her reader that she is not a slave and that her reader, be she black or white, could be her "twin," provided she understood the message.

DIALOGIZING FEMININITY AND AUTHORSHIP

Hannah Craft's reading of other biblical texts and other texts than the Bible—notably gothic novels—comforts her in this trope as she weaves heteroglossia, intertexts and self-ideology into her narrative. The very first chapter of *The Bondswoman's Narrative*, which is headed by a quotation from Song of Solomon: "Look not upon me because I am black; because the sun hath looked upon me" (5), finds Hannah pondering over her role in the micro society around her after she has learnt to read. She starts teaching "little slave children" whom she pities as if she were not a slave herself, believing that since she is now well read, she has already escaped the condition in which they are:

> I pitied their hard and cruel fate very much, and used to think that … if I could so discharge my duty by them that in after years their memories would hover over this as the sunshiny period of their lives I should be amply repaid. … These little children, slaves through they were, and doomed to a life of toil and drudgery, ignorant and untutored, assimilated thus to the highest and proudest in the land—thus evinced their equal origin, and immortal destiny. (11–12)

Moreover, her compassion for them is increased by their ignorance which will not allow them to achieve equality with white people and to get a place in the kingdom of heaven. Therefore, what she proposes is her own definition of slavery: slavery is lack of knowledge *and* lack of belief.

Crafts' own knowledge, including knowledge of literature and its codes, frees her. Thus, in the eighteenth chapter, Hannah finds herself in a forest where she meets two other fugitive slaves: a girl and her brother, who aptly enough is called Jacob. The girl is dying, and Hannah pities the girl "to whom the sweetest influence of religion had become gall and wormwood" (226). As a woman who can read, Hannah can decipher signs that these uneducated children could not. For example, dialogically speaking, caves, forests, and fetters are tombstones to whoever cannot "read" them while Hannah can fight these constructions and therefore frees herself from them. The case in point is the gothic. The palimpsestic relation to the gothic genre is overwhelming for any female, black or white, who could read in the 1850s. Hannah Crafts is precisely in that predicament, as her many allusions to Walpole, Hawthorne and Lewis show.

One particular example of her use of gothic imagery is self-telling. Hannah, who is asked to go upstairs to close the windows of her master's mansion, discovers a gallery of portraits of her master and his ancestors. As very frequently in gothic fiction, pictures are used to expose the surface of things while intimating more hidden truths. Although the 16-year old girl is initially stricken with awe, unlike the heroines of the gothic novels she has read, she does not flee but confronts these frightful representations and studies them in order to assure herself that she is "not a slave," as she puts it: "Though filled with superstitious awe I was in no haste to leave the room; for there surrounded by mysterious associations I seemed suddenly to have grown old, to have entered a new world of thoughts, and feelings and sentiments. I was not a slave with these pictured memorials of the past" (17). With this passage Crafts tells her readers that she does not identify with the heroines of such novels, but rather, since she reads the pictures, with the conscientious readers.

She frees herself from these representations, and frees herself altogether, as a woman desiring to author a text of her own. Thus, Hannah Crafts' references to sentimental novels and the end of her narrative signal that she sides with the narrators of Dickens's *Bleak House* or Charlotte Brontë's *Jane Eyre*. Her protagonist, after many tribulations, is offered the same retribution as Jane Eyre and Esther—marriage. Although she is a female slave, and, as such, should be subjected to the usual representations of a female slave, i.e., someone who has to fight against male assaults[11] or who is culturally depicted as hypersexualized, she escapes those two normative, cultural and racialized notions. Instead, she is offered marriage, which, as she puts it, is "designed for the free," and not for slaves: "Marriage like many other blessings I considered to be especially designed for the free, and something that all the victims of slavery should avoid as tending essentially to perpetuate that system. … I had spurned domestic ties … because it was my unalterable resolution never to entail slavery on any human being" (213). The fact that she never marries a slave, but eventually marries a free negro in the North and then becomes a schoolteacher makes her Jane's and Esther's "twin."

This is how she blackens or "slaverizes" her narrative and "dialogizes" her text in the most subtle manner, although she does not blacken *Bleak House* or propose a negro-centred re-reading of *Jane Eyre*, as Jean Rhys would later do.[12] Like Charlotte Brontë, whose novel *Jane Eyre* was originally subtitled *An Autobiography*, Crafts greatly "novelizes" her own story. In that particular instance, she sides not with Jane Eyre but with Charlotte Brontë, who writes a novelized autobiography. In doing so, Crafts confirms her authority, and authors a new story. Although a negro, Crafts is endowed with the same authority as Dickens and Brontë.

CONCLUSION

The message Hannah Crafts had to drive through to her would-be readers of the time (in a dialogic rendering) was that although a slave, she was not a slave, for at least three reasons. First, her tale fitted the literary canon of the era: she wrote a prototypal sentimental novel for Blacks and Whites. Secondly, her tale also fitted the biblical gnosis of her Black and White contemporaries and she wrote for both of them. Thirdly, she overturned the negative representations Hannah was subjected to as a black woman by making white people blacker or whiter, and black people whiter or blacker.

In his *From Behind the Veil*, Robert B. Stepto, discussing one of his essays, "Distrust of the Reader in Afro-American Narratives," notes that: "This essay seemed ... conspicuous ... principally because it contends that 'Afro-American literature has developed as much because of the culture's distrust of literacy as because of its abiding faith in it'" (Stepto 1991, xi). I believe that Hannah Crafts wrote *The Bondswoman's Narrative* with these two notions in mind. She had to make her readers believe she was literate and well-read in order to escape once and for all from slavery. She could literally pass off as white, and she could thus smuggle herself to the North, but she had to hammer home the message "I can read, therefore I am a slave no more," even if this message was for herself alone since her narrative was not published during her lifetime. The text is full of references that could have been shocking to a black and white activist readership at the time. John Stauffer is right, Hannah Crafts shows ambivalent attitudes towards slavery. She used slavery as a medium to author a text with a message, namely, "however shocking it may seem, you can be free if you can read, write and believe." The same holds true if she had been a white woman, simply because of the culture's distrust of women's literacy. Whatever the identity of the author, the narrative, a hybrid life narrative, tells of the life experienced by a slave or a white woman in the nineteenth century. Whoever Hannah Crafts was she was at least free from any (editorial) bonds, and free to author her narrative.

NOTES

1. See the preface and the appendixes to the 2002 edition.
2. The federal law voted by Congress required that all escaped slaves should be returned to their masters after their capture. It also required officials and citizens of free states to cooperate in this law. If not, they could be subjected to a heavy fine and a prison sentence.
3. Any text from a Black author that was published between 1760 and 1865 went through an editing process which amended the contents to fit the expectations of a white readership. Furthermore, a preface, or a foreword,

or a postscript, or letters of praise from eminent personalities of the time or from the editor were added to certify the particulars of the author and his/her authenticity. Sometimes a set of appendices was also attached to the book, not only to trace the veracity of the textual event but also to avoid fraudulent narratives from authors who had only a second-hand knowledge of what they were narrating. In most cases, editors of such works belonged to anti-slavery leagues or committees and could not afford to stain their reputation and their commitment to a cause.

4. "[My Master] used to read prayers in public to the ship's crew every Sabbath day; and when I first saw him read, I was never so surprised in my life, as when I saw the book talk to my master, for I thought it did, as I observed him to look upon it, and move his lips. I wished it would do so with me. As soon as my master had done reading, I followed him to the place where he put the book, being mightily delighted with it, and when nobody saw me, I opened it, and put my ear down close upon it, in great hopes that it would say something to me; but I was very sorry, and greatly disappointed, when I found that it would not speak. This thought immediately presented itself to me, that everybody and everything despised me because I was black" (cited by Gates 1988, 136).

5. There are many instances in her text of a literary canon that she might have read and used. Judging from her text and from the library of her supposedly last master John Hill Wheeler, whose last entry is 1850, she should/could have read anything from Shakespeare to Dickens. See John Hill Wheeler's Library Catalogue in Appendix C to the *Bondwoman's Narrative* edition of 2002.

6. Brontë's chapter reads as follows: "I soon possessed myself of a volume, taking care that it should be one stored with pictures. I mounted into the window-seat: gathering up my feet, I sat cross-legged, like a Turk; and, having drawn the red moreen curtain nearly close, I was shrined in double retirement."

7. Hannah often escapes punishment or death by accident, while other characters (be they black or white) in the same scene do not.

8. "London. Michaelmas Term lately over and the Lord Chancellor sitting in Lincoln's Inn Hall. Implacable November weather. As much mud in the streets, as if the waters had but newly retired from the face of the earth. ... Fog everywhere. Fog up the river, where it flows among green aits and meadows; fog down the river, where it rolls defiled among the tiers of shipping and the waterside pollutions of a great (and dirty) city" (Dickens 1977, 5).

9. One from Moses, one from Esther, one from Jeremiah, two from Psalms, three from "Bible" (an approximate location in the Bible which signals texts remembered on a personal basis rather than a universal version of the message).

10. "Moreover I will appoint a place for my people Israel, and will plant them, that they may dwell in a place of their own and move no more; nor shall the sons of wickedness oppress them anymore, as previously" (2, Samuel, 7:10).
11. See Harriet Jacobs's narrative, and Delphine Louis-Dimitrov's analysis.
12. Jean Rhys, *Wide Sargasso Sea* (first published 1966).

REFERENCES

Andrews, William L. 1986. *To Tell a Free Story*. Oxford: University of Illinois Press.

Bakhtin, Mikhaïl. 1981. *The Dialogic Imagination: Four Essays*. Ed. Michael Holquist. Austin/London: University of Texas Press.

Bible., King James Version.

Brontë, Charlotte. 1996. *Jane Eyre* (1847). London: Penguin Books.

Crafts, Hannah. 2003. *The Bondwoman's Narrative*. Ed. Henry Louis Gates Jr. New York: Grand Central Publishing.

Dickens, Charles. 1977. *Bleak House* (1853). New York: W.W. Norton & Company.

Douglass, Frederick. 2003. *Narrative of the Life of Frederick Douglass, an American Slave* (1845). New York: Barnes & Nobles Classics.

Fabian, Ann. 2004. Hannah Crafts, Novelist; or, How a Silent Observer Became a 'Dabster at Invention'. In Gates and Hollis, 43–52.

Frye, Northrop. 1973. *Anatomy of Criticism: Four Essays*. Princeton: Princeton University Press.

Gates, Henry Louis Jr. 1988. *The Signifying Monkey: A Theory of African-American Literary Criticism*. New York: Oxford University Press.

———. 2003. Introduction. In *The Bondwoman's Narrative*, XXII–XCII. New York: Grand Central Publishing.

Gates, Henry Louis, Jr., and Hollis Robbins, eds. 2004. *In Search of Hannah Crafts*. New York: Basic Civitas Books.

Genette, Gérard. 1982. *Palimpsestes*. Paris: Editions du Seuil.

Gronniosaw, Ukawsaw. 1772. *A Narrative of the Most Remarkable Particulars in the Life of James Albert Ukawsaw Gronniosaw, an African Prince, as Related by Himself* (1770). Bath: Samuel Hazard.

Jacobs, Harriet. 2001. *Incidents in the Life of a Slave Girl* (1861). New York: W.W. Norton & Company.

Lejeune, Philippe. 1996. *Le pacte autobiographique*. Paris: Editions du Seuil.

Lewis, Matthew. 1985. *The Monk* (1796). London: Oxford University Press.

Rhys, Jean. 2009. *Wide Sargasso Sea* (1966). London: Penguin Books.

Stauffer, John. 2004. The Problem of Freedom in the Bondwoman's Narrative. In Gates and Robbins, 53–66.

Stepto, Robert B. 1991. *From Behind the Veil. A Study of Afro-American Narrative.* Urbana/Chicago: University of Illinois Press.

Walpole, Horace. 2004. *The Castle of Otranto* (first published 1764). New York: Dover Thrift Publications.

CHAPTER 12

Janet Frame's Autobiographical Trilogy: Birth of an Oeuvre

Claire Bazin

INTRODUCTION

The title of this chapter is borrowed from the book *Janet Frame, The Lagoon And Other Stories: Naissance d'une Œuvre* I wrote in collaboration with Alice Braun,[1] itself inspired from Janet Frame's prologue to the first volume of her autobiographical trilogy,[2] where she resorts to the metaphor of birth: "From the first place of liquid darkness, within the second place of air and light, I set down the following record with its mixture of fact and truths and memories of truths and its direction always towards the third place where the starting point is myth" (Frame 2008, 3).[3]

In the beginning was the word. For Janet Frame, the world is a landscape of words. The first volume of her autobiography could actually be entitled "Words," thereby echoing Jean-Paul Sartre's autobiography entitled *Les Mots*. In the second volume, Janet discovers the word "dépôt" (sic), which becomes a source of innumerable images: "with that tiny hat, like a duncecap above the o, which I later learned was a circumflex, sign of a lost 's'; I imagined the ravines in the landscape of words where the lost

C. Bazin (✉)
Department of English, Université Paris Nanterre, Nanterre, France

© The Author(s) 2018
V. Baisnée-Keay et al. (eds.), *Women's Life Writing and the Practice of Reading*, Palgrave Studies in Life Writing,
https://doi.org/10.1007/978-3-319-75247-1_12

letters had fallen" (208). In his *Oxford History of New Zealand Literature in English,* Terry Sturm writes: "Frame has a distinctly tactile sense of the power of words" (Sturm 1991, 97). If this could apply to any writer, it is particularly relevant in Frame's case as she traces her personal itinerary— from the young girl born in 1924 in Dunedin, New Zealand, hungry for words and books, to the famous writer she has become.

I will follow Janet Frame in her itinerary to show how, from an avid reader, she has become a distinguished literary figure. The writer as reader has produced a work that includes poetry, fiction and autobiography (Frame refuses to establish clear-cut distinctions between the different literary genres) before returning to her homeland, New Zealand, after a seven-year exile which enabled her to (re)build herself.

Portrait of the Writer as Reader

In one of the rare interviews she consented to give, Frame declared: "Spoken words in childhood arrive from on high, as high as the sky" (Alley 1991, 156). She is a word-taster. It is said that she wrote her first poem at the age of three, which requires the reader's "willing suspension of disbelief," though it is worth quoting: "Once upon a time there was a bird. One day a hawk came out of the sky and ate the bird. The next day a big bogie came from behind the hill and ate up the hawk for eating up the bird" (Hansson 1996, 5). The bird is a recurrent figure in Frame's poetry and prose, and often emblematizes the figure of the writer. In *Towards Another Summer,*[4] Frame's posthumous autobiographical novel, Grace, the ungraceful heroine, often turns into a migratory bird.

In childhood, Frame is first fascinated by individual words, before discovering texts and books written by others, before being able to find "words of her own," before becoming an author. As French writer Annie Ernaux, a fervent admirer of Janet Frame, puts it in her last book, *Le vrai lieu,* writing is often an extension of reading (Ernaux 2014, 42): I read, therefore I write, as if, through, or thanks to, texts written by others, the reader thought she might be able to do the same. Frame recalls that her friend the writer Frank Sargeson, who became her mentor and offered her accommodation for a while after her internment, used to copy whole pages from *Ivanhoe* when he was a child, convinced that he was the author: "innocently believing he was now writing a book ... He had thought that books belonged to everyone, going in and out of everyone's head, and anyone could write down any book and be a writer" (Frame 2008, 297–298). Reading and writing are closely linked, the first playing the part of a catalyst for the second, fueling the need to write. It is by dint of reading that one becomes a writer, as suggested by Annie Ernaux in *Le vrai lieu*: "I don't think one can write without having read a lot" (Ernaux 2014, 52, my translation). It is as if there couldn't be any writing without years of reading, even indiscriminately. The selection comes later.

When Janet discovers Grimm's *Fairy Tales*, which her friend Poppy had lent her (Poppy is the initiator who had taught Janet the word "fuck"), she is struck by an epiphany: "And that night I took Grimm's *Fairy Tales* to bed and began to read, and suddenly the world of living and the world of reading became linked in a way I had not noticed before" (Frame 2008, 48). Fiction invades reality to the point of being fused and confused with it. Later on, she has the feeling of sharing her life with Tolstoy's heroes: "All Tolstoy's characters lived, and some died in that room with its windows open to the honeysuckled front hedge" (304). At a very early age, Janet Frame is desperately looking for meaning, for signifiers, and she is often shocked at the inadequacy between signifier and signified, and even more so at the general indifference with which this incommensurability is greeted. The title of chapter 10: "OK permanent Wave" (53) is an eloquent, though comic illustration of her reaction. Janet's aunt is going to have "a second permanent wave" (55), which arouses the child's stupefaction, even indignation: "I had supposed that a permanent wave meant just that, and the prospect of a word's lack of truth gave me a feeling of shock" (55). She discovers that the words she so much cherishes can also be traitors, as when she went to the dentist's who told her to "smell the pretty pink towel" (22–23) to put her to sleep, both literally and metaphorically, or later, when she was diagnosed with *schizzofreenier*, as she spells it. The diagnosis that falls like a sentence is both a legitimate source of fear and a source of pride and hope. Her illness becomes her ally in her artistic creation, to the point that when the diagnosis is invalidated three years later at the Maudsley Hospital in London, she feels deprived of a precious shelter, a hiding hide. The unintentional spelling mistake or phonic distortion—of 'phre' into 'free'—turns the illness into a space of freedom.

All her life long, Janet Frame remains fascinated by words, especially by the word "destination": "I remember learning to spell and use these three words: *decide*, *destination*, and *observation*, all of which worked closely with adventure" (37), which sounds like an invitation to travel, though, for lack of money, she cannot do it literally. It is when she realizes, Proust-like, that one can travel in one's mind that she is struck by an epiphany: "I could experience an adventure by reading a book" (35). The very title of the first volume—*To the Is-Land*—is eloquent enough: the phonic distortion "polysemizes" the word, giving voice to the "mute" letter. The capital "I" and the caesura turn it into a land of being, or a land of the present, as opposed to her ancestors' "Was-Land" (7) or the land of the Future (7). The caesura opens a multitude of semantic fields. By changing its spelling, Frame changes the very concept and the word opens like a Pandora's Box, offering the reader undreamt-of riches. As Terry Sturm puts it, "Janet Frame's story is about words, their appearances, their sounds and the relationship between people and words" (Sturm 1991, 97). In spite of her sister's advice to the contrary, Janet insists on pronouncing the word 'island' as it is spelt, daring to challenge the phonetic laws. Valérie Baisnée analyses this resistance to phonetic laws as Frame's first poetic manifesto (Baisnée 1997, 102–3).

The mere word "island" becomes the narration of the adventures through which Frame has discovered it. "Island" even becomes an adjective, qualifying the family of Janet Frame's friend K, whose intimacy and almost Brontëan seclusion Janet envies: "the island state of her family" (Frame 2008, 163). If, to sum up French linguist Saussure's theory, her elder sister Myrtle advocates the respect of "langue," common to all individuals, Janet refuses it in the name of "parole," a sign of individuality. If there are some words that a poet or a novelist has to use to abide by conventions, Janet subverts the codes and chooses her own words, which is best illustrated in the writing of her first poem which she reads aloud to Myrtle before taking it to school:

> At home that evening, the writing of my first poem sparked my first argument over writing as an art, for when I read my poem to Myrtle, she insisted that the words 'touch the sky' should be 'tint the sky': When the sun goes down and the night draws nigh and the evening shadows touch the sky—I disagreed with Myrtle, who then insisted that there were words and phrases you had to use … in deference to her obvious wisdom and wider knowledge I changed the word to 'tint' when I took my poem to school. But later, when I wrote it in my notebook, I reverted to 'touch the sky', having my own way (75)

Poetic conventions prevent individual choice, restrain imagination. It is the very word "imagination" which is, of course, Janet Frame's favourite: "My life had been for many years in the power of words. It was driven now by a constant search and need for what was after all 'only a word'—imagination" (134). The word "imagination" is obviously far more than a mere word for her. The doors of "that world" (the world of imagination) open wide, taking Janet away from her ordinary life ("this world"). Even if what Janet aspires to is more a harmonious cohabitation between "this" world and "that" world than a separation. When she is elected "Dux of the school," she is allowed free access to the local library, the Athenaeum, where she borrows books for her mother who will never read them, both because of her lack of time but also because she views books as so many treasures of a forbidden fruit. In *Le vrai lieu*, Annie Ernaux says that her mother used to wash her hands before touching a book (Ernaux 2014, 49). Frame's mother only strokes the cover as if it were a holy object. It is to the very same mother, however, that Janet owes her taste for words and books: "I wonder in which world I might have lived my 'real' life had not the world of literature been given to me by my mother..." (Frame 2008, 142). With just a change in her tone of voice, Janet's mother is able to transform an ordinary stone into a jewel: "When Mother talked of the present, however, bringing her sense of wondrous contemplation to the ordinary world we knew, we listened, feeling the mystery and the magic. She had only to say of any commonplace object, 'Look kiddies a stone' to fill that stone with a wonder as if it were a holy object" (5). It is the mother who transmits her tastes, hence this significant comparison: "I clung to works of literature as a child clings to its mother" (183). Janet starts from individual words and phrases to end up with books, which she almost literally devours: "we were all hungry for words" (77)—like the sugar inscription on the Christmas cake: "Words and phrases that could be eaten" (89), which is the source of infinite happiness as it consecrates the cohabitation between the written and the real worlds.

When her sister Myrtle drowns in the local swimming pool due to a heart defect, Janet finds refuge in poetry: "What marvellous knowledge of the poets who could see through my own life" (105). The path that leads from reading to writing may be long and arduous, but Janet takes it and that turned out to be a life-ensuring choice in due course. Her native country could have destroyed her with a lobotomy. Frame was saved by her writing.

WRITE I MUST

At the end of the second volume of the autobiography—each volume significantly ends on a departure—Janet embarks for the continent. Her arrival in London, told at the beginning of the third volume, and which marks the first stage of her long journey, is a disaster: her booking letter had not reached its destination and Janet found herself alone, in the London rain, surrounded by her luggage, to which she clung, like a child to its mother. Great Britain was far from being the "Home" her father had described to her before her departure. The fictional possibilities vanish in front of a hostile reality and the arrival is but a real anti-climax. However, thanks to the power of her imagination, Janet flies to the wonderland of literature, where the missing letter transports her, opening for her the world of words and letters, which fills her with joy and excitement: "the thrilling sense" (356). "That" world is definitely more welcoming than "this" world.

She finds herself immersed in fiction and myth in a reiteration of what she had felt on the death of her sister Myrtle. This experience enables her to theorize the relation between fiction and reality. The personal drama of arrival sends her back to a fictional topos. For example, she alludes to Macbeth's letter in Shakespeare's eponymous play which triggers the final catastrophe. Through the initially unfortunate experience, Janet Frame reinscribes Shakespeare in her literary landscape as a guide and prop. The reference to Macbeth sends her back to the childhood play where she had ended up not playing (Frame 2008, 135–136). It is as if this new unpleasant experience was a kind of revenge over a missed opportunity: she is now at last playing the part she had never managed to play as a child, illustrating her creed that "reality (is) the ore of the polished fiction" (356). The lost letter, which she did send, no longer matters and is even forgotten and replaced by the gift of fictional letters.

As she did with the illness, she once again reverses the situation. Her anxiety becomes transcended by "the fictional possibilities and enthusiasms" (356) to the point that she feels grateful to the missing letter. Far from clipping her wings (to pursue the metaphor of the bird), from caging her in the hostile reality of this world, the missing letter enables her to fly away, even if the reference to Plato's myth might express her obsession with internment. But Janet Frame rewrites the platonic myth since, for her, the reflected object is richer than the original and accessible through the power of imagination.

The "mirror cities" she is discovering in London will become 'singularized' in Ibiza to give the third volume of the autobiography its title: "The Envoy from Mirror City." The metaphor acquires a universal status and becomes the realm of Imagination where she has always wanted to live. Her short-lived fictional flight "on the grimy London steps" (355) is framed in by the disastrous experiences of the hostel and the YMCA, where she finally ends up and which reminds her of the psychiatric hospital, with its black and white tiles and its various interdictions: "there were efforts at control in the sheet of rules pinned inside the doors of the bedrooms and bathrooms and lavatories that were in rows, institutional in appearance and smell" (356). But what matters is the mental journey Janet Frame has just made, which helps to her rebirth, "excavated as reality" (356). The epiphany is best expressed in the alliteration that follows: "I felt fleetingly at the back of my mind" (355–356).

She pictures herself as a heroine in fiction, reflecting Valérie Baisnée's insistence on the importance of intertextuality in the writing of an autobiography: "Autobiography can be established through the remembrance of key literary texts" (Baisnée 1997, 123). The literary epiphany, born from, or thanks to, the painful experience, is a means of being reborn: the bane turns into a boon. Following a very Framean process, Janet Frame evokes the complexity and the richness of the moment through an eloquent oxymoron: "the … gift of the loss" (356). However difficult her predicament, she manages to overcome it thanks to the world of literature, the "True Place," to translate Annie Ernaux's title, *Le vrai lieu* (2014).

For the lack of New Zealand literary foremothers and forefathers, apart from Katherine Mansfield (whom Frame tends to reject because she "belongs" to her mother, whose literary tastes she forces herself to despise) and Frank Sargeson, her literary models are the Brontës or their heroines with whom, like Annie Ernaux among others, she identifies, both in their lives and in their writings: "plain Jane," in particular, the eponymous heroine, whose name she almost shares. Janet recognizes herself in the sisters and their alcoholic brother (Janet's is epileptic), but also in Maggie Tulliver, Catherine Earnshaw, Tess or Emma (Frame 2008, 151). We could actually parody Jane Eyre's offensive declaration to her wicked aunt, Mrs. Reed: "*Speak* I must" (Brontë 1971, 30)[5] by turning it into "Write I must." Frame's rebellion is textual.

The other unavoidable model is Shakespeare, though she had first rejected him because he was a "must," but whom she started to love thanks to Miss Farnie, her enthusiastic and competent teacher: "Miss Farnie's approach had converted me" (136). Frame goes as far as to begin the second volume of her trilogy with a quotation from *The Tempest:* "Prospero 'My brave spirit !/ Who was so firm, so constant, that this coil/ Would not infect his reason ? Ariel: Not a soul,/ but felt a fever of the mad; and play'd/ Some tricks of desperation'"[6] (Frame 2008, 172).

She also finds refuge in Shelley's, Keats's and Coleridge's poems, especially on her sister Myrtle's death by drowning: "Only the poets know, only the poets know" (103). She herself wanted to become a poet. But if she did publish some collections of poems, one must admit that she is far better at fiction or autobiography, as the critics have undoubtedly perceived. Apart from a few exceptions (among them Valérie Baisnée), very few have tackled her poetry. What Frame seeks is "a voice of her own," a "writing of her own." As French theoretician Georges Gusdorf puts it: "The writer's task is to write like nobody else with everybody's words" (Gusdorf 1991, 296; my translation).

In the early 1950s, when she was still in New Zealand, and barely out of hospital, Frame published her first collection of short stories, *The Lagoon And Other Stories,*[7] which miraculously spared her the lobotomy she was threatened with, as the surgeon who was about to perform the operation had read about her winning the Hubert Church Award for her book. The narration of the episode in Volume II is resumed, verbatim by Michael King in *Wrestling With The Angel: a life of janet frame:* "Writer wins Prize for Prose: The New Zealand centre of [the writers' organization] PEN announces that the Hubert Church Memorial Award for prose has been won by Miss Janet Frame of Oamaru for her book 'Lagoon and Other Stories'" (King 2000, 112). In volume II, Frame concludes: "It is little wonder that I value literature as a way of life as it actually saved my life" (Frame 2008, 263). It is a matter of give and take. Be it a catharsis, or what Suzette Henke calls a scriptotherapy (Henke 2000, 651–669), or a strategy of resistance, a work has been born.

Birth of an Autobiography

The autobiography appears thirty years later, first in three volumes (1982–1985) before being gathered into one, after a prolific fictional production (13 novels), but also after two autobiographical novels, *Owls*

Do Cry (1958) and *Faces in the Water* (1961) which pave the way to the "official version," as they are fraught with autobiographical details, though Frame claims that she is neither Daphne (the heroine of the first) or Istina Mavet (the second), even if we could hear a phonetic echo in the very initials of the second heroine's name: "I M". If one is to abide by Philippe Lejeune's famous "autobiographical pact" (Lejeune 1975), *Faces in the Water* is not a "proper" autobiography, as author, narrator and main character are not one and the same, which is Lejeune's prerequisite. This is also true in the case of *Owls Do Cry*, even if, once again, there are some biographical elements such as the epileptic brother, who is also a character in the more overtly fictional sequel called *The Edge of the Alphabet* (1962). In *Owls Do Cry*, the eldest sister, who was called Myrtle, and here rebaptized Francie, dies in the flames of the local rubbish dump. As for Daphne, she is lobotomized and ends up working in an unglamorous textile factory. In this case, fiction is less generous than reality, since Daphne, the fictitious heroine, is not to know her creator's fame and is lobotomized. Daphne and Istina are what Lejeune calls "carbon copies" (Lejeune 1975, 15; my translation) of Frame herself: the same with a difference.

Actually, even in the autobiography, Frame seems to be leading the reader up the garden path when she declares: "I've created selves, but I've never written of 'me'" (Frame 2008, 484). There is no pure autobiography, but always a generic mixture. The mere act of writing turns life into writing: "The story of a life is always the fiction of a life," as Brigitte Barry puts it (Barry 1996, 13–28). The three texts—the two autobiographical novels and the autobiography—contribute to the erection of an autobiographical monument. Lejeune insists on saying that in the production of an autobiographer there is not only one (text), but a set of texts which constitute what he calls an autobiographical puzzle (Lejeune 1975, 23; my translation). What is interesting, especially for a reader on the lookout for autobiographical elements, is the movement, the dialogue, between the different texts, which creates a stereographic effect. The experience in psychiatric hospitals spans only seven chapters in the autobiography, as if, and it is certainly the case, it was easier to tell the truth under the guise of fiction. Four of the short stories contained in *The Lagoon*—"The Bedjacket," "Jan Godfrey," "The Park" and "Snap-Dragons"—articulate upon the hospital experiences which cannot but evoke the author's. In *Faces in the Water*, too, the reader learns all that s/he wants to know (or not) about the sad reality of hospitals. Frame's autobiography reads like an analeptic springboard to read or re-read her fiction.

It is the publication of her autobiography (and Jane Campion's film *An Angel at My Table,* 1990, based on the autobiography) that has made her famous, as if, and here I agree with Valérie Baisnée, the autobiography, by giving access to the fiction, had also clarified the reader's perception of it (Baisnée 1997, 97). I disagree with most of Frame's critics, among them Gina Mercer (1994), who consider her autobiography as inferior to her fiction, on the ground that it is too easy to read, as though autobiography was a less prestigious genre than fiction, because it is too self-centered. If Frame's extra-ordinary life is first-rate material—in *Angela's Ashes,* the Irish-born writer Frank McCourt writes that "the happy childhood is hardly worth your while" (McCourt 1997, 1)—it is also true that humour is very much present in Frame's autobiography. André Breton, the French surrealist writer, used to say that "humour is the superior rebellion of the mind" (Breton 1940, 11, cited by Escarpit 1960, 70, my translation). Humour is Frame's weapon and rampart against sentimentalism. Frame only relates the amusing incidents she has witnessed in hospital: the more, the merrier; she only talks about the funny characters: "If I talked of my time in hospital, I described only the amusing incidents and the stereo-types of patients–the Jesus Christ, the Empress" (Frame 2008, 259). In an article on Foucault and Frame, Jean-Jacques Lecercle says that "what pre-vents Frame from falling into the trap of sentimentalism and bad literature is the elliptical narration of the asylum episodes" (Lecercle 2001, 30). Gina Mercer also insists on Frame's "strategies of avoidance," as she resorts to paralepsis, euphemisms and ellipses in the narration of her internment (Mercer 1994, 12; 24).

CONCLUSION: PORTRAIT OF THE ARTIST AS A YOUNG WOMAN

After a seven-year exile, with London and Ibiza as the key landmarks in Frame's journey, she comes back "home," a famous writer. If the official reason for her return is her father's death, it is not the main one. It is only in New Zealand, her native country, that she can completely reconstruct a self that had been seriously shattered. It is also as if she were taking a spec-tacular revenge upon this country that had almost destroyed her. She has to make herself known and renowned at home: "Remember you'll never know another country like that where you spent your earliest years. You'll never be able to write intimately of another country" (496). Unlike other literary figures like Conrad, Nabokov or Beckett, Frame refuses to be a writer in exile, and chooses to offer herself as a "mapmaker," a pioneer who will open the way for other writers, becoming, in her turn, the literary mother she herself didn't have in New Zealand. The "mad woman"—the "mad niece" as she used to call herself (Frame 2008, 342)—has become an artist, realizing her mother's dream for the epileptic brother, whose illness should have been a guarantee of genius. Difference has become Frame's identity, but this difference is the "right" kind of difference, a prestigious difference. Frame is now "within," having entered the literary landscape which she has contributed to draw and has made her own.

NOTES

1. Claire Bazin and Alice Braun, 2010.
2. The autobiography first came out in three volumes: I—*To the Is-Land* (1982), II—*An Angel at my Table* (1984) and III—*The Envoy from Mirror City* (1985), before being published under the title *An Angel at my Table* (1989).
3. All references to Janet's Frame autobiography are to the three-volume autobiography entitled *An Angel at My Table* (London: Virago Press, 2008).
4. Janet Frame, *Towards Another Summer* (Auckland: Random House, 2007).
5. Italics in the original.
6. William Shakespeare, *The Tempest*, Act I, Scene 2 (Shakespeare 2011, 1075).
7. Janet Frame, *The Lagoon and Other Stories*, 1951 (London: Bloomsbury, 1997).

REFERENCES

Alley, Elizabeth. 1991. 'An Honest Record': An Interview with Janet Frame. *Landfall* 45 (2): 154–168.

Baisnée, Valérie. 1997. *Gendered Resistance: The Autobiographies of Simone De Beauvoir, Maya Angelou, Janet Frame and Marguerite Duras.* Amsterdam/Atlanta: Rodopi.

Barry, Brigitte. 1996. Histoire d'une vie, vie d'une histoire : figures autobiographiques chez Janet Frame. In *Confluences 13, Ecrits et Figures*, 13–28. Nanterre: Publidix.

Bazin, Claire, and Alice Braun. 2010. *Janet Frame, The Lagoon and Other Stories: Naissance d'une OEuvre.* Paris: Presses Universitaires de France.

Breton, André. 1940. *Anthologie de l'humour noir.* Paris: Gallimard.

Brontë, Charlotte. 1971. *Jane Eyre* (1847). New York: Norton critical edition.

Campion, Jane. 1990. *An Angel at My Table*. Film directed by Jane Campion. Produced by Grant Major & Bridget Ikin, written by Laura Jones; produced by ABC, Television New Zealand, Channel 4, Hibiscus Film, Sharmill Films. Distributed by Sharmill Films (Australia). Released on 20 September 1990 Australia.

Ernaux, Annie. 2014. *Le vrai lieu. Entretiens avec Michelle Porte*. Paris: Gallimard.

Escarpit, Robert, ed. 1960. *L'Humour, Que Sais-Je ?* Paris: PUF.

Frame, Janet. 1997. *The Lagoon and Other Stories* (1951). London: Bloomsbury.

———. 2007. *Towards Another Summer*. Auckland: Random House.

———. 2008. *An Angel at My Table* (1989). London: Virago Press.

Gusdorf, Georges. 1991. *Lignes de vie. Les écritures du moi, lignes de vie 2, auto-bio-graphie*. Paris: Odile Jacob.

Hansson, Karin. 1996. *The Unstable Manifold: Janet Frame's Challenge to Determinism*. Lund: Lund University Press.

Henke, Suzette. 2000. Jane Campion Frames Janet Frame: A Portrait of the Artist as a Young New Zealand Poet. *Biography* 23 (4): 651–669.

King, Michael. 2000. *Wrestling With The Angel. A Life of Janet Frame*. Auckland: Viking.

Lecercle, Jean-Jacques. 2001. Folie et littérature: de Foucault à Janet Frame. In *La Licorne*, 293–304. Poitiers: Presses Universitaires de Poitiers.

Lejeune, Philippe. 1975. *Le Pacte autobiographique*. Paris: Editions du Seuil.

McCourt, Frank. 1997. *Angela's Ashes*. London: Flamingo.

Mercer, Gina. 1994. *Janet Frame: Subversive Fictions*. Dunedin: University of Otago Press.

Shakespeare, William. 2011. *Arden Shakespeare Complete Works*. Ed. Ann Thompson, David Scott Kastan, and Richard Proudfoot. London: Bloomsbury.

Sturm, Terry, ed. 1991. *The Oxford History of New Zealand Literature in English*. Auckland: Oxford University Press.

PART IV

Reading to Write Herself in the World

Writing Herself as/in Reading the Others in Ruth Ozeki's *A Tale for the Time Being*

Nicoleta Alexoae-Zagni

INTRODUCTION

Ruth Ozeki is an award-winning novelist (author of *My Year of Meats* and *All Over Creation*), filmmaker and Zen Buddhist priest. The work under scrutiny here, *A Tale for the Time-Being* (2013), is one of her most ambitious endeavours as it actually took Ozeki seven years to come up with "the right book."[1] It is not her latest publication, since the book-length essay *The Face: A Time Code*, described by Ozeki on her Facebook page as "a hybrid work, part memoir, part meditation, and part thought experiment" (Ozeki 2015), was released in paperback in March 2016. Hybridity is actually a word that resonates well with Ozeki, who calls herself a "racially hybridized, genetically pluralistic entity, who has never lived in any one place or culture" (Palumbo-Liu 2014)—"half Japanese, half Caucasian-American ethnically or racially ... my citizenship ... Canadian/American so it gets even more complicated" (Kosaka 2013). Ozeki's Man Booker-shortlisted *A Tale For the Time Being* would also be best described as a "hybrid" or, in the words of a puzzled reviewer, a "...this—this what?

N. Alexoae-Zagni (✉)
University of Paris 8 Vincennes-Saint-Denis, Paris, France

© The Author(s) 2018
V. Baisnée-Keay et al. (eds.), *Women's Life Writing and the Practice of Reading*, Palgrave Studies in Life Writing,
https://doi.org/10.1007/978-3-319-75247-1_13

A novel with Japanese footnotes, six appendices and a bibliography; a memoir; a semi-autobiographical meditation on time, climate change, history, or all of these?" (Hendry 2013). The uniqueness of this book lies in the way in which, by means of an inclusive revisiting of history, of literary figures and traditions, of quantum physics and Buddhist practices, spanning territories and realities from Silicon Valley to Japanese temples and remote islands off the coast of British Columbia, it blurs the boundaries between fact and fiction, between what we know and what we project, between past and present, between reading and writing.

It takes indeed a book of an enveloping, capacious caliber to answer the traumatic global call of the real, represented by the earthquake and the tsunami that hit Japan in March 2011, the meltdown at Fukushima and their consequences. And Ozeki, who had at the time finished the first draft of a novel recounting a young Japanese girl's story in the form of a diary and was on the point of submitting the completed manuscript to her editor, felt that *that* book was no longer relevant: "When a catastrophe of that magnitude happens it changes everything. I thought about the book some more, and asked the question—how does a fiction writer respond to something that real? ... How do you respond to that as a fiction writer?" (Doyle 2013) Reworking her material, she broke "the fictional container" and "stepped into the book [her]self" as a "real character," the reader—the "right reader" after several "wrong" ones in previous "terrible," "pre-earthquake/pre-Fukushima" versions (Krevel and Botshon 2016). Reeling on the fault lines between fact and fiction as real author, authorial narrator and fictional character, Ozeki does not merely reflect on realities and conditions: she engages with them and explores the aesthetic possibilities sustained by the search for a narrative form that would accommodate an expression of compelling personal and collective interrogations.

This chapter seeks to shed light on what I consider the lynchpin of this reworked version, the relationship between reading and writing, and to examine how these acts are not only connected, but represent the very mechanism that structures the narrative and sets in motion directions for an exploration of ideas. In so doing, my analyses will equally show the manner in which, by raising questions about the acts of reading and writing and a story's meaning(s), the text itself becomes more complex and less easily definable, a fluid and innovative enactment of life writing that experiments with narrative conventions and strategies as it taps into multiple sources of imagination and memory and crosses various historical and cultural boundaries.

The Author as Reader and Writer of Her Times

Ozeki's final orchestration relies on a deceptively simple plot: a novelist named Ruth, living with her husband Oliver on Cortes Island (off the coast of British Columbia), discovers a collection of artefacts washed ashore in a Hello Kitty lunchbox, apparently from the tsunami that hit Japan. The most significant item is a book whose cover identifies it as *À la recherche du temps perdu* by Marcel Proust and that turns out, upon opening, to be the diary of a 16-year-old girl named Nao. The story alternates between the diary entries and Ruth's ruminations on them and on her own life on the island, where she leads a quiet, but somewhat isolated life; she is a successful novelist, but is stalled on a memoir "about the years she had spent taking care of her mother, who'd suffered from Alzheimer's" (Ozeki 2013, 31).

This systematic interweaving of a first-person narration (Nao) with a third-person one (Ruth as focalizer), with frequent shifts between diegetic present and past recollections, is framed by a narrative structure carefully divided into four parts, each placed, alternately and by means of quotes, under the aegis of thirteenth-century Zen master Dōgen and French writer Marcel Proust. This structural framework clearly draws the attention to the initial act of reading, the original authorial "she" who reads to write herself. Unmistakably, the standalone epigraphs, the footnotes, the six appendices and the final bibliography offer transitions, reflexions, clarifications or verifications, but more interestingly, they create links between the creative methodology and the subjects under scrutiny. The reading activity is evinced as interpenetrated with that of writing, the writer inscribing herself not only by acts of creation but also of reception. Ozeki's writing is indeed a "mirror-talk" with literature—to use Susanna Egan's image that calls to mind "a combination of reflexive practices" and foregrounds "interaction between people, among genres, and between writers and readers ..." (Egan 1999, 11–12). A fundamental instrument of mediation and (self-)understanding, reading provides the writer with narrative modes she can invest, hermeneutical procedures to understand herself, suggestions of characters to mediate experiences or of authorial postures to adopt—"... I think the idea for those ... characters came from this reading and studying that I was doing," Ozeki casually pointed out in an interview on NPR (2013). The book is thus a writerly act meant as a dialogue with narratives of history as well as with literary traditions. The author's "putting herself on the line," as she phrased it for AbeBooks, implies creating a world "like a model of [her] mind and all the things [she] was thinking about at the time" (East 2013), to convey, among others and as remarked by her husband, "her interest in ... autobiography, biographical narratives and I-novels" (Lee 2013).

Therefore, it is important to acknowledge how deliberate formal and aesthetic choices gesture to a dialogue with established cultural forms and pose a challenge to configurations and enactments pertaining to self-writing. Ozeki's book develops its own formal universe, crisscrossing areas defined by genetic configurations, and develops its critical relationship to patterns of thought and representation of the subject offered by literary history.

To pick up, for instance, on the reference to the "I-novel": *A Tale for the Time Being* is clearly—and only among many other things—a nod to *shi-shosetsu*, the "most salient and unique form of modern Japanese literature" (Suzuki 1996, 1) in the words of Tomi Suzuki, whose book *Narrating the Self: Fictions of Japanese Modernity* is part of Ozeki's acknowledged critical apparatus (Ozeki 2013, 420). The I-novel is traditionally defined as a single-voiced narrative recounting the author's lived, personal experience in a thin guise of fiction; many canonical I-novels are actually narrated in the third person. This collapsing of genres commonly regarded in the Western tradition as quite separate and the exploitation of the tension between fictional and non-fictional modes of representation are likely to put an informed reader on the trail of framing cues that have come to define autofiction as well—and critics have aptly pointed out that Tayama Kataï's work *Futon* (1907), generally regarded as the inaugurator of this "new genre," is an "autofiction avant la lettre" (Forest 2005, 289).

Ozeki's writing moves forward by combining generic elements from traditional forms in new and creative ways, laying out a sophisticated discourse of the self. Julia Watson and Sidonie Smith have pointedly remarked upon it in their latest collection of essays on life writing: mentioning Ozeki's use of a pseudonymous character, the two critics bring up her name as a player of the card of "autofiction" in what they have identified as an engagement with the affordances and the "seeming limitations" of the autobiographical and suggest the necessity of more thorough discussions of her work (Smith and Watson 2017).

One protagonist in the novel is indeed called "Ruth," like Ozeki herself; moreover, the real Ruth Ozeki, like her fictitious counterpart, is married to a man called Oliver and had to deal with her mother's Alzheimer's. They also share a common Nisei heritage. Nevertheless, the fictional Ruth is meant to be an "avatar" or a "fictional alter ego," in Ozeki's own words,[2] allowing her first and foremost to respond to a "deeply disturbing event" that made her think about things such as "the ephemeral nature of being" and shook her "entire notion of what time and space are" (Sethi 2013). This fictional Ruth picks her first clues and starts researching Buddhism and the Zen philosophy of Master Dōgen after having read about them in Nao's diary; Ozeki, on the other hand, an ordained Buddhist priest, connects her way of experiencing herself, and the world, pluralistically (in relation to her mixed-race identity) to Buddhism and a vision of interconnectedness and relationality of self and selves, of the self as a collection of fluid, impermanent, interpenetrating interdependencies that change and flow through time. Reflecting on her search for a suitable form to express a unique self, the author relates her spiritual preoccupations to an impossibility to write from a single point of view, or "even stick to a single grammatical person" (Palumbo-Liu 2014). Consequently, the use of multiple points of view and the pronominal shifts—destabilizing a sense of singularity, unicity and omniscience—correspond to an authorial vision of the human being as "trying to integrate and make sense" of "pluralistic elements," the only way of granting access to a "kind of wholeness" (Palumbo-Liu 2014).

If we follow this line of thought and keep in mind how the question of reading is intimately related to an attitude towards cultural heritage, mobilizing notions of intertextuality, *mise en abyme* and critical engagement with the memory of literature and its dynamic, it also leads to precise writers and works that make their presence felt, implicitly or explicitly. And indeed, if we are to understand that everything Ozeki has read has seeped in (as she has pointed out to Felicia R. Lee in the exchange referred to above), I make no apology for hedging my bets that it is also potentially enriching to tease out the multiplicity of references to Maxine Hong Kingston's (1989) *The Woman Warrior. Memoirs of a Girlhood among Ghosts.* This is the narrative that has played a groundbreaking role in the development of self-writing by women and ethnic subjects and, more importantly perhaps, proved a solid challenge to contemporary scholarship on autobiography. Rocío Davis has aptly captured this contribution in her study of "Asian North American autobiographies of childhood":

It obliged us to rethink feminist, postmodern, avant-garde, or ethnic perceptions and enactments of the autobiographical mode. To a large extent,
we can affirm that after Kingston, American autobiography was never the
same. Formal and aesthetic issues have become protagonists of the autobiographical act, serving as ways of signifying. We no longer ask only what the
text is about, but are equally concerned with how processes of self-
representation are articulated. (Davis 2007, 4)

A Tale for the Time Being nods in the direction of conceptualizations of
self-representation that emerge in Kingston's first *opus*, as well as of the
narrative and discursive configurations that sustain them. Kingston had
indeed set the tone in self-referential writing by formulating the impossibility of impermeable borders between facts and stories, truth and imagination. With her, self-writing should not be understood as asserting
certainties, but as trying to negotiate and reconcile meanings; the referential singularity of a univocal enunciative instance is discredited and replaced
by a biographical focalization on other people or characters who are the
inspiration and/or the skeletal structure of the *mise-en-scène* of one's own
self. I also find it significant that Ozeki places her writing, just like her
honored predecessor, within the shadow of Marcel Proust, pointing to an
artistic filiation with a precursor who hasn't finished giving a hard time to
critics, theoreticians and poeticians, even ones as discerning as Philippe
Lejeune[3] or Gérard Genette[4]: "After all, I am not writing history or
sociology, but a 'memoir' like Proust ... a form which can neither be dis-
missed as fiction nor quarrelled with as fact," Kingston had famously
argued when she first took the pen to denounce the "cultural misreadings" of what was to become the most taught book ever in American colleges and universities (Kingston 1982, 64).

It is thus not much of a leap to suggest *A Tale* gestures to *In Search of
Lost Time* as well, with references to Proust's masterpiece being not only
identifiable in the conception of the narrative levels and voices itself, but,
as we shall see, clearly and explicitly asserted throughout the text.
Formulating its own stance, as Kingston's does, on the relations between
self, narrative and time as articulated in and by means of acts of literary
creation, Ozeki's novel is indeed exceptional in the attention that it pays
to the French modernist writer, filtered through an authorial conviction
that "all writing is in search of lost time" (Anita Sethi), the act of reading
an other and the other installed as a necessary prelude to self-writing.

The writer, this writer, is not merely a follower or reproducer of existing scripts, but a conscious reader who would insert herself into them, inflecting them and bringing new cultural complexities to the mix. "Working the boundary of 'fact' and 'fiction'" (Smith and Watson 2017) and experimenting with literary forms and structures to explore the potentials and the limitations of herself/her self in the world and in relation to it, Ozeki's textually (and intertextually) complex undertaking resists and defies generic classifications. It only seems appropriate to conclude this section by saying that any attempt to generically locate *A Tale for the Time Being* should probably allow for the same capaciousness and plasticity as Shirley Geok-lin Lim does in her reading of *The Woman Warrior*: "It is a complex, highly inventive, historically embedded work. It is part biography, part autobiography, part history, part fantasy, part fiction, part myth and wholly multilayered, multivocal, and organic" (Lim 1991, x). The following analyses will allow for an understanding of the ways in which Ozeki's exploration and exploitation of existing and established practices and forms further expand this tradition of subverting recognized modes of self-writing through hybridized practices, to take to yet greater depths textual enactments of individual and collective experiences and concern.

READING AS TIME MAKING

When reading interviews and conversations with Ruth Ozeki, one is offered compelling insights into her belief in art: this belief is sustained by faith, conviction and trust that writing will have enough magical power to lead to truths related to human existence, to reality, to being and to time. Ozeki has, on several occasions, pointed out her interest in the Japanese notion of "kotodama," whereby words and names are endowed with mystical powers (Sethi 2013 and Kosaka 2014) and has her character Nao remark upon it as well—"some words have kotodama, which are spirits that live inside a word and give it a special power" (Ozeki 2013, 98). "Kotodama" bespeaks reliance on words to give access to and stay in contact with the naked, raw reality as well as reach beyond individual experience; "kotodama" conveys the hope that by undertaking a seemingly paradoxical detour by imagination one can reach truths that escape grasping or reasoning and examine the crevices dug in the surrounding universe. These genuine authorial creeds are actually instilled into the two main characters of this book, as both Nao and Ruth find their "superpower" while living the interconnectedness between reading and writing.

Ruth and Nao are not just spatially separated, but also temporally so. Their getting in touch is somewhat *ex abrupto* when the 16-year-old Miss Yasutani goes, surprisingly for one who has decided on a private practice of writing like the diary, in search of another—"Hi! My name is Nao, and I am a time being. Do you know what a time being is? Well, if you give me a moment, I will tell you" (Ozeki 2013, 3)—, and of another's time: "I'm reaching forward through time to touch you" (26). This is more than a monologic situation as someone is being spoken to; and from the beginning, Nao addresses the reader as though she is imagining her into existence, and as though a response were possible. As if to escape its essential and inescapable belatedness—the life led and the life recorded can never be in perfect synchronicity—, the diary has the future as its ultimate addressee and this future is meant to include Nao's—pronounced '*now*'s—temporality as well, the deliberate play on words lending urgency to the story. The hope that her diary will be read by someone sympathetic enough to at least leaf through it—someone who will "make time" for it, so to say—is conveyed with the same urgency as the belief that all humans and non-humans are "time beings," everything and everyone inextricably intertwined. Being "in time," "in one's time," "of one's time" and even "with the times" are actually questions seeping Nao's every reflexion, the young girl's understanding of self in place and time filtered from the onset through the teachings of the thirteenth-century Japanese Buddhist thinker Dōgen Zenji (directly referred to), especially his conceiving of everything and everybody as "time beings," even "words and stories" (Ozeki 2013, 24).

At the present of her writing, as she is struggling with being a being, turned into a nonbeing by her classmates' disregard and bullying, compounded by her parents' aloofness and absence, Nao sees meaning and relevance of her own self and notations in futurity, conceived as someone else's (her reader's) personal time zone, mind and imagination. She inscribes herself in time by means of conversations, talking as much to herself as she entrusts her musings to her reader, an idea conveyed by the overabundant mechanisms of direct address. Deciding that her diary will chart and gain insights into selves and lives, it is there that she will retrace, explore and record the life of the "most important person" she knows, "totally unique and special," her great grandmother Jiko, "a nun and a novelist and New Woman of the Taisho era ... also an anarchist and a feminist" (Ozeki 2013, 5). Proceeding to write about a member of her family who has not left behind any personal account of her life, the young narrator expresses not only a wish to inscribe herself in a meaningful biological filiation but also, more surreptitiously, in a literary one, as her diary is hidden inside the covers of a book entitled *À la recherche du temps perdu*: "[Jiko] told me lots of stories ... and that's when the idea popped into my mind of using Marcel Proust's important book to write down my old Jiko's life" (24).

The quest for a meaningful filiation initiates a reformulation of the reality (essentially biological) of filiation, the symbolic dimension of emancipation and inscription underlying the personal need to find meaning being also intimately related to an attitude towards cultural heritage. The question of writing is here related to legacy and the tangibility of its incarnations and forms, the past not only trickling into or soaking the present, but in full synchronicity with it: "it felt as if me and old Marcel were on the same wavelength," observes Nao (23). The references to the past, compounded by the interrogation of its manifestations and practices, convey disarray in the present and only a renewed dialogue with what happened before can dispel it. Nao's "googling" of Marcel Proust's name and Amazon searches of the sales rates of *In Search of Lost Time* in an effort to understand the importance of this book she has only heard about, have reminded me of another French writer's words, René Char's aphorism that "our inheritance was left to us without a testament."[5] This observation helps elucidate the young girl's undertakings as it expresses both the consciousness of an inheritance—puzzling as it is—and the need to examine the traces left by previous generations.

The highly symbolic use of "Marcel Proust's important book" (Ozeki 2013, 24) may be a means of allying her diary with a canonical and publicly celebrated text as well as of inserting it into an alternate literary trend thriving on experimentation, innovation and a blatant breaking down of boundaries between fiction and non-fiction. There is more to it than meets the eye, however, and not just because Nao's diary is hidden inside covers bearing the title of Proust's masterpiece: recall another famous practitioner who bought diaries and transformed them into vehicles and caches of self-expression—Virginia Woolf. Sally Bayley, who calls this a "scrapbook method of journaling," reports Woolf's idea to bury the pages of her diary inside "the leaves of some worthy & ancient work," which the critic equates to embedding "the life of her writing within the life of something ancient," which will allow it to "fossilise, gather age and strength [and] mature" (Bayley 2016, chapter 2). The first book to be so "desecrated"

(Woolf's term) is a leather-bound volume of Isaac Watts's *Logick: Or The Right Use of Reason*, the gesture clearly one of hacking through and into ancient and canonical "logick" to replace it with the inscriptions of a woman's thoughts and reflexions, a woman who for that matter was constantly struggling with depression. Her choice may thus be further interpreted not only as subverting acceptations of reason or even sanity, but equally as pointing to the inherently palimpsestic nature of women's writing, accurately delineated by Sandra Gilbert and Susan Gubar in *The Madwoman in the Attic*, where they observe that, throughout history, women have "produced literary works that are in some sense palimpsestic, works whose surface designs conceal or obscure deeper, less accessible (and less socially acceptable) levels of meaning" (Gilbert and Gubar 1984, 73). Woolf's diary—and Nao's, by the same token—are thus palimpsests not only in that they erase texts to inscribe their own, disrupting expectations and traditions of writing, but equally insofar as they gesture to layers upon layers of referential traces and connections.

Ultimately, the thread leading to this other diary keeper who consistently made connections between her private diary and the published ones of others as well as wrote reviews and essays on the latter, including on Samuel Pepys's, brings to the forefront an inscription in a literary lineage that prefers conversation to imitation, endeavoring to reach knowledge of oneself through dialogue.

The echoes thus emerge only amplified if one ponders on recurring themes like the acute awareness of living in time, the grip of time or the freedom from the contingencies of time. Interestingly so, Nao's preoccupation with "now"—*NOW* felt like a big fish swallowing a little fish, and I wanted to catch it and make it stop (Ozeki 2013, 98)—acquires deeper valences if read alongside with Virginia Woolf's turning to writing as an attempt to "stay, this moment" (in Ellis 2007, 129) or to Proust's overarching concern with salvaging the transient from the destructive effects of time.

"I'm reaching forward through time to touch you" (Ozeki 2013, 26) Nao writes, apparently conveying something other than what Philippe Lejeune has observed about diarists when he sees them as performing the past for an unforeseeable future (Lejeune 2009, 19) or as managing time (Lejeune 2009, 24). If there is indeed the wish for a dialogue between the writer and the reader implying a "pact of diary performance in time and through time" (Lejeune 2009, 24), what Nao experiences in writing is more of a release from the temporal reality of her self; freed from any order of time, she aims at creating intersubjective relations that would also transcend time and shake lives and consciousnesses at both ends.

Nao and her diary will indeed touch lives in ways more complex than she or her first reader, Ruth, could have foreseen. Ruth appears not to belong to her time herself: "She didn't like talking to people in real time anymore ... Their move to the island was a withdrawal" (Ozeki 2013, 83). Solitary and disorientated, she is drafting and re-drafting a "battered," unsatisfactory memoir of the time she spent looking after her dementia-suffering mother, fearful that she may have inherited the disease.

Ruth's first presumption is that the package washed up after the Japanese tsunami that had taken place only a few months before. After initially considering the reading as "wasting precious hours on someone else's story" (31), as the teenager's world becomes increasingly present in hers she decides to read the diary slowly, at the same speed she imagines Nao wrote it. Reading becomes something that brings the diarist and the reader together, something involving human beings and not exclusively text. In reminiscing, Ruth remembers herself and returns to her own time; in reading, she tries to enter the time of another:

> Ruth closed her eyes. In her mind, she could picture Nao, sitting by herself in the darkened kitchen, waiting for her mother to bring her father home from the police station. What had those long moments felt like to her? ... The metallic clank of the key in the lock must have startled her, but she stayed where she was. Feet scuffled in the foyer. Did her parents speak? Probably not ... She didn't move. Didn't look up. Kept her eyes fixed on her fingers, which lay in her lap like dead things. She listened to her father bathe, and then, as her mother grimly looked on, she listened to him stumble through his confession. (64–65)

Reading becomes time spent together—time for and of being together, at the same time and equally outside time. Reading brings Nao's time into Ruth's time with such an intensity and reality that the latter forgets that they don't live in the same present and that the young diarist may no longer be of this world—either because she carried out her suicide threat or because was a victim of the tsunami that apparently brought her diary to Ruth's shore. Ultimately, reading Nao's diary gives Ruth the capacity to transcend both chronological time and the limits of her own consciousness.

REVERBERATING TIMES

Ruth's story and reflexions are conveyed through her interpretations of the similarities between Nao and herself and prompted by reading passages from the Japanese girl's diary. She pieces out Nao's stories with warmth, compassion, concern and insight, annotates the handwritten pages, translates the kanji permeating Nao's English, and googles the girl's and her family's names desperately and repeatedly for clues about their existence. These gestures propagate to her own life and influence her storytelling and her self-writing. Significantly, Nao's diary invites its addressee not to stick to it, so to speak, but to discuss with it and to assert herself in reaction to it. Not only do Nao's undertaking and questions reverberate in her own mind and are turned into a driving force of life and creativity, but they also make it possible for her to transcend time and space and influence the course of events in Nao's life. The experience of time set in motion by reading appears as the reverberation of one individual experience in another and creates a network of consciousnesses, opening personal memory to other temporalities, of both contemporaries and forerunners.

To illustrate this point with one significant thread developed in the narrative, the young girl's professed purpose in writing is "to tell someone the fascinating life story" of her 104-year-old great-grandmother, Jiko. The grandmother–granddaughter relation is the key to this story. The former's words, both fragile and powerful, give shape and meaning to the latter's quest, in strong contrast to the silence of the girl's parents. The act of attempting to elucidate the traumas that haunt the elderly woman's past invariably leads to an interweaving of Jiko's stories into Nao's articulation of her own cultural displacement and personal desire for a space of belonging. By reassembling pieces of memories rescued from family and collective amnesia, Nao will bear witness to undocumented lives, illusions, failures or wounds to create meaningful genealogies that transcend and overlap temporally and spatially. Therefore, the grandmother's stories become a palimpsest over which her listener, now teller, draws her own narrative. Jiko unveils and stirs up memories, both personal and cultural, individual and collective and, most significantly, instructs Nao in the practice of remembrance, alerting her to the danger of becoming insensitive to one's history, being "heiwaboke" (180). Indifference has silenced memory and it is only as a seeker of an embodied past that Nao is able to connect with those who went before her.

Abstractions dry out the fabric of history and Nao is aware of how dull her sensibilities are, of how impervious and unreal the past is to her and of how difficult it is to connect with it:

> It's hard to write about things that happened a long time ago in the past. When Jiko tells me exciting stories from her life, like … when my great-uncle Haruki #1 died while carrying out a suicide bomber attack on an American warship, the stories seem so real … but later, when I sit down to write them, they slip away and become unreal again. The past is weird. I mean, does it really exist? It feels like it exists, but where is it? And if it did exist but doesn't now, then where did it go? (97)

Reading and writing as interconnected emerge as the most privileged form of relation to another, conceived only as a dialogic experience, waking the character to the promise of a chance of living in her own time if only to prolong her great-uncle's time into hers. Haruki was Jiko's only son, a promising student conscripted into becoming a kamikaze pilot during the last days of the Second World War, who chose to sink his own airplane rather than play an active role in a war he didn't believe in. After receiving his wristwatch as a gift from Jiko, who extracts her promise to wind it every day, Nao becomes increasingly convinced of the necessity to search his time better to understand not only him but herself as well. Self-writing brings together both anteriority and interiority, the young girl's reading of Haruki's letters addressed to his mother while training with the army to become a "sky soldier" charting a search for self that takes a detour to a different search. And this draws a particular form of attention that is less concerned with the factual reconstruction of a life than with the subjective representation that the young inquirer can make of it.

Seeking self-understanding in the interplay between collective and family memory and history, Nao becomes keen on re-establishing a genuine filiation through reflexion and dialogue. A consequence of this development is her refusal to deal with flawed parenthood by "murdering the father"—which can be understood literally here, as the young girl recounts at length her father's suicide attempts and her own initial accepting of them as his "karma"—"… maybe it's just my dad's karma to end up on a park bench feeding crows in this lifetime, and really you can't blame him for causing a human incident and wanting to move along to the next lifetime pretty quick" (52). In quite a surprising twist, a climax is reached when, increasingly glad to "learn … a lot about history and stuff" (262),

Nao confronts this "crazy and unreliable" (74) father who, unemployed and depressed, has become a "hikikomori," a recluse, holed up spending his days reading Western philosophy, constructing origami insects and making failed suicide attempts. She challenges him into refusing to see himself as a passive recipient of fate, no longer in charge of his own life, when he is not, unlike his uncle, truly without an option:

> Jiko Obaachama gave me his letters. You should read them, too, and maybe you'll stop feeling so sorry for yourself. Your uncle Haruki Number One was brave. He didn't want to fight in a war but when the time came, he faced his fate … He was a kamikaze pilot, only his suicide was totally different. He wasn't a coward. He flew his plane into the enemy's battleship to protect his homeland. You should really be more like him! (264)

Deep similarities between the two Harukis' questions, puzzles and anxieties come to life, fragments of disparate times identified, related and articulated as father and daughter proceed, after Jiko's death, to reading together the secret diary of the student-soldier.[6] Nao, who has so far only remarked upon her father's silences and few words, chooses to extensively record his loquacious flow of talk:

> He was still talking. "… so that's why I cried today, when I read Uncle Haruki's diary. I understood how he felt, you see? Haruki Number One made his decision. He steered his airplane into a wave. He knew it was a stupid, useless gesture, but what else could he do? I made a similar decision, also stupid and useless, only my plane was carrying our whole family. I felt so sorry for you, and for Mom, and for everyone, on account of my actions …" (388)

In this deployment of strong moments of a family line the survival of the past acquires meaning in relation to its prolongation into future action: the written traces materializing Haruki Number One's acts help bring to light his namesake's haunting anguishes, as it turns out that the father had actually quit his job when the company he was working for started using the interfaces to design weapons controllers for the US Army. They do more than that as they allow the two, father and daughter, to continue reading—and being together—in a revitalizing process of recovery, mutual understanding and reconciliation. Ultimately here, reading is evinced as not only time regained, the realization of another's time in one's own time, but also as mediating an awareness (or recognition) of oneself in time, as the last entries in Nao's diary attest that they also weave themselves back into the fabric of their being in their present:

> He's stopped reading The Great Minds of Western Philosophy completely, and spends all his time programming, which really is his superpower ... and maybe I've started to find mine, too, which is writing to you ... And maybe you'll be glad to know that for the first time in my life, I really don't want to die. When I wake up in the middle of the night, I check to see if H #1's sky soldier watch is still ticking, and then I check to see if I'm still alive. (389)

Placed under the aegis of Marcel's Proust's musings from *Le temps retrouvé* that "in reality, every reader, while he is reading, is the reader of his own self" and that "the writer's work is merely a kind of optical instrument, which he offers to the reader to permit him to discern what, without the book, he would perhaps never have seen in himself" (109), Ruth's own awareness of selfhood emerges through an interweaving of acts of individual and collective reading and recollection. As she delves deeper into Nao's diary, she not only engages emotionally with this stranger's story but also allows herself to come face-to-face with fragments of her own past and with people from the community she lives in, albeit initially to find help with the deciphering of the other items found with the diary in the Hello Kitty box. If the reader is encouraged to share in the production of meaning, the strategy at work here is, importantly, an ethical device attempting to activate in her a desire for communication and community with others, while preserving rather than obliterating differences. This transformative interaction first draws attention to a reception act conceived as not racially bound. Underlying this formulation of collective and collaborative acts of reading is a metadiscursive refusal to suggest Nao's story is Ruth's alone to handle or Ruth's in the first place because Ruth would be some kind of racial bridge, because she is mixed, because, as "part" culturally Japanese, "part" racially Asian, she could and would have a responsibility to make sense of Nao's story in ways others can't. Here, Ruth alone cannot make full sense of Nao's notations. She continuously needs Oliver's enlightenment on aspects ranging from ocean currents or quantum physics to crow species, as well as his perspective and insight to piece things together; Nao's narrative also benefits from anthropologist

Muriel's clues, and Muriel, we learn repeatedly, is a gossip who shares everything with everyone on the island, so that what Ruth initially wants to see as her own solitary, interior work is never conducted in isolation but always in communal dialogue, whether she likes it or not. Her reading act, in fact, expands to become a gradual opening to a dialogic process, with her admitting that she also needs the help of Benoît and Kimi to translate from French and from Japanese, respectively, or that of Dr. Leistiko to provide backstory about Nao's father, Haruki #2. Throughout all this, never do Ruth's racial identity and cultural heritage eclipse other lines of interest. They are part of a spectrum of connections, just as Ruth is part of a larger community of engagement—each member, because of a variety of reasons, race among them, having differential access to Nao's narrative or to Ruth's mediation of it. Ruth reaches a sense of the truth of the human essence in being-with-others, engaged in participatory and collective reading and sharing of stories.[7] Recovery and redemption from personal disaster happen in time in a movement that becomes one of communion occurring paradoxically between irreducibly separate existences that nevertheless call and answer each other and, finally, for each other. Dora, who, as secretary of the community club on the island, is in charge of the cemetery as well, warns Ruth "not to forget" to water the Japanese dogwood she wants to plant near her parents' graves (372) and Muriel the "old-timer" takes her to task for not having marked her mother's grave with at least "a small memorial ... [i]f not for her, for everyone else" who knew and loved her (374). Ruth needs them all, with all of their curiosity and frustration and inquisitiveness, to be of her own time and to transcend self-consciousness. Without embarking on the adventure of other existences—and times—she will not reach a sense of self-understanding that transcends chronologies and realities.

"'I need a supapawa.' She closed her eyes again. Her mind was her power. She wanted her mind back" (185)—Ruth is reported to have cried out and longed for during one of those moments when she could only stare at her "battered" manuscript and "notice and admire the uninhibited flow of the girl's language" (37). Her engagement with other lives and stories will allow her to perform that which was most difficult before, when she was stranded in a disconnected present: being a daughter and an artist who can only inscribe her own existence from the prism of lives intersecting and connecting.

CONCLUSION

It seems befitting to conclude by reminding the reader that Ruth's memoir comes through not as it was initially meant to—a reverberant space of a very personal quest, centered on her "own feelings and reactions" while observing "the gradual erosion of her mother's mind" (64)—but as a palimpsestic and multivocal narrative. Emerging as polyphonic and dialogical, outward and community focused, encompassing and claiming other "I"s of real and/or imagined figures, it testifies to the power of written words to save things from total oblivion and disappearance, to become bearers of memory and means of making time concrete. If *A Tale for the Time Being* itself does not leave us with the certainty of powers retrieved, it provides at least a promise of their being reactivated via an active and empathetic engagement with reading and writing, my reflexions here an enactment of these very movements of the mind.

NOTES

1. In a Skype interview and discussion with the participants in the session dedicated to her work at the *European Association for American Studies Conference* in April 2016, Ozeki meticulously outlined the different stages of a strenuous writing process involving several moments of "unzipping" and "breaking into" the book's "fictional container" (Krevel and Botshon 2016).
2. As pointed out in the interviews with Anita Sethi (2013) and John Endo Greenaway (2013), respectively.
3. Philippe Lejeune recalls the two noted occurrences of the first name "Marcel" in the diegesis as well as the suggestion of the hypothesis of giving the narrator the same first name as to the author; in his opinion, this installs the text in an "ambiguous space" (Lejeune 1975, 29).
4. After having for decades pondered on the genre of *In Search of Lost Time* and clarified, time and again, his take on it, Genette seems to capitulate before the generic ambiguity of the Proustian text. In *Bardadrac* (1982, 2006), which is not a theoretical work in the classical sense of the term, but a collection of alphabetically classified mini-essays, he returns to propose the designation of "autofiction"—which he had already used in 1982 in *Palimpsestes* only to invalidate it subsequently! Real or strategic abdication on his part, the question deserves to be asked…
5. "Notre héritage n'est précédé d'aucun testament" (Char 1946, 62).

6. The diary appears, mysteriously for them, in Haruki #1's remains box in Jiko's temple. The limited space available here does not allow for an examination of their turning up there and of the supernatural twist in the plot accommodating it.

7. This echoes Maxine Hong Kingston's search for "a community of like minds" to overcome the paralysis of her mind after the tragedy of the Oakland fire—"I do not want the aloneness of the writer's life. No more solitary. ... The Book of Peace, to be reconstructed, needs community" (Kingston 2003, 61–62).

References

Bayley, Sally. 2016. *The Private Life of the Diary: From Pepys to Tweets.* [Kindle version]. Retrieved from http://www.amazon.com.

Char, René. 1946. *Feuillets d'Hypnos.* Paris: Gallimard.

Davis, Rocío G. 2007. *Begin Here: Reading Asian North American Autobiographies of Childhood.* Honolulu: University of Hawai'i Press.

Doyle, Jessica. 2013. An Interview with Ruth Ozeki. *AbeBooks.* http://www.abebooks.co.uk/books/authors/ruth-ozeki-interview.shtml.

East, Ben. 2013. The Tide Turned for Ruth Ozeki with *A Tale for the Time Being. The National,* March 19. http://www.thenational.ae/arts-culture/books/the-tide-turned-for-ruth-ozeki-with-a-tale-for-the-time-being.

Egan, Susanna. 1999. *Mirror Talk: Genres of Crisis in Contemporary Autobiography.* Chapel Hill/London: The University of North Carolina Press.

Ellis, Steve. 2007. *Virginia Woolf and the Victorians.* Cambridge/New York: Cambridge University Press.

Forest, Philippe. 2005. *La beauté du contresens et autres essais sur la littérature japonaise.* Nantes: Éditions Cécile Defaut.

Genette, Gérard. 1982. *Palimpsestes. La littérature au second degré.* Paris: Éditions du Seuil.

———. 2006. *Bardadrac.* Paris: Éditions du Seuil.

Gilbert, Sandra M., and Susan Gubar. 1984. *The Madwoman in the Attic: The Woman Writer and the Nineteenth-Century Literary Imagination* (1979). New Haven/London: Yale University Press.

Greenaway, John Endo. 2013. Ruth Ozeki: Stepping into Character for Her Latest Novel. *The Bulletin: A Journal of Japanese Canadian Community, History + Culture,* April 16. http://jccabulletin-geppo.ca/ruth-ozeki-stepping-into-character-for-her-latest-novel/.

Hendry, Diana. 2013. *A Tale for the Time Being,* by Ruth Ozeki—review. *The Spectator,* March 30. http://www.spectator.co.uk/books/8872631/on-the-beach-5/.

Kingston, Maxine Hong. 1982. Cultural Mis-readings. In *Asian and Western Writers in Dialogue: New Cultural Identities*, ed. Guy Amirthanayagam, 55–65. London: Macmillan.

———. 1989 (1976). *The Woman Warrior: Memoirs of a Girlhood Among Ghosts*. New York: Vintage International, Vintage Books, Random House.

———. 2003. *The Fifth Book of Peace*. New York: Alfred A. Knopf.

Kosaka, Kris. 2013. Ozeki's Work Reflects Her Complex Identity. *The Japan Times*, November 23. http://www.japantimes.co.jp/culture/2013/11/23/books/ozekis-work-reflects-her-complex-identity/#.VVTAIZMvvps.

———. 2014. Nineteen Questions: Ruth Ozeki. *Nineteen Questions*, January 6. https://nineteenquestions.com/2014/01/06/ruth-ozeki/

Krevel, Mojca, and Lisa Botshon. 2016. Reading Ruth Ozeki in the New Millennium: Two Views and an Interview. (personal communication, forthcoming).

Lee, Felicia R. 2013. What the Tide Brought In. *The New York Times*, March 12. http://www.nytimes.com/2013/03/13/books/ruth-ozekis-new-novel-is-a-tale-for-the-time-being.html.

Lejeune, Philippe. 1975. *Le pacte autobiographique*. Paris: Éditions du Seuil.

———. 2009. *On Diary*. Ed. Jeremy D. Popkin and Julie Rak, trans. Katherine Durnin. Manoa: University of Hawai'i Press.

Lim, Shirley Geok-lin. 1991. *Approaches to Teaching Kingston's "The Woman Warrior"*. Ed. Shirley Geok-lin Lim, ix–xi. New York: MLA.

NPR Author Interview. 2013. Tsunami Delivers a Young Diarist's 'Tale' of Bullying and Depression. *NPR*, March 13. http://www.npr.org/2013/03/17/174215667/tsunami-delivers-a-young-diarists-tale-of-bullying-and-depression.

Ozeki, Ruth. 2013. *A Tale for the Time Being*. Edinburgh/London: Canongate.

——— 2015. In *Facebook*. Retrieved 23 July 2015. https://www.facebook.com/ruth.ozeki?fref=ts.

Palumbo-Liu, David. 2014. Where We Are for the Time Being with Ruth Ozeki. *Los Angeles Review of Books*, September 16. http://lareviewofbooks.org/interview/time-ruth-ozeki.

Sethi, Anita. 2013. Meet the Author. *The Guardian*, March 7. http://www.theguardian.com/books/2013/mar/07/ruth-ozeki-interview-time-being.

Smith, Sidonie, and Julia Watson. 2017. *Life Writing in the Long Run: A Smith & Watson Autobiography Studies Reader*. [E-reader version]. https://doi.org/10.3998/mpub.9739969.

Suzuki, Tomi. 1996. *Narrating the Self: Fictions of Japanese Modernity*. Stanford: Stanford University Press.

CHAPTER 14

Haunting Books and Stories in Janice Kulyk Keefer's Postethnic Family Memoir *Honey and Ashes* (1998)

Corinne Bigot

INTRODUCTION

In the beginning were stories. In the prologue to *Honey and Ashes: A Family Story*, the Canadian writer Janice Kulyk Keefer explains that she wrote the memoir because she wanted to collect and write down the stories about "the Old Place" that had filled her childhood, but had vanished from her consciousness as an adult (Kulyk Keefer 1998, 4). The stories which fed her feeling of, and desire for, difference, were told by her grandmother, mother and aunt and evoked their lives in Staromischyna (in today's Ukraine) before they left for Canada in 1936. Writing down the stories turned into composing a family memoir—Kulyk Keefer evokes her own childhood in Toronto, and writes the lives of her grandparents, mother and aunt in pre-multicultural Canada in the 1940s and 1950s, and their lives in Eastern Europe. Like other forms of life writing, a narrative of family is "a set of shifting self-referential practices that, in engaging the

C. Bigot (✉)
University of Toulouse II Jean Jaurès, Toulouse, France

© The Author(s) 2018
V. Baisnée-Keay et al. (eds.), *Women's Life Writing
and the Practice of Reading*, Palgrave Studies in Life Writing,
https://doi.org/10.1007/978-3-319-75247-1_14

past, reflect on identity in the present" as the author is at the same time the observing subject and the object of investigation (Smith and Watson 2010, 1). Janice Kulyk Keefer, whose name on the cover is a conscious choice that signals her "split self" (Kulyk Keefer 2016, 25),[1] has written an immigrant family narrative that is centrally concerned with ethnicity. As Sidonie Smith and Julia Watson point out, "immigrant narratives ... have long been sites through which formerly marginal or displaced ethnic ... subjects explore the terms of their cultural identities and their diasporic and transnational allegiances" (Smith and Watson 2010, 156). The memoir, which entwines the meaning of the "I" with the "we" of collective memory, is a poignant exploration of personal, familial and historical memories. Kulyk Keefer reads and writes about her family's homeland's tragic history,[2] which she claims to have inherited. Thus, the memoir is centrally concerned with the kind of memory Marianne Hirsch calls post-memory—the memory of the child of survivors (Hirsch 1997, 22) who is haunted by his or her family's past, which she tries to reconstruct. The stories, that are both seductive and full of holes, trigger a desire to know more, which results in an investigation, with Kulyk Keefer commenting on her readings, and a reconstruction, in which the reader is included, notably through Kulyk Keefer's comments on the family photographs that are included in the memoir.

This chapter intends to show that *Honey and Ashes*, a postmodern narrative that draws attention to its author's gathering, perusal and interpretation of family documents as well as history books and novels, is centrally concerned with reading—both reading lives and reading herself home—and the exploration of the relationship between literature and haunting.

My analysis will focus on the author's careful reading and/or examination of her sources and her attempt to create a "postmodern space of cultural memory composed of leftovers, debris ..." that are interwoven "to tell a variety of stories, from a variety of often competing perspectives" (Hirsch 1997, 13). I will also examine Kulyk Keefer's attempt to produce an alternative form of memory work by weaving her family's story into (Canadian and Eastern European) History, and her attempt to write a postethnic story that speaks "across borders." Finally, I will show that Kulyk Keefer's belief in a "continuum of experience and imagination" (7) is linked to her belief in the power of literature to move and touch human beings, and to haunt them.

THE FIRST STRANDS OF THE WEAVE

I read *Honey and Ashes* as a postmodern family narrative, constructing a family story through careful analysis of its myths. It is constructed as a weave, the women in her family having inspired the running metaphor— Natalia, Janice's mother, who entered the Toronto School of Design and became a talented clothes designer; Olena, her grandmother, who was a gifted seamstress; and their foremothers, who were weavers in Staromischyna. Janice Kulyk Keefer evokes women who washed and dried the stalks of flax and hemp that they later wove into thread: "all winter long the women's looms hum and clatter" (19). The metaphor of the weave also transpires when she evokes the objects Olena brought to Canada—quilts, cushions, kilims, a wall hanging, and a *poyas*[3] she had woven herself (113), the list evoking the threads that compose the family story/ies.

The first chapter focuses on the stories Olena, Vira (her aunt) and Natalia (her mother) told Janice throughout her childhood, and the powerful impact they had: they were "like the books in which [Janice] lost herself" (299). They conjured up a world that was more real to her than the world of TV cartoons whose characters' adventures "paled beside the stories [her] mother told of her childhood in a village named Staromischyna, or 'the Old Place'" (12–13). The Old Place, in the immigrant's memory, is always a paradise, as Eve Hoffman, who left Poland at 13, points out in her own memoir, *Lost in Translation* (1998, 5). As immigrants whose "past is home, albeit a lost home" (Rushdie 1992, 9), Olena, Natalia and Vira have created fictions, an "imaginary homeland" (Rushdie 1992, 10) which Janice inherits. They conjure up a fairy tale village, complete with thatched houses, horses and carts, geese, storks, fields and orchards; in the stories, their house is "not a house but a world" (23). The untranslatable words that evoke it make it even more fantastic and real: "you enter the house by the *siny* … you pass the *komora* with it sacks grains and flour … two stoves, one for cooking and a tall clay *pich* … The *bambatel*, with its grand wooden floor …" (24). The world of stories was, like the world of fairy tales, a world the child could return to in her mind and imagination, since it never left her. In the first section of the memoir, Kulyk Keefer uses the stories she remembers to conjure up and imagine the lives Natalia, Vira, Olena and Tomasz (her grandfather) had before they emigrated to Canada.

Stories, however, are only one strand of the weave since Kulyk Keefer examines family photographs, documents and even objects, trying out different ways to read them and relate them to the stories, in order to tell the story of the family. So doing she creates a "postmodern space of cultural memory composed of leftovers, debris, single items in order to tell a variety of stories, from a variety of often competing perspectives" (Hirsch 1997, 13). Another layer of reading is added when Kulyk Keefer reads the documents she inherited from Tomasz and connects them to the stories. These documents—passports, cards, boat tickets, birth and death certificates—are said to be her "most precious possessions" (16) and their reading, with the help of a friend who speaks Polish, is also foregrounded. Some documents "validate the existence" (53) of characters in the stories, enabling her to see them: "Petro suddenly comes alive for me: Petro, who was struck dead ... when he was only seventeen" (53). They help her understand the plight of her family better: Tomasz's 1931 boat ticket and his stamped passport provide her with the dates of his single visit to Staromischyna during the family's seven-year separation (73–74).

Yet some documents force her to see that "stories speak one language: documents another" (52). Thus, one document reveals a six-year legal battle after Olena's father's death that contradicts the moving story of his deathbed bequest to Olena (53). Kulyk Keefer's examination of official documents in Latin, Ukrainian, Polish and English enables her to retrace Tomasz's journey from Poland to Canada and to find the truth about the births and deaths of his children. Comparing the dates on the birth and death certificates to the date on the boat ticket leads to the discovery that the moving story of his having left home on the very day the twins were born and his son died is untrue (61). Yet she sees that stories do not really lie—Olena's story repairs the wrong before the judge did since Olena's father intended to give her his property, and the second one creates meaning as Tomasz's departure for Canada is "mirrored" by his son's birth and death (62) while making the father's plight easier to picture. Thus, Kulyk Keefer does not oppose documents to stories or truth to fiction, rather she weaves them together.

READING PHOTOGRAPHS AND WRITING THE FAMILY MYTH

Family photographs regularly feature in family memoirs[4] and *Honey and Ashes* includes a 14-picture family album which Kulyk Keefer comments on. As Roland Barthes has shown, one "reads" pictures (Barthes 1977,

32–51; 52–68), and as Marianne Hirsch demonstrates, family photographs can be "read" (Hirsch 1997, 10) as part of family narratives. On a first, simple, level, Kulyk Keefer reads the pictures by relating them to the stories: some photographs enable her to suddenly see fabled characters such as Melania, Olena's cruel mother, who looms large in Olena's stories. More interestingly, she reads them critically, since, as Marianne Hirsch argues, photography "perpetuates family myths while seeming merely to record actual moments in family history" (1997, 7). While Kulyk Keefer reads and deconstructs the family narrative through family photographs, she also foregrounds her participation in its construction, through appropriation: "we appropriate [people in the pictures] for our purposes, making mysteries or moral fables out of the way they stand" (Kulyk Keefer 1998, 59). She is aware that family photographs "locate themselves precisely in the space of contradiction between the myth of the ideal family and the lived reality of family life" (Hirsch 1997, 8): for instance, she reads the snapshot of a family gathering in which Vira and Natalia wear smart dresses as evidence of their mother's belief in the obligation to be well dressed for a photograph, although the family had very little to eat (Kulyk Keefer 1998, 136). She sees what the photograph hides (their poverty) and relates it to a larger context by quoting Margaret Forster's working-class memoir in which Forster writes of the significance of dressing well (136).

Family pictures (and the order in which they appear) enable her to both read and write the family myths, for instance a series of pictures featuring Vira and Natalia, from 1937 to 1949, from the classroom at Charles Fraser School to Vira's graduation, tells the story of the girls' successful integration in Canada. She also uses a photograph she calls "the best" family portrait (156) to write Tomasz and Olena's narrative. In the snapshot, taken two years after Olena and the girls joined Tomasz in Toronto, Olena, Vira and Natalia stand behind Tomasz, who is seated. Kulyk Keefer reads the picture—her family's smiles, their impeccable clothes, the crease of Tomasz's trousers, and their shining shoes—as evidence of the family's success. She also connects it to the wedding photographs that should have been taken, but were not, due to the bride's parents' opposition to the marriage, and writes the family portrait into the family myth. She does not only see it as evidence of a happy life, she reads it as the conclusion of a fairy-tale-like narrative: "here, then, is the happy ending of the courtship in that moonlit orchard seventeen years ago" (156).

Kulyk Keefer also draws attention to the construction of the family myth by exposing the seam of a photograph. A studio portrait featuring Tomasz, Olena, Vira and Natalia is described, commented on and included in the book, dated "1928?" (np). It used to hang in the grandparents' bedroom, and for years Janice believed it was taken in Toronto, after the women arrived. But her investigation (comparing dates) proves that the photograph "tells a lie" (84), which her careful examination of the picture confirms. She finds the seam that joins the two photographs—Tomasz's, taken in Toronto, and the women's, taken in Pidvolochysk. So it speaks of the family's seven-year separation, through its "scar": "though the tinting has been done by a skilful pair of hands, it can't disguise the scar between presence and absence" (85). While the photograph creates the family myth, the seam exposes its construction. It is also evidence of a silent repair, revealing a desire to change the story.

DRAWING THE READER IN

I believe Kulyk Keefer's comments on the photographs she has included to be a device meant to draw the reader in, encouraging her to try her hand at reading them too. This reader is brought in, encouraged to participate in the weaving of the story, through the compelling force of the pictures. For instance, commenting on the studio portrait of her aunt and mother taken in the early 1940s, four years after their arrival in Toronto, Kulyk Keefer draws attention to the girls' unusual pose (they stand back to back, their shoulders touching), proudly asserting that they are sisters (102). Read in connection with the chapters devoted to Natalia's and Vira's "journeys," from their first days in Toronto when they arrived at the ages of 14 and 12 with no knowledge of English, to their graduations from design school (Natalia) and university and medical school (Vira), the picture and the next two snapshots are part of the narrative of the immigrant family's successful journey, or, in Hirsch's terms, the family myth. Yet I find that the girls' portrait yields another interpretation: reading it with the chapter in which Kulyk Keefer calls the girls "survivors" (105) and describes the many diseases—scarlatina, typhoid fever and diphtheria—that killed many children in Staromischyna, including the girls' sister, I see two survivors who stand together and *alone*: "after the death of the twins, they have to be everything to one another, for better or worse" (105). I also follow Kulyk Keefer's reading of the family myth through the wedding photographs (Olena's, Natalia's and Vira's) she comments on and includes, and add my own reading. Kulyk Keefer evokes the *poyas* that Olena brought from home for her daughters to wear on their wedding days, concluding that the *poyas*, embroidered blouses and skirts were nowhere to be seen on these days, as evidenced by the pictures. I see that the wedding photographs reveal the girls' successful integration in Canadian society *and* the cultural gap with their previous lives, yet my eyes are drawn to a *punctum*, a piece of embroidered cloth on Olena's arms, suggesting her connection to the past.

READING AND WEAVING THE FAMILY HISTORY INTO CANADIAN HISTORY

As she describes herself reading the family documents and photographs, Kulyk Keefer writes them into the larger context of Canada's immigration history. In the early to mid-twentieth century, Halifax and Quebec were Canada's two major ports of entry for immigration from Europe, which the Solowskis' journeys illustrate. Interestingly, at the time when Kulyk Keefer was composing the memoir, the Canadian government was constructing a site of memory [*lieu de mémoire*][5] (Nora 1996, 194) of its own—Canada's Museum of Immigration in Halifax.[6] The museum opened on the very site where immigrants used to be processed upon arrival, and has become a symbol of the memorial heritage of Canada's immigrant communities.

Collecting, reading, describing and quoting from the family documents and photographs, reading them in connection with the stories, Kulyk Keefer creates her own place of memory to write the family's experience of exile into Canada's history of immigration. She uses Tomasz's boat ticket as well as official documents stating that Tomasz was "legally admitted" at the Port of Quebec in 1927 and certifying he had been "passed by the surgeon" to retrace his journey from Danzig to Saskatoon via Cherbourg, Quebec and Halifax (62) and to evoke immigration from poverty-stricken Europe. She narrates Olena, Natalia and Vira's departure from Poland and arrival in Halifax in 1936 and also the medical inspection they endured from Vira's point of view. She links Vira's trachoma to an article from the *Halifax Herald,* April 4, 1903, claiming that sixty of the 160 Canada-bound passengers from Eastern Europe on one liner were held up for trachoma (115). The article helps her to understand why Olena needed to have Vira's trachoma treated before they left Poland, although the treatment was barbaric. The success story does not cancel out the hardships the family experienced, both during the journey and once in Toronto, nor the reasons why they left "the Old Place." Kulyk Keefer recalls the objects her grandmother took with her from home, those remainders and reminders of the past that always spoke of exile and loss. She evokes Olena's first sewing machine in Toronto, which was encased in a box "like a relic" (30), and fascinated her. It was understood to be inferior to the black and golden machine Olena had in the village, and so reminded her of their exile. The Canadian machine was also evidence of their first years in Toronto, when Olena started earning paltry sums sewing shirts for another more successful immigrant. As an adult, Kulyk Keefer reinterprets the fabled black and golden machine as the result of dire poverty and forced immigration: it was bought with the money Tomasz had earned in Canada, and enabled Olena to sew clothes for their children, "whose very existence ha[d] forced her husband to live so far away" (30).

POSTMEMORY

As a postmodern life narrative focusing on ethnicity and legacy, *Honey and Ashes* is an attempt to "resituate the autobiographical 'I' within an ethnic 'we' as the meaning of her 'I' is entwined with and must be read with the 'we' of collective memory" (Smith and Watson 2010, 176–177). In a telling scene, Kulyk Keefer describes the experience of seeing her face in her grandmother's pictures, a resemblance she accentuates by putting on a headscarf. So doing she turns into "any woman from the Old Place, sixty or six hundred years ago" (47–48). This strengthens her belief that there is no clear break between past and present. The scarf, she sees, is both shelter and halter, both a shell and a noose (48). It reveals her attachment to her family and to her family's past, however tragic the past was.

The memoir reveals "a compulsion to tell" that marks second-generation Canadian Ukrainians (Ledohowski 2013, 198–216). Collecting the stories Kulyk Keefer comes across silences, denial, and memory losses, which become blatant when she starts reading history books: "[t]his curiosity meant that following what had been private images, family myths, into the vortex of context—a public world full of other people and events that the storytellers of my childhood had never known, or had forgotten, or suppressed" (Kulyk Keefer 5). *Honey and Ashes* is concerned with postmemory, which, as Marianne Hirsch explains, is inherited, "delayed, indirect, secondary" (Hirsch 1997, 13). Hirsch's concept is linked to Henri Raczymows's concept of *mémoire trouée*, a memory full of holes which also defines the indirect and fragmentary nature of second-generation memory (Hirsch 1997, 23).

The memoir shows that, as Hirsch argues, photography and postmemory are related (12–13; 19). Describing the family portrait that used to hang in her grandparents' bedroom Kulyk Keefer confesses, "all my life I've been haunted by this photograph" (85). She sees more than the seam in it, she sees Vira and Natalia as haunted by the deaths of their siblings: "sometimes it seemed as if the pallor of the children who'd survived was an act of revenge ... by the ones who'd died" (85).[7] Although Janice has never known the twins, nor seen any photographs of them, they are haunting presences in her imagination, and with them, countless, nameless infants who died of typhoid fever, scarlatina or diphtheria in the Old Place. *Honey and Ashes* is a testimony about being haunted by absent presences, through stories that are half-remembered and half-forgotten. Kulyk Keefer narrates the story of Olena's sister's tragic death as told by her grandmother. The 15-year old died in a Russian punitive raid during the First World War (151–152). Like everyone in the village the girl was forced to dig trenches in the cold all day; she was later discovered to have a fever and alarmingly swollen legs. As the girl refused the only solution she was offered—amputations—she died of gangrene. Janice is haunted by the fact that no one remembers her name: "all we can call her is 'the girl'" (152). Memories and stories are full of holes which, coupled with the striking images survivors evoke, increase their haunting effect. Natalia remembers only one night of terror when they had to hide from the Polish militia (181). However partial the story is, it haunts Janice's postmemory, as evidenced by an isolated one-sentence paragraph that repeats Natalia's description of her cousin who had been savagely beaten to death: "A mess of red jelly, crusted with flies" (181).

READING HISTORY

Kulyk Keefer claims she has inherited "the burden and gift" and a past which she sees as "an equal spill of beauty and blood" (14) and explains that to claim Ukrainian descent is to belong to "the most tragic nation in Europe" (199). Remembering the stories resulted in questions about her family's homeland's history and the family narrative turns into an investigation. Her intention, as she explained elsewhere, was to "go into the intersection of history and [her] family's personal history" (Kulyk Keefer and Zakydalsky 1996, 10). She describes herself reading history books and the *Encyclopedia Britannica* to learn about the history of Galicia (Kulyk Keefer 1998, 167). She later reads books about the history of the Jewish community in Poland and Ukraine. History books yield intellectual comfort, proving that the Poles and Ukrainians were encouraged to fight against each other by their rulers (169) or showing that the prejudices against the Jews were not the products of genetics but were motivated by economics and empire (202).

Yet history books prove to be too "abstract" (202) and do not help her to "see" people. So she draws connections between the history books she reads and the personal and familial stories she was told, since what matters to her is the intersection between History and family history, which is accessed through stories. She relates Tomasz's life to the history of Eastern Europe: when he turned 18, in 1918, Galicia, which was part of Austria, became part of Poland (167); when he married Olena, Poland's rights to Western Galicia were confirmed by the League of Nations (178). She finds Tomasz and Olena's exile in a paragraph stating that starvation in Galicia resulted in forced immigration (171). She compares sources, multiplying perspectives. She reads about "the pacification of Ukraine" when it became part of Poland after the 1818–1819 war—in books, in an article from *The Guardian* dated October 1930 that explains that "the pacification" of Ukraine meant "punitive expeditions" (179), and in a booklet dated 1931 and published by the Ukrainian Review, which describes Polish brutalities in Eastern Galicia (179–180). This she relates to Natalia's story about finding her cousin's body after a raid.

History books also provide her with knowledge that confirms her own feeling of having inherited a tragic history. A complex history of colonization, invasions, changing borders, and violence, including pogroms, emerges. History books, however, do not devote many pages to the Ukrainian–Polish War (1918–1919) which for her is "one of these crucial places where private and public history, family memory and public record intersect" (174). Tomasz, whose father was Polish, joined the Ukrainian Galician army, and thus fought against his father's people during this war. While history books tell her that Galicia became a killing field, and that thousands of civilians were killed (170), family (hi)story cruelly reminds her that brothers fought with and killed one another.

The references to the encyclopaedia's entry on "Galicia" serve other purposes. They prick the reader's interest since she is unlikely to have come across the name Galicia, encouraging her to read on. Referring to the region as "Galicia" also reveals how impossible it is to call it either Poland or Ukraine. It highlights an impossibly complex weave of ethnicities and nationalities—Goths, Slavs, Hungarians, Ruthenians, Ukrainians, including ethnic Jews—and a complex coexistence of languages—Yiddish, Polish, Ukrainian, Russian, German.

A Postethnic Memoir

Like all chronicles of diaspora, *Honey and Ashes* "interrogate[s] and undermine[s] any simple or uncomplicated sense of origins" (Chambers 1994, 16). Kulyk Keefer makes a clever use of the paratext to shift the ground of reference for identity: two maps, meant to be read together, shift boundaries as Staromischyna moves from the Polish–USSR Ukrainian border to Ukraine (x, xi). Her explanation that "Staromischyna" is a rendering from Cyrillic into English of the Ukrainian name, while the name that appears on prewar Polish documents is spelt differently (xiii) and her mention of reading family documents written in Polish *and* Ukrainian shifts the ground further. *Honey and Ashes* belongs to a recent trend in family narratives that explore "a postethnic identity" (Smith and Watson 2010, 157) and challenge the single story of fixed identity. Her own grandfather offers a case in point when she asks, "was he Polish or Ukrainian, Tomasz Solowski?" (Kulyk Keefer 1998, 173), and she uses family documents to prove her point: "My grandfather's name as it appears on official documents is perfectly Polish" (173).

Kulyk Keefer makes it clear that for her ethnicity is linked to history, rather than culture, and is neither a cultural choice, nor an intellectual one: "for me ethnicity has been no voluntary affair of food and dress but a mesh of old place and new, of personal and public history—a mesh that cuts deeps into the skin" (7). As Lisa Grekul points out, the figurative bridge of blood that exists between Kulyk Keefer and her family's history is a recurring image (Grekul 2005, 150), but I find the image of the mesh cutting into her skin equally crucial. Since she often refers to borders, defines herself as "a Ukrainian-Canadian with a thread of Polishness in her" who wishes to tell a story that speaks "across any number of borders" (7), I read her metaphor with Gloria Anzaldúa's metaphor of the border as an open wound: "the U.S.–Mexican border es una herida abierta where the Third World grates against the first and bleeds" (Anzaldúa 2012, 25). In *Honey and Ashes*, the wound breaks where the past grates against the present and bleeds into it.

The memoir is meant to draw connections between people, across borders and ethnic divides, in an attempt to create "a common space" (7). The memoir challenges "the single story"[8] by refusing to take sides, by showing equal concern about the victims of the Polish-Ukrainian war, pogroms,[9] and the Holocaust, by showing how prejudice spreads, and by adopting multiple sources and perspectives. Thus, she tries "to see things from the Polish side" (179), that is to say her readings enable her to analyse the difficulties the new Republic of Poland that the Allies "pulled out" of their hats after 150 years of colonial rule faced: to understand how the attempt to build the nation led to defining its people by their language and their faith, and that denials of human rights and perversions of justice were doomed to occur. Above all, reading about the 1918–1919 Polish–Ukrainian war enables her to understand that the Ukrainian school she attended taught them "the single story": "it was understood that the Poles were our enemies" (173). She also explains that she was traumatized by an American novel she read in her twenties, at a time when she lived in England and had decided to become Janice Keefer. Louis Begley's novel, *Wartime Lies,* which details "the long Polish struggle against the Ukrainian invaders" (200–201), is both the other side of the story she was used to hearing about at Ukrainian school and a single story that feeds into *and* fuels prejudices. The novel, which made her feel close to despair (200), had the power to conjure up a world whose burden overwhelmed her, and confirmed her desire to flee from her own past.

A Continuum of Imagination: Literature and Painting

Kulyk Keefer explains that her choice to study English literature in England was a way for her to escape from her ethnic identity (221), hence her choice to write a PhD dissertation on Henry James, "that arch-Anglophile" (221); however, she discovered that he expressed exactly what she was desperately running from—"the imagination of disaster" (221) that haunted her family. It was Toni Morrison who later taught her that imagination is bound up with memory (7). The memoir makes it clear that literature puts words to her feelings, and helps her define what she believes in. As a writer who had previously written a novel about a woman haunted by Woolf's novels, and would later use T.S. Eliot's *Waste Land* as a haunting sounding board to a poem conveying her worries about the new millennium,[10] Janice Kulyk Keefer expresses her belief in literature when she says she believes in "a continuum of experience and ... imagination" that can bring people together (1998, 7).

She believes that books can make us "read ourselves home" (233) and so she reads herself home, even when quoting the Caribbean-Canadian poetess Dionne Brand's impossible longing for home (326). She recognizes the Zbruch (Staromischyna's river) in Isaac Babel's story "Crossing the Zubrich" (18; 202). She relates to Chekhov's stories, whose setting and characters evoke the peasant culture she comes from in a much more truthful, albeit frightening, way than sentimentalized images on greeting cards (91). As she is writing the memoir and reading about the hostilities against Jews in Ukraine, she re-reads Isaac Babel, with whom she fell in love in her twenties. "Crossing the Zubrich" enables her to imagine Olena's Jewish friends of whose fate nothing is known (202–203).

The "continuum of imagination" implies the capacity to touch and be touched: Babel's story hurts her because it has the power to touch: "it's as though he were writing with the tip of a knife, nicking not paper, but skin" (203). Virginia Woolf's words wring her heart (16). A chronicle about a princess in Kiev who was forgotten in a labyrinth-like palace when her family fled the Mongol slaughters "gnaws" at her (169), as it evokes her father's sisters who were left behind when their parents fled to Canada in 1914. She can endow objects with the power to tell stories of people's lives/deaths. One object in a British Museum's display of jewellery hidden and found in Kiev moves her because it conjures up "the warmth and softness of the skin that wore it" (161). The mention of the woman's skin reminds me of her relation to the miniature cupboard that used to sit on a shelf in her mother's house: "a replica, holding ... the touch of the hands that had fashioned it" (26). The key word, I think, is "touch," a word with a double meaning, tactile and emotional (Sedgwick 2003, 17). Eve Sedgwick argues that to touch is always to reach out, to fondle, and "always to understand other people," "if only in the making of the textured object" (14), and this is shown by Kulyk Keefer's attempts to reach out to people in the memoir. The attention she pays to people's faces, photographs, objects or books she remembers from her childhood or encountered in her investigation reminds me of Jean-François Lyotard's idea that Walter Benjamin's childhood stories do not describe events from childhood, but "capture the childhood of the event and inscribe what is uncapturable about it" (Lyotard 1992, 106). Lyotard defines the encounter/event thus: "What turns an encounter with a word, a smell, place, book, or face into an event is not its newness ... it is its very value as initiation. You only learn this later. It cut open a wound in the sensibility. You know this because it has reopened since and will reopen again" (106). While many such encounters/events with people, artefacts, stories and book pepper *Honey and Ashes*, one in particular deserves careful attention—the encounter with *The Diary of a Young Girl*, which she read at age 12.

The experience is so intense we might call it love at first reading as Anne Frank and her diary become one with Janice: "it became my companion, my shadow self" (194). She recalls a strong sense of identification, although Anne Frank was German and Dutch, and a Jew: "we were the same somehow" (194). She identified with Anne as a girl, whose thoughts and "desires" she shared (194), and as one who like herself was "other" (194). She recalls that the introduction to the diary shocked her into understanding what genocide was, which she related to her own family's history, further reading her life in Anne's: "Anne had been murdered, along with millions of other people, just for being. What happened to the Franks could have happened to us; Anne's death could have been my own" (194). The diary was also the first reading experience of hearing two voices, the girl's and "the voice of History with a capital H" (194), which led her to start reading history books, which was also the first intimation, if not step, of her larger, relentless investigation. The diary is a "bridge of words" that speaks across borders. It contains all that matters to her and which *Honey and Ashes* retraces: the intersection of the personal and the historical, a voice that had to capacity to touch her readers across borders, and finally, a haunting child.

The final section of *Honey and Ashes* is devoted to her own visit from Poland to Ukraine, all the way to the "Old Place." It reveals another crucial encounter with paintings by Natalka Husar, a Ukrainian-Canadian artist, who painted the *Black Sea Blue* series after her own journey to Western Ukraine. Janice took the catalogue with her on her journey, along with maps and guidebooks, suggesting they meant as much to her and guided her as much as books could. She inserts several titles into the narrative, and describes several paintings, but only includes one reproduction. On the surface (literally) *Pandora's Parcel to Ukraine* tells the story of the thousands of parcels Ukrainian-Canadians sent to the region (228). Beneath the surface, through the technique of underpainting, another story appears: one can see Chernobyl children,[11] whose bodies are already showing signs of disease (228). These children, which Kulyk Keefer has elsewhere called fireflies,[12] join a host of ghostly presences—Vira and Natalia's siblings, her mother's cousin, "the girl" whose name no one remembers, a cousin called Petro, Anne Frank, among others—that haunt her imagination and the memoir, and prompt her to write.

While works of literature and art are shown to be crucial to Janice Keefer as a human being and as a writer, Greek myths and literature are granted a special role. *Honey and Ashes* starts with and returns to Greek myths, from Orpheus and Odysseus (16) to Odysseus and Persephone (283), because they illustrate what we seek, they warn us but also express a writer's most meaningful attempt: to write of the dead. Kulyk Keefer reads her own venture in the myth of Orpheus: "what Orpheus attempted: to bring back the dead from an underworld of silence and forgetting" (16).

CONCLUSION

Honey and Ashes is both a postethnic family memoir and a postmodern life narrative, whose narrator comments on her readings and the role they played in her life and sense of identity. The memoir grants equal importance to family documents, photographs and stories and to history books and novels, all of which are part of the "weave." The metaphor of the woven cloth that runs throughout the memoir reads at first as a woman's tribute to her female ancestors, most of whom worked at their looms in the village, and to her mother and grandmother, who were seamstresses. But it also enables a writer and lover of world literature to place her life narrative inside its larger tradition, as Greek mythology and literature are rife with weavers from Arachne to Philomela to Penelope.

Although Kulyk Keefer started with the intent of writing of "her" dead, the memoir, through collective memory and history, speaks of the haunting presence and lives and deaths of many others. As she writes the memoir, she understands that writing is an act of exorcism that sabotages itself since it turns into "one more form of haunting" (16). *Honey and Ashes* is a form of memory work that comprises both reading lives, from her parents to strangers, through encounters, and writing these lives, all the while "fight[ing] against the cicatrisation of the event," as Lyotard puts it (1992, 106) to preserve the haunting. *Honey and Ashes* also establishes a strong connection between literature and haunting as the passion for stories, books and reading goes with the desire to be haunted.

NOTES

1. In "Language Lessons," she explains that she started to call herself Janice Keefer after her marriage to Michael Keefer, only to see that this proved no solution to her "problematic sense of identity" and so decided on "an unhyphenated" name that would be an acknowledgement of her split self. (Kulyk Keefer and Zakydalsky 1996, 25).
2. As the memoir will show, situating the village, and more largely, this region of Eastern Europe, is a loaded issue. Galicia is a historical and geographic region in Central-Eastern Europe, once a small kingdom that straddled the modern-day border between Poland and Ukraine. Kulyk Keefer cites the Polish thinker Adam Michnik who calls it "the most tragic nation in Europe" (Kulyk Keefer 1998, 199).
3. A piece of cloth to be wrapped around the waist, to mark off the blouse from the skirt.
4. For instance, Michael Ondaatje's *Running in the Family* (1982), which Kulyk Keefer evokes as the kind of family memoir she intends to write (Kulyk Keefer and Zakydalsky 1996, 10), includes several family pictures.
5. The concept of memory sites (*lieu de mémoire*) was popularized by the French historian Pierre Nora in his three-volume collection *Les Lieux de Mémoire* (1982–1984), published in English as *Realms of Memory* (1996).
6. Canada's Museum of Immigration at Pier 21 in Halifax opened in 1999. It occupies part of a former ocean liner terminal and immigration shed. Family documents such as tickets, passports or photographs, and personal objects such as suitcases, are on display, to illustrate and retrace the story of Canada's European immigration, and to evoke the fates of the thousands of immigrants who arrived from Europe, and, more largely, immigrants. The museum offers visitors the possibility to trace their ancestors' history. Its purpose is to make Canadian proud of their ancestry and history, which stands in sharp contrast to the experience immigrant communities had, as Kulyk Keefer's memoir reveals.
7. The twins were born in 1927; Ivan died aged six months, and Marusia a year and a half later. The photograph was taken around 1928.
8. I borrow this metaphor from the Nigerian writer Chimamanda Ngozi Adichie who used it to refer to prejudices, in particular ethnic prejudices, in her 2009 Ted Talk. See https://www.ted.com/talks/chimamanda_adichie_the_danger_of_a_single_story.
9. One section of the memoir is devoted to her confrontation with another aspect of her family's homeland's history, that proves equally tragic, equally haunting: "to claim Ukrainian descent is to belong to what Polish thinker Adam Michnik has described as the most tragic nation in Europe. ... the tragedy has to do with an equally vicious anti-Semitism that became part of my life" (199).
10. *Rest Harrow*, 1993. "The Waste Zone," 2001. See Olinder 2009.

11. The nuclear plant accident occurred on 26 April 1986 at the Chernobyl Nuclear Power Plant near Pripyat, in what was then part of the USSR but is now Ukraine.
12. Janice Kulyk Keefer wrote about the Chernobyl children in her 1996 novel, *The Green Library*. In the novel, the father of one of the victims calls the children "fireflies" (Kulyk Keefer 1996, 213).

References

Adichie, Chimamanda Ngozi. 2009. "The Danger of the Single Story". Ted Talk. https://www.ted.com/talks/chimamanda_adichie_the_danger_of_a_single_story. Last Accessed 21 May 2017.

Anzaldúa, Gloria. 2012. *Borderlands/La Frontera*. San Francisco: Aunt Lute Books.

Barthes, Roland. 1977. *Image, Music, Text*. Trans. Stephen Heath. London: Fontana Press.

Chambers, Iain. 1994. *Migrancy, Culture, Identity*. London/Oxford: Routledge.

Grekul, Lisa. 2005. *Leaving Shadows. Literature in English by Canada's Ukrainians*. Edmonton: University of Alberta Press.

Hirsch, Marianne. 1997. *Family Frames: Photography Narrative and Postmemory*. Cambridge, MA: Harvard University Press.

Hoffman, Eva. 1998. *Lost in Translation*. London: Vintage. First published 1989.

Kulyk Keefer, Janice. 1996. *The Green Library*. Toronto: Harper Perennial.

———. 1998. *Honey and Ashes: A Story of Family*. Toronto: Harper Flamingo Canada.

———. 2016. Language Lessons. In *Canada Unbound*, ed. Lisa Grekul and Lindy Ledohowski, 23–40. Toronto: University of Toronto Press.

Kulyk Keefer, Janice, and Oksana Zakydalsky. 1996. Interview: Governor General's Award Nominee Janice Kulyk Keefer. *The Ukrainian Weekly* 45: 5–10. Sunday November 10.

Ledohowski, Lindy. 2013. The Compulsion to Tell Falls on the Next Generation. Ukrainian Canadian Literature in English and Victims of the Past. In *Reconciling Canada. Critical Perspectives on the Culture of Redress*, ed. Jennifer Henderson and Pauline Wakeman, 198–216. Toronto: University of Toronto Press.

Lyotard, Jean-François. 1992. *The Postmodern Explained to Children: Correspondence 1982–1985*. London: Turnaround.

Nora, Pierre, ed. *The Realms of Memory*. Trans. Arthur Goldhammer. New York: Columbia University Press.

Olinder, Britta. 2009. Images of Canada in a Post-national Perspective. Janice Kulyk Keefer's 'The Waste Zone'. In *Canada: Images of a Post/national Society*, ed. Gunilla Florby et al., 277–288. Brussels: Peter Lang.

Rushdie, Salman. 1992. *Imaginary Homelands*. London: Granta Books.

Sedgwick, Eve Kosofsky. 2003. *Touching Feeling*. Durham: Duke University Press.

Smith, Sidonie, and Julia Watson. 2010. *Reading Autobiography: A Guide for Interpreting Life Narrative*. Minneapolis: University of Minnesota Press.

CHAPTER 15

Reading Fathers, Writing Self: Selfhood Dissolved in Maxine Hong Kingston's Poetic Memoir *I Love a Broad Margin to My Life*

Joan Chiung-huei Chang

Introduction

The Woman Warrior, published in 1976, established Maxine Hong Kingston as a writer who challenged literary genres, including life writing. *The Woman Warrior* has succeeded in refuting and reframing conventions of ethnic ideology and cultural understanding in an innovative manner while encouraging readers to see literature and culture from an unprecedented perspective. Her latest book, *I Love a Broad Margin to My Life,*[1] is a 229-page memoir in one poem; published in 2011, it received mixed reviews.[2] For example, American poet and critic William Logan criticized Kingston's poetic craftsmanship, claiming: "if you're going to write a long poem … you ought to possess some ear for the poetic line. Kingston is a prose writer who lives with ghosts (as well as a mob of banalities), writing in a form she doesn't understand" (Logan 2010, 62). David Orr also

J. C.-h. Chang (✉)
National Taiwan Normal University, Taipei, Taiwan
e-mail: joanchang@ntnu.edu.tw

© The Author(s) 2018
V. Baisnée-Keay et al. (eds.), *Women's Life Writing and the Practice of Reading*, Palgrave Studies in Life Writing,
https://doi.org/10.1007/978-3-319-75247-1_15

expressed disapproval: "the book lacks a formal structure that can accommodate the burden of so many pages" (Orr 2011, 16). Why did Kingston choose to write a free-verse memoir? This essay aims to show that *ILBM* is Kingston's most recent attempt at pursuing unconventional life writing, a path she has been exploring for decades. By analysing the role played by intertextuality and intratextuality in *ILBM*, this essay argues that Kingston not only pays tribute to her literary and biological fathers, but also stretches generic possibilities through parody, tracing journeys to the East and to the West, so as to present a plural (auto)biography with multiple subjectivities. It will show that Kingston's life narrative, which promotes her pacifism, eventually succeeds in dissolving selfhood.

WRITING HER LIFE IN VERSE

Both Logan's and Orr's criticism of *ILBM* are related to Kingston's choice of poetry for her memoir. Yet Kingston is not a pioneer in adopting verse to compose an autobiographical narrative. Many examples prove that a number of poets have resorted to this "lyrical-meditative utterance," which combines "reminiscence and meditation" (Stelzig 2012, 57) to reflect upon their lives: William Wordsworth, with *The Prelude* (1805), John Clare, with "I Am" (1848), Carl Sandburg, with "Memoir of a Proud Boy" (1918) and Lawrence Ferlinghetti, with "Autobiography" (1958). Kingston began writing *ILBM* when she was about to turn 65, a time when she felt anxious about ageing and threatened by death. Kingston gave at least two reasons for her decision to turn to poetry for this life narrative. In *To Be the Poet* (2002), Kingston announced her determination to become a poet on turning 60: "I want the life of the Poet. I have labored for over twelve years, one thousand pages of prose. Now, I want the easiness of poetry ... I won't be a workhorse anymore; I'll be a skylark. Free of obligations" (Kingston 2002, 3).[3] *To Be the Poet* is a step-by-step manual of poetry writing, a chronicle of Kingston's practice in poetry writing, and a prelude to *ILBM*. She returns to these reasons in *ILBM,* stating that writing verse is faster than writing prose: "I have fears on my birthdays. Scared. / I am afraid, and need to write. / ... / I want poetry as it came to my young self / humming and rushing, no patience for / the chapter book" (Kingston 2011a, 26). Kingston's assertion that writing poetry is faster and easier than writing prose should not be taken at face value. We should remember Robert Frost's idea that "a poem begins with a lump in the throat, a sense of wrong, a homesickness, a lovesickness" (Frost & Untermeyer 1963, 22); or Ishmael Reed's belief that "writing poetry is the hard manual labor of the imagination" (Reed 1993, 106). I believe that Kingston has written *ILBM* with a determination to celebrate the ideal of liberation that poetry suggests, and to reflect on what it is to be a poet, rather than to cultivate conventional poetic skills such as diction, rhyme, meter, or imagery.

Kingston explained the differences between writing poetry and writing prose fiction in a 2008 interview: "When I write prose fiction, I fill all the space. In poetry, I can leap about, give just a taste, a bit of color, a sound, a sighting that suggest worlds. I don't have to show a whole scene. I don't have to plot" (Shan 2008, 57). Kingston is convinced that by becoming a skylark poet, she could free herself from spiritual and physical limitations, and from the constraints of literary conventions and criticism, as she argued in *To Be the Poet*: "Poets do whatever they like ... The poem comes unworked for" (Kingston 2002, 6); "Have fun, and the poems come" (11). In a reading of excerpts from *ILBM* at the University of California in Berkeley, held on April 14, 2011, Kingston further explained: "When you're writing prose, you have no control over the margins. Whatever the printer, or whatever your computer does, that is the margin. At poetry, you the writer, the poet, controls where the line begins and ends. ... Isn't that great?" ("Story Hour," University of California, Berkeley). As Christine Lorre-Johnston observes, the very form (poetry) "also acts as a creative space in a different way, because of the wide margins it leaves on each side of the page" (Lorre-Johnston 2013, 89). Obviously, Kingston has chosen poetry for the sake of freedom from literary form, independence from literary criticism, and the hope of contending with the challenge of time.

I Love a Broad Margin to My Life must also be understood in the context of Kingston's dedication to two poets, one American and the other Chinese, one being her literary father and the other her biological father. The title is an open dedication to Henry David Thoreau, quoting his famous line "I love a broad margin to my life" from the chapter "Sounds" in *Walden* (Thoreau 2003, 90). Just as "Sounds" praises the beauty of leisure time and the enjoyment of idleness, Kingston is seeking freedom from the pressure of time through writing in free verse. *ILBM* also demonstrates Kingston's desire to build literary links with her biological father. As she turns 65, Kingston makes a bucket list for the rest of her working life, which includes:

> Translate Father's writing into English.
> Publish fine press editions of the books
> with his calligraphy in the margins and
> my translations and my commentary
> on his commentary, like the I Ching.
> (Kingston 2011a, 19)

Kingston explains that her father has been annotating his daughter's narratives "in the flyleaves and wide margins of the Chinese editions" (18), using the Chinese language. A most reticent and reserved man, Kingston's father seeks communication with his daughter in a scholarly and poetic style. Kingston's choice of writing in verse is actually a response to his feedback on his reading of her books "in the tradition of poetry answering poet" (218). In *ILBM*, by calling her father a poet and by speaking to her father as one poet to another, Kingston destigmatizes his identity as a stowaway and coolie, and shows respect for him as a poet and scholar. Therefore, in addition to claiming Henry Thoreau as a literary father and praising him for his enlightenment on what the "broad margin" in life is, in *ILBM* Kingston also pays tribute to her biological father and honours his text annotations in the margins of her books.

As Elliott Shapiro points out, Kingston can turn borders (here the margin) "from zones of exclusion into regions of possibility" (Shapiro 2001, 8). By emphasizing a "broad" margin, Kingston juxtaposes the primary text and the secondary text (the annotations), the father's and the daughter's stories, successfully establishing a space for dialogue and intimacy, and speaking for equality and collaboration.

A MEDITATION UPON AGEING AND DEATH

Yet the pivotal issue at the core of *ILBM* is the narrator's anxiety over human mortality. As the review from *NPR Books* (2011) puts it, this book is "a meditation on growing old." In *ILBM*, she explains that eight days before her 65th birthday, she attended the funeral of John Mulligan, a writer who "died without / finishing his book, *MLAmerica*" (Kingston 2011a, 8). As she confesses that she is aware of the threat of death, Kingston expects poetry to help with speeding up her writing. Already reaching seniority, Kingston expresses her evident desire to become part of the literary canon. In an interview with Paul Skenazy in 1989, she compared her writing to those of Jane Austen and Virginia Woolf; in an interview with Nicoleta

Alexoae-Zagni in 2006, Kingston explained that her writing was deeply influenced by the writers Pearl Buck, Jade Snow Wong, William Carlos Williams, Virginia Woolf, Walt Whitman, and Norman Mailer (Alexoae-Zagni 2006, 105–106). In *ILBM*, she compares and contrasts her writing experiences and works to those by writers, including Jane Austen (7), Sylvia Plath (25), Dylan Thomas (25), Cervantes (24), and, above all, Henry David Thoreau (9–10). Estimating the number of years she might still have on Earth, Kingston refers to her wishes to be as prolific and successful a writer as these canonical writers.

This anxiety over ageing and dying seems personal and simplistic, but is actually communal and complex. *ILBM* begins with the advent of Kingston's 65th birthday:

> I am turning 65 years of age.
> In two weeks I will be 65 years old.
> I can accumulate time *and* lose
> time? I sit here, writing in the dark—
> (Kingston 2011a, 3)

This birthday is shadowed by the deaths of many people, and conveys Kingston's fears about her own death. *ILBM* ends with a list called "My Dead," evoking people who passed away during the four years of her composing this memoir. In fact, *ILBM* is tinted with melancholy throughout the whole book, as Kingston ponders over human atrocity and untimely deaths, making the book almost elegiac. At the beginning of *ILBM*, Kingston reveals: "I have a superstition that as long as I, / any writer, have things to write, I keep living" (8). Towards the end, she offers: "That my writing give life, / to whomever I write about, / as Shakespeare promised" (205).

Kingston also compares the lives and deaths of her characters to tragic heroes, and, by so doing, pays homage to anonymous war victims through her intertextual references. Soon after saying that her writing would give life to whomever she writes about, Kingston suddenly announces the "suicide of Fa Mook Lan." Fa Mook Lan, the daughter transvestizing herself as a man in order to answer the draft call for her father in *The Woman Warrior*, "killed herself. / She had P.T.S.D; her soldier's heart broke, / and she fell upon her sword" (211). On the one hand, the death of the woman warrior clearly alludes to a Greek hero—Ajax, who kills himself out of dignity and sorrow by jumping upon his sword; on the other hand,

Fa Mook Lan (a variant on Fa Mu Lan) embodies all the soldiers who killed themselves after returning from wars. Due to Fa Mook Lan's androgynous identity, Kingston shows that both men and women can be victims of wars and traumatized by wars. Kingston is in agony over these deaths and laments: "Each one who dies, I want to go with you. / I feel your pull into death. / I want to join my dead" (217). To heal herself, she makes up a list of reasons for living on.

However, at the end, she suggests that poetry has failed to fulfill her expectations and needs: "I regret always writing, writing. / ... / I wanted to write. / That desire is going away. / I've said what I have to say" (221). She realizes: "Poetry, which makes / immortality and eternity, did not stop / time" (214). Despite the fact that poetry or art could be eternal, she sees that human beings, including herself, are mortal; Kingston the writer is thus humbled.

Has Kingston killed poetry? Why write and refute poetry at the same time? Linda Hutcheon—who refers frequently to *The Woman Warrior* in *A Poetics of Postmodernism*—argues that postmodernism is a "contradictory phenomenon" which "uses and abuses, installs and then subverts, the very concepts it challenges" (Hutcheon 1988, 3). Hutcheon's analysis applies to *ILBM*, and explains why the writer both upholds and denies poetry in *ILBM*. In one respect, Kingston wants her readers to appreciate the freedom and leisureliness offered by poetry for narrating her life; but in another, she reminds them that this literary construct provides little assistance for many events in real life. To drive her point home, Kingston makes a drastic call: she kills off her literary mother, Fa Mu Lan, the historical figure whom Kingston has often alluded to as a role model for female empowerment and autonomy. First, she changes her name: Fa Mu Lan in *The Woman Warrior* becomes Fa Mook Lan in *ILBM*; as "mook" often implies stupidity and meanness, Kingston replaces the woman warrior's heroic attributes with frailty and vulnerability. Then, she announces the suicide of Fa Mook Lan; therefore, she renounces selfhood in autobiographical writing.

KINGSTON'S JOURNEYS TOWARDS EMANCIPATION

My contention is that in *ILBM* Maxine Hong Kingston renounces and dissolves selfhood, since "everybody" becomes more significant than her personal welfare, as Kingston endeavours to bring peace to all human beings. Yun-hua Hsiao argues that *I Love a Broad Margin to My Life*, which the author claims will be her last book, closes the loop of Kingston's discussion on war and peace, which had started with her very first book, *The Woman Warrior* (Hsiao 2013, 88). Parody is the thread that weaves Kingston's works together—also as books of peace. Hutcheon notices that postmodernist contradictory texts are "parodic in their intertextual relation to the traditions and conventions of the genres involved" (Hutcheon 1988, 11) and that "parody is a perfect postmodern form, in some senses, for it paradoxically both incorporates and challenges that which it parodies" (11). Kingston has parodied one text after another, including those by others as well as by herself. For example, Kingston's first book, *The Woman Warrior* (1976), should be read with her second, *China Men* (1980). Blurring boundaries between fiction, autobiography and biography, these two books represent two sides—a female version and a male version—of the same text, each proposing a pacifist agenda of protest against racial, sexual and cultural discrimination in American society. Her third book, *Tripmaster Monkey: His Fake Book* (1989), is a fictional work, which describes a mission carried out by the cowboy-like protagonist Wittman Ah Sing, and stages an anti-war play, *Viet Rock,* to protest against the Vietnam War. Kingston's fourth book, *The Fourth Book of Peace,* was also supposed to be a fictional work advocating peace, composed by a writer pen-named "Maxine Hong Fiction." Unfortunately, the Oakland-Berkeley Hills Fire in 1991 consumed Kingston's draft of this book, a disaster which made her realize the limitation of fiction: "after the fire, I could not re-enter fiction" (Kingston 2004, 61). Retrieved from memory and supplemented with imagination, her fifth, *The Fifth Book of Peace* (*FBP*), a hybrid text of memoir and fiction, finally came out in 2003. Written in a conversational and stream-of-consciousness style, this book details the process of Kingston's recomposing the story of *FBP*, and recovering from the trauma of the fire accident. *FBP* should be read together with a book edited by Kingston, *Veterans of War, Veterans of Peace* (2006), a collection of autobiographical writings by participants in Kingston's veteran workshops, including war veterans, gangsters, drug addicts, domestic violence victims, and draft evaders—mostly victims of post-traumatic stress disorder (PTSD).

Both *FBP* and *Veterans of War* are healing texts, and Kingston's endeavour to bring peace to "everybody" is made clear when she explains it through a Chinese idiom: as "everybody" in Chinese ideography means "big families," she claims that all human beings are actually one big family (Kingston 2004, 241). Virtually, Kingston's wordplay with the translation of Chinese idiom and English expression is what Jonathan Shaw terms a "textual moment" when "ethnic and racial affiliation and literary culture come together" (Shaw 2011, 180). This textual moment makes Kingston aware of the limitation of fiction and the need to face the issue of war as a hard reality. It also brings about an epiphany: the significance of her life writings does not lie in her personal welfare, but in that of everybody/the big family, and this ideal autobiographical text would not be realized until her completion of *I Love a Broad Margin to My Life*.

ILBM belongs to Kingston's corpus of pacifism as it picks up the same themes and resurrects actual and fictional characters from her previous peace books, including Wittman Ah Sing, Fa Mook Lan, Kingston's father and mother, no-name aunt, Yue Fei, Ts'ai Yen, among others. Besides, it relates Kingston's actual arrest and prison stay after a demonstration against the war on Iraq on International Women's Day in 2003 as a crucial event that makes her feel closer to her literary and biological fathers. Firstly, Kingston claims this experience brings her closer to her father who was imprisoned for running a gambling house, and was actually a regular inmate in the local prison: "Now I'm on the trip / my father went on. In a paddy wagon to jail. / I'm reliving his arrests. I'm knowing his feelings" (Kingston 2011a, 143). Secondly, Kingston's "literary father," Henry David Thoreau, also inspires and encourages her. Thoreau, who was jailed by the government for tax evasion, considers the night he spent in prison "novel and interesting" (Thoreau 2007, 839). In a similar manner, Kingston claims that the day of peace protest turns out to be "the most beautiful day of our lives" (Kingston 2011a, 150). Through inspiration from both Henry Thoreau and her own father, Kingston explores the possibility of liberation from corporeal incarceration, and the prospect of transcending mortality. *ILBM* is a captivity narrative; however, it is also a text of freedom showing how one's spirit could not be subject to physical confinement. Alice Walker, Kingston's cellmate in the 2003 protest, said that "writing saved me from the inconvenience of violence—as it saves most writers who live in 'interesting' oppressive times and are not afflicted by personal immunity" (Walker 2000, 123). Similarly, Kingston's corpus of pacifism promotes a pursuit of emancipation from time and space, and of freedom from violence and wars through writing. At the end of *ILBM* Kingston reveals that she has to make up reasons why she should live on in order to stay true to Thoreau's instruction that one should "live deliberately" (218). Kingston understands that to believe that literature/writing could advocate peace is too utopian to be effective, so a new strategy should be applied for obtaining peace.

ILBM also depicts an odyssey of many journeys, with characters and narrators departing from home, travelling eastbound to different places in Asia, and then returning home in the West. Thematically, *ILBM* is indebted to two texts: the sixteenth-century Chinese classic *Journey to the West*[4] and Kingston's novel *Tripmaster Monkey: His Fake Book* (1989). *ILBM* is the parody of a parody, as it parodies *Tripmaster Monkey*, which is a parody of *Journey to the West*. *Tripmaster Monkey* features Wittman Ah Sing's adventures in the American West, mainly California, which also alludes to the immigrant history of the Chinese from China/the East to the US/the West. In addition to parodying the Chinese classic *Journey to the West*, *Tripmaster Monkey* also appropriates several other American texts. This is a significant writing feature of Kingston's, who always rewrites, revises or represents existing stories, legends, or literature in her works.[5]

Just like the Monkey King in *Journey to the West* who can perform 72 polymorphic transformations in his pilgrimage of seeking sacred texts for enlightenment, Wittman Ah Sing embarks on a crusade, and successfully transforms himself from the cynical hippie into a peace lover. However, at the end of the book Wittman claims: "There is no East here. West is meeting West. This was all West. All you saw was West. This is The Journey *In* the West" (Kingston 1990, 308). *Tripmaster Monkey* relies on a motif from *Journey to the West*, but Wittman's mission is to demystify his exotic characteristic and justify his American identity. Wittman has created a new version of the frontier story of the American West, not only presenting his own "Song of Myself" but also aligning Chinese immigrant experience with American westward history. Carrying on the storyline of *Tripmaster Monkey*, *ILBM* sends Wittman Ah Sing on an odyssey-like trip to the East. This time the "sacred texts for enlightenment" he must seek are peace tactics. While *Tripmaster Monkey* is devised as a journey *in* the West, *ILBM* depicts how Wittman Ah Sing undertakes a journey *to* the East, delineating Wittman's departure from the US to visit Vietnam, Hong Kong, and Mainland China, on a crusade seeking salvation and reconciliation for people of different nationalities and cultures.

In *ILBM*, Kingston and Wittman travel together to the East, but it becomes increasingly difficult to tell the narrative voices apart. In her review Joan Frank points out that while Kingston "traces her own ancestry in fact and imagination," Wittman Ah Sing is also wandering "portions of China in search of his original identity" (Frank 2011, np) and Heller McAlpin notes that "his travels blur with hers" (2011, np). In an interview with David Ulin, Kingston admits that Wittman is actually "my alter ego, who is more interesting than I am" (Ulin 2011, np). This technique corresponds to the motif of the shape changer in *Journey to the West*, i.e., the fluid identity of the shape-changer, and stretches generic possibility by presenting a plural (auto)biography with double subjectivities—one female and one male, one real and one imaginary—forming what Susanna Egan characterizes as "a mirror talk" in autobiography:

> The contemporary autobiographer turns with great frequency to double voicing, double vision, or that fluid and encompassing activity both personal and generic that I am calling mirror talk. Not privileging one perspective over another, but transforming the narcissistic by means of the corrective lens of the other, developing linguistic strategies that enable plural voices and that contain the oral and the written within each other. (Egan 1989, 25)

While in *Tripmaster Monkey* Kingston is the strict master disciplining her naughty disciple Wittman,[6] in *ILBM* the relationship between Kingston and Wittman has become more lenient, more equal and also more mutually supportive: "Wittman, son, brother, imaginary friend, / I need you. Help me again" (Kingston 2011a, 211). Finally, "the woman warrior" and "the Chinatown cowboy" are now on friendly and cooperative terms. The journey to the East helps Kingston to reflect on the issue of wars in the world, and pursue peace in interpersonal and international contexts. If we say that in *Tripmaster Monkey*, Kingston has transformed Wittman Ah Sing to become a pacifist just like her, then in *ILBM* Kingston has transformed herself to be more like Wittman Ah Sing—a cynical, loud, inventive angry young man who is nevertheless loving and supportive of the disadvantaged people in society.

CONCLUSION: SELFHOOD DISSOLVED

One could argue that *ILBM* is a dark book, eulogizing deaths and hinting at depression. Towards the end, Kingston suggests she might stop writing: "I'll stop, and look at things I called / distractions. Become reader of the world, / no more writer of it.... I shall begin taking / my sweet time to love the moment-to-moment beauty of everything. Every one. Enow" (Kingston 2011a, 221). Or else, as Joan Frank says, her drive to write is waning.[7]

Rather, as I see it, Kingston is suggesting the possibility that the self can dissolve even while writing her life, yet another step in her experimentations with life writing. Ever since her first book, Kingston has been playing with, experimenting, challenging, and even inventing new genres. As Derek Royal observes, Kingston's works are "using established forms of expression in a way that will subvert or open up the forms" (Royal 2004, 148). *ILBM* is a memoir by name, and by nature a heterogeneous self-display, juxtaposing Kingston's self-portrait with those of war victims. It stages war scenes and peace protests. It mingles the stories of others with her own. In many respects, this book is also a product of hybridity. As we have seen, firstly it gathers protagonists from Kingston's previous books, such as Fa Mulan from *The Woman Warrior* and Whittman Ah Sing from *Tripmaster Monkey*. Secondly, in addition to fusing facts and imagination, Kingston synthesizes generic elements from fiction, poetry, theatre, autobiography and memoir in composing this peculiar piece of life writing. Thirdly, *ILBM* is both poetry and memoir, with a clear political intent. In this respect, it is true to the experiment she conducted in *To Be the Poet*. In his review of *To Be the Poet* Lewis Klausner argues that Kingston's choice of the poetic form can be seen as politically motivated: "The verse ... has become a vehicle that frees Kingston from the constraints of writing a novel or history and to report instead on the free play of impressions and ideas in her mind, the trivial and silly alongside the serious" (Klausner 2003, 354). In other words, rather than mastery in poetry, what Kingston desires is an opening up of form, a liberation from generic determination, and freedom in literature. In *ILBM*, poetry is used to free her from any literary form demanding rigid and fixed conventions.

Finally, thanks to inspiration from her father, Kingston learns that "I" can be dissolved in life writing. *ILBM* tells how Kingston's father composes his "19th song for a barbarian reed pipe" as a sequel to Ts'ai Yen's peace song "Eighteen Stanzas for a Barbarian Reed Pipe" without using "I": "But BaBa did not write 'I.' / ... / How be American unless 'I'? Crossing / languages, crossing the sky of life and death, / Daughter will help father" (219). When Kingston concludes her memoir with the words: "Every one. Enow" (221), she is reminding us of her promotion of "everybody is the big family," a song combining English letters and Chinese ideogram, echoing Ts'ai Yen's bonding Chinese lyrics with Western music, which is also how "Daughter will help father." Instead of "I," Kingston is presenting "everyone" as the subjectivity in this memoir; she has not only put one of her alter egos, Fa Mulan, to death, but has also cancelled herself by effacing her writerly identity because she will not continue being a writer any more. With her first memoir, *The Woman Warrior*,

Kingston has undermined the conventions of life writing and foregrounded subjectivity as pluralistic and relational; with *ILBM*, she succeeds in dissolving selfhood. By enlarging "individualism" to include "everybody," Kingston has called for welfare and peace for not only one being, but all human beings.

NOTES

1. Hereafter abbreviated as *ILBM*.
2. Joan Frank claims that "Kingston's swift, effortlessly flowing verse lines feel instantly natural in this fresh approach to the art of memoir" (Frank 2011, np). For other positive reviews, see Donna Seaman (2010) and Carmela Ciuraru (2011).
3. In an interview about *To Be the Poet*, Kingston revealed that since she began her writing career as a poet, *To Be the Poet* was actually a return for her: "*The Woman Warrior* began as a poem. All my prose works began as poems. In a way I'm just wanting to go back to a short form" (Tsang 2002, 6).
4. *Journey to the West* is a Chinese novel published in the sixteenth century and attributed to Wu Chen'en. In English-speaking countries, the novel is widely known as *Monkey,* the title of its popular translation by Arthur Waley (first published in 1942). *Journey to the West* is an extended account of the legendary pilgrimage of the Buddhist Monk Xuanzang who traveled to Central Asia and India, to retrieve Buddhist sacred texts and returned home after many trials and tribulations.
5. For a detailed discussion on the appropriation in *The Woman Warrior, China Men* and *Tripmaster Monkey*, see Shapiro 2001.
6. In *Tripmaster Monkey*, as John Leonard puts it, Kingston's narrator is "usually affectionate, always ironic, occasionally annoyed—looks down on him. ... Though seldom a bully, she does at one point tell Wittman to shut up" (Leonard 1989, 770). Sometime Kingston plays the role of Kuan Yin, the Chinese goddess of mercy, and brings the Tripmaster Wittman under her control. The narrative is characterized by a complex medley of different voices: from Kingston as observer, Kingston as participant, Wittman as protagonist and Wittman as narrator. Debra Shostak remarks that the narrator of the novel "often makes herself visible as both observer and participant in the narrated action, and the result is that the boundaries between narrator and object of narration become vague" (Shostak 1998, 68).
7. Joan Frank seems pessimistic about it as she observes that after finishing *ILBM*, Kingston's "drive to write, she confesses, is waning" (Frank 2011, np); for his part, David L. Ulin argues that *ILBM* "may be her last book" (Ulin 2011, np).

REFERENCES

Alexoae-Zagni, Nicoleta. 2006. An Interview with Maxine Hong Kingston. *Revue française d'études américaines* 110 (4): 97–106.

Ciuraru, Carmela. 2011. Woman Warrior Looks at Aging, Writerly Self. *Boston. com*, January 25. https://www.highbeam.com/doc/1P2-27777419.html. Accessed 10 Aug 2017.

Egan, Susanna. 1989. *Mirror Talk: Genres of Crisis in Contemporary Autobiography*. Chapel Hill: University of North Carolina Press.

Frank, Joan. 2011. *I Love a Broad Margin to My Life*: A Review. *The Chronicle*, January 16. http://www.sfgate.com/books/article/I-Love-a-Broad-Margin-to-My-Life-review-2478442.php. Accessed 10 Aug 2017.

Frost, Robert, and Louis Untermeyer. 1963. Robert Frost to Louis Untermeyer, 1 January 1916. In *The Letters of Robert Frost to Louis Untermeyer*, 21–23. New York: Holt Rinehart.

Hsiao, Yun-hua. 2013. *From War to Peace: Maxine Hong Kingston's* Tripmaster Monkey, The Fifth Book of Peace *and* I Love a Broad Margin to My Life. *Peer English* 8: 81–92.

Hutcheon, Linda. 1988. *A Poetics of Postmodernism: History, Theory, Fiction*. London/New York: Routledge.

Kingston, Maxine Hong. 1990. *Tripmaster Monkey: His Fake Book* (1987). New York: Vintage.

———. 2002. *To Be the Poet*. Cambridge: Harvard University Press.

———. 2004. *The Fifth Book of Peace* (2003). New York: Vintage.

———. 2006. *Veterans of War, Veterans of Peace*. Kihei: Koa.

———. 2011a. *I Love a Broad Margin to My Life*. New York: Alfred A. Knopf.

———. 2011b. Story Hour in the Library: *I Love a Broad Margin to My Life*: A Reading. 14 April 2011. University of California, Berkeley. *YouTube*, April 21. http://www.youtube.com/watch?v=s3DtBRZeMq8. Accessed 10 Aug 2017.

Klausner, Lewis. 2003. Review of *To Be the Poet* by Maxine Hong Kingston. *Women's Studies* 32: 353–355.

Leonard, John. 1989. Of Thee Ah Sing. *The Nation*, June 5, pp. 768–772.

Logan, William. 2010. Weird Science. *The New Criterion*, December, pp. 61–68.

Lorre-Johnston, Christine. 2013. Thoreau's Heritage in *I Love a Broad Margin to My Life* (2011) by Maxine Hong Kingston; or, East and West Meet—Again. *Revue française d'études américaines* 137 (3): 80–93.

McAlpin, Heller. 2011. Making Room for a 'Broad Margin' to Life, in Verse. *NPR Books*, February 1. http://www.npr.org/2011/02/01/133303006/making-room-for-a-broad-margin-to-life-in-verse. Accessed 10 Aug 2017.

Orr, David. 2011. A Life in Verse. *New York Times Book Review*, March 13, p. 16.

Reed, Ishmael. 1993. *Airing Dirty Laundry*. Boston: Da Capo.

Royal, Derek Parker. 2004. Literary Genre as Ethnic Resistance in Maxine Hong Kingston's *Tripmaster Monkey: His Fake Book*. *MELUS* 29 (2, Summer): 141–156.

Seaman, Donna. 2010. Review of *I Love a Broad Margin to My Life*, by Maxine Hong Kingston. *Booklistonline.com*, October 15. https://www.booklistonline.com/I-Love-a-Broad-Margin-to-My-Life-Maxine-Hong-Kingston/pid=4362322?pid=4362322. Accessed 10 Aug 2017.

Shan, Te-Hsing. 2008. A Veteran of Words and Peace: An Interview with Maxine Hong Kingston. *Amerasia* 34 (1): 53–63.

Shapiro, Elliott H. 2001. Authentic Watermelon: Maxine Hong Kingston's American Novel. *MELUS* 26 (1): 5–28.

Shaw, Jonathan Imber. 2011. 'A Lot You Know About Us Monkeys': Representation and Reference in Kingston's *Tripmaster Monkey: His Fake Book*. *MELUS* 36 (1): 177–194.

Shostak, Debra. 1998. Maxine Hong Kingston's Fake Books. In *Critical Essays on Maxine Hong Kingston*, ed. Laura E. Skandera-Trombley, 51–76. New York: Hall.

Stelzig, Eugene. 2012. 'Lives Without Narrative': Romantic Lyric as Autobiography. *The Wordsworth Circle* 43 (1): 56–58.

Thoreau, Henry David. 2003. *Walden* (First published as *Walden, or Life in the Woods* in 1854). New York: Barnes and Noble.

———. 2007. Resistance to Civil Government. In *The Norton Anthology of American Literature*. Shorter 7th ed., ed. Nina Baym, Wayne Franklin, Philip F. Gura, et al., 829–844. New York: W. W. Norton & Company.

Tsang, Lori. 2002. From Warrior to Poet: An Interview of Maxine Hong Kingston. *The Women's Review of Books* xix.10–11: 6.

Ulin, David L. 2011. David L. Ulin Talks to Maxine Hong Kingston. *Los Angeles Times*, February 6. http://latimesblogs.latimes.com/jacketcopy/2011/02/david-l-ulin-talks-to-maxine-hong-kingston.html. Accessed 10 Aug 2017.

Walker, Alice. 2000. One Child of One's Own: A Meaningful Digression Within the Works. In *The Writer on Her Work*, ed. Janet Sternburg, vol. 1, 121–140. New York: W. W. Norton & Company.

"A 'Warrior Woman' Confronts Mortality, In Verse." 2011. Rev. of *I Love a Broad Margin to My Life*. *NPR Books*, January 20. http://www.npr.org/2011/01/20/133086352/A-Warrior-Woman-Confronts-Mortality-In-Verse. Accessed 10 Aug 2017.

PART V

Reading Herself Through Oral and Written Traditions

Homemade Tales of Homespun Lives: The Shared Search for Identity in Culinary Memoirs

Virginia Allen-Terry Sherman

INTRODUCTION

Starting from the simplified premise that authors construct autobiographical narratives in collaboration with the reader and that, for the narrator, these narratives serve as a mode of self-reading as much as self-writing (Al-Hassan Golley 2003, 58), we will discuss a specific genre of self-writing often referred to as culinary or food memoirs. My exploration of themes of authorial intention invites the use of the term "culinary," as it embodies the notion of preparation as well as consumption of food, central to questions of identity, and to the participative relationship between narrator and reader.

Helen Buss, in her work on the reading of memoirs written by contemporary women, rightly claims that the memoir form requires an active role on the part of the reader (Buss 2002, xxiv). To contextualize Helen Buss' theory, and to explain its importance to our current argument, let us look

V. Allen-Terry Sherman (✉)
Université Grenoble Alpes, Grenoble, France

© The Author(s) 2018
V. Baisnée-Keay et al. (eds.), *Women's Life Writing
and the Practice of Reading*, Palgrave Studies in Life Writing,
https://doi.org/10.1007/978-3-319-75247-1_16

271

briefly at what we can determine to be the differences between the autobiographical genre and that of the memoir and how we can consider the memoir reader is able to play that active role.

Memoirs are, by nature, more selective than autobiographies and, due to their discriminatory nature, fictional in construct. While autobiographies attempt to rewind the clock on a chronology of past events, memoirs are historically more permissive, narrating personal recollections against an intermittent backdrop of factual events. Episodic, and sometimes parenthetical in nature, a memoir often tells a story *from* a life, employing touchstones that mark turning points in an author's experience, while an autobiography can be seen to tell the story *of* a life. Sidonie Smith and Julia Watson have described the memoir genre as targeting one moment or period of experience, "characterized by density of language and self-reflexivity about the writing process, yoking the author's standing as a professional writer with the work's status as an aesthetic object" (Smith and Watson 2010, 4). This association can be seen in memoirs in the mix of the personal with the contextual, the autobiographical narrative intersecting with history. Smith and Watson have highlighted this characteristic in their citation of Nancy K. Miller's exposure of the dynamic postmodern nature of memoirs, oscillating between the "private and the public, subject and object" (Smith and Watson 2010, 4). This fluctuation requires an active stance on the part of the reader, coupled with an act of the imagination. The reader stands alongside the narrator as witness, adopting, we may conclude, one of the tripartite voices of memoir that Buss identifies, who observes and records the actions from a localized viewpoint (Buss 2002, 16). For the reader as well as the narrator, "the memoir form is a discursive practice that brings together material realities and imaginary possibilities" (Buss 2002, 185).

Sidonie Smith and Julia Watson also refer to Julie Rak's focus on discursive forms of storytelling centred around Western notions of identity-seeking, as a way of counterbalancing the exclusionary nature of autobiography; Rak sees the memoir genre as linked to popular forms of life writing that tell stories about unacknowledged aspects of people's lives, often by anonymous authors (Smith and Watson 2010, 3–4). Culinary memoirs exemplify a popular form of memoir by proposing creative mechanisms for self-searching through their focus on homespun food, culinary traditions and the inclusion of family recipes. They are a recent, essentially Anglophone and feminine literary phenomenon, that occupy a place within the evolution of the culinary imagination, as described by Sandra Gilbert (Gilbert 2014), offering a narrative framework for writers to explore memories. They (re)define home and identity, while inviting the reader to experience the author's food ways through descriptions of food preparation and recipes proposing first-hand experience.

We will explore the relationship the memoirist has with the act of reading and writing—or rather self-reading and self-writing, to embrace autobiographical discourse—as well as the influence of literature and reading on the will to write. We will also analyse the role of the reader as both the writer's mirror and actor within the text. Both the works we will discuss, by American authors, are evocations of home, whether physical or spiritual, either long sought or already found. They offer literary complementarity, as well as telling divergences and parallels. The first is *Dream Homes: From Cairo to Katrina, an Exile's Journey* (2008) by English Studies professor, Joyce Zonana; the second, *A Homemade Life: Stories and Recipes from My Kitchen Table* (2009) by food writer and blog author, Molly Wizenberg.[1]

Joyce Zonana describes her quest to discover her roots and understand the heritage of her immigrant Egyptian Jewish family. In her search for home, she weighs her ambivalent relationship to food against her chosen counterweight of literature. Molly Wizenberg tells a coming-of-age story, growing up amidst the pages of cookbooks in the kitchen, a place she asserts is her home, and recommends to her reader. Zonana, born in 1949, turned away from the kitchen early, in an age when women had to challenge their mothers' domestically defined lives, while for Molly Wizenberg, born in 1978, feminist advances had already reclaimed the kitchen as worthy territory for creativity. Molly Wizenberg's story is a profusion of memories and recipes, and a celebration of home as self-defining. Zonana learns that losing material possessions, homes, even memories, leads her to the realization that home can be anywhere one is at peace with one's sense of identity.

Autobiographical Self-Performance: The Shared Role of Writer and Reader

James Olney asserts that autobiography is the literature that offers us an increased awareness, of ourselves and our share in the human condition through an understanding of another life (Olney 1972, vii). When we seek unity within the stories of others, the acts of writing and reading work together to create order from chaos (Anderson 2011, 118). Moving beyond trauma narratives to contemporary concerns about identity, other people's narratives are, for the reader, as Sidonie Smith explains, guides to self-understanding, self-improvement and self-healing (Anderson 2011, 231).

The cultural obsession with the personality, that adheres to an ideology of individualism, accounts for the popularity of memoirs as personal story-telling since the 1990s (when the publication of culinary memoirs began its ascension): "[t]he contemporary fascination with confession and other modes of personal storytelling derives in part from the tenacious hold that the ideology of individualism has on Westerners" (Smith and Watson 2010, 124). The response also manifests a need to interact in *ad hoc* communities. As Boris Cyrulnik said, when a group hears a shared story, each person feels reassured by the presence of the others. This is why stories, myths and prayers recited side-by-side are excellent cultural tranquilizers (Cyrulnik 2012, 188, my translation).[2] The celebratory recipes that create rhythm in the memoirs under discussion offer the comfort of community prayers through their repetitive form and language.

This performative act, which echoes the self-performance of the memoir itself, implicates the reader who both accepts the autobiographical pact defined by Philippe Lejeune in which a form of authenticity takes precedence over veracity and reads stories to learn about herself: "As readers we go to history [and I would add *histories*], to learn more not about other people and the past but about ourselves and the present" (Olney 1972, 36). A memoir is as much the reader's performance as the playing out of the narrator's identity, declares Buss (2002, 35). Within this contract of sincerity, the author determines the way the text will be read, according to Jean-Pierre Carron (Carron 2002, 21, my translation).[3] Buss explains that the dominant place of the witness transforms authenticity so that it is no longer an "essentialist value but rather an effect of selection and shaping of detail" (Buss 2002, 17), which culinary memoirists attain through the choice of memories, anecdotes, recipes and rituals. Its achievement requires an active stance and an act of the imagination, for as Buss also asserts "[t]he writing of memory is a literary enterprise" (19).

Acts of personal remembering are social-interactional activities that emphasize interpersonal relatedness through participative activities. Several critics emphasize the importance of the role of the reader: "[s]haring our past experiences with others is an important part of creating shared histories and interpersonal bonds" (Fivush et al. 1999, 356), and, more specifically, as Sidonie Smith and Julia Watson claim, "life-writing requires an audience to both confirm the writer's existence in time and mark his or her lived specificity, distinctiveness and location. This autobiographical truth resides in the intersubjective exchange between narrator and reader aimed at producing a shared understanding of the meaning of a life" (Smith and Watson 2010, vii). Indeed, hermeneutical theory asserts that alone "we cannot grasp our own 'horizon of understanding' as there will always be unstated blind spots" (Moi 2002 (1985), 43). "Blind spots" subsist because, on a literary level, the memoir allows a piecemeal construction of the past which, by its nature, sacrifices objective distance to focus on detail, while on a psychological level, the narrator's memory and, more so, pen are selective, particularly in recalling childhood memories in which other people's imaginative constructions interfere with one's own.

Wizenberg audaciously proposes her life story at the age of 31,[4] although she adds to *A Homemade Life*, the discreet subtitle *Stories and Recipes from My Kitchen Table*. As a narrative of personal enterprise and self-affirmation, her *bildungs*-memoir is used to vehicle convictions about the virtues of a homemade life. It takes the form of an enthusiastic conversation with her companion-reader. Her self-reading and self-writing are, Wizenberg comes to realize, of altruistic intention in offering a homemade formula against the current of self-help culture, a culture of contemporary individualism. Her intense home focus is perhaps the literary blind spot that the reader can help her to see beyond, by reminding her that eating is ultimately a larger social act. We bake cakes, she asserts, because "That's the best we can ever hope to do, to win hearts and minds, to love and to be loved" (*HL*, 311). To authenticate this notion, we read a corresponding scenario on Wizenberg's blog, *Orangette*, in which a friend, in helping her to understand a major life change, invites her to re-read the closing words of her book *Delancey* (2015), wherein she expresses a deep-set fear of change, that elucidates her attachment to home and homemade: " ... I got to discover something in myself ... I have never been good at change. But I thought somehow that, by throwing myself into Delancey, I could trick my system, beat change at its own game. I couldn't."[5]

These blind spots take the form of paradoxes. Wizenberg's cooking is symptomatic of the solitary self-searching of youth, constantly seeking culinary perfection, while at the same time emphasizing her family's contribution: "What follows is a result of our pooled memories and my own trial and error" (*HL*, 39). Cooking is always, in essence, a collective effort. Although demanding of herself, she confesses to a strong desire to please, which she considers a weakness. It keeps her revising her recipes, her eyes fixed on her reader (*HL*, 98). "It wouldn't be right for me not to tell you about the fresh ginger cake ... I made eight different versions before I found the right one" (*HL*, 71, 87).

Joyce Zonana shares with her reader her persistent identity trauma that has kept her searching for home for years. However far she moves from her immigrant family she fails to shed her feeling of marginality in American society: "I had never been able to shake the sense of being indelibly 'other', incurably alien ... No matter what I did, I remained to myself an anomaly, a strange amalgam of ancient custom and contemporary ambition" (*DH*, 144–145). Throughout the narrative, the reader accompanies Zonana's awareness of the diasporic nature of rootless nomadic existence: "Was this how my parents felt when they moved to the United States? Separated from family, friends, familiar objects and places; scents, sounds, customs and tastes. Alone, with no support or guidance? Was this a reprise of *their* dislocation?" (*DH*, 147).

As works of autobiographical intention, these memoirs can be understood to embody an implicit contract based on the narrative and its paratexts in which author, reader and text operate in a triangle of mutual intentions. Paratexts, as Vincent Jouve reminds us, are "the collection of indications and signs that reveal the way in which the book should be read, [and] constitute a pact or a reading contract" (Jouve 2007, 28, my translation).[6] They influence the reader's horizon of expectation increasing the climate of intimacy between reader and writer, and orienting interpretations. Smith and Watson explain that Janet Varner Gunn describes two pivotal moments in reading: the first when the autobiographer reads her life; the second when the reader encounters the text and reads her own life by association (Smith and Watson 2010, 207). In effect, author and reader are each engaged in their own autobiographical act.

Rich with entertaining details, the three full pages at the beginning of *A Homemade Life* are an integral part of the narrative in which the author explicitly reveals to the reader not just selected intimacies intrinsic to a memoir, but also, in effect, the "making of" her performative autobiographical act (*HL*, v). On a purely textual level, her lengthy personal acknowledgments at the beginning of the book attest to the collective "homemade" origins of Wizenberg's narrative and convey a sense to the reader of being part of that same crowd of well-meaning bystanders, perhaps even a literary mentor. Wizenberg recognizes their constant support, even during moments of creative uncertainty: "Whenever this book gave me trouble, I worked instead on the acknowledgments. It was the easiest part to write" (*HL*, v). On a literary level, the reader is cast as a necessary accomplice in the telling of Wizenberg's food tales. Her seemingly casual tone engages the reader in a compelling conversation while teaching home life skills. She often addresses the reader directly using the second person pronoun: "It's a lot better, I swear, than it sounds. I'll tell you more about it later" (*HL*, 42); "... there was cake, of course, which I'll tell you about in a minute ..." (*HL*, 302); "You want to keep it nice and hot, but not smoking" (*HL*, 40).

In her acknowledgments, Zonana also admits that writing, no doubt conceived as an individual academic exercise, turned out to be not a solitary enterprise but, as she explains, "an intensely communal adventure, bringing [her] into ever-deepening contact with an ever-widening circle of people" (*DH*, 1). She adds, "Through the act of writing I found my home in the world" (1). It is implicitly understood that the reader is part of that community of resources that helped her to write, as part of a concerted rescue effort. The acts of writing, rereading and being read lead her home.

We find that same concord in the culinary memoir, *Under the Tuscan Sun* (1997), in which an American professor of literature, Frances Mayes, engages in a quiet conversation with her reader who implicitly shares cultural and, above all, culinary pleasures with her:

> My reader, I hope, is like a friend who comes to visit, learns to mound flour on the thick marble counter and work in the egg, a friend who wakes to the four calls of the cuckoo in the linden and walks down the terrace paths singing to the grapes; who picks jars of plums, drives with me to hill towns of round towers and spilling geraniums, who wants to see the olives the first day they are olives. (Mayes 1997, 3)

The reader becomes her mirror and the roles are reversed as Mayes "reads" what the reader has done and discovers herself in the narrative.

Autobiographical Literary Intention in Women's Memoirs

When a woman writes about herself she is immediately engaged in "a double process of writing and rewriting the stories already written about her as a woman, as being passive or hidden" (Al-Hassan Golley 2003, 61). In culinary memoirs, we witness this double act of self-discovery and self-making, in the form of self-reading and self-writing. Writing for women is a "process and a quest for dialogue, social change and the possibility of saying we as well as I" (61).

Wizenberg, the author of an award-winning blog, *Orangette*, perpetuates its informal style and literary intention of intimacy in her memoir, exemplified through the level of complicity with her reader. The expectations of dialogue transmitted through the narrative style and peritextual contract are aligned with those of her blog, a forum which, for her, is like "opening a window" onto the world:

> ... a place to tell my stories and a crowd of people who, much to my surprise seemed eager to listen, and share. What started as a lonely endeavour came to feel like a conversation: a place where like-minded people could swap recipes and dinner plans, a kind of trading post where cakes and chickpeas are perfectly valid currency. I'm not the only one, I learned, who believes that the kitchen, and the food that comes from it, is where everything begins. (*HL*, 5)

Wizenberg explains that her blog is a literary exercise and, understanding her expressed passion for writing, we can assume that this memoir fulfils a similar purpose. She describes *Orangette* as a place for her to store recipes and "the long-winded tales that spun from them" (*HL*, 5), the inspiration for her book,[7] and an extension of herself and of her home. She admits to it being a memory store where she can re-read her stories, and make sense of her life: "[p]art of what I love about writing is that is helps me to remember things ... sometimes when I sit down to write, the stories are already half-gone" (*HL*, 184). She writes with the intention of re-reading herself, to explore her memories with the objectivity of reader.

Or perhaps it would be truer to say that she writes to hear herself talk. Her extrovert fast-paced stream of anecdotes suggests that telling tales about herself is central to her existence. Although ostensibly composed as segmented stories, the chapters tell a roughly chronological narrative, each anecdote seamlessly concluding with a food story and associated recipe. Her episodic narrative marks the literary evolution of an oral form of transmission of culinary traditions. As with all shared homemade projects, it is implied that one can reproduce the culinary and literary endeavours, emphasizing that reading and writing are, by implication, interdependent. The act of reading the memoir in itself offers readers access to her lifestyle and values.

The recipes supply a further level of intimacy, allowing the author to dialogue directly with the reader in a gesture of sharing. The positions of both reader and writer are negotiated, in culinary memoirs, through the dual role of recipes. They are, at once, an integral part *and* a paratext of the narrative. The narrator pauses in the narrative to guide the reader in the realization of a recipe, cooking, symbolic of the performative act of autobiographical writing itself. They also represent the ritual of the shared meal, the breaking of bread together, a spiritual dimension that evokes archaic memories, as well as what can be perceived as a gift shared between author and reader.

Culinary memoirs thus stage their own reception through the weaving of autobiographical fragments around recipes, inviting the reader to share the author's perception of food preparation and traditions and to participate in creating and consuming—a two-way metaphor for reading. With the recipes as an open door (or, indeed, window) into the author's world, the reader plays an active role in discovering other—or even her own—traditions.

While Zonana's autobiography is a coming to terms with contradictory and anachronistic aspects of her family's identity that she had previously rejected, her recipes can be considered her family's legacy, particularly given the fragility and ephemerality of her material inheritance exposed to multiple house moves and even natural disasters. She associates herself with her family and community in her food tales: "Need I say, we like it lemony, salty, generously spiked with cumin" (*DH*, 209; 218). Throughout a nomadic existence in which she trails and finally loses meagre diasporic remnants of exile that embody fragments of her inheritance, she learns to cook her favourite childhood dishes, such as tabbouleh, and, above all, to take sensual pleasure in their preparation: "When I had finished, I would gratefully lick my fingers, savouring the bits of bulgur and parsley, the tang of lemon, and the warmth of the cumin" (*DH*, 137).

Her recipes are somewhat sterile postscripts compared to the exuberant and sensual food preparations in the text, but they remain nonetheless an integral part of the tale, their presence authenticating her search for identity. Their post-narrative placement is symptomatic of Zonana's difficulty in making food preparation and celebration a totally inclusive part of her life. She is ambivalent about the place that she wants to give them in her life, held back by the shadow of her mother's diasporic sacrificial dedication to recreating the food of her Egyptian past.

While food descriptions are hesitant, even understated in Zonana, Wizenberg allows recipes to pace the narrative (*HL*, 19) as an elemental part of the text. Her idealistic vision of food and cooking inspires her to insist that recipes are to be shared like stories, because it makes the world a better place and confirms that we are all part of a bigger chain:

> Sharing a recipe is how you pay back fate—in the karmic sense—for bringing you something so tasty in the first place … And isn't cooking about making people … feel good? It seems to me, then, that it only makes sense to give people the means to continue feeling good. By which I mean the recipe. (*HL*, 177)

Consequently, each recipe is charged with emotional and gastronomic pleasure. This memoir is her personal recipe book, confirmed by her admission, in a recent blog,[8] to always keeping her memoir and other books to hand on her kitchen, the writer-cook as reader of cookbooks and memoirs, and self-critic too, putting herself in the place of her own reader.

In female memoirs, the contract between writer and reader becomes a relationship of what Pam Morris calls literary intimacy (Morris 1993, 60). In culinary memoirs, women create a kinship within a genre. The role of the subjectivity of the female reader is crucial to the evolution of the narrator. She mediates between her perspective and that of the writer (Schweickart 1991, 540–545). While (as pointed out by Smith and Watson) Gayatri Spivak argues that autobiography may not be an ideal means for postcolonial female writers to express themselves in the context of universal individualism and possessive masculinity (Smith and Watson 2010, 129), Linda Hutcheon argues that postmodernism coincides with a "feminist re-evaluation of non-canonical forms of discourse," including family biographies and memoirs (Hutcheon 1989, 23). Food writing makes an implicit pact with readers in which memoirs become a shared venture with other women. The reader is warmly invited into the kitchen to engage in what we could describe, using Toril Moi's definition, as a non-subordinate intersubjective exchange between narrator and reader (Moi 2002, 31).

Women that work together on food projects exchange and share intimacies that enable them to protect their identity; readers become partners in reinforcing their role as good women in each other's eyes (Moi 2002, 32). Within the home, that represents a microcosm of society, Moi claims that women control the social mores and the symbolic language of food, determining what food will say about themselves, their families and the world (49). Using Carole Counihan's premise that providing food defines the nature and extent of female power (Counihan 1999, 32), sharing recipes and food traditions empowers women, allowing dysfunctional families, such as Zonana's, to perpetuate traditions. Culinary memoirs thus extend the reach of women whose power is typically exerted uniquely over family members.

Zonana's mother was not a liberated woman, but her pride in her role strengthened her identity. Described by Zonana as powerful and sensual, her mother must channel her energy into her domestic interior and create a world within the confines of her physical home and diasporic social space (*DH*, 111). Zonana rebelled against this, leaving the kitchen and rejecting the community's social isolationism, but remaining, herself, in a sort of no-(wo)man's land, occupying a professional role as academic, but unable to find a social niche for herself which could take into account her multifaceted identity.

SELF-WRITING AS A CREATIVE HEALING FORCE

The women authors of culinary memoirs are typically well educated, bookish and employed in literary professions as writers, journalists or teachers. Their approach to the transcription of culinary traditions is often forged in archaic childhood memories where reading and writing became intimately rooted (*HL*, 221), rather than in experiential culinary experiences. Recording culinary traditions is indissociable from food ways as contributing sources to locating home. Nonetheless, as we have seen, it is Zonana's act of creative self-writing, rather than her bibliographic grounding, that helps her to understand her place in the world (*DH*, 3). Indeed, memoirs for academic women—a common profile among culinary memoirists—enable them to repossess a sense of themselves as women, without sacrificing their identities as intellectuals (Buss 2002, xxv). They offer the possibility to find a balance which respects their inevitable multiplicity of self, avoiding the dichotomy of traditional identity patterns.

Zonana grew up with a dream of writing, believing that books and reading could save a person struggling with an inherited identity. Reading was her childhood evasion, a world of adventure centered around romantic wilderness homes far from her culturally suffocating neighbourhood (*DH*, 113). The escape to imaginary exotic places through the fantasy world of her books shapes her adult conscience. For Zonana, words and literature become the sacrament that cooking was for her mother. She writes "[c]ooking was my mother's art, her sacrament. She dreamed food, lived it, even as today I dream words, seeking sustenance" (*DH*, 25). As reader and writer, she weighed and evaluated words, just as her mother weighed and evaluated food: "'Hunger,' I said to myself, 'appetite, craving, greed.' 'Identity,' I pondered, 'agreement, likeness, self'" (*DH*, 30). The hunger for a sense of home and belonging that was assuaged by words as a child is satisfied by food traditions as she undertakes her journey as a writer, inviting the reader on an endotic "exile's journey," a quest in search of a home and identity. Drawn towards the intellectual world of words, she runs away from food as symbolic of domestic slavery. Searching for a physical home, she discovers an imaginary one, as she stumbles upon the "ancient home of dreams—a resting place, a cure" (*DH*, 181), at the synagogue in Cairo where her mother prayed for a child. Her journey ultimately comes to a cathartic end as she flees Hurricane Katrina and discovers that a spiritual home delimited by cultural traditions is more solid than a material one can ever be.

Exploring food traditions as a way to reach home, Zonana thus learns that food for her parents was not the slavery she initially believed. Despite the long preparation, the tightly wrapped stuffed vine leaves, a poetic symbol of the imbricated memories of the memoir itself, are a pact of self-discovery and self-realization. In the gesture, she has a similar sense of belonging and being at home that her parents felt when they bought the ingredients for her father's *ful medammes* 'chez les Arabes' on Atlantic Avenue, an outing that, as a child, bore the "aura of a pilgrimage" (*DH*, 35). The accents and aromas brought peace: "For a moment I knew who I was" (*DH*, 35), recalling a parallel shopping scene on Atlantic Avenue, when culinary memoirist Colette Rossant exclaims: "I finally felt that New York was my home" (Rossant 1999, 165).

Wizenberg's homemade life is equated with moral and emotional stability, and as such the antithesis of Zonana's diasporic journey. Wizenberg was, in a sense, never lost and therefore already "home," but she had to first find her food writing way through the academic corridors and library shelves of diverse academic departments. She evangelizes the homemade life to her readers, while validating her own choice. The kitchen is a reassuring home and her book is its celebration, a homemade project already completed. Describing herself as a "wordy teenager" lost in a world of books, poems and recipes, she reveals that the motivation to write was an early driving force reflected in her teenage compositions. An extract from her school essay on fresh ginger cake shows, even then, her informal, homespun blogger style: the delicious cake is indeed "... incredible—mark my words" (*HL*, 74). With the conception of her blog, she spends her abandoned PhD research months in Paris reading cookbooks in the Luxembourg Gardens and writing emails home about her daily food experiences (*HL*, 163). Her multiple trials for each recipe are preceded by the reading of an equal number of cookbooks. Both as a child and a student, reading serves as the inspirational springboard from which she jumps into practical projects, galvanized into action through the seductive power of words.

Culinary memoirs unite reading, writing, tasting and savouring in a creative performance between author and reader, in which the act of reading is a trope for eating: the memoir is consumed—devoured or savoured.[9] By reading and, in effect, consuming the book, the reader endorses the value of the written word. Her presence allows the writer to step outside her work and view it through the reader's eyes. Not only are these personal memories submitted, foremostly, for publication, they are also subjected to narrative manipulation to render them imaginatively appealing, as well as seeing their importance equated with, or even subordinated to, storied recipes. The reader substantiates this subjective process. While Zonana's reflective style invites meditative savouring, Wizenberg's extravagantly tasty tale has to be devoured. One finds proof of Smith and Watson's assertion that the subjectivity of another is in effect "cooked up, reproduced and tasted" (Smith and Watson 2010, 150).

Zonana's memoir evokes hunger, initially for books and later for food, while Wizenberg's tale describes appetite that is always generously satiated. This perspective gives us an insight into the place of reading for each writer: Zonana's pre-memoir reading gave her the sustenance to write, while, for Wizenberg, her current memoir is in itself the source of the nourishment she requires, confirmed in her own daily practical use of her cookbook memoir. Wizenberg considered the written word precious enough to have stored her teenage poems in the freezer, symbolic of long-term conservation, as well as quick and easily accessible nourishment (*HL*, 72). Her writing, a metaphor for food and eating, finds a common language between herself and reader. Like her academic and literary career, Zonana's search is long and painstaking, taking time to reach maturation in a slow conversion towards culinary traditions.

Despite initially running away from traditional food preparation, Zonana's first written assignment was for a cookbook of inexpensive ethnic restaurants. Believing that her chosen academic career would, she writes, "lead her away from home and food preparation and its ambiguities of identity, [she was] unaware that in the end it would guide [her] even more inexorably back" (*DH*, 31). Food was the common language between her and the immigrants she interviews for the book. Ironically, she learns to cook from surrogate mothers, driven not by a love of food but rather by a desire to write (*DH*, 30). This experience led her eventually to learn how to feed herself, both literally and metaphorically (*DH*, 31). Food and language are subconsciously intertwined with a strong symbolic resonance: in a highly sensual evocation, she describes how, drawn by a desire to reconnect with her roots, she yearns to learn Arabic, the language of her family's birthplace and of her Jewish, Sephardic, Egyptian origins, hoping to "be able to nourish [her]self with words, aromatic words that fill [her] mouth with their rich consonants and moist vowels, words that fill [her] belly with the sweet, rich juice of communion" (*DH*, 41). *Dream Homes* ends with a Rosh Hashanah meal heralding the Jewish New Year. Alongside the traditional foods of her inherited identity are her creative inventions reflecting her honed, hybrid identity: "It is not at all what my mother would have made, but it is what I want just now" (*DH*, 203). She humbly realizes that home is not necessarily a final destination, and, more particularly, that books do not have all the answers.

In front of the derelict synagogue in Cairo, Zonana has a sensation of homecoming (*DH*, 178). It is a place of healing where she was spiritually conceived and her wandering diasporic soul finds a home. Although she never found her mother's childhood house, she did find her "true birthplace" (*DH*, 180). While her mother's only memories are through sensual evocation—smells and tastes of food that evoke memories of Cairo—Zonana discovers memories that she hadn't recalled at the outset of her journey, of re-discovered culinary traditions. They are a positive, life-enhancing force that resists static, painful or inaccessible memories (*DH*, 113). The self-exploration in *A Homemade Life* is antithetical to the literal and symbolic journey in *Dream Homes*. Wizenberg advances from the outset with the certitude that "[i]n the simple acts of cooking and eating, we are creating and continuing the stories that are our lives" (*HL*, 6). Home is not the root but the stage where one plays out the story of one's life in the present instance, she thus claims: "I write about my life some, too, since it intersects with food roughly three times a day. ... For me, the two are inseparable" (*HL*, 195). While Zonana slowly connects food to her life, and current experience to memories, Wizenberg, with gentle irony, benevolently relates life to food for her readers, and ties memories to experience for herself.

Constructing her memoir is likened, by Zonana, to the long, slow process of preparing the stuffed vine leaves, fragments rolled into tight packages and simmered in the juice of imagination. Language, she believes, will make her past present, full of the flavour of the food of her family's traditions. The dish, a gift that is so painstakingly long to prepare, is made in the spirit of authenticity, of remembrance and of nostalgia, as the symbolic participative act involving the reader (*HL*, 22–23). Zonana cooks the dish as much for herself as for her guests, just as she writes the book as much for herself—for both the act of writing and reading—as for her readers, making sense of her past reading and her present writing. Her autobiographical act and vocation are validated in the dynamic interaction between text and reader, exemplary of the genre, wherein the reader oscillates between involvement and observation, narrative and recipes, recalled memories and experiential moments.

CONCLUSION

Both works propose a coming together of life and food around the home, of combining ingredients for healing, making sense of the whole, and thus making whole. While Zonana's convoluted construction of memories through the intricate preparation of stuffed vine leaves is profoundly symbolic, Wizenberg's uninhibited cooking up of memories is a literal invitation. The synergy expressed between life and food is not a mere autobiographical device: although Wizenberg says, "I don't think any of us are terribly interested in recipes that have no stories or real-life context" (*HL*, 195), their life stories require the recipes—their roots—as much as the recipes require their memories. For both authors, the presence of the reader is indispensable, yet the distance at which the narrator places her is telling. Wizenberg invites her to sit at the kitchen table, while Zonana seeks a discreet companion on her circuitous journey that circumnavigates the kitchen, concluding with a Rosh Hashanah table that celebrates tradition and invention, a sign that commensality will triumph over individualism. Zonana's reader is an observer, the mirror, rather than the actor that Wizenberg needs, the one role no less creative than the other.

NOTES

1. These works are henceforth referenced in the text as *DH* and *HL*, respectively.
2. The original French reads, *Quand dans un groupe, on partage un même récit, chacun est sécurisé par la présence de l'autre. Raconter la même histoire, croire aux mêmes représentations crée un sentiment de grande familiarité. C'est pourquoi les récits partagés, les mythes racontés, les prières récitées côte à côte sont d'excellents tranquillisants culturels* (Cyrulnik 2012, 188).
3. *L'auteur détermine les manières de lire un texte et influence les effets qu'un texte produit lorsqu'il devient public* (Carron 2002, 21).
4. Wizenberg was born in 1978.
5. From Wizenberg's November 30, 2016 blog, *Orangette*. http://orangette. net/2016/11/november-30/.
6. *L'ensemble des indications ou signaux qui indiquent selon quelles conventions le livre demande d'être lu, constitue le pacte ou le contrat de lecture* (Jouve 2007, 28).
7. From Wizenberg's "Frequently Asked Questions" on her blog *Orangette*. http://aboutorangette.blogspot.fr/.
8. From Wizenberg's July 23, 2015 *Orangette* blog "We'll go from left to right." http://orangette.net/2015/07/well-go-from-left-to-right/.
9. See "Ecrire, lire, déguster, savourer" by Simone Vierne (Vierne 1989, 92).

REFERENCES

Al-Hassan Golley, Nawar. 2003. *Reading Arab Women's Autobiographies: Shahrazad Tells Her Story*. Austin: University of Texas Press.

Anderson, Linda. 2011 (2001). *Autobiography*. London: Routledge.

Buss, Helen M. 2002. *Repossessing the World: Reading Memoirs by Contemporary Women*. Toronto: Wilfrid Laurier University Press.

Carron, Jean-Pierre. 2002. *Ecriture et identité: Pour une poétique de l'autobiographie*. Brussels: Eurorgan.

Counihan, Carole M. 1999. *The Anthropology of Food and Body: Gender, Meaning and Power*. London/New York: Routledge.

Cyrulnik, Boris. 2012. *Sauve-toi, la vie t'appelle*. Paris: Odile Jacob.

Fivush, Robyn, Catherine Haden, and Elaine Reese. 1999. "Remembering, Recounting, and Reminiscing: The Development of Autobiographical Memory in Social Context." In *Remembering Our Past: Studies in Autobiographical Memory*, ed. David Rubin, 341–359. Cambridge: Cambridge University Press.

Gilbert, Sandra M. 2014. *The Culinary Imagination: From Myth to Modernity*. New York: WW Norton & Company.

Hutcheon, Linda. 1989. *The Politics of Postmodernism*. New York: Routledge.

Inness, Sherrie A. 2006. *Secret Ingredients: Race, Gender and Class at the Dinner Table*. New York: Palgrave Macmillan.

Iser, Wolfang. 1979. *The Act of Reading*. London: Routledge, Kegan, Paul.

Jauss, Hans Robert. 1978. *Pour une esthétique de la réception*. Trans. Claude Maillard. Paris: Gallimard.

Jouve, Vincent. 2007. *La poétique du roman*. Paris: Armand Colin.

Lejeune, Philippe. 1975. *Le pacte autobiographique*. Paris: Seuil.

Mayes, Frances. 1997. *Under the Tuscan Sun*. New York: Broadway Books.

Miraux, Jean-Philippe. 1996. *L'autobiographie: L'écriture de soi et sincérité*. Paris: Editions Nathan.

Moi, Toril. 2002 (1985). *Sexual/Textual Politics*. London: Methuen.

Morris, Pam. 1993. *Literature and Feminism*. Oxford: Blackwell Publishers.

Olney, James. 1972. *Metaphors of Self: The Meaning of Autobiography*. Princeton: Princeton University Press.

Rossant, Colette. 1999. *Apricots on the Nile: A Memoir with Recipes*. London: Bloomsbury.

Schweickart, Patrocinio P. 1991. "Reading Ourselves: Towards a Feminist Theory of Reading." In *Feminism: An Anthology of Literary Theory and Criticism*, ed. Robyn R. Warhol and Diane Price Herndl. New Brunswick: Rutgers University Press.

Smith, Sidonie, and Julia Watson. 2010. *Reading Autobiographies: A Guide for Interpreting Life Narratives*. Minneapolis: University of Minnesota Press.

Vierne, Simone. 1989. *L'imaginaire des nourritures. Textes présentés par Simone Vierne*. Grenoble: Presses Universitaires de Grenoble.

Waugh, Patricia. 1989. *Feminine Fictions: Revisiting the Postmodern*. London: Routledge.

Wizenberg, Molly. 2009. *A Homemade Life: Stories and Recipes from My Kitchen Table*. New York: Simon & Schuster.

Zonana, Joyce. 2008. *Dream Homes: From Cairo to Katrina, an Exile's Journey*. New York: The Feminist Press at The City University of New York.

CHAPTER 17

Reading Culture(s) in American Indian Women Writers' Autobiographical Essays

Ludmila Martanovschi

INTRODUCTION

This study aims at investigating contemporary American Indian women writers' contributions to the volume *Here First: Autobiographical Essays by Native American Writers*, edited by Arnold Krupat and Brian Swann and published by The Modern Library, New York in 2000. The volume, preceded by *I Tell You Now: Autobiographical Essays by Native American Writers* (1987) produced by the same editors, stands on its own and it is of particular interest since it brings to light autobiographical texts prepared on the cusp of the twenty-first century by writers who became established years after the Native American Renaissance of the late 1960s laid the

I would like to thank Prof. P. Jane Hafen (Taos Pueblo) for introducing the collection *Here First: Autobiographical Essays by Native American Writers*, edited by Arnold Krupat and Brian Swann, as part of the bibliography for the course "Gender and Literature" dedicated to Native American women's autobiographies at University of Nevada, Las Vegas and allowing me to attend her class as Fulbright grantee (2003–2004).

L. Martanovschi (✉)
Ovidius University, Constanta, Romania

© The Author(s) 2018
V. Baisnée-Keay et al. (eds.), *Women's Life Writing and the Practice of Reading*, Palgrave Studies in Life Writing,
https://doi.org/10.1007/978-3-319-75247-1_17

foundation for Native writing in the United States of America. The writers included in the volume *Here First* offer fresh and nuanced perspectives on American Indian identity, and thus contribute to broadening the reader-ship's exposure to the central issues in the field of American Indian Studies.

In their introduction to the volume, the two editors, Arnold Krupat and Brian Swann, mention the fact that the contributors were asked "to speak of their lives and their relation to their art" (Krupat and Swann 2000b, xii), which resulted in many authors' decision to include information on their Native descent and tribal affiliations as well as their formative years and journey to becoming published writers. The outcome is poly-phonic, multidimensional and sometimes even contradictory, as the editors themselves notice:

> Reading and rereading these essays, what has emerged for us most power-fully is, on the one hand, how many different ways there are today to be Indian, and, on the other hand—no surprise, given that our contributors are creative writers—how many different ways there are to *write about* being Indian. (Krupat and Swann 2000b, xiv)

The 26 essays, 15 of which are signed by women, often refer to the roles of reading in the subjects' lives, precisely because the contributors are writers who dedicated their lives to working with words. Thirteen of the pieces belonging to female authors are particularly relevant for the topic under discussion here since they include reflections on the practice of reading as well as confessions about the first attempts at producing texts that could become reading material for oneself and others, all being highly revealing of American Indian worldviews and contexts.

The collection as a whole benefited from having been published by The Modern Library, a publisher which had had a mainstream readership for decades and gave the volume a chance to be known to a much wider pub-lic than that of a small press to which individual Native writers often had found themselves forced to resort to previously. The flourishing of American Indian literary production and the institutionalization of American Indian programs at university level in the second half of the twentieth century definitely contributed to making the publication of such a volume not only possible, but also auspicious.

The phrase in the title of the current study, "reading culture(s)," seeks to encompass two acceptations. On the one hand, it refers to an active process as contemporary women writers "read" or, in other words, decode the Native culture or cultures they are affiliated to, discussing quintessential knowledge, myths, practices, values, worldviews that define the families, communities, tribal nations and/or other indigenous networks that have shaped their lives. In their essays the authors often aim at capturing the core elements of their respective cultures and at perpetuating orality, a fundamental dimension of the American Indian world. On the other hand, the same phrase refers to the reading culture or cultures that American Indian women engage with on their way to becoming writers. These usually include mainstream American frameworks through which they develop their reading skills and passion for books such as the education system from primary school to post-graduate level studies, other institutions that have enabled them to access books, professional environments, especially the academia, where they thrive as readers and writers. The current analysis demonstrates that most female autobiographers in the volume strive to achieve a sense of balance between "reading" their own oral culture(s) and reading written literature, both forces contributing to their becoming writers.

As scholars concerned with the history and the specificity of American Indian life writing by women have emphasized, the defining element is connectedness between the autobiographer's experience and that of the community, which often goes hand in hand with circular narratives and the organization of the material along storytelling patterns. In *American Indian Women, Telling Their Lives* (1984), Gretchen M. Bataille and Kathleen Mullen Sands established that "female Indian autobiographers tend to integrate some elements of historic, ceremonial, and social importance into the narratives but concentrate on everyday events and activities and family crisis events—birth, naming, puberty, marriage, and motherhood" (Bataille and Sands 1984, 8). The first chapter in the volume, "American Indian Women's Narratives: The Literary Tradition," surveys the various forms in which life narratives have emerged, from as-told-to autobiographies (written by an author using information from personal conversations with the subject), with their marked ethnographic content, to contemporary written autobiographies, concluding that they all "reflect the strength and endurance of American Indian women as they face drastic changes in their own cultures and work to preserve traditional values and ways in themselves and pass them on to their children" (Bataille and Sands 1984, 24). These considerations are also valid for the contemporary women writers included in the volume *Here First*, as they grapple in their essays with the same issues that stand at the core of book-length works. Their contributions to the collection represent a coming of age of the autobiographical genre, their self-assuredness and maturity reflecting the fact that previous stages such as the one described in what follows have been surpassed: "as Native peoples developed the genre of autobiography and connected it to tribal literatures, they began to define their own space in relation to mainstream literature, utilizing colonial education to create a critical and oppositional space" (Hafen 2002, 237).

WOMEN WRITERS' READING OF AMERICAN INDIAN CULTURE(S)

Throughout the volume *Here First* the women autobiographers feel compelled to engage unapologetically in a decolonizing process and illuminate their American Indianness in their own terms, thus confirming Hertha Sweet Wong's observation according to which "[m]ost contemporary Native autobiographers interweave their personal stories with cultural myths and histories, emphasizing a specific subjectivity and the continuity of oral traditions" (Wong 2005, 142). Finding the one element in one's tribal culture that is revealing of its creation myth and historical evolution, of past and present, of the communal and the personal proves to be an effective strategy. Anna Lee Walters,[1] of Pawnee-Otoe descent, constructs her essay around the image of the buffalo, which informs all the dimensions of the two Plains tribal cultures she is affiliated to, as she explains:

> For many centuries on the Plains, perhaps as far as back as paleo times, the Pawnees (of Caddoan linguistic stock) and the Otoe-Missourias (of Siouan linguistic stock) followed the buffalo as a way of living purposefully with the workings of the sky and earth. The buffalo brought order, teachings, values, ethics, aesthetics, and life. The languages of these groups reflect long associations with the buffalo; literary forms and literature grew out of them. The peoples' experiences with the buffalo were holistic and visionary. (Walters 2000, 372)

Walters takes upon herself the role of "translating" or making what she has learned or read about her people intelligible to a wider audience who might not be aware of the many ramifications of the buffalo's traditional role in the tribe's ordinary and ceremonial living, especially given the fact that for decades "the buffalo road" has been more of a metaphor than a physical reality. She traces her origins as a writer in the songs and the prayers at the heart of the Pawnee and Otoe hunting traditions, and this particular choice of literary filiation is specific to her experience and heritage.

One more revealing example can be found with the case of Elizabeth Woody, who is an enrolled member of the Confederated tribes of the reservation of Warm Springs, Oregon. She places weaving at the centre of her artistic universe and considers it a defining experience for her tribal community and herself. Weaving serves as a metaphor for the very practice of storytelling, which is bringing all the strands of the narrative together. Also, since weaving has both a functional and an artistic dimension, it points to the fact that storytelling itself contains both a functional, didactic strand and an artistic, aesthetic strand. She expresses her literary manifesto in poetic terms, considering that "[i]t is still possible for the poet, the storyteller, the singer, the maker, and the healer to revisit the inner location of occurrences or the innovation" (Woody 2000, 382). Very importantly, she identifies the source of poetry in stories and songs, recognizing the technical dimension involved in the making of art and its therapeutic function. Knowledge drawn from her tribal background amounts to principles of poetics that have preoccupied literary minds for centuries.

A third voice who brings forward her tribal culture's creation myth in order to centre the essay included in *Here First* is Anita Endrezze, who speaks proudly about her Yaqui paternal grandparents' coming from Sonora, Mexico: "In the Yaqui story of creation, Yomumuli creates everything out of love and joy. She guides both people and animals and offers them free will within a set of moral laws" (Endrezze 2000, 141). The importance of the mythical female figure in the process of creation becomes the note that resonates throughout Endrezze's whole work. Her essay testifies to an alternative way of valorizing femininity and an emphasis on the power of women in the tribal tradition she is familiar with, which are echoed in various other contributions to the collection since American Indian women writers often choose to delimit themselves from mainstream feminism, given the distinct positions women occupied in their tribal cultures.

Irrespective of the image they embrace as organizing principle for their self-presentation—the buffalo, weaving, a female creator and law-giver—, the autobiographers in the volume connect their individuality to that of their community, resorting time and time again to tribal knowledge, mythology and practices; thus, a rich variety of American Indian cultures from across the United States of America is being brought to the readers' attention. One constant element is that the Native women writers represented in the collection under scrutiny here define themselves as storytellers, a pan-Indian trait, and thus insure their sense of continuance with family, community and tribal nation.

LeAnne Howe's personal experience deserves special attention as she was raised by adoptive parents who fortunately belonged to the family of Southeastern tribes in which her biological mother was born. Today, the writer and scholar Howe is an enrolled member of the Choctaw tribe, and in her autobiographical essay she acknowledges the fact that she was introduced to storytelling by her adoptive Cherokee family:

> My adopted Cherokee grandmother made sure that I would become a storyteller. In a way I am the bridge between blood and adopted community. By tradition and birth, I am a storyteller. I hope that I am doing what all my ancestors want me to do. In a way I am trying to tell you now, what I know from my breath and mind. (Howe 2000, 227)

Her writer's creed emphasizes the indelible connection to her family. She practices writing as storytelling, ensuring the survival of the oral tradition that she chooses to pursue programmatically. Her journey as a writer is informed by the trust she places in her role as continuator of her predecessors' way of being in the world, since storytelling represents a form of passing on knowledge as well as a mode of relating to the others ceremonially but not only.

In her turn, Kimberly M. Blaeser (Anishinaabe) testifies to the powerful identification between storytelling and American Indian identity as she says: "The stories we remember and tell have a mysterious way of journeying with us. We become the stories we tell, don't we? They inhabit us. We become the people and places of our past, because our identity is created from their stories. Looped together: memories, stories, being" (Blaeser 2000, 82). She gives poetic expression to the role of memory for identity formation. In the case of an American Indian tribal context the urgency of keeping communal memory alive in the face of the myriad threats to the existence of the tribal nation that have occurred over the centuries is paramount. The tribal stories that are transmitted from one generation to the next are not only myths, but also genuine history lessons that educate tribal members about who they are and help them preserve a sense of pride despite the colonial forces still exercising pressures. The figure of the grandmother is again intrinsic to the process of identifying one's path in life and of connecting the past to the future: "If I have found a way to balance the various loyalties with which my child's heart was early impressed, it was partly my grandmother who showed me the way" (Blaeser 2000, 89).

Vicky Sears, a Cherokee speaker who also remembers her paternal grandmother's stories, more specifically rabbit trickster tales, credits them with having a therapeutic effect on her. Storytelling is considered to have healing powers as the child grows up and makes the conscious decision to use those powers in her own writing: "My head kept returning to Elisi's stories to remember what was warm, practical, and good. Without those tales I don't believe I would have been able to survive many of the things I was to see and experience" (Sears 2000, 313). The Cherokee author discloses traumatic experiences growing up and being sent from one foster home to another, after the disintegration of her parents' marriage. At the same time she identifies the source of her sanity and well-being in her grandmother's teaching via storytelling, since she claims that the stories remembered serve as guiding principle and palliative treatment. The natural course for her is to transform her own use of storytelling filtered into her writing for the same purposes, as she confesses: "Much of what I write is about healing, especially from abuses. ... I do know that writing has always been an essential way for me to heal" (Sears 2000, 314). Her testimony enters a tradition of autobiographical writing in which the violence of the past is negotiated and about which theoreticians explain that "Narrators suffering from traumatic or obsessional memory may see the act of telling as therapeutic in resolving troubled memories, acknowledging how the process of writing has changed the narrator and the life story itself" (Smith and Watson 2010, 28). Sears concentrates on trauma that is linked both to personal history and communal experience as the problem of broken families, dysfunctional foster homes and adoption outside the tribe is a matter of deep concern for American Indian nations in general, and American Indian women writers[2] in particular. Also, life writing as a way of coping with trauma resonates with most writers as they address the history of their individual tribe's relationship with colonizing powers, a history often marked by violence, suffering and loss.

AMERICAN INDIAN WOMEN'S ADHERENCE TO READING AND WRITING CULTURES

As mentioned from the very beginning, all the Indigenous authors publishing in English have also been introduced to reading written texts (as opposed to reading oral cultures) from an early age, but their experiences concerning the acquisition of reading skills, irrespective of the fact that English represented their first language or not, differed to a great extent. Joining a reading culture almost always constituted an essential step towards becoming a writer.

One of the essays in which the transition from a world of orality to a world of writing is presented as having occurred smoothly is Luci Tapahonso's piece "They Moved over the Mountain," in which the Diné language is acknowledged as the writer's mother tongue. She considers that her Diné parents understood the importance of preserving one's identity, while adapting to the mainstream's way of life: "our success as adults depended upon formal education, as well as being knowledgeable about Diné family history and culture" (Tapahonso 2000, 343). With poetic propensity for visual detail, she recreates the actual circumstances in which she first encountered written words in an improvised private "library," while growing up on a farm north of Shiprock, New Mexico in the Southwest: "About fifty yards from our main house was an old storage shed, which was lined with bookshelves. My parents read to us in the dim coolness of the shed. We weren't allowed to take books from the shed because they might be lost or damaged. We learned to care for books so that everyone would have a chance to enjoy them" (Tapahonso 2000, 343). So gradually, the children in her family get acquainted not only with the Diné stories and songs, but also with English written words, read out loud to them. The special care and attention that books enjoy in the familial context seem to contribute to the speaker's own respect for published matter and choice to become a writer.

Tapahonso further narrates her initiation into English, which becomes identified with the academic sphere and writing. The preparations her parents had previously offered are viewed as helpful:

> It became clear that the two settings, school and home, were distinctly different places and incompatible. Yet because my parents had prepared us, and had read to us from storybooks, *Life* magazine, and *National Geographic*, I was intrigued by the surprises and mysteries the written word held, and learning to read and write came easily. (Tapahonso 2000, 344)

The interest in reading texts in English matches the process of acquiring writing skills, and the two activities are viewed as interconnected. Later, she mentions that at the Navajo Methodist Mission School in Farmington, she came to love reading and studying. Reading becomes a favourite pastime outside the classroom and, interestingly enough, it is viewed as an alternative to the school's focus upon religion: "I began reading books to fill spare time between school and meals as the fascination with the playground wore off after a month or two, and primarily because I couldn't understand the Christian religion" (Tapahonso 2000, 347). Proclaiming the incomprehensibility of Christianity is synonymous with rejecting it[3] and to clinging to the religious beliefs learnt at home, in her tribal context. The passion for extracurricular reading is gradually complemented by the interest in writing her own texts, which is encouraged by a high school teacher's appreciation of her first attempts at creative writing.

The use of the two languages she was raised with is reflected upon: "I learned to associate the physical act of writing with English, and Diné occupied an entirely different sphere in my daily life" (Tapahonso 2000, 347). Diné and English have been perpetuated into her mature years, as her books written primarily in English often include Diné lines. It is one of her critics' opinion that "Tapahonso's writing actively and consciously combines English prose and poetry with Navajo phrases to highlight the relevance of Navajo worldviews and values, and to reproduce the rhythms and styles of the oral storytelling tradition" (Tillett 2007, 89). When discussing her art, Tapahonso ruminates about the realms of the two languages, actually reflecting on the confluence between the oral and written strands in her work:

> The writing process begins as thoughts and feelings in the Diné language, which are then translated. As I think of, or remember, incidents to write about, the initial idea or "telling" is in Diné, then it is literally translated in the physical act of writing or typing. The idea of writing means writing in English, but the Diné language is the language of basic emotions. (348)

Even if perfectly bilingual, the writer confesses to the fact that Diné comes first and it is a repository of raw feeling and initial thought, while English seems to require an effort of translating all that into writing, and inevitably the process contains a form of filtering.

If, for Tapahonso, the transition to school and writing is smooth, for Blaeser the sense of wholeness that she associates with family and home gets painfully disrupted when she has to be introduced to formal education:

"I think the first real heartache of my life came when I had to leave the safe, still center to enter school. In many ways I have been homesick ever since" (Blaeser 2000, 85). This displacement is defined in terms of separation and loss: "Education has always been for me a dangerous cutting away. The academic perspective implies a distance, a distance that cannot be fully retraced" (Blaeser 2000, 85). Even if she is successful academically, Blaeser seems to admit courageously to the rift that her schooling caused in her relationship with her tribal culture and the nostalgia she feels for her beginnings. The alienating effect of having to perform in a different environment than the familial one, which used to provide a sense of security and confidence, is described accurately. It can only be hoped that as a scholar and teacher herself, she can help others make the transition less painfully.

The use of English for the purpose of expressing familial, communal and tribal concerns is sounded in Charlotte DeClue's essay. As a statement of her strong connection to her roots, she mentions the naming ceremony held for her by her relatives and makes clear from the very beginning: "I was given the Indian name, Kawashinkashinsay, Kawashinsay for short, which means 'ponytail'" (DeClue 2000, 111). The author, whose ancestors are Osage and Kiowa, both being Plains tribes, reminisces that the family history used to be recorded in a book called *The Good Red Road*, a phrase which also becomes the title of her essay. Considering the practice of inscribing various family members' life events in that book "a good source of learning" (DeClue 2000, 111), she further explains: "It was there I learned the value of writing in a language I would eventually inherit from the non-Indian world. But it was for our people that we first wrote" (111). This is a powerful testimony to "reinventing the enemy's language," as defined by Joy Harjo and Gloria Bird: "We are coming out of one or two centuries of war, a war that hasn't ended. Many of us at the end of the century are using the 'enemy language' with which to tell our truths, to sing, to remember ourselves during these troubled times" (Harjo and Bird 1997, 21). The appropriation of the colonizer's language for decolonizing purposes as well as the transformation of that language for communicating to the world the colonizer's truth and revolt remain the objectives declared throughout American Indian writing.

Reading and writing in English gain new meanings with each author. For Betty Louise Bell (Cherokee), reading is acquired outside the home, as a means of escaping the prospect of "poverty, illiteracy, domestic labor"

(Bell 2000, 33), conditions shared by relatives in the autobiographer's social environment. Reading, and later writing, enable class mobility, as the reference to Stanford University, seen as "the home of books and learning, gentility and power" (32), reveals. Bell defines herself as an avid reader from the very beginning of her essay: "Everything I know, I was proud to say, I learned from books. At the age of six, I remember declaring my ambition to be a reader. In a house where both parents were semiliterate, where I read and wrote letters for relatives who could not read or write, I knew no greater ambition than to read" (31). She further mentions her familiarity with Charlotte Brontë and George Eliot, whose characters Jane Eyre and Maggie Tulliver came alive for her, explaining that her dissertation in college many years later focused on Victorian women novelists. The fascination with strong female characters constitutes a form of training in recognizing and articulating discourse about noteworthy feminine qualities in her immediate surroundings. Her insight into the Western canon[4] is complemented by the need to write about realities that are close to her and that need to be rendered into literary form: "I began to remember that I had had a life, not the life of Dickens, Brontë, or Eliot, but a life shaped and haunted by its own unwritten but not untold stories" (35). Thus, Bell documents the fact that she used her training in order to give voice to the powerful feminine presences in her memories: "Ironically, my first novel came not from the canons of English and American literature but from the Oklahoma voice of my mother and my great aunt" (35). Relying, for one's writing, on Native women's lives whose stories are made known from an inside perspective becomes not only an act of decolonization, but also an instance of repositioning women in their rightful place. Bell programmatically counters representations by outsiders and reverses the process of silencing and distorting women's experience.

Nora Marks Dauenhauer shares a similar trajectory, but the writers that make up her list of role models, or else literary influences, are different. Raised in a traditional Tlingit setting, she went on to attend Alaska Methodist University (AMU) in Anchorage, obtaining a BA in anthropology. The readings she acknowledges include Greek, English and Icelandic epic poems, as well as representatives of American, Japanese and Chinese poetry: "While I was at the university I read *Beowulf* and *Njal's Saga*. They seemed so Tlingit to me in their concern with funerals and family trees. I read Homer, Ferlinghetti, e. e. cummings, Basho, John Haines, Gary Snyder, Dennis Tedlock, and Han Shan. They became some of my teachers" (Dauenhauer 2000, 106). Again, being introduced to World Literature constitutes a stage onto her becoming a writer. At the same time Dauenhauer implies that renowned European texts such as *Beowulf* and *Njal's Saga* share certain thematic similarities with Tlingit tales, thereby implying that the latter are worthy of being considered literary classics due to their scope and significance. She continues to emphasize the merit of literature originating with tribal cultures and to blur the boundaries between Native and non-Native influences on her work when mentioning her discovery of American Indian fiction and poetry writers publishing in English with a fair amount of visibility: "Later, as younger Native American writers began to appear in print, I became excited and inspired initially by their work, and subsequently by meeting in person Simon Ortiz, James Welch, Joy Harjo, Luci Tapahonso, and others. I also began to discover the work of earlier writers such as D'Arcy McNickle" (107). Here she is actually formulating an American Indian canon whose members are mentioned again and again throughout the autobiographical essays in the volume. All of these writers along with several others are invoked as friends, guides, teachers, supporters, inspirers and pathfinders who have helped younger colleagues find their way into print. To give just a couple of additional examples, Bell pays homage to Gerald Vizenor in her piece, while Tapahonso talks about Leslie Marmon Silko's mentorship when the former attended the University of New Mexico and started writing.

Simon Ortiz (Acoma Pueblo), Leslie Marmon Silko (Laguna Pueblo), James Welch (Blackfeet-Gros Ventre), Joy Harjo (Muscogee), Gerald Vizenor (Anishinaabe) are often listed as representatives of the Native American Renaissance, a label used to capture the fact that after N. Scott Momaday's *House Made of Dawn* (1968) won the Pulitzer Prize, several authors found interested publishers and readers, Native American literature enjoying unprecedented appreciation. However, the phrase is sometimes rejected "because it might imply that Native writers were not producing significant work before that time or that these writers sprang up without longstanding community and tribal roots" (Ruppert 2005, 173). As a matter of fact, Native works constantly echo their being grounded in the tradition of storytelling and in written productions by predecessors who were publishing before the middle of the twentieth century, such as D'Arcy McNickle (Cree/Flathead), whose fiction and non-fiction became "college classroom staples in many infant Native American Studies programs" (Hafen 2002, 239). As if intent on demonstrating her reliance on an earlier tradition, Vickie Sears does mention discovering reading and being exposed to texts written by Native writers, E. Pauline Johnson (Mohawk) and Charles Eastman (Sioux), both of whom were publishing around the turn of the twentieth century. The latter is particularly famous for his autobiographical work in which he tried "to offer a cultural explanation of Sioux history and values" (Hafen 2002, 238), an effort still present in Native life writing today.

A completely different tradition, but a predictable one—if American Indian identity issues are seen as connected to those of other minorities on the territory of the United States of America and even to other groups worldwide, is discussed by Gloria Bird (Spokane): "Along the way, I have been influenced by the personal narrative writing styles of African American feminist writers, and began writing criticism that attempted to *read* Native American literatures as a product of colonization, looking at ways that Native peoples have internalized colonial attitudes and beliefs about themselves that appear in their creative work" (Bird 2000, 69). As a matter of fact, she prefaces her essay entitled "Autobiography as Spectacle: An Act of Liberation or the Illusion of Liberation?" with a quote from Aimé Césaire, thus extending even further the sense of relatedness she feels and the correlations she finds relevant. Even if certain theoretical considerations from adjacent Ethnic Studies fields lend themselves to being applied in the case of Native American Studies, recently there has been an increasing emphasis on the specificity of this domain, and the need for disassociation from sweeping perspectives in connection to multiethnic issues that often provide more traps than revelatory elements.

Reading and writing as significant components of decolonization and resistance are relevantly tackled in "On the Tip of My Tongue: An Autobiographical Essay". The author, Evelina Zuni Lucero, whose parents are from the Pueblo Nations of New Mexico, focuses on her younger self's experience when moving from a Bureau of Indian Affairs tribal school in her native state to a public school with an ethnically diverse student population in Colorado, far from her grandparents and their tribal homelands. Excelling academically becomes a way of fighting discrimination. Reading and writing, which are clearly important dimensions of her "military tactics," are mastered by the young girl for the purpose not only of affirming personal worth, but also demonstrating the fact that Native students can equal and surpass the performance of their peers, as Lucero explains: "Looking back now, I can see how this was a serious undertaking—my goal was to prove Indians could beat whites at their own game. I was reacting not only against being made to feel bad about myself, but also against the message implicit in textbooks and the classrooms: Indians are inferior" (Lucero 2000, 251).

Her family's move to Nevada occasions the confrontation with a new challenge, that of attending a public high school in Carson City as a teenager, this time the percentage of Native students being even smaller. As Lucero testifies, she applied the same strategy: "Native Students were not expected to do well in school and most didn't. I became the anomaly, but once again it was out spite, out of a struggle to hold my own that I worked to do well" (257). The high school experience laid the ground for what Lucero calls her "politics of resistance" (259), which she perfected while attending Stanford University. Lucero's essay is one of the many in the collection which confront stereotypes about American Indians and detail their offensive force, while providing solutions for deconstructing them.

To come full circle to the issue of bilingualism that emerged in the case of Tapahonso and to explore one more aspect of a Native woman autobiographer's engagement with the culture of reading and writing, the analysis finally introduces the essay by Ofelia Zepeda (Tohono O'odham), who testifies to writing as a mode of enabling language preservation, advancing language teaching and affirming the survival of Native tribal nations. Zepeda discusses her work with the American Indian Language Development Institute at the University of Arizona. There educators are urged to write creative pieces in their Native languages in order to use them in their language classes:

> Through the AILDI, I, along with other faculty, have been successful in convincing Native speakers of some American Indian languages that it is possible to express creativity through writing just like one would in the English language. And finally, that it was possible to publish writing in the Native language so that their own versions and translations of their tribal stories and their poetry and songs could be available to large numbers of readers, including non-Indian ones. (Zepeda 2000, 419)

The importance of striving to keep Indigenous languages alive cannot be overemphasized and such efforts are often considered forms of activism that lead to the empowerment of tribal communities across the United States of America. Leading scholars in the field of American Indian

Studies discuss the situation of Native languages in the twenty-first century and urge Native people to sustain the struggle for the retention of their tribal languages as vibrant means of communication and repositories of identity:

> Although students may learn their tribe's language and some of the culture at school, the most effective learning and reinforcement takes place at home. Since it is not always possible to learn these things at home, in many areas of Native America there has been a surge of interest in revitalizing languages. Tribes across the country encourage kindergarden through high school classrooms to incorporate Native languages. (Mihesuah 2003, 149)

As explained here, home environments should be complemented by school environments in order to sustain the acquisition and active use of Indigenous languages today. The availability of contemporary technology and the youth's fascination with the media have to be channeled towards such worthwhile objectives. Creativity, resourcefulness and constant reinvention are needed more than ever for the continuance and thriving of American Indian cultures into the future.

CONCLUSION

In following the experiences that shaped them as writers as well as their artistic creeds, the current study has traced American Indian women's ways of "reading" the core elements of their own tribal cultures and of taking over storytelling as thematically and stylistically emblematic for their work. At the same time, the analysis has stressed the autobiographers' involvement in reading cultures as their essays represent the first contact with school, most often enabling the development of reading skills, the discovery of one's passion for books and joining kindred networks, the connection to various literary models as well as the transition to writing with its connective, professional, militant, therapeutic and/or aesthetic functions. American Indian women writers reveal themselves as (grand)daughters, storytellers, creators, searchers, visionaries, healers, scholars, guides, warriors, craftswomen, continuators, mediators, and spokespersons for their communities since they capitalize on preserving their respective Native languages, passing on tribal knowledge and practices, establishing American Indian literatures and translating Native worldviews for a mainstream readership, as proven by the discussion of the contributions to *Here First*.

NOTES

1. Walters is the author of a book-length autobiography, *Talking Indian: Reflection on Survival and Writing* (1992), which is considered to express "direct resistance to ongoing and pervasive forces of assimilation" (Tillett 2007, 80), which she has space only to address briefly in the contribution to the volume *Here First*.
2. The repercussions of the 1978 Indian Child Welfare Act are discussed in one other essay in the volume as the contributor subsumes the issue of adoption to her focus on identity politics (Hilden 2000, 194–5).
3. A different approach to religion appears with Roberta Hill (Oneida) as she speaks about her Catholic background. In her case the practice of confession is intrinsic to self-reflection and the acquisition of writing skills: "Learning to confess was my earliest training for learning to write" (Hill 2000, 199).
4. The writers in the collection confess to having been attracted to popular children's texts, accessible as they were growing up, such as *Uncle Arthur's Bedtime Stories* by Arthur S. Maxwell (Tapahonso 2000, 347) or *Little House on the Prairie* by Laura Ingalls Wilder (Sears 2000, 313), which are familiar to American readers of the first half of the twentieth century.

REFERENCES

Bataille, Gretchen M., and Kathleen Mullen Sands. 1984. *American Indian Women Telling Their Lives*. Lincoln/London: University of Nebraska Press.

Bell, Betty Louise. 2000. Burying Paper. In *Here First: Autobiographical Essays by Native American Writers*, ed. Arnold Krupat and Brian Swann, 30–40. New York: Random House.

Bird, Gloria. 2000. Autobiography as Spectacle. An Act of Liberation or the Illusion of Liberation? In *Here First*, ed. Krupat and Swann, 63–74.

Blaeser, Kimberly. 2000. Rituals of Memory. In *Here First*, ed. Krupat and Swann, 75–90.

Dauenhauer, Nora Marks. 2000. Life Woven with Song. In *Here First*, Krupat and Swann, 91–109.

DeClue (Kawashinsay), Charlotte. 2000. The Good Red Road. In *Here First*, ed. Krupat and Swann, 110–119.

Endrezze, Anita. 2000. A Journey to the Heart. In *Here First*, Krupat and Swann, 120–142.

Hafen, P. Jane. 2002. Native American Literatures. In *A Companion to American Indian History*, ed. Philip J. Deloria and Neal Salisbury, 234–247. Malden: Blackwell Publishers.

Harjo, Joy, and Gloria Bird. 1997. Introduction. In *Reinventing the Enemy's Language. Contemporary Native Women's Writings of North America*, ed. Joy Harjo and Gloria Bird, 19–31. New York: W.W. Norton and Company.

Hilden, Patricia Penn. 2000. Displacements: Performing *Mestizaje*. In *Here First*, ed. Krupat and Swann, 182–196.

Hill, Roberta. 2000. A Soul Like the Sun. In *Here First*, ed. Krupat and Swann, 197–211.

Howe, LeAnne. 2000. My Mothers, My Uncles, Myself. In *Here First*, ed. Krupat and Swann, 212–228.

Krupat, Arnold, and Brian Swann, eds. 2000a. *Here First: Autobiographical Essays by Native American Writers*. New York: Random House.

———. 2000b. Introduction. In *Here First*, ed. Krupat and Swann, xi–xvii.

Lucero, Evelina Zuni. 2000. On the Tip of My Tongue: An Autobiographical Essay. In *Here First*, ed. Krupat and Swann, 247–261.

Mihesuah, Devon Abbott. 2003. *Indigenous American Women: Decolonization, Empowerment, Activism*. Lincoln/London: University of Nebraska Press.

Ruppert, James. 2005. Fiction: 1968 to the Present. In *The Cambridge Companion to Native American Literature*, ed. Joy Porter and Kenneth M. Roemer, 173–188. Cambridge/New York: Cambridge University Press.

Sears, Vickie. 2000. Wind Circles. In *Here First*, ed. Krupat and Swann, 310–320.

Smith, Sidonie, and Julia Watson. 2010. *Reading Autobiography: A Guide for Interpreting Life Narratives*. Minneapolis: The University of Minnesota Press.

Tapahonso, Luci. 2000. They Moved over the Mountain. In *Here First*, ed. Krupat and Swann, 337–351.

Tillett, Rebecca. 2007. *Contemporary Native American Literature*. Edinburgh: Edinburgh University Press.

Walters, Anna Lee. 2000. The Buffalo Road. In *Here First*, ed. Krupat and Swann, 370–380.

Wong, Hertha Sweet. 2005. Native American Life Writing. In *The Cambridge Companion to Native American Literature*, ed. Joy Porter and Kenneth M. Roemer, 125–144. Cambridge/New York: Cambridge University Press.

Woody, Elizabeth. 2000. The Child Before Memory: Recognition of the 'Maker'. In *Here First*, ed. Krupat and Swann, 381–404.

Zepeda, Ofelia. 2000. Autobiography. In *Here First*, ed. Krupat and Swann, 405–420.

CHAPTER 18

"Books. Why?" Staging the Reading Act in Louise Erdrich's Autobiographical Texts

Elisabeth Bouzonviller

INTRODUCTION

Louise Erdrich waited for 11 years and an established position as an American poet and novelist before publishing a first autobiographical text in 1995 entitled *The Blue Jay's Dance: A Birth Year*, which was then followed by a second one in 2003, *Books and Islands in Ojibwe Country*, both being listed as "nonfiction" in the peritext of her works. Being evocations of short, specific periods of her own life, these texts cannot exactly be considered as autobiographies; rather, they are life narratives. Since she defines herself, in interviews, first as a mother, then as a writer and a mixed-blood "Indian",[1] both texts necessarily explore these facets of the identity she claims as hers. Actually, they both tackle the main subject of maternity and writing as *The Blue Jay's Dance* is a one-year maternal adventure at home

---

Erdrich 2003, 4.

E. Bouzonviller (✉)
Université Jean Monnet, Saint Etienne, France
e-mail: elisabeth.bouzonviller@univ-st-etienne.fr

© The Author(s) 2018
V. Baisnée-Keay et al. (eds.), *Women's Life Writing and the Practice of Reading*, Palgrave Studies in Life Writing,
https://doi.org/10.1007/978-3-319-75247-1_18

307

from pregnancy to birth and early motherhood, while *Books and Islands* deals with a family journey through Ojibwe land with her 18-month-old daughter, Nenaa'ikiizhikok, and the child's father, Tobasonakwut. Both texts are teeming with references to books the narrator reads or has read, confirming Alberto Manguel's idea in his *History of Reading* that "we are what we read" (Manguel 1996, 173) and showing therefore an author/narrator who "reads to write herself." In fact, both these life narratives seem to offer a woman's postcolonial life narratives through books that challenge established white patriarchal ways in politics and literature. We shall first focus on these life narratives as motherhood memoirs with a feminist "coming to voice" trope aspect, to borrow Smith and Watson's reference to "the thematics of speech and silence" from the last decades of the twentieth century (Smith and Watson 2010, 84–85), a female point of view that remains intricately linked with literary creation in Erdrich's case. Then we shall consider the quest for origins at stake in those life narratives, which enlarges the autobiographical reference from an individual to a collective scope. Eventually, we shall conclude on the essentially hybrid nature of these life narratives, a main component of what Gerald Vizenor calls "survivance" (Vizenor 2011, 69).

From Motherhood to Literature

Both texts are meditations on the narrator's maternal link with a daughter before and after birth. In both texts, although fathers are mentioned and present at times, what the narratives focus on is clearly a female experience that links motherhood and literature, whether it is through reading or writing. *The Blue Jay's Dance* focuses mainly on writing as the first chapter defines this life narrative as "a set of thoughts from one self to the other—writer to parent, artist to mother" (*BJD*, 5). Unlike female writers from former generations, the narrator may be lucky to have a room of her own—a "small gray [writing] house"—(6) beside the family home, yet once her daughter is born, she endlessly lacks time and space to devote herself to writing. On the other hand, in *Books and Islands,* the more mature mother has plenty of time to read during the trip. This text even includes the pencil drawing of a self-portrait representing the narrator as a reading nursing mother, books offering a soothing conclusion to her worries about being a mother close to menopause:

... I was struck by the awful burden of it all. How would I do it? I don't suppose the Virgin Mary felt sorry for herself, but I did. Then suddenly, I thought of a most wonderful consolation.
Books. Why?
To read and read while nursing a baby. (*B&I*, 17)

In *The Blue Jay's Dance*, despite her busy days as a mother, the narrator celebrates maternity and details the intricate links between writing and motherhood, valuing their common imprint on the future: "The need to write and to reproduce are both all absorbing tasks that attempt to partake of the future" (*BJD*, 79). She insists on a lack of interest granted to mothers' heroic labors that goes back to biblical times (35) and, in a way, this life narrative devoted to pregnancy and early motherhood may be perceived as filling this gap as she enlarges her individual experience to a universal, timeless female one: "... this sense of my sex, an overwhelming consciousness of the simple fact of my femaleness, assails me" (189). She offers her female version of life, her female narrative, a liberated voice, both personal and political, as requested in the following lines: "A woman needs to tell her own story, to tell the bloody version of the fairy tale. A woman has to be her own hero" (104). As explained by Smith and Watson, this "'coming to voice' mean[s] articulating an emergent subjectivity outside or against the repressive constraints of asymmetrical gender relationships" (Smith and Watson 2010, 85).

Claiming that "[e]very female writer starts out with a list of other female writers in her head" (Erdrich 2002, 144), the narrator goes on with a long list, from Jane Austen to Jane Smiley, including paratactic biographical details about marriage and children (144), the humorous conclusion being: "Reliable birth control is one of the best things that's happened to contemporary literature ..." (145). Wondering about the specificity of "writing as a mother," she resorts to the examples of two Nobel Prize female novelists and their 'ruthless' female heroines, American Toni Morrison's Sethe and Norwegian Sigrid Undset's Kristin Lavransdatter (146–147). Eventually, despite the obstacles motherhood may place on a female writer's way, she concludes on writing as a substitute for the perfect wholeness and plenitude nursing mothers experience and she refers to several male writers who have expressed their longing for this type of sensation through the scriptural act:

> One day as I am holding baby and feeding her, I realize that this is exactly the state of mind and heart that so many male writers from Thomas Mann to James Joyce describe with yearning—the mystery of an epiphany, the sense of oceanic oneness, the great *yes*, the wholeness. There is also the sense of a self merged and at least temporarily erased—it is death-like. ... Perhaps we owe some of our most moving literature to men who didn't understand that they wanted to be women nursing babies. (*BJD*, 148)

It is not surprising, therefore, that the narrative should end on an image of the newly-born daughter's growth that seems to replicate the fate of any literary work to be published and abandoned to its readers along the "death of the author's motif."[2] The insistent anaphora "She will walk" (222–223) forecasts the child's long way toward independence, but also the fate of any accomplished book, the mother-writer's conclusion being "She will walk until her sense of balance is the one thing left and the rest of the world is balanced, too, and eventually, if we do the growing up right, she will walk away from us" (223).

In both texts, books invade the narrator's environment and there are many instances of the *mise en abyme* of the reading act. In *The Blue Jay's Dance*, "books line the walls" of her small writing house (7) while, in *Books and Islands*, she explains that she and her daughters "have a lot of books in [their] house" (*B&I*, 9). Books invade the page through the physical description of their home and the constant references to certain works—whether they are dictionaries, canonical novels and contemporary ones, works on religion, psychology, history, children's literature, etc.— but also through the obsessive repetition of the term "book" itself and the various illustrations representing them (*B&I*, 4; 17; 121; 141), which is not surprising for a writer and the owner of an independent bookstore, Birchbark Books. The Minneapolis bookstore is also mentioned and sketched in the text itself (*B&I*, 138–139).

Back home in her bookstore, at the end of *Books and Islands*, she exclaims: "I love to be among the books ...." (*B&I*, 139). Even though this narrative is a travelogue, books are never left behind: "Books. Another reason. I can take home along anywhere in the person of a book, and I do" (10). Thus, the travelers do not travel light, books are part of their luggage, as is clearly detailed in the heterogeneous list of adult and children works they take along (10). Moreover, one of the goals of the trip is Ernst Oberholtzer's library of rare books on Mallard Island, in the middle of Rainy Lake, an area which straddles the border between Minnesota and Ontario. The final goal of the trip is clear in the title and the first sentences of the narrative: "My travels have become so focused on books and islands that the two have merged for me. Books, islands. Islands, books" (3). What is at stake is not only a spatial move in quest of reading, but also an internal one. The chiasmus evoking the narrator's double obsession and replicating the title itself is followed by this statement:

> ... I can't travel aimlessly. I always seem to have a question that I would like to answer. Increasingly, too, it is the same question. It is the question that has defined my life, the question that has saved my life, and the question that most recently has resulted in the questionable enterprise of starting a bookstore. The question is: Books. Why? The islands are only incidental. (4)

This question—"Books. Why?"—recurs then like a chorus throughout the text, and several answers are provided which all point out the human desire for contact, transmission and survival in life and beyond (*B&I*, 6; 55; 95; 99; 141). Although the narrator pretends that her destination is "incidental," her quest about the meaning of literature remains closely linked with a quest for origins, to be found in the "Ojibwe country" of her maternal ancestors, the map of which precedes the first chapter; thus, this double quest recalls Roland Barthes asking: "Isn't telling stories always a matter of looking for one's origins, telling about one's problem with the law, getting into the dialectic of love and hate?"[3]

A Quest for Origins

In Erdrich's life narratives, writing about herself, writing about motherhood, is also a search for her Ojibwe roots, whether they are realistic or more desired ones, and this search relies on traveling but also on reading, whether it is based on texts or other types of media. A section of *The Blue Jay's Dance* is entitled "Three Photographs" (*BJD*, 138–140). It describes family photographs which draw a family tree over three generations and compose a kind of family narrative that echoes the visual narrative of much older roots to be found in the description of the petroglyphs from Lake of the Woods in *Books and Islands* (*B&I*, 49–81). Thus, her two autobiographical texts become tools of exploration focusing on the recollection of family history, which is often a synecdoche for her tribal history, but also on the reconstruction of a desired past in a typical autofictional process. For example, during a kind of reverie, the narrator imagines how her daughter's paternal grandmother may have met her own relatives (*B&I*, 12–13), but also how her own ancestors may have painted the petroglyphs before moving to the Great Plains (80-81). These family evocations are obviously based on a spiritual wandering inspired by the northern environment and the desire for a deeply rooted "tribal" (Bacon 2001, np) lineage.

The references to food are also linked to this quest for origins. Smith and Watson explain that Rosalia Baena "proposed th[e] term [gastrography] to designate life writing in which the story of the self is closely linked to the production, preparation, and/or consumption of food" (Smith and Watson 2010, 271). *The Blue Jay's Dance* partly relies on this type of life narrative, as it includes long passages resembling the pages of a recipe book (*BJD*, 17–18; 125–132; 204–210). This interest in food, which can easily be related to the image of the nurturing mother, also recalls the cultural aspect of food and the sense of community it implies when the narrator exclaims: "This fabulous menu includes my favorite Ojibwa traditional food—wild rice" (*BJD*, 125). Traditional wild rice beds (Erdrich 2003, 51–54) are precisely among the places the narrator visits in Ojibwe country and, in *Books and Islands*, she even reproduces the petroglyph of the wild rice spirit she has seen up North (*B&I*, 53).

The visit to these petroglyphs is part of the goal of her trip in Ojibwe country. They offer another kind of embedded reading scenes as the narrator describes, draws and tries to decipher them, thus being involved in a paperless reading pertaining to the maternal side of her family. From a linguistic point of view, she appropriately explains that the terms "book" and "rock painting" have a common root in the Ojibwe language: "Mazina'iganan is the word for 'books' in Ojibwemowin or Anishinabemowin, and mazinapikiniganan is the word for 'rock paintings.' ... [b]oth words begin with 'mazina.' It is the root for dozens of words all concerned with made images and with the substances upon which the images are put, mainly paper or screens" (*B&I*, 5). The petroglyphs of "The rice spirit" and "The horned man" are carefully reproduced within the text (53; 54) as the narrator tries to read them and informs the ignorant reader in the light of her newly acquired Ojibwe knowledge. She tries to decipher these petroglyphs like texts and wonders about writing as a linking trace, thus relating these former scriptural signs to more modern ones:

> I am standing before the rock wall of Painted Rock Island and trying to read it like a book. I don't know the language though. ... Once you know what it is, the wild rice spirit looks exactly like itself. (51)

The line is a sign of power and communication. It is sound, speech, song. The lines drawn between things in Ojibwe pictographs are extremely important, for they express relationships, usually between a human and a supernatural being. (56)

In front of these rock paintings, she may lack precise ethnological knowledge, but she immediately relates them to family, tribe, tradition and transmission and suggests their similarity with writing in its polysemous and didactic nature:

One thing certain is that the paintings were made by the ancestors of the present-day Anishinaabeg, for the ancient symbols on the rocks are as familiar and recognizable to Tobasonakwut as are, say, highway and airport and deer crossing signs to contemporary Americans. Of course, the rock paintings are not just pointer signs. They hold far more significance. They refer to a spiritual geography, and are meant to provide teaching, and dream guides to generations of Anishinaabeg. (49–50)

In the end, her reading extends to the whole landscape, which she tries to decipher like a book, as planned at the beginning of the narrative when she said: "So these islands, which I'm longing to read, are books in themselves" (*B&I*, 3). The importance of the land, the meaning of which must be read by the curious narrator, is not surprising in a postcolonial context where displacement and dispossession have played a major role and it conjures up the idea of eco-autobiography developed by Peter F. Perreten (Smith and Watson 2010, 268).

The Blue Jay's Dance also stages this variety of reading acts, ranging from nature to more conventional written texts, when the narrator imagines she can read, in her garden, the "narrative of flowers" left by an unknown previous female occupier of the house: "Over the years, I have seen her hand in the places where plants still bloom" (*BJD*, 106). Moving from this natural reading, she eventually discovers a scrap of paper, as if bequeathed by this woman's ghost, which she reads and quotes in the narrative and which evokes human loss and grief (108).

Reading, whatever the medium, text, plants, petroglyphs or landscape, is therefore presented as the way to establish a link with the past, as she understands after seeing the petroglyph of the horned man: "Books. Why? So we can talk to you even though we are dead. Here we are, the writer and I, regarding each other" (*B&I*, 55). Thus, the narrator's personal history becomes a collective story of loss and recovery through reading and it is quite fitting that her youngest daughter, the promise of a new generation of mixed-blood Americans from Ojibwe origins, should have been read herself by her mother, like a book, when she was born:

> ... I couldn't make out her features. I had to adjust her to my reading distance.
>   It occurs to me, now, that I now do this constantly. If reading is taken to mean comprehending, I step back often. I focus; to my great relief, I have a little more patience. ... Already she is making sense of things and I am making sense of her. (*B&I*, 132)

HYBRIDITY AND "SURVIVANCE"

In his "Postscript to *The Name of the Rose*" Umberto Eco claims that "books always talk about other books, and each story tells a story that has already been told."[4] In Erdrich's case, the first part of this statement is obvious, as we have seen, but given her mixed-blood origins, the second part is more questionable as she precisely offers a new perspective that is both female and "Indian" (White and Burnside 1994, 111), or rather "mixed-blood" (Feyl and Chavkin 1994, 238). Even though Lionel Larré sustains that the first Native autobiographies from the nineteenth and early twentieth centuries were acts of resistance through their inner dialogism (Larré 2009, 56), they were nevertheless very much caught in the constraints of a white, colonial society that imposed its rules through its translators and editors. On the contrary, Erdrich's life narratives offer a reflection on both her personal experience and on an ethnic group that baffles these colonial and patriarchal limitations. They point out another facet of America's history through a hybrid writing that takes into account the narrator's gender and her various family origins both European and Native, thus giving a voice to the 'subaltern' who used to be silent, as demonstrated by Spivak. Erdrich's rhizomatic identity, which is typical of composite cultures, as developed by Deleuze and Glissant, entails life narratives typical of what Françoise Lionnet calls "métissage," not only in their range of interests and knowledge, but also in the very nature of the texts themselves (Lionnet 2001, 23). Through their linguistic and intertextual hybridity, hers are stories of survival, or rather "survivance" in Vizenor's terms, as they occupy what Bhabha defines as a "third space of enunciation" (Bhabha 2006, 157). Her autobiographical texts, which rely on the idea of in-betweenness, can be viewed as "autoethnographies," as they "both collaborate with and appropriate a colonizer's (or dominant culture's) discursive models, thereby transculturating them into indigenous idioms and producing hybrid forms of collectivized life narrative," thus "contest[ing] the traditional Western limits of individuality and normative discourses" (Smith and Watson 2010, 259).

While Erdrich constantly stages the reading act in her life narratives, it is meaningful that, in the first chapter of *Books and Islands,* she should make the following statement linking her tribe and Ojibwe ancestors with the origin of literature:

> The Ojibwe had been using the word mazinibaganjigan for years to describe dental pictographs made on birchbark, perhaps the first books made in North America. Yes, I figure books have been written around here ever since someone had the idea of biting or even writing on birchbark with a sharpened stick. Books are nothing all that new. People have probably been writing books in North America since at least 2000 B.C. (*B&I*, 5)

Thus, she debunks the scornful idea that "Indians" (White and Burnside 1994, 111) were savages or that, at best, their traditions were restricted to the transience of orality. A sense of pride is definitely felt here, as well as when she adds: "The meaning that I like best of course is Ojibwe from the verb Ozhibii'ige, which is 'to write.' Ojibwe people were great writers from way back and synthesized the oral and written tradition by keeping mnemonic scrolls of inscribed birchbark. The first paper, the first books" (*B&I*, 10–11). According to Erdrich, writing as a trace left from human life, as a testimony about "tribal" existence (Bacon 2001), would therefore go back to much earlier than the first "Indians" who went to school under colonial rule or the first successful and innovative "tribal" novelists from the late 1960s.

It is not surprising that the texts of a narrator who travels with her Ojibwe dictionary (*B&I*, 10), since this language is not her mother tongue but a social and political commitment, should include various references to the Ojibwe language, thus creating a new hybrid language specific to the one who defines herself as "an emissary of the between world, that increasingly common margin where cultures mix and collide" (Bacon 2001). These references have increased in number, with time, in her fiction and this is also the case in these two life narratives. *Books and Islands* was published later than *The Blue Jay's Dance* and it precisely includes many more Ojibwe terms.

As her texts mix languages, they also mix oral and written traditions. Although the narrator constantly stages reading scenes of herself, she nevertheless confesses that she is "an instinctive mother, not a book-read one" (*BJD*, 64). Moreover, while books are sources of pleasure and information that are quoted or summarized, she also relies, in her narratives, on oral storytelling, as valued in tribal tradition, through relatives, friends and chance meetings. To present her daughter's father's family history, for example, she first refers to Jacques de Noyon's seventeenth-century *coureur des bois* written testimony about his encounter with this tribe, but she then shifts her point of view to her personal knowledge of her partner's family history acquired orally through him (*B&I*, 32).

In *Books and Islands*, books themselves relate not only to the Western world. Oberholtzer's library may contain rare originals, but the library itself is rooted in Ojibwe country, and Oberholtzer himself was an ecologist deeply interested in Ojibwe culture who "loved the books in the people. He loved the oral tradition of story-telling" (*B&I*, 125). In a *mise en abyme* process, one of the books the narrator intends to read there is a first edition of *Tristram Shandy*, the eponymous character's pretended autobiography, and what she claims to be "the first novel in the English language" (120). Thus, while writing about her own life, the narrator indicates her desire to read a book about a character's account of his life, a fictional life narrative within a true life narrative. Failing to find Laurence Sterne's work, she discovers other literary interests and eventually falls "in love with a corny purple edition of Catlin's journals" (121). Catlin having immortalized life on the Great Plains through his nineteenth-century paintings and "Indian Gallery,"[5] the literary shift from the Western to the "tribal" world is thus obvious. Moreover, as if to balance the Sterne English literary reference, the narrator also recalls her fascinated youthful reading of John Tanner's 1830 captivity narrative, *The Falcon, a Narrative of the Captivity and Adventures of John Tanner During Thirty Years Residence among Indians in the Interior of North America* (42), a work for which she contributed an introduction in 1994 for the Penguin edition and which her sister Lise describes as "the only true sequel to that great American novel, *The Adventures of Huckleberry Finn*" (43). Once again, literature and Ojibwe origins intertwine, as the narrator recalls that she and her sisters enjoyed this autobiography thoroughly, which mentions briefly one of their ancestors (43) and can be considered as "the first narrative of native life from an Ojibwe point of view" (46), although it was not written by an Ojibwe by birth. Eventually, *Books and Islands* ends on the multiple aspects of literature. Recalling the hero of the movie *Cast Away*, the narrator tries to imagine the best book to have on a desert island and decides on the equal power of traditional storytelling and the resourcefulness of books: "A dictionary would be a good thing to have arrived in the FedEx box. But even better to be like Oberholtzer and to store up 11,000. Or to be an Ojibwe raised on stories and to contain many books in mind. Or me, with a bookstore" (*B&I*, 140). Thus, relying on her mixed-blood family's influences, Erdrich celebrates both aspects of literature, oral and written, which her family seems to embody in an ironical inversion of cultures, when she says: "My mother read, my father told [stories] to me. Lots of stories" (Spillman 2009, np).

Books and Islands is a travelogue that follows a circular pattern relying on books: it opens at home with the packing of books (*B&I*, 10) and ends home in Minneapolis again, after the travellers' return, with the reading of the end of *Austerlitz* (133–134), which the narrator started reading in a motel during the trip (95–97). This particular book offers a kind of *mise en abyme* of the idea of genocide with its protagonist, a surviving Jew from Prague, and its final pages, which are a reference to a book by Dan Jacobson, another survivor from the Holocaust, whom Erdrich knew as a professor in London when she was a student there (134). The narrator of *Books and Islands* describes *Austerlitz* as "the reconstruction of [Jacques Austerlitz's] memory" and shows him digging for "the truth of his origins," through traveling and photographs in particular (95), which is obviously what Erdrich does herself in her life narratives (*BDJ*, 138–140; *B&I*, 12–13). Thus, Sebald's narrative echoes Erdrich's family and tribal quest, and what Elise Marienstras calls a "'genocide' in the 'plural.'"[6] But unlike the narrator of Austerlitz, Erdrich refuses the idea of a "vanished past" (*B&I*, 134). Indeed, whereas this reading leads her to think of the "Natives'" fate in North America, the final words of this section devoted to her reading of Sebald's novel are for the hope embodied by her youngest mixed-blood daughter, the term "yet" presenting a visual and linguistic contrast and opposition with the historical disasters mentioned before:

... when I look past a generation or into the past of Tobasonakwut's world there is a lightlessness, too, for the nine of every ten native people perished of European diseases, leaving only diminished and weakened people to encounter what came next–the aggressions of civilization including government policies and missionaries and residential schools. Yet, here, as I turn to Kiizhikok sprawled in sleep beside me, is a light. (*B&I*, 134–136)

Like Erdrich's hybrid culture and writing, her child embodies their tribe's survival and resistance, its "survivance."

CONCLUSION

In *Books and Islands,* the narrator's daughter owns a Chinese-made toy called Alpha-Bug which can produce sounds and even combine letters into words, but her older daughters have noticed its limited capacity at producing these combinations, especially if they are "suggestive or swear words" (*B&I*, 129). Unlike this industrialized and limited language producer, in her life writing, as in her fiction and poetry, Erdrich explores the endless possibilities of language and literature. A tool to embark on a personal and tribal quest, her life narratives celebrate the fruitful combination of cultures and words. The texts seem then to offer a remapping of America as Indian country where the narrator evolves beyond the usual limits of Ojibwe land, but she also embeds the writing act within the female, and especially maternal, experience, thus offering a writing metaphor beyond culture. Apart from her tribal attachment and her perpetual genealogical and ethnic quest, she also insists on a writing experience defying limits as she perceives it rooted in feelings beyond will, in the same way she describes[7] a writer's lack of control over his/her story when it is good: "Because we can't control the fixation of love and desire, we experience emotional mayhem—stories, fiction, works of art results" (*BJD*, 105–106). Given this statement about art, and literature in particular, Erdrich's constant use of the verb "save" (*BJD*, 104; *B&I*, 4; 99) to refer to books, whether from a writer's or a reader's point of view, comes as no surprise and her mentioning Bradbury's dystopian novel *Fahrenheit 451* (*B&I*, 125) should stand as a warning about the importance and power of books in our lives.

NOTES

1. Interviewed by Bill Moyers, she said "… I'm always a mother. That's my first identity, but I'm always a writer too. I have to write. I have to be an artist" (Moyers 2010). In an interview with White and Burnside, she also insisted on the importance of her "Indianness": "Being Indian is something we're terribly proud of" (White and Burnside 1994, 111), and she told Feyl and Chavkin: "There are times I wish that I were one thing or the other, but I am a mixed-blood. *Psychically doomed,* another mixed-blood friend once joked. The truth is my background is such a rich mixed bag I'd be crazy to want to be anything else" (Feyl and Chavkin 1994, 238).

2. See Roland Barthes 1984, 63; 69, Michel Foucault 1969, 78 or Maurice Blanchot 1955, 12.
3. My translation from the original French, which reads as follows: *Raconter, n'est-ce pas toujours chercher son origine, dire ses démêlés avec la Loi, entrer dans la dialectique de l'attendrissement et de la haine?* (Barthes 1973, 75).
4. My translation from the French (Eco 1987, 517).
5. George Catlin (1796–1872) was a painter, writer and indigenous art collector, who gave lectures and presented his "Indian Gallery," an exhibition about Indian life, in the main American and European cities. He thus paradoxically reinforced the romantic vision of the "Noble Savage" and contributed to the development of certain stereotypes while at the same time trying to fight for the recognition of a culture which had been ignored, or even scorned, till then.
6. Historian Elise Marienstras declares: "It seems rather difficult to deny the term genocide ..."; "As for the genocide, we should talk about it in the plural, as regards specific cases, like the one of the Pequots in the seventeenth century, the ones against the Native tribes from California against whom its Governor launched an Indian hunt in the nineteenth century." My translation from the original French, which reads as follows: *Il semble bien difficile de réfuter le terme génocide; Quant au génocide, on devrait en parler au pluriel, concernant des cas précis, comme celui qui a été mené contre les Pequots au XVIIe siècle, ceux contre les tribus autochtones de Californie, dont le gouverneur a appelé à la chasse aux Indiens au XIXe siècle* (quoted by Garrait-Bourrier 2015, 135).
7. "The story starts to take over if it is good. You begin telling, you get a bunch of situation characters, everything together, but if it's good, you let the story tell itself. You don't control the story" (Bruchac 1994, 104).

REFERENCES

Bacon, Katie. January 14, 2001. An Emissary of the Between-World. *The Atlantic.* http://www.theatlantic.com/doc/200101u/int2001-01-17.

Barthes, Roland. 1973. *Le Plaisir du texte.* Paris: Éditions du Seuil.

———. 1984. *Le Bruissement de la langue. Essais critiques IV.* Paris: Éditions du Seuil.

Bhabha, Homi. 2006. Cultural Diversity and Cultural Differences. In *The Post-colonial Studies Reader,* ed. Bill Ashcroft, Gareth Griffiths, and Helen Tiffin, 155–157. Oxford: Routledge.

Blanchot, Maurice. 1955. *L'Espace littéraire.* Paris: Gallimard.

Bradbury, Ray. 1993. *Farenheit 451* (1953). New York: HarperCollins.

Bruchac, Joseph. 1994. Whatever Is Really Yours: An Interview with Louise Erdrich. In *Conversations with Louise Erdrich and Michael Dorris,* ed. Allan Chavkin and Nancy Feyl Chavkin, 94–104. Jackson: University Press of Mississippi.

Catlin, George. 1841. *Letters and Notes on the Manners, Customs, and Condition of the North American Indians*. London: Tosswill and Myers.

Deleuze, Gilles. 1993. *Critique et clinique*. Paris: Éditions de minuit.

Deleuze, Gilles, and Félix Guattari. 1980. *Mille plateaux*. Paris: Éditions de Minuit.

Eco, Umberto. 1987. Postille al Nome della Rosa. *Alfabeta* 49, June 1983. Apostille au Nom de la Rose. Trans. M. Bouzaher. Le Nom de la Rose (1980). Trans. J.N. Schifano, 509–544. Paris: Grasset.

Erdrich, Louise. 2002. *The Blue Jay's Dance: A Birth Year* (1995). New York: Harper Perennial.

———. 2003. *Books and Islands in Ojibwe Country*. Washington: National Geographic Society.

Feyl, Nancy Chavkin, and Allan Chavkin. 1994. An Interview with Louise Erdrich. In *Conversations with Louise Erdrich and Michael Dorris*, ed. Allan Chavkin and Nancy Feyl Chavkin, 220–253. Jackson: University Press of Mississippi.

Foucault, Michel. 1969. Qu'est-ce qu'un auteur ? *Bulletin de la société française de philosophie* 3: 73–104.

Garrait-Bourrier, Anne. 2015. Du génocide 'éprouvé' à l'ethnocide affirmé. Les Indiens d'Amérique aux confins des définitions. In *Témoigner. Entre histoire et mémoire*, ed. Philippe Mesnard, vol. 120, 122–135. Paris: Éditions Kimé.

Glissant, Édouard. 1990. *Poétique de la relation*. Paris: Gallimard.

———. 1996. *Introduction à une poétique du divers*. Paris: Gallimard.

Larré, Lionel. 2009. *Autobiographie amérindienne. Pouvoir et résistance de l'écriture de soi*. Pessac: Presses Universitaires de Bordeaux.

Lionnet, Françoise. 2001. *Autobiographical Voices: Race, Gender, Self-Portraiture*. Ithaca: Cornell University Press.

Manguel, Alberto. 1996. *A History of Reading*. New York: Viking/Penguin.

Moyers, Bill. 2010. *Bill Moyers Journal*. April 9. http://www.pbs.org/moyers/journal/04092010/profile.html.

Smith, Sidonie, and Julia Watson. 2010. *Reading Autobiography. A Guide for Interpreting Life Narratives*. Minneapolis: University of Minnesota Press.

Spillman, Robert. 2009. The Creative Instinct. The SALON Interview, March 3. http://www.salon.com/weekly/interview960506.html.

Spivak, Gayatri Chakravorty. 1988. Can the Subaltern Speak? In *Marxism and the Interpretation of Culture*, ed. Cary Nelson and Lawrence Grossberg, 24–28. London: Macmillan.

Sterne, Laurence. 2013. *The Life and Opinions of Tristram Shandy, Gentleman* (1759). London: Random House Vintage Classics.

Tanner, John. 1994. *The Falcon, a Narrative of the Captivity and Adventures of John Tanner During Thirty Years Residence Among Indians in the Interior of North America* (1830). London: Penguin.

Vizenor, Gerald. 2011. Native American Indian Literature: Critical Metaphors of the Ghost Dance. In *Native American Writing*, ed. A. Robert Lee, 61–69. London/New York: Routledge.

White, Sharon, and Glenda Burnside. 1994. On Native Ground: An Interview with Louise Erdrich and Michael Dorris. In *Conversations with Louise Erdrich and Michael Dorris*, ed. Allan Chavkin and Nancy Feyl Chavkin, 105–114. Jackson: University Press of Mississippi.

General Bibliography

Alvermann, Donna E., Norman Unrau, and Robert B. Ruddell, eds. 2013. *Theoretical Models and Processes of Reading*. Newark: International Reading Association.

Anderson, Linda. 2001. *Autobiography*. London: Routledge.

Andrews, William L. 1986. *To Tell a Free Story: The First Century of Afro-American Autobiography, 1760–1865*. Urbana: University of Illinois Press.

Benjamin, Walter. 2000. The Storyteller. In *Theory of the Novel: A Historical Approach*. Ed. Michael McKeon, 77–93. Baltimore/London: The John Hopkins University Press.

Bennett, Andrew, ed. 1995. *Readers and Reading*. London: Longman.

Buss, Helen M. 2002. *Repossessing the World: Reading Memoirs by Contemporary Women*. Toronto: Wilfrid Laurier University Press.

Carron, Jean-Pierre. 2002. *Ecriture et identité: Pour une poétique de l'autobiographie*. Brussels: Eurorgan.

Cavallo, Gugliemo, and Roger Chartier. 2001. *Histoire de la lecture dans le monde occidental*. 2ème ed. Paris: Editions du Seuil.

Charles, Michel. 1977. *Rhétorique de la lecture*. Paris: Editions du Seuil.

Chute, Hillary L. 2016. *Disaster Drawn: Visual Witness, Comics, and Documentary Form*. Cambridge, MA/London: Belknap Press of Harvard University Press.

Clayton, Jay, and Eric Rothstein, eds. 1991. *Influence and Intertextuality in Literary History*. Madison: The University of Wisconsin Press.

de Certeau, Michel. 1988. Reading as Poaching. In *The Practice of Everyday Life* [1984]. Trans. S. Rendall. Los Angeles/London: University of California Press.

© The Author(s) 2018
V. Baisnée-Keay et al. (eds.), *Women's Life Writing and the Practice of Reading*, Palgrave Studies in Life Writing,
https://doi.org/10.1007/978-3-319-75247-1

Eakin, Paul. 1999. *How Our Lives Become Stories: Making Selves*. Ithaca/London: Cornell University Press.

———. 2008. *Living Autobiographically: How We Create Identity in Narrative*. Ithaca/London: Cornell University Press.

Eco, Umberto. 1979. *Lector in Fabula*. Milan: Bompiani.

Egan, Susanna. 1999. *Mirror Talk: Genres of Crisis in Contemporary Autobiography*. Chapel Hill/London: The University of North Carolina Press.

Felski, Rita. 1989. *Beyond Feminist Aesthetics: Feminist Literature and Social Change*. Cambridge, MA: Harvard University Press.

Fetterley, Judith. 1978. *The Resisting Reader: A Feminist Approach to American Fiction*. Bloomington: Indiana University Press.

Flint, Kate. 1993a. *The Woman Reader, 1837–1914*. Oxford: Clarendon Press.

———. 1993b. *The Woman Reader, 1837–1914*. Oxford: Clarendon Press.

Galtier, Brigitte. 1997. *L'Écrit des jours. Lire les journaux personnels*. Paris: Honoré Champion.

Golden, Catherine. 2003. *Images of the Woman Reader in Victorian British and American Fiction*. Tallahassee: The University Press of Florida.

Goulemot, Jean Marie. 2003. De la lecture comme production de sens. In *Pratiques de la lecture*, ed. Roger Chartier, 119–131. Paris: Payot & Rivages.

Gusdorf, Georges. 1991. *Lignes de vie. Les écritures du moi, lignes de vie 2, auto-bio-graphie*. Paris: Odile Jacob.

Hirsch, Marianne. 1997. *Family Frames: Photography Narrative and Postmemory*. Cambridge, MA: Harvard University Press.

Iser, Wolfang. 1979. *The Act of Reading*. London: Routledge, Kegan, Paul.

Jauss, Hans Robert. 1978. *Pour une esthétique de la réception*. Trans. Claude Maillard. Paris: Gallimard.

Kadar, Marlene, ed. 1992. *Essays on Life Writing: from Genre to Critical Practice*. Toronto: University of Toronto Press.

Larré, Lionel. 2009. *Autobiographie amérindienne. Pouvoir et résistance de l'écriture de soi*. Pessac: Presses Universitaires de Bordeaux.

Lawrence, Karen. 1994. *Penelope Voyages: Women and Travel in the British Literary Tradition*. Ithaca: Cornell University Press.

Lejeune, Philippe. 1975. *Le pacte autobiographique*. Paris: Éditions du Seuil.

———. 1989. *On Autobiography*. Trans. Katherine Leary. Minneapolis: University of Minnesota Press.

———. 2009. *On Diary*. Ed. Jeremy D. Popkin and Julie Rak, trans. Katherine Durnin. Manoa: University of Hawai'i Press.

Lionnet, Françoise. 2001. *Autobiographical Voices: Race, Gender, Self-Portraiture*. Ithaca: Cornell University Press.

Littau, Karin. 2006. *Theories of Reading: Books, Bodies and Bibliomania*. Cambridge [u.a.]: Polity Press.

Macé, Marielle. 2011. *Façons de lire, manières d'être*. Paris: Editions du Seuil.

Mangel, Alberto. 1996. *A History of Reading*. New York: Viking/Penguin.

Marcus, Laura. 1994. *Auto/Biographical Discourses: Theory, Criticism, Practice*. Manchester: Manchester University Press.

Miller, Nancy K. 1991. *Getting Personal: Feminist Occasions and Other Autobiographical Acts*. New York: Routledge.

———. 1994. Representing Others: Gender and the Subjects of Autobiography. *Differences: A Journal of Feminist Cultural Studies* 6 (1): 1–27.

Miraux, Jean-Philippe. 1996. *L'autobiographie: L'écriture de soi et sincérité*. Paris: Editions Nathan.

Olney, James. 1972. *Metaphors of Self: The Meaning of Autobiography*. Princeton: Princeton University Press.

Pearson, Jacqueline. 1999. *Women's Reading in Britain, 1750–1835: A Dangerous Recreation*. Cambridge: Cambridge University Press.

Rubin, David C., ed. 1999. *Remembering Our Past: Studies in Autobiographical Memory*. Cambridge: Cambridge University Press.

Schweickart, Patrocinio P. 1995. Reading Ourselves: Toward a Feminist Theory of Reading. In *Readers and Reading*, ed. Andrew Bennett, 66–93. London: Routledge.

Smith, Sidonie, and Julia Watson, eds. 1998. *Women, Autobiography, Theory: A Reader*. Madison: The University of Wisconsin Press.

———, eds. 2010. *Reading Autobiography: A Guide for Interpreting Life Narratives*. Minneapolis: University of Minnesota Press.

———, eds. 2012. *Interfaces: Women, Autobiography, Image, Performance*. Ann Arbor: University of Michigan Press.

———, eds. 2017. *Life Writing in the Long Run: A Smith & Watson Autobiography Studies Reader* [E-reader version].

Steele, Kathryn Lenore. 2008. *Navigating Interpretive Authorities: Women Readers and Reading Models in the Eighteenth Century*. Dissertation, Rutgers University, New Brunswick.

Index[1]

---

[1] Note: Page number followed by 'n' refer to notes.

© The Author(s) 2018

V. Baisnée-Keay et al. (eds.), *Women's Life Writing and the Practice of Reading*, Palgrave Studies in Life Writing, https://doi.org/10.1007/978-3-319-75247-1

Printed by Printforce, the Netherlands